Introductory Statistics for Criminal Justice and Criminology

Jon L. Proctor
Indiana University, South Bend

Diane M. Badzinski

Prentice
Hall

Upper Saddle River, New Jersey 07458

Library of Congress Cataloging-in-Publication Data

Proctor, Jon L.
    Introductory statistics for criminal justice and criminology / Jon L. Proctor, Diane M. Badzinski.
        p.   cm.
    Includes bibliographical references and index.
    ISBN 0-13-014292-1
        1. Criminal justice, Administration of—Research—Methodology.   2.
    Criminology—Research—Methodology.   3. Criminal statistics—Methodology.   I.
    Badzinski, Diane M.
    HV7419.5 .P76 2002
    519.5'024'364—dc21

                                                                    2001021761

Publisher: Jeff Johnston
Senior Acquisitions Editor: Kim Davies
Editorial Assistant: Sarah Holle
Development Editor: Kelly Curtis
Managing Editor: Mary Carnis
Production Management: Stratford Publishing Services
Production Editor: Judy Ashkenaz, Stratford Publishing Services
Interior Design: Stratford Publishing Services
Production Liaison: Adele M. Kupchik
Director of Manufacturing and Production: Bruce Johnson
Manufacturing Buyer: Cathleen Petersen
Cover Design Coordinator: Miguel Ortiz
Formatting: Stratford Publishing Services
Marketing Manager: Ramona Sherman
Marketing Assistant: Barbara Rosenberg
Marketing Coordinator: Adam Kloza
Printer/Binder: R.R. Donnelley and Sons, Inc.
Copy Editor: Laura Lawrie
Proofreaders: Alice Vigliani, Kathleen Traynor
Cover Design: Denise Brown
Cover Illustration: Denise Brown/Judy Wingerter, Stratford Publishing Services
Cover Printer: Phoenix Color Printers

Prentice-Hall International (UK) Limited, *London*
Prentice-Hall of Australia Pty. Limited, *Sydney*
Prentice-Hall Canada Inc., *Toronto*
Prentice-Hall Hispanoamericana, S.A., *Mexico*
Prentice-Hall of India Private Limited, *New Delhi*
Prentice-Hall of Japan, Inc. *Tokyo*
Prentice-Hall Singapore Pte. Ltd.
Editora Prentice-Hall do Brasil, Ltda., *Rio de Janeiro*

10 9 8 7 6 5 4 3 2 1
ISBN 0-13-014292-1

We dedicate this text to our daughters,
Alyssa and Hannah, and to our son, Luke.
Children truly are a blessing from the Lord.

Contents

List of Figures and Tables

Figures

Tables

Preface

Goals of the Text

We strongly believe that it is impossible to study criminal justice and criminology without some understanding of statistics. In our experience, however, students often fail to see the connection between taking a course in statistics and fulfilling their desire to learn about the workings of the criminal justice system. This text will introduce students to the essentials of statistics in order to heighten their understanding of the role statistics play in the study of criminal justice. Students will see how statistics can be used to implement change in the criminal justice system, shape public policy, and develop and test theories of crime. They will see the role of probability theory in statistics and, most central, will learn how to perform various statistical tests to meet specific research objectives. Step-by-step demonstrations are provided for calculating statistics using both hand calculators and computer technology.

Special Features of the Text

Special features of *Introductory Statistics for Criminal Justice and Criminology* include the following:

Excel Application

It is important that students at least try some computer computations in order to understand the technology that is available and the ways in which technology has simplified computing of basic statistical procedures. Because more and more students have access to personal computers and software, this book presents computer calculations using Excel. Although most texts select other statistical packages, such as SPSS and SAS, for computer demonstrations, we believe that the majority of undergraduate students are better served using software that is less sophisticated and more common in both the home and the workplace. If an instructor so chooses, the computations can be completed using other available software packages.

Problem–Solution Format

The beginning of each chapter introduces the chapter topic with a scenario in which a problem and a solution are presented. This problem–solution format reinforces the process involved in conducting criminal justice research, in which researchers often must define problems and seek ways to address them. Further, the problem–solution format reemphasizes the link between the study of crime and the study of statistics. In many instances, criminal justice workers rely on statistics to address specific problems.

ExploreIT! Boxes

Students are ushered into each chapter with an ExploreIT! box introducing them to the information presented in the chapter. ExploreIT! is meant to get readers thinking about the chapter contents and whet their appetites for the material.

TryIT! Boxes

To reinforce key concepts, TryIT! boxes are inserted throughout the text. The TryIT! boxes are designed to allow students to review the material and, when applicable, to practice the different calculations.

Key Terms

Throughout the book, key terms are introduced in boldface type and are defined in boldface italics; the terms appear in the margin next to the paragraph where they first appear in the text. Key terms also are listed at the end of each chapter.

Problem Sets

Most chapters end with problem sets to aid students in calculating and interpreting the different statistics. When applicable, we recommend that the problems be done using both hand calculations and Excel. We specifically used small sample sizes for ease of calculation.

Ancillary to the Text

An instructor's manual and a student workbook accompany *Introductory Statistics for Criminal Justice and Criminology*. The instructor's manual contains an outline of each chapter and a test bank of examination questions, including multiple-choice, true–false, matching, and short-answer items. As a unique feature, the manual includes a set of Excel problems and answers. To provide maximum flexibility for instructors in selecting the way in which the problems are calculated, the problem sets can be completed using a hand calculator or another software package, as well as in Excel.

Acknowledgments

We wish to thank the many people at Prentice Hall, Stratford Publishing Services, and Ohlinger Publishing Services who contributed to the development and production of this book. In particular, we would like to thank our senior editor at Prentice Hall, Kim Davies, as well as Adele Kupchik, our production liaison at Prentice Hall; Kelly Curtis, managing editor at Ohlinger Publishing Services; and Judy Ashkenaz at Stratford Publishing Services. We thank the copyright holders who allowed us to use their material in this textbook—Pearson Education Limited, Oxford University Press, and the Biometrika trustees. Finally, we wish to thank our colleagues who reviewed this text and gave us suggestions and advice: Gregory Russell of Washington State University, Ellen Cohn of Florida International University, Lee E. Ross of the University of Wisconsin–Parkside, and Kimberly Tobin of Westfield State College.

About the Authors

Jon L. Proctor received his bachelor's and master's degrees in criminal justice from the University of Nebraska and his doctorate in sociology from the University of Nebraska. His teaching interests are primarily in the areas of research methods, statistics, and corrections-related courses. His research focuses on a variety of correctional issues, including classification, parole, and institutional control of inmate populations.

Diane M. Badzinski received her bachelor's degree from St. Cloud State University, her master's degree from the University of California, Santa Barbara, and her doctorate from the University of Wisconsin–Madison. After ten years of teaching at the University of Nebraska–Lincoln, she resigned her position and now teaches part-time. Although her teaching interests and responsibilities often lie in research methods and statistics, she also enjoys teaching a variety of communication courses.

Purpose of Statistics

ExploreIT!

- About 79% of National Collegiate Athletic Association athletes were subjected to hazing during the 1998–1999 school year (Rosellini, 2000, p. 102).

- Smokers who drink regularly are nearly twice as likely to have genetic mutations associated with lung cancer as are smokers who don't drink (MacNeil, 2000, p. 63).

- Seventy-three percent of respondents support the death penalty; 38% say that only the most brutal murderers should be executed ("They're on Death Row. But Should They Be?," 2000, p. 26).

- In a statistical study of appeals in capital cases, it was found that 68% of the cases had prejudicial errors and should be reversed (Gergen, 2000, p. 76).

- Nebraska is ranked number one in college football ("Scouting Reports," 2000, p. 51).

- According to the Bureau of Justice Statistics, in 1999 the crime rate index fell for the eighth straight year, to its lowest level since 1978 (Bureau of Justice Statistics, 2000).

Are the statements in the ExploreIT! box accurate? Is hazing really that prevalent among college athletes? Should the American Lung Association now advertise "Don't drink and smoke?" Should Nebraska be ranked number one in college football? How much confidence should we have in the studies showing a decline in the crime rate? How should you go about evaluating such statistical claims? How do researchers make such statements? This course and your text, *Introductory Statistics for Criminal Justice and Criminology*, will equip you with the information and the tools you will need for evaluating and making statistically based claims. Whether you are interested in the incidences of hazing on college campuses, the probability of your team winning the national championship, or tracking the number of violent crimes, the role of statistics can not be ignored.

This chapter has three purposes. First, we illustrate the importance of statistics for the criminal justice student. We argue that it is impossible to study crime without a basic understanding of statistics. Second, we define basic statistical terms and concepts. These concepts will be used repeatedly throughout the remainder of this text. Therefore, it is essential that you have a general understanding of their meaning and application. Our final goal is to encourage you to process the material in this text actively. We *do not* want you simply to sit back, relax, and enjoy this book. We want you to read the text with a pencil and calculator in hand, pausing to complete the examples and problem sets. After you have grasped the information and performed hand calculations, we hope you will try completing some of the problem sets using a computer program, to see how technology has made computing statistical procedures much less complex. Do you have access to a computer at school or at home? Most computers are loaded with Excel or a similar spreadsheet program. We demonstrate statistical procedures using Excel, although your instructor may choose to use other available statistical packages.

1.1 Studying Crime and Taking Statistics

Why are you interested in the study of crime and the criminal justice system? There is no doubt that crime is intriguing. Stories of victims are heart-wrenching. Senseless murders and inescapable injustices speak to the very core of our humanity. Crime fascinates all of us. There is no doubt that crime sells. About one-third of all newspaper coverage and up to one-half of local news programming is about crime (Stepp, 1998). Detective stories and cop shows are among the most popular TV genres. Although the drama presented by the media often distorts reality, people turn to mass media for information about crime. There is no doubt that the job outlook for the criminal justice student is bright. In a recent projection of job growth occurring over the first decade of the twenty-first century, an upward trend is expected for a wide range of criminal justice occupations, including corrections officers, paralegals, detectives, police officers, and investigators. In fact, a faster than average rate of growth is expected for corrections officers (Melchionno and Steinman, 1998). There is no doubt that the field of criminal justice needs committed individuals working to provide solutions to the social and economic problems rooted in crime.

The question that remains to be answered is, "Why are you taking a course in statistics?" Our experience tells us that students often do not see the connection between their interest in the criminal justice system and the need to take a course in statistics. They often do not see how statistics can be used to color and shape perceptions of criminal justice practices. Perhaps most important, they do not see the role of statistics in establishing procedures and implementing public policies. It is essential to understand that our criminal justice systems, including their procedures, operations, and policies, are

statistics   based on **statistics**—*the science of collecting, describing, analyzing, and interpreting observations.*

Let's look at some examples to illustrate the role of statistics in studying crime. After reading about public school shootings in Arkansas, Colorado, Kentucky, and Oregon, you may want to know the extent of violence in public schools. Finding an answer to this question requires collecting information and making meaningful comparisons of the prevalence of such violence in schools across our country at different time periods. You also may want to know whether a gun inspection program would be effective in reducing violence in schools. Statistics are necessary to examine the prevalence of violence in public schools and to evaluate the effectiveness of the gun inspection program.

Let's consider an example in which statistics are needed to address a criminal justice policy adequately. As a result of the slaying of the young girl named Megan by a twice-convicted sex offender, over 30 states have adopted "Megan's Law." Is this law effective in deterring future sex offenders? Answering this question necessitates collecting and interpreting various forms of observations, including the number of repeated sex offenders. Is the law effective in notifying neighbors of convicted sex offenders living in their neighborhood? Once again, the use of statistics is necessary to answer this question.

Statistics is the foundation of the study of crime. Therefore, the *study* of crime necessitates an understanding of statistics. We hope that you will begin to see the role of statistics in all facets of your study of crime, whether it be the need for community-oriented policing, increasing the number of police officers, reducing the number of offenders on parole, developing strategies for heightening awareness of road rage, or adopting a law to deter stalking.

1.2 Descriptive and Inferential Statistics

There are two classes of statistics, descriptive and inferential. Your research goal determines the type of statistics you will use. Is your goal to describe your observations? For example, is the purpose of your study to describe types of 911 calls? If so, you

descriptive   can accomplish your task by using descriptive statistics. We use **descriptive statistics**
statistics   to *describe and summarize observations, often involving the grouping of those observations and identifying a value or values best representing the observations.* As a

TABLE 1.1 Police Emergency Log

January 13, 2000

0800:	domestic dispute	131 Lake Drive
0830:	car accident	corner of Park and Western
0929:	car accident	68 Woodsong Road
1231:	domestic dispute	1617 Aldrich Avenue
1541:	domestic dispute	Foodmart
1614:	pedestrian accident	3 South Street
1700:	fire alarm	Ely Hall, Westfield State College
1831:	car accident	1341 Main Street
1900:	car accident	4 North Avenue
2200:	car accident	70 Michael Drive

researcher interested in describing types of 911 calls, as illustrated in Table 1.1, you could make a log of all the calls during a particular period.

You also could group the type of calls and report the percentage of each type of call as follows: 50% car accidents, 30% domestic disputes, and 20% other. In both cases, you are describing your observations, but only the second option involves calculating descriptive statistics. You should note that simply logging the types of calls does not involve the use of statistics. It is when you go beyond listing your observations and begin summarizing your observations in meaningful ways that you need descriptive statistics. Chapters 3, 4, and 5 are devoted to descriptive statistics.

Is your goal to go beyond describing your particular sample of observations and make some statements about what is occurring in a given population? If so, you can accomplish your task by using inferential statistics. It is impossible to collect information on the entire population of 911 calls. **Inferential statistics**, which *are used to make generalizations about what is happening in a given population based on a sample of observations*, make it possible to draw some inferences about these 911 calls.

inferential statistics

Inferential statistics are extremely common in criminal justice research. A recent study, for example, explored the attitude of juveniles toward police officers (Leiber, Nalla, and Farnworth, 1998). Even though the researchers surveyed only 337 delinquent youths, we can—with some caution—generalize their findings to youths not part of the actual study. Another study examined people's knowledge of sex-offender notification laws by surveying 335 residents of Massachusetts (Johnson, Badzinski, and Proctor, 1999). Inferential statistics made it possible for the researchers to draw generalizations about how much residents of Massachusetts know about such laws, based on a small sample of all residents. Although much of the text is devoted to inferential statistics, it should be noted that descriptive statistics form the foundation of inferential statistics. That is, inferential statistics often involve calculating some descriptive statistics; thus, knowledge of descriptive statistics can be viewed as a prerequisite to understanding inferential statistics.

We further classify inferential statistics into two groups: parametric and nonparametric. **Parametric statistics** *involve some key assumptions concerning the level of measurement of the data as well as the distribution of the data in the population.* These assumptions require that the data be measured at the interval or ratio level and that the observations be normally distributed in the population. We will discuss each of these assumptions in more detail later in the text; for now, however, we simply note the differences between the two categories of inferential statistics. **Nonparametric statistics** *make no assumptions concerning the level of measurement or the distribution of the data in the population.* Which group of inferential statistics is preferred? If the assumptions of parametric statistics are met, they generally are preferred over nonparametric statistics, as they provide more powerful and efficient methods of analysis.

Throughout this text, we have inserted TryIT! boxes. The boxes contain problems to aid in the review of key text material and, when applicable, to provide an opportunity to practice the different calculations. The answers to the problems presented in the TryIT! boxes are found at the end of each chapter. Please do not skip these boxes—they are a tool to facilitate mastery of the material. Active involvement with the material is the key to success in understanding statistics. As "maximum learning is always the result of maximum involvement" (Hendricks, 1987, p. 53), you must be active participants in the process of learning statistics. We encourage you not to simply read your text but rather wholeheartedly dig into the pages of this book and be sure to complete each of the TryIT! boxes—begin now with TryIT! Box 1.1.

(margin notes) **parametric statistics**

(margin notes) **nonparametric statistics**

TryIT!   BOX **1.1**

Below are three proposed research projects. For each proposal, decide whether the researcher's goal can be met using descriptive or inferential statistics.

1. A police commissioner needs to provide the city council with a report summarizing the number and types of all arrests made during the summer of 2000. In accomplishing this goal, the commissioner is using _____ statistics.

2. A report is issued listing the names of all prisoners on death row. The researcher classifies the prisoners in terms of geographical location. To accomplish this goal, she will most likely use _____ statistics to summarize the information.

3. MADD (Mothers Against Drunk Drivers) is interested in addressing whether a particular advertising campaign is effective in reducing drinking and driving among teenagers in the United States. To accomplish their goal, MADD most likely will rely on _____ statistics.

1.3 From Samples to Populations

sample   A **sample** is *a subset of the people or objects of interest, drawn from and representing the*
population *larger population,* whereas a **population** is *the entire collection of the people or objects*
of interest in the study. Notice that it is impossible to draw a sample prior to clearly
defining our population. For example, a researcher might define the population of
"emergency calls" as all 911 calls received by a city police department during a specific
two-week time period. Although other definitions could be advanced, the point is that
the sample could not be drawn without a clear definition of the population. Hence, the
sample will be drawn from the population, identified as all 911 calls during the specified two-week period. It is also important to note that the term *population* is not
restricted to people but often refers to a well-defined collection of objects, such as emergency calls, police dramas, misconduct reports, or court transcripts.

In the 911 illustration in Table 1.1, the ten 911 calls are an example of a sample representing a larger collection of emergency calls. Researchers are usually interested in
learning about populations. That is, the researcher is not keenly interested in the sample
of 911 calls, but, rather, she is interested in making some claims about emergency calls
in general. As it may be too difficult, too time-consuming, or impossible to obtain information on a population, it is often more practical to study a sample rather than a population. And the good news is that it is possible to make claims about the population
based on the sample, provided that the sample accurately represents the population.

What do we mean when we say that the sample is representative of the population?
Ideally, a sample should have the same characteristics as the population. If 80% of
police officers in the population are male, then 80% of the police officers in our sample
should be male. As a more complex example, if 75% of emergency police calls occur
between 2:00 P.M. and 6:00 P.M., then 75% of the calls in our sample should be made
during that peak period. We must strive to make our sample as similar to the population as possible. Take a moment and try to distinguish between samples and populations by completing TryIT! Box 1.2.

TryIT!   BOX 1.2

For each of the research situations listed below, identify the sample and the population
that is being studied.

1. A researcher surveys 25% of the freshman class at a local high school regarding
   their attitudes toward illegal drugs.

2. A researcher studies the number of burglaries committed during the past year by a
   group of convicted burglars.

3. Approximately 250 Washington State residents over 18 years old were asked, "How
   many times were you victimized by crime during the previous 24 months?"

4. A marketing firm conducts a study with 35% of the car dealerships in a major city to determine how many cars on their lots had been vandalized within the past 30 days.

sample   popul

5. Researchers followed 25 out of 150 juveniles who participated in a crime prevention program for three months after the program, to see how many crimes they had committed.

sample

6. A researcher contacts 15% of the individuals who visited the local jail during the past 12 months (1999) to determine how the jail administration might improve visiting time.

1.4 Mathematical Operations

One of the main obstacles we have found when teaching statistics is that students think they must be highly proficient at math. Although it is impossible to avoid mathematical operations in performing statistics, it is not necessary to be a mathematical genius to master statistics. For the most part, the statistical formulas presented in this text simply require basic mathematical operations of addition, subtraction, multiplication, and division, as well as the additional operations of squaring values and taking the square root of values. We recommend that you purchase a calculator with the capability to perform these basic mathematical functions.

As statistics involve performing mathematical operations, it is necessary to establish a few rules for performing calculations. The rules we use throughout this text are as follows:

1. The first rule is to carry all calculations out two places past the decimal point. For example, 3 divided by 4 should equal .75 (¾ = .75). Do not round up to .8. For values that only go one place past the decimal point, you should simply add a 0 to the second place past the decimal point. Thus, 3 divided by 5 equals .60 (⅗ = .60). We simply added a 0 after the .6 to correctly read as .60.

2. The second rule is to round up or down for those values that are more than two places past the decimal point, depending on the value of the third value. For example, 5 divided by 3 equals 1.666. If the value of the third value past the decimal point is 5 or higher, you must round the second value up. In this example, the correct answer is 1.67. If the value of the third value is less than 5, then you should simply drop the third value. To illustrate, 7 divided by 3 equals 2.333, which will require dropping the third value past the decimal point. In this example, the correct answer is 2.33.

3. The third rule is that values that are whole numbers should remain as whole numbers. For example, 10 divided by 5 equals 2. We leave this value as 2, being careful not to proceed two places past the decimal and write 2.00.

In many instances, you will be performing several calculations prior to arriving at the final answer. If you are using a calculator or computer, the values may not be rounded in terms of the same guidelines. In such cases, you should simply continue with the problem, making sure that the final answer is taken to two places past the decimal point. Given this issue of rounding, answers may vary slightly among students as well as between students and the text. These rules, however, should help in terms of simplifying calculations and producing accurate answers.

1.5 Computer Technology and Statistics

It is important for you to at least try some computer computations to understand the technology available and to grasp how technology has made computing statistics less complex. Most of the examples and problem sets presented in this text will allow both hand and computer calculations. We encourage you to do both. Hand calculations are useful for understanding the specific steps involved in performing a particular statistical procedure. Computer calculations allow researchers to conduct statistical analyses more efficiently, analyze data sets too large to be reasonably calculated by hand, and perform advanced statistical procedures too complex for hand calculation.

Many excellent statistical programs exist for analyzing descriptive and inferential statistics using your computer. We have elected to demonstrate computer applications using Excel for several reasons. First, this software, or a similar spreadsheet program, is common in the workplace. If you have access to a computer—at home, school, or work—it is highly likely that you will be able to find this type of computer software. Second, Excel allows you to type in a particular statistical formula and to visualize the step-by-step manipulations involved in the calculations. Third, the program has many unique features—such as the "function wizard" and the "data analysis tool"—to aid in the ease of calculations. Finally, Excel is a versatile and user-friendly program that we believe you will enjoy mastering.

A word of caution: The accessibility of statistical programs, coupled with the ease of using these programs, makes it tempting to perform different kinds of analyses without a sufficient grasp of their proper application. It is essential that you fully understand the purpose and the assumptions of the different statistical methods prior to performing the techniques.

1.6 Summary

This chapter documents the importance of statistics for studying crime. Although it is possible to study statistics without a knowledge of crime, we believe it is impossible to study crime without a knowledge of statistics. Whether researchers use descriptive and/or inferential statistics will depend on their research goals. Descriptive statistics are used to describe and summarize observations. Inferential statistics are used to draw conclusions about a population based on a subset of that population. Typically, studies report both descriptive and inferential statistics. There are two classes of inferential statistics, referred to as parametric and nonparametric. If certain assumptions about the data distribution can be met, it is generally preferable to use the more powerful parametric procedures. Both classes of statistics are discussed in detail in the following chapters.

A discussion of both descriptive and inferential statistics requires us to make a distinction between a sample and a population. A population is the entire collection of people or objects of interest in the study. In contrast, a sample is a representative subset of the people or objects of interest drawn from the larger population. An understanding of statistics will require you to process the information actively. We strongly suggest that you complete the problems in the text using both hand and computer calculations. We hope you find the TryIT! boxes a helpful learning tool.

Key Terms

statistics

descriptive statistics

inferential statistics

parametric statistics

nonparametric statistics

sample

population

TryIT! Answers

Box 1.1

1. descriptive

2. descriptive

3. inferential

Box 1.2

1. *Sample:* 25% of the freshmen who were surveyed. *Population:* all freshmen at the high school.

2. *Sample:* group of convicted burglars. *Population:* all convicted burglars.

3. *Sample:* 250 Washington State residents over 18 who were asked the question. *Population:* all Washington State residents over 18 years.

4. *Sample:* 35% of car dealerships studied by the marketing firm. *Population:* all car dealerships in the city.

5. *Sample:* 25 juveniles who participated in the program and were followed for three months. *Population:* all 150 juveniles who participated in the program.

6. *Sample:* 15% of individuals who visited the jail during the past 12 months (1999) contacted by the researcher. *Population:* all individuals who visited the jail during 1999.

Foundations of Research

ExploreIT!

In response to an increase in the number of alcohol related crimes on college campuses, the dean of students at the local college has hired you to study alcohol consumption on campus. As the researcher, you need to determine what specific information concerning alcohol consumption would be useful. Is it important to know the number of students who drink? Is it important to know what types of students drink? Is it important to know whether there is a relationship between alcohol consumption and crime? In addressing these questions, you will be specifying the purpose of your research, identifying variables, determining levels of measurement, and formulating testable hypotheses.

2.1 Goals of Science

The goals of social science research are varied. Criminal justice research, however, typically serves one of four general purposes: exploration, description, explanation, or

explor-atory research
application (Maxfield and Babbie, 1998). **Exploratory research** *is usually reserved for the study of "new" behaviors and/or phenomena about which little information is known.* For example, during the last decade of the twentieth century, carjacking grabbed national attention as a new type of criminal behavior that combined the elements of robbery and auto theft. Exploratory research on carjacking might involve any number of issues, including characteristics of offenders, types of victims, and location of incidents.

descriptive research
Descriptive research *focuses primarily on describing events and/or situations.* The Uniform Crime Reports (UCR) are an excellent source of descriptive research. These reports provide detailed information on a variety of issues, including state and city crime rates, frequencies and rates of index crimes, number of arrests made, and number of law enforcement personnel. Monitoring the Future (MTF), another source of descriptive research, provides information on drug use, involvement in criminal acts, and victimization data for the nation's high school seniors (Maxfield and Babbie, 1998).

explan-atory research
Explanatory research *goes beyond description in an attempt to explain why.* Why does one city have a higher crime rate than another city? Why are convenience stores more frequently robbed than banks? Why do so many offenders fail on parole? Explanatory research attempts to answer these types of questions. For instance, in a study of attitudes toward authority, researchers sought to explain "why" some juveniles have negative attitudes toward the police. Results showed that racial and cultural factors explained differences in attitudes. Specifically, nonwhite juveniles and those committed to delinquent norms expressed more negative attitudes toward the police than did White youths or those committed to conventional norms (Leiber, Nalla, and Farnworth, 1998).

applied research
Finally, criminal justice research may be of an applied nature. **Applied research** *typically involves the evaluation of programs and/or policies.* It is designed to assess whether programs have achieved their goals. For example, a city that developed and implemented a community policing program designed to reduce citizens' fear of crime might want information about the program's success. Researchers could then evaluate the impact of the community policing program on citizens' fear. Many criminal justice programs are designed to decrease certain types of criminal behaviors. For instance, a study of domestic violence in Minneapolis discovered that arresting abusers resulted in lower rates of domestic violence recidivism than did either counseling suspects or sending them away from the home (Sherman and Berk, 1984). The results of this study led to the adoption in many states of mandatory arrest policies for domestic violence abusers. Despite the deterrent effect of arrest on recidivism found in the Minneapolis study, follow-up studies of domestic violence in other cities produced mixed results.

For example, in Omaha and Charlotte, offenders who were arrested for domestic violence had higher rates of repeat offending than did those who were not arrested, whereas offenders arrested in Colorado Springs and Miami-Dade were less likely to reoffend compared to offenders who were not arrested (Sherman, 1992).

In an evaluation of the impact of Prison Fellowship Ministries (PFM) on recidivism, researchers found offenders who had a high level of participation in PFM-sponsored Bible studies were significantly less likely to be rearrested than inmates who did not participate in Bible studies (Johnson, Larson, and Pitts, 1997).

Regardless of one's research purpose, certain foundational blocks must be understood before using statistics in research. This chapter is devoted to laying the foundations of research that will enable you—the criminal justice student—to read, understand, and perform research in your particular area of interest. The foundations of research include variables and attributes, levels of measurement, and hypothesis construction.

2.2 Variables and Attributes

variables

attributes

qualitative variable

quantitative variable

Researchers collect data to measure associations between variables and their attributes. **Variables** are *characteristics that vary in quality and/or quantity among individuals.* Specifically, variables take on values that reflect different qualities (e.g., male and female) and different quantities (e.g., zero arrests, three arrests, six arrests). **Attributes** are those *qualities or quantities that describe the variable:* Male and female are attributes of the variable "sex." Zero arrests, 3 arrests, and 12 arrests are attributes of the variable "number of arrests."

Variables and their corresponding attributes may be separated into two general types: qualitative and quantitative. A **qualitative variable** consists of *attributes that vary in quality or kind.* In contrast, a **quantitative variable** consists of *attributes that vary in degree or magnitude.* Consider the following example. Let's suppose that seven convicted offenders were given one of four possible criminal sentences: probation, house arrest, community service, or boot camp. As shown in Figure 2.1, three offenders received probation, two offenders received house arrest, and so on. The variable "criminal sentence" is a qualitative variable comprised of attributes representing different kinds of sentences. Making a slight change in our example, let's propose that all seven convicted offenders received a probation sentence. The first offender received 14 months' probation, the second offender received 23 months' probation, the third offender received four months', and so on. As illustrated in Figure 2.1, there are no differences among the subjects in terms of the kind of sentence received—all received probation. There are differences, however, in the amount of time each subject is sentenced to probation. This is an example of a quantitative variable, as the attributes represent different degrees of the variable "criminal sentence."

FIGURE 2.1 Qualitative and quantitative variables for criminal sentence

Criminal Sentence Qualitative	Criminal Sentence Quantitative
Probation (3 offenders)	Offender 1: 14 months' probation
House Arrest (2 offenders)	Offender 2: 23 months' probation
Community Service (1 offender)	Offender 3: 4 months' probation
Boot Camp (1 offender)	Offender 4: 8 months' probation
	Offender 5: 16 months' probation
	Offender 6: 4 months' probation
	Offender 7: 6 months' probation

Take a moment and try distinguishing between qualitative and quantitative variables by completing TryIT! Box 2.1.

TryIT!   BOX **2.1**

Identify each variable as either qualitative or quantitative.

Variables

1. Number of officer complaints

2. Frequency of drug usage

3. Type of drugs used

4. Number of prior offenses

5. Dollar amount of stolen property

6. Type of weapon used to commit a crime

7. Police officer rank

8. Prison security level

2.3 Levels of Measurement

In criminal justice research, the importance of measurement can not be overstated. The collection of data involves the measurement of observations. For example, if we are interested in the variable "arrests," we could measure this as simply yes or no, depending on whether or not an individual has ever been arrested. Another option would be to measure how many times an individual has been arrested. The level of measurement determines the kinds of statistical calculations we can perform and the kinds of research questions we can answer. In the previous section, variables were referred to as either qualitative or quantitative. Measurement of variables can be further refined into four specific levels: nominal, ordinal, interval, and ratio.

Nominal Level

nominal-level

A **nominal-level** variable consists of *a set of attributes that have different names or labels describing the categories*. For example, we could use a nominal-level variable to indicate the "type of sentence" an offender received. Some of the possible attributes of this variable would include prison, boot camp, and probation. Another example of a nominal measure is "type of crime," including attributes such as robbery, burglary, larceny, and arson. *Attributes* and *categories* are interchangeable terms that describe the different characteristics of a variable.

Two important features of nominal-level variables must be addressed. First, the categories must be mutually exclusive. That is, each subject must fall into only one category. Second, the categories must be exhaustive: Every subject must fit into at least one of the categories. The previous two examples, "type of sentence" and "type of crime," satisfy the mutually exclusive requirement. The categories of each variable are distinctly different and do not overlap. Unfortunately, neither example satisfies the exhaustive requirement. In considering "type of sentence," there are certainly other sentences that an offender could receive, such as house arrest, fine, and community service, to name a few. Additionally, robbery, burglary, larceny, and arson are not the only types of crimes. Let's assume we asked 300 inmates what crime they were most recently convicted of, and the results were as follows: 50—robbery, 50—burglary, 50—arson, 50—larceny, and another 100 involving 25 other types of crimes. To make our list exhaustive, we could add the other 25 crimes to our list of attributes, or we could simplify the process by adding one additional category, labeled other. The first 200 inmates remain in the original four categories, with the final 100 inmates falling into the fifth category labeled other.

Ordinal Level

ordinal-level

An **ordinal-level** variable *has a set of different attributes with a rank ordering among the categories*. The definition is the same as the nominal level, with the additional requirement of an implied order. Specifically, the attributes differ in terms of quality—that is, whether they have more or less of the variable. For instance, asking respondents how fearful they are of crime using the following attributes—not at all fearful, somewhat fearful, very fearful—indicates an ordinal level of measurement for the variable "fear of crime." The quality of the variable changes among the attributes from no fear to some fear to a lot of fear. Another example would be the job title among security personnel in a correctional institution. The variable "job title" consists of the following attributes: major, captain, lieutenant, sergeant, corporal, and officer. It is important to note that the ordering of the attributes is from highest rank to lowest rank.

Although ordinal-level variables have an implied ordering among the attributes, the distance or magnitude between the categories is not measurable. We know that very fearful indicates more fear than somewhat fearful, but how much more is unknown. We cannot know if very fearful is twice as fearful as somewhat fearful, or if the difference between very fearful and somewhat fearful is the same as the difference between somewhat fearful and not at all fearful. Similarly, we know that corporals are higher in rank than officers and that sergeants are higher in rank than corporals. We cannot assume, however, that the difference in rank between officers and corporals is the same as the difference in rank between corporals and sergeants.

A final note on nominal- and ordinal-level variables: Whether you are reading a research article or looking at a computer data file, you will notice that the categories are usually labeled with numerical values. These values merely represent *codes* for the different attributes or categories of the variable and do not have any mathematical meaning. Computer programs read and analyze numbers requiring us to define our attributes with numerical values. For the nominal variable "type of sentence," we could code our attributes in the following manner: "1" = prison, "2" = boot camp, "3" = probation. A researcher also could code "type of sentence" as "1" = probation, "2" = prison, "3" = boot camp. For nominal variables, the *order* of the numbers does not matter.

For ordinal variables, the order of the numerical values does matter. For example, for the variable "fear of crime," we could use the following numerical codes to define our attributes: "1" = not at all fearful, "2" = somewhat fearful, "3" = very fearful. As the attributes for our ordinal-level variable are rank-ordered from lowest fear to highest fear, so, too, the codes also must be ordered from lowest value to highest value. Notice that the lowest numerical value corresponds with the lowest level of fear, the next value in numerical order corresponds with the next level of fear, and the highest numerical value corresponds with the highest level of fear. The actual numbers we use to label our attributes are of little consequence as long as the order of the values corresponds with the order of the attributes (lowest numerical value = lowest level of the variable). For example, we could use the following codes for our variable: "13" = not at all fearful, "27" = somewhat fearful, and "78" = very fearful. It is much simpler, however, to use smaller numbers in successive order—1, 2, 3, and so on—to label our attributes.

Interval Level

interval-level

An **interval-level** variable *has a set of different attributes that are rank-ordered and have equal intervals between the attributes that can measure distance among the numerical values.* Thus, a variable measured at this level has distinctively different attributes, an implied order among them, and equal intervals that can measure distances between the attributes. The requirement of equal intervals indicates that dis-tances between the attributes are measurable and clearly defined. One of the most com-monly used examples of an interval-level variable is the variable "temperature." The difference between 50° and 40° is the same as the difference between 90° and 80°—a difference of 10°. At any point on the temperature scale, we can calculate the difference in terms of the amount of degrees between any two temperatures.

Recall that in the previous example we used "fear of crime" as an ordinal-level vari-able consisting of three ordered attributes. To convert this variable into an interval-level measure, we could construct a scale in which respondents are asked the following ques-tion: "How fearful are you of crime?" The attributes of this variable could range between 1 = not very fearful and 10 = very fearful. Thus, the variable comprises ten equal attributes defined in units of one. Notice that in this example, the quantity of the level of fear distinguishes the attributes of the variable. Criminal justice researchers commonly treat scales as interval-level measures.

One limitation of interval-level variables is the lack of an absolute zero point. What this means is that although we can add and subtract different numerical values repre-senting the attributes of a variable to indicate the degree to which one value is greater or less than another value, we cannot multiply or divide the scores to compute ratios. Using a 10-point interval scale, we cannot say that a "4" indicates twice as much fear as a "2." In many instances, however, you may see an interval-level variable using a scale, for example, ranging from 0 to 10. This zero represents an arbitrary, not an absolute, zero point. In our example, the meaning of the zero would indicate the lowest level of fear, not the absence of fear itself. We say this to caution you—the fact that one of the attributes is 0 does not mean that the 0 represents an absolute zero point.

Ratio Level

ratio-level A **ratio-level** variable *has a set of different attributes with a rank ordering, equal inter-vals between the attributes, and an absolute zero point indicating the absence of the variable.* That is, a "zero" can be meaningfully interpreted as representing the absence of the variable. A variable measured at this level has (a) distinctively different attrib-utes; (b) an implied order among them; (c) equal intervals that can measure distances between the attributes; and (d) an absolute zero point indicating the absence of the variable. An example of a ratio-level variable is "misconduct reports" among incar-cerated offenders. We could simply count the number of official misconduct re-ports received by ten incarcerated offenders. As illustrated in Figure 2.2, the attributes would consist of a numerical value (e.g., number of misconduct reports) for each offender.

Like an interval-level variable, the attributes of a ratio-level variable indicate differ-ences in the quantity of the variable. Unlike an interval-level variable, however, a vari-able measured at the ratio level allows us to compute ratios in terms of assessing differences between the values of the attributes.

FIGURE 2.2 Ratio-level variable for misconduct reports

Offender	Misconduct Reports
1	0
2	8
3	12
4	0
5	9
6	4
7	15
8	9
9	1
10	24

Using our example of misconduct reports, we can say that offender 2 has twice as many misconduct reports as offender 6 and that offender 10 has six times as many misconduct reports as offender 6. The addition of an absolute zero point allows us to use multiplication and division when comparing the different values of our variable.

Several final notes on measurement are worth mentioning. First, nominal and ordinal variables are generally classified as categorical measures because the attributes consist of labeled categories. Interval- and ratio-level variables are generally referred to as numerical measures, because the attributes are defined with numerical values in which mathematical calculations may be performed. Second, although many variables may be measured in a variety of ways, we advise measuring the variable at its highest possible level. As shown in Figure 2.3, we could measure the variable "arrests" using either a nominal or a ratio scale.

There are two advantages to measuring a variable at its highest level. First, the types of statistics used for numerical variables are generally more powerful than those used for categorical variables. Second, we can convert numerical values into categories through simple computer manipulations; however, we cannot convert categories into numerical

FIGURE 2.3 Comparison of nominal- and ratio-level variables for arrest record

Nominal Level	Ratio Level
Have you ever been arrested?	How many times have you been arrested?
0 = no	_____ (write in value for each respondent)
1 = yes	

values. To illustrate, let's begin with a ratio level of measurement and ask 100 respondents to indicate the number of times they have been arrested. We find that 50 respondents had been arrested zero times and 50 respondents had been arrested at least once, with the number of arrests ranging from 1 to 20. We could later convert the information to categories by simply assigning a value of 0 to the 50 respondents who indicated *no* arrests and a value of 1 to the respondents who had between 1 and 20 arrests. If we began with categories (0 = no arrests, 1 = one or more arrests), it would be impossible to later convert the categories to a ratio level of measurement.

Levels of Measurement in Review

Nominal: Variables consisting of a set of attributes that have different names or labels describing the categories.

Ordinal: Variables comprising a set of different attributes with a rank ordering among the categories.

Interval: Variables with different attributes that are rank-ordered and have equal intervals between the attributes that can measure distances among the numerical values.

Ratio: Variables having different attributes with a rank ordering, equal intervals between the attributes, and an absolute zero point indicating the absence of the variable.

You are now ready to determine the specific level of measurement for a group of variables. Complete TryIT! Box 2.2 before moving on to the next section.

TryIT!   BOX **2.2**

Identify the level of measurement used for each variable.

Variable	Attributes
1. Parole decision:	1 = grant parole 2 = deny parole *nominal*
2. Number of prior convictions:	_____ (value for each respondent) *ratio*
3. Prison sentence:	1 = 1–12 months 2 = 13–36 months *ordinal* 3 = 37–60 months 4 = more than 60 months
4. Correctional officer stress level:	Lowest Highest 1 2 3 4 5 6 7 8 9 10 *interval*
5. Number of index crimes for each state in 1998:	_____ (value for each state) *ratio*

2.4 Hypothesis Construction

hypothesis   As noted early in this chapter, criminal justice research is concerned with measuring associations or differences between variables and their attributes. Conducting research typically involves formulating hypotheses among variables. A **hypothesis** is *a statement regarding the effect or influence of one variable on another variable.* Specifically, a hypothesis proposes a relationship between two or more variables (Hoover, 1988). We also might hypothesize that a set of variables has a particular effect on another set of variables. Whether we are dealing with a simple relationship between two variables or a more complex one involving several variables, statistics are used to test the hypotheses we have formulated. Based on the statistics we have calculated, we make a decision: If the hypothesis is supported, we conclude that the proposed relationship does in fact exist. If the hypothesis is not supported, then we conclude that the proposed relationship is nonexistent.

Before proceeding with some examples of hypotheses, we must first turn our attention to another distinction that must be made concerning our variables—whether a **independent variable** variable is defined as independent or dependent. An **independent variable** is *a variable that produces a change in another variable*—that is, one that will influence, determine, or cause changes in the dependent variable. A **dependent variable** is *a variable* **dependent variable** *that is influenced or affected by the independent variable.* Criminal justice researchers attempt to explain variation or changes in the dependent variable as a result of the influence or effect of an independent variable. For example, a researcher may think that an offender's age may affect the likelihood of being granted parole. In this example, "age" is the independent variable and "parole decision" is the dependent variable. Once our independent and dependent variables have been defined, we are ready to formulate a hypothesis.

Let's assume that we are interested in the dependent variable "arrests." Additionally, we have decided to measure "arrests" on a ratio scale by asking 100 respondents, "How many times have you been arrested?" Let's further assume that the average number of arrests for our sample is 1.8, with a low of 0 (some people will have never been arrested) and a high of 6 (some people will have been arrested several times). Our goal in research is to try to explain this variation in our dependent variable. That is, why were some people arrested more than others? We do this by developing and testing hypotheses between some independent variables that we, as researchers, believe are associated with our dependent variable. Using "age" and "employment status" as two independent variables, we formulate the following two hypotheses:

Hypothesis 1: Younger respondents are more likely than older respondents to have been arrested.

Hypothesis 2: Unemployed respondents have a higher average number of arrests than employed respondents.

Once our hypotheses have been formulated, we are ready to conduct statistical tests to assess whether the proposed relationships between our independent variables and dependent variable exist.

It is important to remember that variables are neither independent nor dependent by nature but are defined by the researcher in accordance with the research question. For example, the variable "prison sentence" can be used as either an independent or a dependent variable. We might predict that "prior convictions" influences or affects "prison sentence." Specifically, as the number of prior convictions increases, so does the prison sentence. In this case, "prior convictions" is the independent variable and "prison sentence" is the dependent variable. This is illustrated in Figure 2.4a. "Prison sentence" also may be used as an independent variable, as demonstrated in Figure 2.4b. In this example, we hypothesize that offenders with longer prison sentences have a higher average number of misconduct reports.

Notice how our variable "prison sentence" is measured as a numerical variable in Figure 2.4a and as a categorical variable in Figure 2.4b. This further demonstrates the latitude we have in decision making not only in defining variables as independent or dependent but also in how we choose to measure them.

In the foregoing examples, we considered the effect of one independent variable on one dependent variable. Because we are attempting to explain or predict changes in the dependent variable, researchers typically look at the effects of several independent variables on a dependent variable. Let's return to our example involving alcohol

FIGURE 2.4a Prison sentence as a dependent variable

Prior Convictions	Prison Sentence (average)
0	16.7 months
1–3	25.8 months
4–6	36.4 months
7 or more	45.7 months

FIGURE 2.4b Prison sentence as an independent variable

Prison Sentence	Misconduct Reports (average)
1–12 months	1.2
13–24 months	1.8
25–49 months	2.6
50 months or longer	5.7

consumption on a college campus, at the beginning of this chapter. Using "alcohol consumption" as the dependent variable, we want to identify some independent variables that we believe influence "alcohol consumption." We can choose to measure alcohol consumption in a variety of ways; however, for our purpose, let's assume we are interested in *how much* students drink. To measure the quantity of alcohol consumption, we might ask respondents the following question: "In the past seven days, how many alcoholic beverages have you consumed?" Because we are asking for a numerical value, we know that this variable is a quantitative variable. Furthermore, it is possible that some respondents do not drink alcohol or have not had any alcohol in the past week. Thus, zero is a meaningful value, which makes this variable a ratio-level measure.

What independent variables do you feel influence or affect the quantity of drinking? We might believe that "age," "sex," and "parental use of alcohol" influence students' consumption of alcohol. Once we have identified our independent variables and specified how they will be measured, we will want to formulate some testable hypotheses between our independent variables and the dependent variable, as follows:

Hypothesis 1: Males are more likely to drink alcohol than females.
Hypothesis 2: Students whose parents use alcohol are more likely to drink alcohol than students whose parents do not use alcohol.
Hypothesis 3: Older students have a higher average number of drinks per week than younger students.

Each one of these hypotheses can now be tested to assess the impact of the independent variable on our dependent variable, "alcohol consumption."

We also may want to look at the effect of "alcohol consumption" on involvement in "campus crime." In this case, "alcohol consumption" now becomes our independent variable, and "campus crime" is our dependent variable. Remember, we need to determine how we are going to measure campus crime before we can formulate a testable hypothesis. For instance, we could use a nominal measure by asking respondents the following question: "Have you ever committed a crime on campus?" (1 = yes, 2 = no). We also could measure crime as an ordinal-level variable by asking respondents, "How many crimes have you committed on campus?" (0 = none, 1 = 1–3, 2 = 4–10, 3 = more than 10). Once we have decided what level of measurement we are going to use, we can then construct a hypothesis and conduct a statistical test to assess whether there is a relationship between "alcohol consumption" and "campus crime."

Practice identifying between independent and dependent variables by completing TryIT! Box 2.3.

Role of Theory

Determining what variables should be included in a research project and how those variables might be related can be a difficult issue for criminal justice research. Both criminological and criminal justice theory serve as a map that guides us in our under-

TryIT!

BOX 2.3

Below are several hypotheses indicating a relationship between two variables. For each hypothesis, identify the independent and dependent variable.

Hypothesis 1: Juveniles from single-parent families are more likely to commit status offenses than are juveniles from two-parent families.

Hypothesis 2: Correctional facilities with higher security levels have lower rates of inmate escapes.

Hypothesis 3: Respondents with higher levels of education are more supportive of Megan's Law than respondents with lower levels of education.

Hypothesis 4: Offenders who participate in drug counseling are more likely to succeed on probation than are offenders who have not participated in drug counseling.

Hypothesis 5: Violent offenders are less likely to be paroled than nonviolent offenders.

---

standing of variables and their relationships. We do not have to guess about the importance of variables and their relationships but, rather, can use theory to inform us as to how variables are interrelated. Thus, theory serves as a guide that determines

> . . . where one looks when searching for facts. In general, a theory is a way of understanding or "making sense" of a phenomenon.
>
> VOLD AND BERNARD, 1986, p. 342

Suppose we are interested in studying crime patterns among different neighborhoods of a particular city. A few questions readily come to mind: How will we measure crime? What distinguishes one neighborhood from another? What would we expect the relationship to be between neighborhood characteristics and crime? Fortunately, we can rely on theory to help us answer these questions. For example, social disorganization theory informs us that disorganized neighborhoods are characterized as having high unemployment, poor health care, inadequate housing, deteriorating schools, a high percentage of single-parent families, and a high poverty rate. These factors, in turn, weaken the ability of informal social controls such as families, churches, and schools to control criminal behavior (Shaw and McKay, 1942).

Thus, we can use social disorganization theory to help us identify important neighborhood characteristics that are associated with criminal behavior. Our purpose, then, is to understand how neighborhood characteristics influence criminal behavior. Each characteristic of a neighborhood that we define serves as a potential independent variable for our study. Suppose we believe that "unemployment" and "poverty" have a major effect on criminality. Suppose also that we have chosen to use the "crime rate" within each neighborhood as our dependent variable. We are now able to construct some hypotheses concerning the neighborhood characteristics of unemployment and poverty with crime. Thus, we might hypothesize the following:

Hypothesis 1: As the level of unemployment in a neighborhood increases, the crime rate also increases.

Hypothesis 2: The crime rate is higher in high-poverty neighborhoods than in low-poverty neighborhoods.

Once we have constructed our hypotheses, we can now use statistics to test them and to make conclusions about the relationship between neighborhood characteristics and crime.

In many instances, criminal justice research involves directly testing the assumptions of a particular theory. For example, according to Gottfredson and Hirschi's "A General Theory of Crime" (1990), criminal behavior is the result of low self-control resulting from inadequate parental control over the lives of children. Children who are not disciplined for misbehavior will fail to develop self-control, and their behavior will tend toward criminality. In a recent study of this theory, researchers selected a self-control scale as the independent variable and analyzed its effect on several dependent variables, including criminal behavior, victimization, and noncriminal behaviors such as drinking, smoking, and speeding (Forde and Kennedy, 1997). Theory guided the researchers in their selection of the variables to be measured and in the development of the following hypotheses:

Hypothesis 1: According to the general theory, the aspects of self-control will tend to come together to affect imprudent behavior and crime directly.

Hypothesis 2: Drawing on routine-activities theory, we expect that the importance of self-control measures will be mediated by opportunities afforded by risky lifestyles.

After applying statistical tests to their hypotheses, the researchers concluded that low self-control did not directly affect criminal behavior but, rather, had an indirect effect on offending through noncriminal behaviors such as drinking and smoking (Forde and Kennedy, 1997).

Often, theory does not adequately address a particular topic of interest. That is, we may be unable to use a particular theory as a guide for our study but must rely on a **research** research question instead. A **research question** is *a formal question designed to guide* **question** *our research inquiry* (Frey, Botan, and Kreps, 2000). When no substantive theory is available, a research question typically suffices to guide us in variable selection and hypothesis construction. For example, we might ask the following research questions:

Question 1: What factors influence public support of Megan's Law?

Question 2: What is the relationship between parole officer supervision style and parole outcome?

Question 3: How does the prison environment affect institutional adjustment?
Question 4: What effects does a police crackdown have on citizens' perceptions of the police?

Each of these questions gives us a general idea of what variables should be studied in order to answer our research question adequately. For example, to answer question 2, we know that we need to include variables that measure parole officer supervision style and parole outcome. We might, for instance, elect to measure "supervision style" as either strict, moderate, or lenient, and "parole outcome" as either success or failure. Once we have determined what variables to include and how they will be measured, we can then construct a hypothesis, such as:

Hypothesis: Officer supervision style influences parole outcome.

Research question 3 informs us that we need to have variables that measure adjustment and the prison environment. Suppose we decide to use "security level" and "percentage overcrowded" as measures of the prison environment, and "misconduct reports" and "participation in programs" as measures of institutional adjustment. We can now construct hypotheses:

Hypothesis 1: Maximum-security institutions have higher levels of misconduct than medium- and minimum-security institutions.
Hypothesis 2: As overcrowding increases, the level of participation in programs increases.

Once again, we can apply some statistical procedures to test our hypotheses and then make conclusions about our research questions based on the results. For example, if we find that our hypotheses are supported, then we answer our research question by discussing "how" the prison environment affects adjustment.

Whether we are using theory as a guide in the selection of variables and construction of hypotheses, testing the validity of a specific theory, or simply asking a research question, statistics are an integral component of the research process, enabling us to make theoretical conclusions and answer research questions.

2.5 Summary

In this chapter, we provided you with the foundational blocks of criminal justice research. We began by introducing the various purposes of research followed with a discussion of variables and attributes, levels of measurement, and hypothesis construction. It is vitally important that you have a thorough understanding of the foundations of research for both performing and interpreting statistical analyses.

Recall that variables take on values that reflect either different qualities or quantities. Attributes, by contrast, are those qualities or quantities that describe the variable. Variables may be described in general terms as either qualitative (categorical) or quantitative (numerical). A qualitative variable is comprised of attributes representing differences in quality or kind, whereas the attributes for a quantitative variable differ in degree or magnitude.

Variables may be defined further, regarding the specific level of measurement. These levels may be thought of as falling on a continuum moving from the lowest level of measurement—nominal—to the highest level of measurement—ratio. Nominal variables have different names or labels that describe the categories. Ordinal variables have different categories that are rank ordered. Not only do variables measured at the interval level have different categories that are rank ordered, but the distance between the numerical values representing the attributes can be measured. Ratio-level variables have all of the characteristics of interval variables with the addition of an absolute zero point.

We also discussed the importance of formulating testable hypotheses between our variables. In constructing a hypothesis, the researcher identifies an independent and dependent variable. An independent variable influences or causes changes in the dependent variable. A dependent variable is influenced or affected by an independent variable. A hypothesis is a statement concerning the effect of an independent variable on a dependent variable.

Finally, we hope you can appreciate the wide latitude of discretion that researchers use in conducting criminal justice research. It is the researcher who determines the independent and dependent variables, how best to measure them, and what hypotheses are important to test.

Key Terms

exploratory research	**nominal-level**
descriptive research	**ordinal-level**
explanatory research	**interval-level**
applied research	**ratio-level**
variables	**hypothesis**
attributes	**independent variable**
qualitative variable	**dependent variable**
quantitative variable	**research question**

TryIT! Answers

Box 2.1

1. Quantitative	5. Quantitative
2. Quantitative	6. Qualitative
3. Qualitative	7. Qualitative
4. Quantitative	8. Qualitative

Box 2.2

1. Nominal	4. Interval
2. Ratio	5. Ratio
3. Ordinal	

Box 2.3

Hypothesis 1: *Family status:* Independent variable. *Status offenses:* Dependent variable.

Hypothesis 2: *Security level of facility:* Independent variable. *Inmate escapes:* Dependent variable.

Hypothesis 3: *Education level:* Independent variable. *Support of Megan's Law:* Dependent variable.

Hypothesis 4: *Drug counseling:* Independent variable. *Probation outcome:* Dependent variable.

Hypothesis 5: *Offender type:* Independent variable. *Parole decision:* Dependent variable.

2.6 Problems

1. Identify the purpose of research for each of the following research situations:

    a. A study of arrest rates among several different cities.
    b. An evaluation of a drug counseling program and its effect on recidivism.
    c. A study of why females commit shoplifting at a higher rate than males.
    d. A multistate study of state-level changes in the juvenile criminal code.

2. For each of the following variables and their corresponding attributes, identify the general level of measurement as either qualitative or quantitative and the specific level of measurement as nominal, ordinal, interval, or ratio.

  a. Employment status
      0 = employed
      1 = unemployed
      — nominal
      — quantitative

  b. Ever convicted of a crime
      0 = no
      1 = yes
      — nominal

  c. Number of times arrested
      _____ (write in number)
      — quantitative
      — ratio

  d. How satisfied are you with the police?
      0 = not at all satisfied
      1 = somewhat satisfied
      2 = very satisfied
      — nominal
      — qualitative

  e. Indicate your level of agreement with the following statement:

      The purpose of prison is to rehabilitate convicted offenders.

      Strongly
      disagree

      Strongly
      agree   *interval / quantity*

      1   2   3   4   5   6   7   8   9   10

  f. Amount of money lost due to property crime
      _____ (write in dollar amount)
      ratio / quantitative

  g. Number of times victimized by crime in the past year
      0 = none
      1 = 1–3 times
      2 = 4–6 times
      3 = 7 or more times
      ratio / quantitative

3. In a study of court decisions, a researcher believes that type of attorney, prior record, and making bail influence trial verdicts. Identify the dependent and independent variables and write a testable hypothesis for each of the independent variables in relation to the dependent variable.

   dep.   *indep.*

4. In a study of police officer satisfaction, Zhao, Thurman, and He (1999) examined the relationship among three factors—the work environment, education level, and years of service—and job satisfaction. Identify the dependent and independent variables.

   dep.   *Ind*

5. The following independent variables were used in a study of the effect of race on juvenile processing: race, prior arrests, living arrangements, and age (DeJong and Jackson, 1998). For each variable, identify the specific level of measurement.

a. Race: White, Black, Hispanic, Other — *nominal*
b. Age: 12 and below, 13, 14, 15, 16, 17, and above   *interval*
c. Living arrangements: mother only, both parents, other arrangements   *ordinal*
d. Prior arrests: 0, 1, 2, 3, or more   *ratio*

6. Write a testable hypothesis for the following independent and dependent variables:

   a. Age (independent) and rule violations (dependent)
   b. Education level (independent) and arrests (dependent)
   c. Participation in prison programs (independent) and parole decision (dependent)
   d. Family status (independent) and delinquency (dependent)
   e. Severity of crime (independent) and length of prison sentence (dependent)

7. Demonstrate how the variable "misconduct reports" can be measured, using the four different levels of measurement. *by # of reports, records (nominal, ordinal, ratio)*

8. For each variable listed below, identify four possible attributes:

   a. Race : *white, Black, korean ...*
   b. Type of residence : *appt., house ..*
   c. Number of misconduct reports : *1 - 10,*
   d. Length of sentence (in months) : *1 - 4, 5 or more*
   e. Prison programs :
   f. Court personnel : *Clerk, Judge, Lawyer, Judge ass.*

9. A researcher believes that the number of merit awards influences police officer satisfaction. She has decided to measure "merit awards" using the following attributes: none, some, and many. She measures "officer satisfaction" using a 20-point scale, with "1" being not at all satisfied and "20" being very satisfied. Identify the independent and dependent variable and the level of measurement used for each. *1) merit awards - Ind.} nominal   2) off. satisf-I } ordinal   # - dep.   # - Dep.*

10. Identify the level of measurement for each of the variables listed below.

    a. Arrests—number of times arrested *ratio*
    b. Satisfaction with police services—not at all satisfied, somewhat satisfied, very satisfied *nominal*
    c. Involvement in block watch program—1 = not very involved, 10 = very involved *ordinal*

Data Organization

ExploreIT!

As a student in a criminal justice statistics class, you have been assigned a class project to present some descriptive information concerning campus crime to the student government association. In order to convey this information to your audience, you will want to arrange your data in a visually appealing and understandable manner. This is likely to involve reporting the frequencies and percentages of different types of crimes occurring on campus in both tabular and graphical formats. Tabular representations of data include single, frequency, grouped frequency distributions, and cross-tabulations. Graphical presentations include histograms, line graphs, and pie charts.

In the previous chapter, we discussed the importance of determining levels of measurement and the development of testable hypotheses. This chapter focuses on organizing data by presenting several methods for constructing tables and graphs for displaying information. The use of tabular and graphical formats makes the dissemination of data more understandable, less cumbersome, and more visually appealing.

We begin by presenting three different types of data distributions—single, frequency, and grouped—commonly used to describe the attributes of a variable. Next, four descriptive statistics frequently used to describe data distributions are discussed. These statistics include proportions, percentages, ratios, and rates. Cross-tabulation, a method for assessing the relationship between two variables within a single table, is then addressed. The chapter concludes with a discussion of graphical methods of data representation, including histograms, line graphs, and pie charts.

3.1 Data Distributions

Single Data Distribution

single data distribution   The simplest type of distribution for representing raw data is known as a **single data distribution**, in which *the number of listed attributes is equal to the number of subjects in the sample*. Both categorical and numerical data may be represented in this format. For instance, let's assume that we asked seven inmates the crime for which they were currently incarcerated. We could present this information in a single data distribution, as shown in Figure 3.1. Notice that the variable "type of crime" is a categorical variable such that each attribute represents a different kind of crime. Since there are seven crimes listed, and each of those crimes (e.g., attributes) represents one subject in our sample, we know that our sample size is equal to 7.

Similarly, we could also present a numerical variable, such as "number of prior offenses," in a single data distribution. Every value that is listed represents a single

FIGURE 3.1 Single data distribution for type of crime

Type of Crime
Robbery
Second-degree arson
Forgery
Burglary
Auto theft
Assault
Drug possession

FIGURE 3.2 Single data distribution for prior offense

Prior Offenses
3
0
7
2
3
1
4

subject's attribute for the variable. As shown in Figure 3.2, there are seven values listed for our variable; therefore, our sample size is equal to 7. Even though some values may be duplicated—for example, 3 appears twice—each value represents only one subject. Once again, our sample size is based on the number of values in the distribution, not the actual values themselves.

Single data distributions are useful when at least one of two conditions is present. First, this organizational format works well when the sample size is small. A second condition, often related to the first, occurs when there are very few duplicate values among the attributes. This is more likely when the sample size is smaller. Returning to the data in Figure 3.2, we see that there are six different values for our sample of seven inmates. If we were to ask 50 inmates how many prior offenses they have committed, the number of values would probably increase; however, there would be many instances of duplicate values among the sample. In this instance, it would make little sense to use a single data distribution to represent our variable. Furthermore, criminal justice research does not typically involve such small sample sizes. Therefore, a more common type of distribution used to represent our data is a frequency distribution.

Frequency Distribution

frequency distribution

A **frequency distribution** *lists the attributes of a variable along with their frequency of occurrence.* This format may be used for both categorical and numerical variables and is generally preferred over a single data distribution, especially when the sample size is large. Suppose we asked 200 criminal justice professionals to identify their current occupation. The use of a frequency distribution for a nominal-level variable is illustrated in Table 3.1. Notice that we now have two columns with the first column listing our variable "occupation" and its attributes, and the second column labeled "frequency" consisting of the number of subjects having each attribute. Of the 200 subjects in our sample, 97 indicated they were police officers, 45 said they were corrections officers, and so on. If we were to represent this information in a single data distribution, we

TABLE 3.1 Frequency Distribution for Occupation of Criminal Justice Professionals

Occupation	Frequency
Police officer	97
Corrections officer	45
Parole officer	33
Probation officer	25
Total	200

would have to list each attribute the number of times that it occurs. For example, we would list police officer 97 times, corrections officer 45 times, parole officer 33 times, and probation officer 25 times. To present the information this way would be time-consuming as well as awkward and confusing.

A frequency distribution is also useful for representing numerical data. Suppose a sample of 50 state patrol officers were given a weapons proficiency test at the state police firing range. Officers were given ten shots at a target and the number of hits represents the attributes of our variable "weapons proficiency." Table 3.2 shows how we can represent this information in a frequency distribution. Notice some values—5, 4, 3, and 1—are missing from our attributes. We could have included these values in our table along with a zero under the frequency column; however, since none of the officers had any of these attributes, it makes little sense to include those values in the distribution.

There are instances where we may have a large sample with a lot of variation in the responses such that our frequency distribution is rather large. For example, many state correctional departments require potential employees to pass a written test before being hired. Let's assume that 150 individuals took a 100-point state correctional officer exam in the fall of 1999. Because we would like some information about those exam scores, we could construct a frequency distribution. Notice, that with a large sample

TABLE 3.2 Frequency Distribution for Police Officer Weapons Proficiency Test

Weapons Proficiency	Frequency
10	8
9	5
8	12
7	19
6	5
2	1
Total	50

TABLE 3.3 Frequency Distribution for Correctional Officer Exam Scores

Score	Frequency	Score	Frequency	Score	Frequency
100	3	88	18	78	12
99	2	87	1	75	16
98	4	86	5	74	10
95	6	83	7	70	8
92	1	81	1	69	15
91	11	80	2	63	13
89	6	79	8	60	1
Total					150

size and a wide range of variation between the minimum and maximum values (0–100) we are likely to encounter a large distribution table as illustrated in Table 3.3. This represents somewhat of a problem when we try to present a lot of information in a concise, easy-to-read manner. In this example, our scores range from a low of 60 to a high of 100. Once again, notice that we have not included those scores that had a frequency of zero. If the scores on the exam had actually ranged from 0 to 100, you can imagine how large our table would need to be to represent all of the scores and their related frequencies. An instance such as this makes it difficult to use a frequency distribution as an adequate representation of our variable and its attributes. This is not to say that we cannot use a frequency distribution but rather to suggest that an alternative method of data representation is preferred. A common approach used to remedy this situation is to construct a grouped frequency distribution.

Grouped Frequency Distribution

grouped frequency distribution

A **grouped frequency distribution** is a *frequency distribution in which single numerical values are grouped into class intervals or categories along with their frequency of occurrence*. Simply put, we reduce the number of attributes of our variable by combining several separate values into a range of values. Returning to our example of correctional officer exam scores, we see that there are 21 different scores. We can combine these scores into several categories, effectively reducing the number of attributes and simplifying our representation of the data.

We have decided to construct a grouped frequency distribution using four categories consisting of the following range of scores: 90–100, 80–89, 70–79, and 60–69. To accomplish this task, we need only to take all of the scores falling within a particular range and add up their frequencies. For example, the range 90–100 is comprised of six

TABLE 3.4 Grouped Frequency Distribution of Correctional Officer Exam Scores

Range	Frequency
90–100	27
80–89	40
70–79	54
60–69	29
Total	150

scores—100, 99, 98, 95, 92, and 91. Each of the six scores has a frequency attached to it, such that three people scored 100, two people scored 99, and so on. Summing up the frequencies of the six scores equals 27. Thus, we have just reduced six attributes (scores) to one attribute (range of scores) with the total number of individuals scoring within that range (frequency). Our second attribute consists of the range 80–89 and comprises seven scores with a total frequency of 40. Table 3.4 illustrates a grouped frequency distribution using the data from Table 3.3. A comparison of Table 3.3 with Table 3.4 clearly demonstrates the value of using a grouped frequency distribution for large sample sizes, with a wide range of variation among the values. The information has successfully reduced 21 different attributes (individual scores) to four (range of scores), making the presentation of our data more compact and visually appealing.

There are two important considerations to keep in mind when using a grouped frequency distribution. The first concern involves the number of intervals to be used. In our example, we selected four categories that typically represent letter grades assigned to a numerical exam score such that a score of 90–100 is usually assigned an A, 80–89 typically assigned a B, and so on. Generally speaking, one wants to have enough intervals to illustrate a pattern among the values and yet not too many intervals to render the use of grouped data meaningless. Of course, the number of intervals is intrinsically tied to the research objective as well as the range of variation of the variable. With this in mind, using anywhere between 5 and 20 intervals is usually sufficient to adequately represent a variable and its attributes.

Once you have decided on the number of intervals to be used, you can determine the width for each interval (e.g., the number of scores in the interval) by dividing the range of the data set (highest value minus lowest value) by the number of intervals. For example, returning to our correctional officer exam scores, we see that the highest value was 100 and the lowest value was 60. The range, therefore, is equal to 40 (100 − 60). As we want four intervals, we simply divide the range (40) by the number of intervals (4), and determine that the width of each interval should equal 10. Each range of scores, therefore, is comprised of ten values, with the exception of the 90–100 range, which has 11 values. If we want ten intervals, the width of each interval would have been four scores (40/10 = 4). Thus, our first attribute would consist of the range 97–100, with a frequency of 9, followed by the range 92–96, with a frequency of 7, and so on through the last range of values.

The second point is that whenever a variable's attributes comprise categories, either labels or numerical intervals, our categories must be mutually exclusive and exhaustive. Notice that in Table 3.3 there is no score of 90. Although it is acceptable to exclude those values in a frequency distribution that have a frequency of zero, we must include those values in a grouped frequency distribution so that our intervals are mutually exclusive and exhaustive. Specifically, every possible value of the variable must be included into one and only one category, even if that value was not an actual value received by any of the subjects.

Although a grouped frequency distribution is the preferred method of data representation for large samples with a lot of variation, note that its use results in less precision. Looking at the frequency distribution in Table 3.3, we can see the exact numerical score for each respondent. That is, three respondents scored 100, two scored 99, four scored 98, and so on. When we convert this information into a grouped frequency distribution, we can no longer determine the exact score of each respondent but only the range of scores in which each respondent falls. As shown in Table 3.4, we know that 27 respondents scored between 90 and 100; however, we do not know how the scores are distributed between the 11 values. For instance, it is possible that all 27 respondents received the same score such as 99, or that 13 respondents had the lowest score (90), whereas 14 had the highest score (100), with none occurring in the middle. Thus, our distribution is less precise in terms of knowing the respondents' exact numerical scores.

Some final words about the organization of a frequency distribution are needed. For a nominal-level variable, the order of the attributes and/or the frequency of their occurrence is a discretionary decision. Because nominal variables do not have any ordering among the attributes, the order in which they are listed does not matter. Returning to our example in Table 3.1, we find that the attributes are ordered from highest occurrence (police officers = 97) to lowest occurrence (probation officers = 25); however, we could have easily listed the attributes in any other order, such as parole officers followed by probation, corrections, and police. Although the order is irrelevant, we find it more visually appealing to list the attributes in either ascending or descending order of their frequency of occurrence.

Because ordinal-level variables have a rank ordering among the attributes, the format of the frequency distribution should be reflective of the order. For example, if we asked a group of respondents to indicate their level of agreement with the statement, "Crime is a problem in my neighborhood," using the following attributes—strongly agree, agree, neither agree nor disagree, disagree, strongly disagree—then we want to make sure that the order of the attributes is either from the most agreement to the least agreement (as indicated above) or from the least agreement to the most agreement (reverse order of above).

Interval- and ratio-level variables also have an implied order among the attributes. Recall from Chapter 2 that the attributes for these variables are represented by numerical values. Once again, the organization of the frequency distribution should represent the ordering inherent in the attributes. Specifically, the numerical values should be listed in order from either highest to lowest or lowest to highest, as shown in Tables 3.2 through 3.4.

Now that you have a good understanding of how data distributions are constructed, take a few moments and complete TryIT! Box 3.1.

TryIT!   BOX **3.1**

A sample of 42 inmates recently admitted to a state penitentiary were classified by category of drug usage. Each attribute listed represents the type of drug an inmate was using during the commission of his/her crime. Using the data below, construct a frequency distribution for the variable "drug type."

Drug Type (X)

Cocaine	Cocaine	Marijuana	Crack	Alcohol	Alcohol
Heroin	Alcohol	Heroin	Alcohol	Cocaine	Crack
Marijuana	Cocaine	Crack	Alcohol	Marijuana	Crack
Cocaine	Marijuana	Crack	Alcohol	Cocaine	Cocaine
Marijuana	Alcohol	Cocaine	Marijuana	Crack	Marijuana
Alcohol	Cocaine	Alcohol	Alcohol	Alcohol	Alcohol
Alcohol	Heroin	Cocaine	Heroin	Alcohol	Marijuana

3.2 Descriptive Statistics

Up to this point we have demonstrated how variables and attributes may be presented in different tabular formats. We now turn our attention to some descriptive statistics that are commonly included in data distribution tables, which allow criminal justice researchers to make meaningful comparisons among variables and their attributes. These statistics include proportions, percentages, ratios, and rates.

Proportions

proportion   A **proportion** is defined *as the frequency of any single attribute divided by the total frequency of all the attributes*. We use this statistic to compare the proportion of the total cases falling within each attribute. The following formula demonstrates how we convert a frequency into a proportion:

$$\text{Proportion}\left(p\right) = \frac{\text{Frequency}\left(f\right)}{\text{Total}\left(n\right)}$$

Let's assume that a sample of 75 parole officers were asked to identify their supervision style as either strict, moderate, or lenient. We could construct a normal frequency distribution, for example, as in Figure 3.3, with an additional column containing the proportion of cases falling within each attribute. We simply take the frequency of each attribute divided by the total frequency. Thus, we see that the highest proportion of parole officers considered themselves to be moderate in their supervision style (37/75 = .49). Knowing the proportion of cases for a single attribute tells us more about the distribution of our variable than does knowing the frequency of the attribute. For example, if the only information we had was that 37 officers were identified as moderate, we really would not know if this was large or small when compared to the other categories. By knowing the proportion, we can say that nearly half of the officers in our sample ($p = .49$) were moderate in their supervision style. This is true, because the total proportion of cases must equal 1. Although proportions are an appropriate statistic to use for making comparisons among the attributes of a variable, they are rarely included in a frequency distribution. Criminal justice researchers more commonly use percentages in place of proportions.

FIGURE 3.3 Calculating proportions for a frequency distribution

Supervision style	Frequency	Proportion
Strict	23	.31
Moderate	37	.49
Lenient	15	.20
Total	75	1.00

Percentages

percen-
tage

A **percentage** is defined as *the frequency of any single attribute divided by the total frequency of all the attributes, then multiplied by 100.* We use the following formula to calculate a percentage:

$$\text{Percentage}\left(\%\right) = \frac{\text{Frequency}\left(f\right)}{\text{Total}\left(n\right)} \times 100$$

The formula for a percentage is the same as that used for a proportion, with the additional step of multiplying the proportion by 100. Using the example of parole officers' supervision style, we can convert our proportion to a percentage (0.49×100) and say that 49% of the officers in our sample report a moderate supervision style. Similar to proportions, the total percentage of our attributes must equal 100. Both ungrouped and grouped frequency distributions usually have a percentage column reporting the percent of the sample falling within each attribute.

We now return to our example of the state police weapons proficiency test. Table 3.5 includes an additional column of percentages. Knowing that 16% of the officers received a perfect score of 10 is much more informative than knowing that the frequency of officers receiving a perfect score is eight. Reporting percentages is an effective method of standardizing values in order to make comparisons among attributes. To say that 16% of the officers had a perfect score is accurate whether the sample size is 10 or 200. That is, the sample size is controlled when comparing percentages. Saying that eight officers had a perfect score, however, does not provide us with as much information. That number might be exceptionally good compared to the frequencies of the other attributes if the sample size was 12 (67%); however, it would be really bad if the sample size was 200 (4%).

Two other statistics commonly reported in grouped and ungrouped frequency distributions include the cumulative frequencies (*cf*) and cumulative percentages (*cp*). A **cumulative frequency** is *the summed total of the frequency of any given numerical value or range of values plus the frequencies of all the other numerical values or range of values falling below it*. Similarly, a **cumulative percentage** is *the summed total of the percentage of any given numerical value or range of values plus the percentages of all the other numerical values or range of values falling below it*. Simply put, we are merely adding the frequencies and percentages as we move from the lowest values to the highest values, thereby constructing a running total of the frequency and percentage columns.

cumulative frequency

cumulative percentage

TABLE 3.5 Frequency and Percentage Distribution for Police Officer Weapons Proficiency Test

Number of Hits	Frequency	Percentage
10	8	16
9	5	10
8	12	24
7	19	38
6	5	10
2	1	2
Total	50	100

TABLE 3.6 Cumulative Grouped Frequency and Cumulative Percentage Distribution for Correctional Officer Exam Scores

Range	Frequency	Percentage	Cumulative Frequency	Cumulative Percentage
90–100	27	18	150	100
80–89	40	27	123	82
70–79	54	36	83	55
60–69	29	19	29	19
Total	150	100		

Table 3.6 illustrates the use of cumulative frequencies and percentages for our example of correctional officer exam scores. The lowest range of values is 60–69, which corresponds with a frequency of 29, followed by the next lowest range of values, 70–79, which has a frequency of 54, and so on up to the highest range of values (90–100). The cumulative frequency for the 60–69 range is 29, which is the same as the frequency. The cumulative frequency for the 70–79 range is 83, which is the sum of the frequency of that range plus the cumulative frequency of the 60–69 range (54 + 29 = 83). The cumulative frequency for the 80–89 range is the sum of the frequency of that range plus the cumulative frequency of all the other lower range of values (40 + 83 = 123). Finally, we add the frequency for the highest set of values to the cumulative frequency of all the other values below it to obtain a *cf* value of 150 (27 + 123), which incidentally must equal the sample size.

The cumulative percentages are obtained in exactly the same manner with the exception of summing the percentage column, instead of the frequency column, as we move from the lowest set of values to the highest. The use of cumulative frequencies and percentages provides an efficient and quick method for discovering certain characteristics within our data. For example, if we want to know the percentage of respondents who scored less than 80%, we need only to look at the cumulative percentage column, where we find the value of 55% in the 70–79 row. Remember, this means that 55% of the respondents scored 79 or lower on the exam. Although it may not be readily apparent from the above example just how valuable these cumulative statistics are, consider an example where we had a sample of 1,500 respondents and a variable with 11 attributes. It would be much more difficult, as well as time-consuming, to determine the number and percentage of respondents scoring above or below certain values if we did not have these statistics readily available.

Take a few moments to practice calculating proportions, percentages, cumulative percentages, and cumulative frequencies by completing TryIT! Box 3.2.

TryIT!

BOX **3.2**

Consider the following number of technical violations committed by a sample of 500 parolees. Calculate the proportions, percentages, cumulative percentage, and cumulative frequency for the distribution.

Technical Violations	Frequency	Proportion	Percentage	Cumulative Percentage	Cumulative Frequency
6	15				
5	16				
4	20				
3	68				
2	47				
1	132				
0	202				
Totals	500				

Ratios

ratio

A **ratio** is *a statistic that is used to compare the frequency of one attribute with the frequency of another attribute.* To calculate a ratio, we use the following formula:

$$\text{Ratio} = \frac{\text{Frequency}_1}{\text{Frequency}_2}$$

Ratios are particularly useful for comparing the frequencies for a dichotomized variable—that is, a variable having only two attributes. For instance, we might want to know the ratio of adult to juvenile arrests. To determine this, we need only to divide the frequency of adult arrests by the frequency of juvenile arrests. According to the Bureau of Justice Statistics (1998), there were 25,656 adult arrests and 7,931 juvenile arrests for index crimes in the state of Massachusetts in 1996. Therefore, our ratio is equal to 25,656/7,931 = 3.23. This means that there were approximately three adult arrests for every juvenile arrest.

Rates

rate

A more common method of comparison in criminal justice research that controls for population differences is the use of rates. A **rate** is defined as *the total frequency of cases that occurred, divided by the total possible frequency at risk of occurring, multiplied by any standard number.* The following formula is typically used to calculate crime rates:

$$\text{Rate} = \frac{\text{Frequency of Occurrence}}{\text{Total Frequency at Risk}} \times 100,000$$

Rates allow us to make comparisons of events across different populations. For example, we may wish to compare the amount of crime in two cities to determine which city is safer. In 1996, there were 52,918 index crimes in Miami compared to 57,100 in Oklahoma City (Bureau of Justice Statistics, 1998). At first glance, we might think that Miami is safer because it had fewer crimes than Oklahoma City; however, we must take into account the total population at risk in each city in order to make any meaningful comparisons. The total population in Miami is 384,976, whereas the total population in Oklahoma City is 469,362. Using the total number of index crimes as the numerator (frequency of occurrence) and the total population as the denominator (total frequency at risk), we are now able to convert the total number of index crimes reported into a rate in the following manner:

Miami

$$\frac{52,918}{384,976} \times 100,000 = \textbf{13,745.79}$$

Oklahoma City

$$\frac{57,100}{469,362} \times 100,000 = \textbf{12,165.45}$$

From this comparison, we can see that Oklahoma City has a lower crime rate. Specifically, 12,165.45 index crimes were committed per 100,000 persons in Oklahoma City in 1996 compared to 13,745.79 in Miami.

It is not necessary to use 100,000 as the standard number of comparison. In many cases, it may not make sense to use such a large number. If we wanted to compare crime rates across several cities with populations ranging from 25,000 to 50,000, it would seem more logical to calculate the rate based on either 10,000 or 1,000. Whatever standard number we choose, we must make sure that we use that same value for all of our comparisons. In essence, we want to compare apples to apples and not apples to oranges. To say that the crime rate in Miami is 13,745 per 100,000 persons compared to a rate of 1,216 per 10,000 in Oklahoma City renders our comparison awkward at best, because we are using two different values as multipliers.

Additionally, it is important to realize that the denominator represents the frequency at risk and will not always be the population of individuals in a particular area. For example, if we want to calculate the commercial robbery rate, the total frequency at risk is comprised of the total frequency of commercial establishments. If a city had 2,700 commercial establishments and there were 135 robberies, then the commercial robbery rate would be calculated by dividing the number of robberies (135) by the total number of commercial establishments (2,700), and multiplying by a standard number. As there are only 2,700 establishments, we may want to calculate a robbery rate per 500 by using the following formula:

$$\text{Rate} = \frac{135}{2,700} \times 500 = 25$$

Thus, we conclude that there were approximately 25 robberies committed for every 500 commercial establishments. Now that you understand the calculations for both ratios and rates, complete TryIT! Box 3.3.

TryIT!

BOX 3.3

Calculate the violent crime rate and property crime rate for each city listed below. In addition, calculate the ratio of property crimes to violent crimes.

City	Population	Violent Crimes	Property Crimes	Violent Rate	Property Rate	Ratio
Los Angeles	3,621,680	49,201	137,080			
Indianapolis	759,689	8,624	39,356			
Boston	559,631	7,427	27,554			
Dallas	1,089,178	15,952	86,022			
Miami	372,949	9,505	35,661			
Boise	159,050	579	7,974			
Seattle	538,105	4,475	48,577			

Source: Uniform Crime Reports (1998).

Cross-tabulations

Up to this point, we have discussed different types of data distributions involving one variable and its corresponding attributes. You have already learned that criminal justice research often involves the study of the effect of an independent variable on a dependent variable. One method in which we assess the relationship between two variables is **cross-tabulation** the use of cross-tabulations. A **cross-tabulation** is *a table that combines two separate frequency distributions into one table to examine the impact of an independent variable on a dependent variable*.

Let's assume that we asked 500 respondents the following two questions, "How safe do you feel being out alone at night?" and "Have you been the victim of a crime within the past 12 months?" We could construct a frequency distribution illustrating the frequencies and percentages for each variable as shown in Figures 3.4a and 3.4b. Approximately one in four respondents (25.40%) felt not at all safe, whereas a plurality of respondents (38.60%) felt very safe.

With regard to our second variable, 34% indicated that they had been victims of a crime compared to 66% who said they had not been victims. Certainly this

FIGURE 3.4a Frequency distribution and percentages for safety at night

Safety at Night	Frequency	Percentage
Very Safe	193	38.60
Somewhat Safe	180	36.0
Not at All Safe	127	25.40

FIGURE 3.4b Frequency distribution and percentages for victim of crime

Victim of Crime	Frequency	Percentage
Yes	170	34
No	330	66

information is useful in describing the attributes of our variables. We might believe, however, that how safe one feels is a function of whether one has been the victim of a crime or not. Therefore, we construct the following hypothesis:

Hypothesis: Respondents who have been victims of a crime are less likely to feel safe being out alone at night than are respondents who have not been victimized.

Our primary interest is to see if there are differences in the levels of fear between those who have been victims of crime and those who have not. In Table 3.7, we have put the independent variable (X) in the columns and the dependent variable (Y) in the rows. Therefore, we want to calculate column percentages to assess the impact of X on Y. Recall that our formula for calculating a percentage is to divide the frequency of an attribute by the total frequency multiplied by 100. In cross-tabulations, we use the term **cell frequencies** to refer to the frequency of two attributes occurring simultaneously. For example, in Table 3.7, the cell frequency of 28 refers to the number of individuals who said yes, they had been the victim of a crime, *and* who felt very safe at night. The number of cell frequencies is always equal to the number of attributes of the independent variable multiplied by the number of attributes of the dependent variable.

cell fre-quencies

To calculate the column percentages for the yes column, we divide the cell frequency of each attribute of our dependent variable by the total frequency of the column. Thus, of the 170 respondents who indicated they were the victim of crime, 28 said they felt very safe ($28/170 \times 100 = 16.47\%$), 45 said somewhat safe ($45/170 \times 100 = 26.47\%$), and 97 said not at all safe ($97/170 \times 100 = 57.06\%$). We use this same process to calculate the column percentages for those who have not been the victim of a crime. For example, of the 330 respondents who had not been the victim of a crime, 165 said they felt very safe ($165/330 \times 100 = 50\%$), 135 said somewhat safe ($135/330 \times 100 = 40.90\%$) and 30 said not at all safe ($30/330 \times 100 = 9.09\%$).

column marginal

row marginal

The column total, known as the **column marginal**, represents *the frequency and percentage of respondents falling within each category of the column variable*. Likewise, the row total is officially known as the **row marginal**, which is *the frequency and percentage of respondents falling within each category of the row variable*. In our example, the column marginal is the frequency distribution of our variable "safety at night" (see Figure 3.4a). The row marginal is the frequency distribution of our variable "victim of crime" (see Figure 3.4b).

Once we have calculated the column percentages, we are ready to interpret the results. We want to compare the percentages for each column of the independent vari-

TABLE 3.7 Cross-tabulation for Safety at Night by Victim of Crime Using Column Percentages

Safety at Night (Y)	Victim of Crime (X)		
	Yes	No	Row Total
Very safe	28	165	193
	16.47%	50.0%	38.60%
Somewhat safe	45	135	180
	26.47%	40.90%	36.0%
Not at all safe	97	30	127
	57.06%	9.09%	25.40%
Column total	170	330	500
	100%	100%	100%

able within each row of the dependent variable. Looking at Table 3.7, we see that over half of the victims (57%) indicated that they did not feel safe at all being out alone at night compared to only 9.09% of nonvictims. Put another way, 90.90% of nonvictims felt somewhat or very safe (50% + 40.9% = 90.90%) compared to 43% of victims (16.47% + 26.47% = 42.94%). Our results support our hypothesis that those who have been the victim of crime feel less safe being out alone at night.

In the above example, we placed the independent variable (X) in the columns and the dependent variable (Y) in the rows and proceeded to compare the column percentages to assess the effect of X on Y. We now reverse the order and place the independent variable in the rows and the dependent variable in the columns. Furthermore, let's assume that we believe that how safe one feels being out alone at night (X) has an effect on whether one carries a weapon such as mace or a firearm (Y). Our specific hypothesis might look like:

Hypothesis: Respondents who do not feel safe being out alone at night are more likely to carry a weapon than respondents who feel safe.

Because our independent variable—safety at night—is now in the rows and not the columns (Table 3.8), we need to calculate the row percentages in order to assess the effect of X on Y. To calculate the row percentages for the very safe row, we divide the frequency of each attribute of our dependent variable by the total frequency of the row. Thus, of the 193 respondents who said they felt very safe, 12 said they carried a weapon (12/193 × 100 = 6.22%) and 181 said they did not carry a weapon (181/193 × 100 = 93.78%). Among the 180 respondents who indicated that they felt somewhat safe, 14 carried a weapon (14/180 × 100 = 7.78%) and 166 did not carry a weapon (166/180 ×

100 = 92.22%). For those 127 respondents who said not at all safe, 57 carried a weapon (57/127 × 100 = 44.88%) and 70 did not (70/127 × 100 = 55.12%).

Now that we have calculated row percentages, we are ready to interpret the results. We want to compare the percentages across the three rows for each column. Table 3.8 shows little difference in the percentage of respondents who carried a weapon between those who felt either very safe (6.22%) or somewhat safe (7.78%). Among those who felt not all safe, however, 44.88% indicated that they carried a weapon, a much higher figure than for the other two categories. Once again, the results of the cross-tabulation support our hypothesis that those who do not feel safe are more likely to carry a weapon than those who feel safe being out alone at night.

The question that now arises is: Should the independent variable be in the columns or in the rows? Our recommendation—and it appears to be somewhat standard practice in criminal justice research—is to place the independent variable in the columns (see Table 3.7). If you consistently adopt this approach, it will become easier to know and calculate the right percentages and thereby simplify the analysis further. There may be situations in which the number of attributes for the independent variable far outnumber those for the dependent variable. In this case, you may want to place the independent variable in the rows, strictly because it may be easier to format the table. Once again, it is perfectly all right to do that. Keep in mind, however, that we always want the percentages of the independent variable, whether it is in the columns or in the rows, because we want to assess the effects of different levels of the independent variable (X) on each level of the dependent variable (Y). One final point: If we are comparing column percentages, the total column percentage must equal 100. Likewise, if we are comparing the row percentages, the total row percentage must equal 100.

TABLE 3.8 Cross-tabulation for Carrying a Weapon by Safety at Night Using Row Percentages

	Carry a Weapon (Y)		
	Yes	*No*	
Safety at Night (X)			*Row Marginal*
Very safe	12	181	193
	6.22%	93.78%	100%
Somewhat safe	14	166	180
	7.78%	92.22%	100%
Not at all safe	57	70	127
	44.88%	55.12%	100%
Column marginal	83	417	500
	100%	100%	100%

As you have learned, cross-tabulation tables are useful for combining two frequency distributions into a single table in order to assess the impact of an independent variable on a dependent variable. Before moving on to Section 3.3, take a few minutes to complete TryIT! Box 3.4.

TryIT!   BOX **3.4**

Using the following cross-tabulation table, calculate the row marginal and column marginal. In addition, determine the percentage of the independent variable within each attribute of the dependent variable to assess the effect of grade level on delinquency.

	Grade Level (X)			
	Eighth	*Tenth*	*Twelfth*	Row Marginal
Delinquent Acts (Y)				
None	54	48	67	
1–3	22	35	85	
4–10	5	10	17	
11 or more	0	1	8	
Column marginal				

Now that you have a good understanding of some basic statistics commonly used to describe variables and attributes, we would like to turn your attention to the use of computer technology to assist you in performing these statistical calculations.

3.3 Using Excel to Compute Descriptive Statistics

This section explains the methods for calculating descriptive statistics using Excel. Although our focus is on the calculation of the statistics previously explained in the chapter, we would like to take a moment to explain how to enter data into Excel. It is important to understand that statistics are calculated by means of mathematical operations. Additionally, to calculate statistics using a computer program such as Excel, the data we enter into the spreadsheet must be in numerical form. This is not to say that we cannot write labels or names for our variables and attributes in Excel—we can and should. For example, let's assume that we want to enter data for the following variables into Excel: "region"—West, Southwest, Midwest, Northeast, Southeast; "crime rate"—124.53, 156.34, 122.12, 144.76, 199.20; and "police agencies"—240, 147, 110, 120, 210. Our purpose at this point is simply to walk you through some basic steps for entering labels and data into Excel.

First, open Excel by clicking on the Microsoft Excel icon located on the menu bar or open up Excel through the start menu. Once the program has opened, you will be

TABLE 3.9 Excel Spreadsheet

	A	B	C	D	E	F	G	H
1	TABLE 3.9 Excel Spreadsheet							
2								
3								
4								
5								
6								
7								
8								
9								
10								
11								
12								
13								
14								
15								

looking at a spreadsheet like that shown in Table 3.9. The cursor will be located in cell a1*
and can be moved across columns and rows by using the arrow keys on the keyboard or by
moving the cursor to the desired cell and clicking the mouse. We labeled the spreadsheet
Table 3.9 simply by typing "Table 3.9 Excel Spreadsheet" in cell a1. (In this text, Excel
spreadsheets will show the table title in cell a1, where you would type it, and above the
table as well.) Words that are longer than the cell width will cross over into the next col-
umn(s). If you want to keep a word or value within a particular cell, you can increase the
cell width by placing the cursor on the line separating two columns and dragging the cursor over to increase the width. The same can be done for the depth of the rows.

Next, format cell justifications and font size in the spreadsheet. The default options
on Excel align numeric values on the right of the cell (right justification) and words on
the left of the cell (left justification), both using the 10 point font. You can change these
options by highlighting the entire spreadsheet (click on the top left-hand gray-shaded
cell above row 1 and left of column A) and using the menu options to set the font size
and cell justification. Although we suggest doing this step prior to entering your data,
you can do it after the data has already been entered, if necessary.

We are now ready to type in our labels and enter our data values. Place the cursor in
cell a3 and type the word Region and hit the right arrow key to move the cursor to cell

*Columns are labeled A, B, and so on in the tables; in text, cells are referred to as a1, b1, and so on.

b3. Type the words Crime Rate in cell b3 and Police Agencies in cell c3. Notice that both Crime Rate and Police Agencies do not fit within the current cell width. Therefore, we expanded the cell width by clicking on the line separating columns b and c and dragging the cursor over until Crime Rate fits within cell b3. We do the same procedure for Police Agencies in cell c3. Using the arrow keys, place the cursor in cell a4 and type the word West. You can either hit return or use the down arrow key to go to cell a5. In cell a5, type the word Southwest, followed by the return key. Once you have entered all the regions in column a, move the cursor to column b and begin entering the data values for the variable "Crime Rate." For example, in cell b4, we typed 122.53, which is the crime rate for the West region. Type in the rest of the values for column b, and then move the cursor to cell c4 and type in the values for the variable "Police Agencies." Our spreadsheet should now look like that in Table 3.10.

TABLE 3.10 Excel Spreadsheet–Sample Data

	A	B	C	D
1	Table 3.10 Excel Spreadsheet—Sample Data			
2				
3	Region	Crime Rate	Police Agencies	
4	West	122.53	240	
5	Southwest	156.34	147	
6	Midwest	122.12	110	
7	Northeast	144.76	120	
8	Southeast	199.20	210	

Now that you understand the process for entering data, let's turn our attention to calculating descriptive statistics using Excel. Assume that a sample of 1,556 respondents were asked, "How safe do you feel walking alone in your neighborhood at night?" The data is presented in Table 3.11.

Proportions

Recall our formula for calculating a proportion is given as:

$$\text{Proportion } (p) = \frac{\text{Frequency } (f)}{\text{Total } (n)}$$

Step 1: Place the cursor in cell c4 and write the following formula: =b3/b8.

b3 is the cell location for the frequency of the attribute—very safe.
b8 is the cell location for the total frequency of respondents (*n*).

/ is the symbol for division.

$ holds the column (b) and row (8) constant.

Step 2: Click on the lower right-hand corner of cell c4 containing the proportion for the first attribute of safety (e.g., "very safe") and drag the cursor to cell c8. This will automatically create the rest of the proportion column for each row.

.28   ←

Percentages

To calculate a percentage, we use the following formula:

$$\text{Percentage} \left(\%\right) = \frac{\text{Frequency}\left(f\right)}{\text{Total}\left(n\right)} \times 100$$

Step 1: Place the cursor in cell d3 and write the following formula: =(b3/b8)*100.

b3 is the cell location for the frequency of the attribute—very safe.
b8 is the cell location for the total frequency of respondents (*n*).
/ * are the symbols for division and multiplication, respectively.
$ holds the column (b) and row (8) constant.

Step 2: Click on the lower right-hand corner of cell d3 and drag the cursor to cell d7. This automatically will create the rest of the percentage column for each row.

TABLE 3.11 Feel Safe Walking Alone at Night in Own Neighborhood

	A	B	C	D	E	F
1	TABLE 3.11 Feel Safe Walking Alone at Night in Own Neighborhood					
2	Safety Ratings (X)	Frequency	Proportion	Percentage	Cumulative Percentage	Cumulative Frequency
3	Very safe	440	0.28	28.28	100.00	1556
4	Fairly safe	629	0.40	40.42	71.72	1116
5	Fairly unsafe	204	0.13	13.11	31.30	487
6	Very unsafe	252	0.16	16.20	18.19	283
7	Not sure	31	0.02	1.99	1.99	31
8	**Sum (*n*)**	**1556**	**1.00**	**100%**		

Cumulative Percentage

Step 1: Place the cursor in cell e7 and write: =d7. This will automatically copy the percentage value in cell d7 to cell e7.

Step 2: Place the cursor in cell e6 and write: =e7+d6. This will add the percentage in cell d6 to the cumulative percentage in cell e7.

Step 3: Click on the lower right-hand corner of cell e6 and drag the cursor up to cell e3. The rest of the cumulative percentage column will automatically be created.

Cumulative Frequency

Step 1: Place the cursor in cell f8 and write: =b8. This will automatically copy the frequency value in cell b8 to cell f8.

Step 2: Place the cursor in cell f6 and write: =f7+b6. This will add the frequency in cell b6 to the cumulative frequency in cell f7.

Step 3: Click on the lower right-hand corner of cell f6 and drag the cursor up to cell f4. The rest of the cumulative frequency column will automatically be created.

Rates

A professor is considering accepting a faculty position at one of six universities. Before making her decision, she would like some descriptive information concerning the amount of crime in each city. Using the data in Table 3.12, we calculate the crime rate per 10,000 persons for each city using the following formula:

$$\text{Rate} = \frac{\text{Frequency of occurrence}}{\text{Total frequency at risk}} \times 10,000$$

Step 1: Place the cursor in cell d3 and write the following formula: =(c3/b3)*10000.

c3 is the cell location for the frequency of index crimes for Topeka, KS.
b3 is the cell location for the population at risk for crime in Topeka, KS.
*10000 converts the proportion into a rate per 10,000 persons.

Step 2: Click on the lower right-hand corner of cell d3 and drag the cursor to cell d8, which corresponds with the last city in our table (e.g., Lansing, MI). This will automatically create the rest of the rate column for each row.

1267.05

By converting the number of index crimes to a rate that controls for population differences, we are now able to compare the amount of crime across the six cities. We can see that Vallejo, CA, has the lowest crime rate at 795.62 index crimes per 10,000 people, whereas Topeka, KS, has the highest (1,267.05 per 10,000).

TABLE 3.12 Calculating Crime Rates per 10,000

	A	B	C	D
1	Table 3.12 Calculating Crime Rates per 10,000			
2	City	Population	Crime Index	Crime Rate
3	Topeka, KS	121495	15394	1267.05
4	Vallejo, CA	113069	8996	795.62
5	Waco, TX	110213	11553	1048.24
6	Salem, OR	119822	10732	895.66
7	Macon, GA	113802	14011	1231.17
8	Lansing, MI	120821	9744	806.48

Source: Bureau of Justice Statistics (1998).

3.4 Graphical Representation of Data

Up to this point, we have discussed various methods, such as frequency distributions and cross-tabulation tables, for representing our data in tabular format. In many instances, it may be more desirable to present our data in graphical form to aid in the interpretation and understanding of the information. Some of the most commonly used graphs in criminal justice research include histograms, bar and line graphs, and pie charts.

Histograms

histogram A **histogram** is *a chart that describes a numerical variable in which the height of the bars represents the frequencies of the attributes*. It is most common to represent the frequency of each attribute along the vertical axis with the numerical value, or range of values, along the horizontal axis. The bars, representing the different attributes, are connected. That is, there is no space separating the vertical bars. Histograms are especially useful for making comparisons among the different attributes of a variable.

Assume that a sample of inmates took an educational exam on arrival in a state prison facility. The warden wants to know how well the inmates did on the exam. We could, of course, construct a frequency distribution listing the range of scores and their

FIGURE 3.5 Histogram for educational exam score

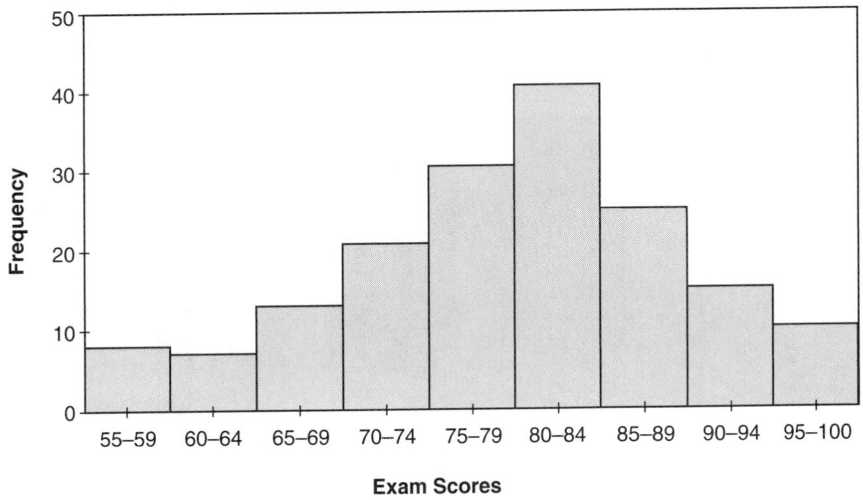

corresponding frequencies; however, we decided to present the data graphically, using a histogram (see Figure 3.5). The attributes for our variable are defined as a range of numerical scores, listed along the horizontal axis (e.g., 55–59, 60–64 . . .), whereas the frequency of individuals falling within each range is listed on the vertical axis. Looking at the histogram, we immediately can see that the highest bar is associated with the 80–84 range, indicating that more inmates scored in this range than any other. We determine the number of inmates falling within each range by comparing the height of each bar with the frequency labels on the vertical axis. For example, nine offenders scored between 55 and 59, eight offenders scored between 60 and 64, and so on. The advantage of a histogram is that the frequencies associated with the attributes of a variable are easily identified by comparing the height of the bars. The higher the bar, the greater the frequency of respondents falling within that interval.

Bar Graphs

bar graph   An alternative to the frequency histogram is the bar graph. A **bar graph** is *a chart that describes a categorical variable in which the bars are separated by spacing and the height of the bars represents the percentages or frequencies of the attributes.* As shown in Figure 3.6, the highest percentage of offenders (32%) is classified as community custody simply by comparing the height of the bars. A pattern also is evident in the chart; the percentage of offenders falling within each custody level decreases as the custody level increases from less secure to more secure. Put another way, a higher percentage of offenders are classified at lower custody levels. The bars are no longer connected, indicating that our variable is categorical and not numerical.

FIGURE 3.6 Bar graph for custody level

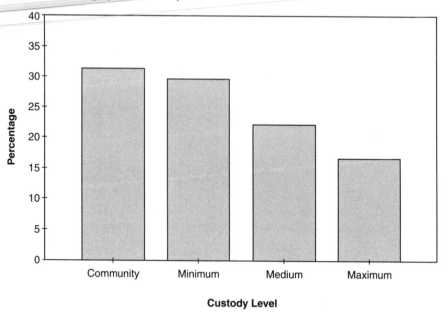

An additional advantage of a bar graph is that it allows us to compare two variables and their attributes in a single graph. Using the above example of custody level, we may want to compare the frequency and percentage of males and females within each custody level. Therefore, instead of having one bar representing the total percentage of males and females combined within each custody level, we will now have two bars representing males and females, respectively, for each category of custody level. Figure 3.7 demonstrates that more males were classified as minimum custody than any other custody level, and among females, the highest frequency is shown for community custody. Although the frequency graph allows us to compare males and females across custody levels, it does not allow us to compare males versus females within custody levels. We may be tempted to make this comparison using Figure 3.7, in which case we might say that the number of males is greater than females for each level of custody. Technically, this is true; however, it is true simply because there are more males than females in the sample.

A more meaningful comparison is to calculate the percentage of males and females within each custody level. As shown in Figure 3.8, a higher percentage of females than of males are classified as community and medium custody. This is not what we would have concluded had we used the frequency graph. The pattern illustrated for males and females across custody levels is the same in Figures 3.7 and 3.8.

A final comment on histograms and bar graphs: In the foregoing examples, we have placed the attributes of our variables (e.g., labels and numerical values) along the horizontal axis and the frequencies/percentages along the vertical axis. Although this is probably the most common method of illustrating graphs, we could just as easily have reversed the order by placing the attributes on the vertical axis and the frequencies/percentages on the horizontal axis. How you display your data graphically is really a matter of personal preference.

FIGURE 3.7 Frequency bar graph for custody level by gender

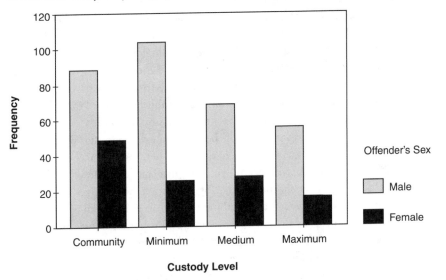

FIGURE 3.8 Percentage bar graph for custody level by gender

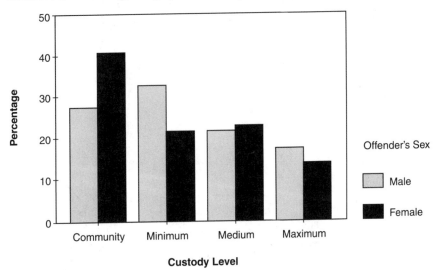

Line Graphs

line graphs   Criminal justice research often uses **line graphs** as an alternative method for graphically representing data. Such graphical representations are ideal for demonstrating trends. A **frequency polygon** is *a line graph that describes a numerical variable in which a dot over each attribute represents the frequency of that attribute*. The dots are then connected by a line to illustrate the different values of our variable. As with the histogram, the frequencies are plotted on the vertical axis and the values for the attributes are placed on the horizontal axis.

frequency polygon

Figure 3.9 illustrates a frequency polygon for the variable "minimum monthly sentence." Our attributes are defined as six-month intervals, with the dot for each interval representing the frequency of offenders falling within that particular interval. For instance, 8 offenders were sentenced to 1 to 6 months, compared to 28 offenders who were sentenced to 7 to 12 months. The graph further illustrates a sharp increase in the number of offenders sentenced from 1 to 6 months up to 13 to 18 months, followed by a dramatic decrease for those sentenced to 25 to 30 months.

There are several variations of the frequency polygon that we could use to illustrate our data, including cumulative frequencies, percentages, and cumulative percentages. The pattern for a percentage polygon is much like that shown in Figure 3.9; however, the dot represents the percentage of subjects falling within each interval. Polygons using cumulative percentages and frequencies do not have an up-and-down pattern like that in Figure 3.9 but, rather, have an upward pattern as we move to ever-increasing values for our attributes. In Figure 3.10, there is no downward pattern, simply because we are adding the frequency of the previous intervals to each successive interval. For example, the dot above the interval 19–24 comprises the frequency of the interval (78)

FIGURE 3.9 Frequency polygon for minimum monthly sentence

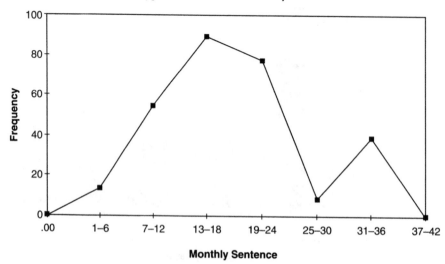

FIGURE 3.10 Cumulative frequency polygon for minimum monthly sentence

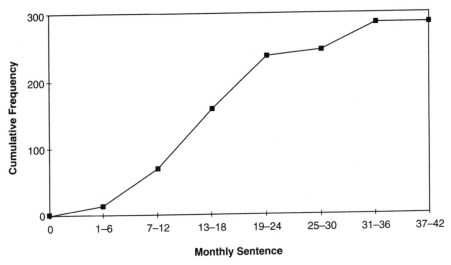

plus the summed frequency of the three previous intervals—1–6, 7–12, 13–18 (159), thus representing a cumulative frequency of 237.

Although it is impossible to have a downward pattern in cumulative frequency or percentage polygon, it is possible to have a flat line from one point to another. This occurs when we move from one attribute to another in which the frequency for the next attribute is zero, thus causing our cumulative frequency to be unchanged. As shown in Figure 3.10, the cumulative frequency for the 31–36 interval is approximately 286, which remains unchanged as we move to the next interval—37–42—because the frequency for this interval is zero.

Frequency polygons also can be used to compare averages and rates, more than one variable in a single graph, and changes in a variable over time. Although these comparisons are common, researchers typically refer to these graphs as line charts, not frequency polygons. The line chart in Figure 3.11 displays the budget for the U.S. Marshals Service from 1981 to 1997. The graph illustrates a steady increase in the budget over the course of 17 years, with the most dramatic increases occurring from 1994 through 1997.

At times, we want to compare more than one variable within a single graph. In Figure 3.12, the comparison involves three variables and their corresponding attributes. The comparison involves two independent variables—sex and education—on one dependent variable—misconduct reports. Simply put, we are comparing the average number of misconduct reports between males and females at various levels of education. The line for females starts at seven years of education, whereas that for males starts at six years. This is because no females in the sample had the value of six years of education; therefore, no average can be computed for females at this level of education.

FIGURE 3.11 Line chart for U.S. Marshals' budget by year

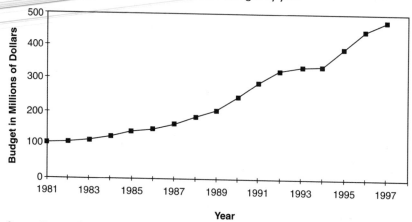

Source: Bureau of Justice Statistics (1998). *Sourcebook of Criminal Justice Statistics* (Washington, DC: U.S. Government Printing Office).

FIGURE 3.12 Line chart for average misconduct reports by sex and education

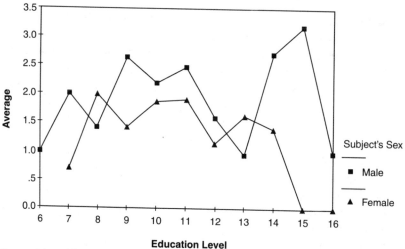

Source: Adapted from Proctor (1999).

Pie Charts

pie chart   A final type of graph that is commonly used in criminal justice research is the pie chart. This type of graph is ideal for displaying proportions and percentages. A pie chart is a circular graph that is divided into different sections representing the attributes of a variable. Whereas line graphs are used for numerical variables, pie charts are used primarily with categorical variables, whereby each slice of the pie represents the percentage of cases falling within a particular category.

FIGURE 3.13 Pie chart for parole board decision

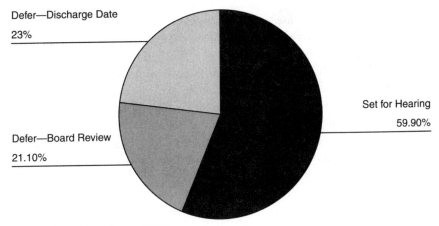

Defer—Discharge Date
23%

Set for Hearing
59.90%

Defer—Board Review
21.10%

Source: Adapted from Proctor (1999).

As shown in Figure 3.13, the larger the slice of the pie, the larger the percentage of cases having that attribute. Because the total area of the pie is equal to 100%, we can see that 55.90% of the inmates were "set for a hearing," which covers slightly more than half of the total area of the pie. More specifically, the percentage of cases within a category is equal to the percentage of the area covered in the pie.

Now that you have a thorough understanding of the different types of graphs commonly used in criminal justice research, construct a bar graph using the data in TryIT! Box 3.5.

TryIT!   BOX **3.5**

Using the following data, construct a bar graph to represent the frequency of offenses committed by juveniles within each age group for single- and two-parent families.

Single-Parent		Two-Parent	
Age (X)	Frequency (f)	Age (X)	Frequency (f)
9–10	5	9–10	2
11–12	15	11–12	5
13–14	25	13–14	7
15–16	42	15–16	18
17–18	35	17–18	10
Total	122		42

3.5 Summary

This chapter has focused on various formats for organizing and presenting criminal justice data. We began by looking at three different types of tabular data distributions: single, frequency, and grouped frequency distributions. You will recall that a single data distribution is one in which each attribute listed represents one subject's value or label on the variable. A frequency distribution lists the values of the attributes in one column, with their frequency of occurrence in another column. A grouped frequency distribution comprises attributes that are defined by a range of values instead of a single value. Single data distributions and frequency distributions may be used for both categorical and numerical data, whereas grouped frequency distributions are only used for numerical data.

Next, we discussed some descriptive statistics that are commonly used to make comparisons between variables and their attributes. Specifically, we defined and described how to calculate proportions, percentages, ratios, and rates. We extended this discussion further by incorporating these statistics into our data distributions, thereby increasing the amount of information that could be gained. The usefulness of cumulative frequencies and percentages was also addressed. Cross-tabulations provide a method for comparing frequencies and percentages of two variables and their attributes within one table. We then demonstrated how using computer technology can simplify our calculations, by illustrating the calculation of these statistics using Excel.

Various methods of graphical representations for criminal justice data were discussed. A histogram is a bar chart describing the frequency or percentage of a numerical variable, whereas a bar graph is a chart that describes the frequency or percentage of a categorical variable. Frequency polygons and line charts are line graphs that describe some characteristic (e.g., frequency, percentage, average) of a variable in which the dots, representing the value within each attribute, are connected by a straight line. Pie charts are useful for visualizing the percentages of each attribute as covering a percentage of the area within the pie. Both bar charts and line charts provide the opportunity to make comparisons of multiple variables within a single graph.

Key Terms

single data distribution	cumulative percentage	row marginal
frequency distribution	ratio	histogram
grouped frequency distribution	rate	bar graph
proportion	cross-tabulation	line graphs
percentage	cell frequencies	frequency polygon
cumulative frequency	column marginal	pie chart

TryIT! Answers

Box 3.1

Drug Type (X)	Frequency (f)
Alcohol	14
Cocaine	10
Marijuana	8
Crack	6
Heroin	4

Box 3.2

Technical Violations	Frequency	Proportion	Percentage	Cumulative Percentage	Cumulative Frequency
6	15	0.03	3	100	500
5	16	0.03	3.20	97%	485
4	20	0.04	4	93.80%	469
3	68	0.14	13.60	89.80%	449
2	47	0.09	9.40	76.20%	381
1	132	0.26	26.40	66.80%	334
0	202	0.40	40.40	40.40%	202
Totals	500	1.00	100		

Box 3.3

City	Population	Violent Crimes	Property Crimes	Violent Rate	Property Rate	Ratio
Los Angeles	3,621,680	49,201	137,080	1358.51	3784.98	2.79
Indianapolis	759,689	8,624	39,356	1135.20	5180.54	4.56
Boston	559,631	7,427	27,554	1327.12	4923.60	3.71
Dallas	1,089,178	15,952	86,022	1464.59	7897.88	5.39
Miami	372,949	9,505	35,661	2548.61	9561.90	3.75
Boise	159,050	579	7,974	364.04	5013.52	13.77
Seattle	538,105	4,475	48,577	831.62	9027.42	10.86

Box 3.4

| | Grade Level (X) | | | |
	Eighth	Tenth	Twelfth	
Delinquent Acts (Y)				Row Marginal
None	54	48	67	169
	66.69%	51.06%	37.85%	
1–3	22	35	85	142
	27.16%	37.23%	48.02%	
4–10	5	10	17	32
	6.17%	10.64%	9.60%	
11 or more	0	1	8	9
	0%	1.04%	4.52%	
Column Marginal	81	94	177	352
	100%	100%	100%	

Box 3.5 Frequency Bar Graph for Offenses by Age and Parental Status

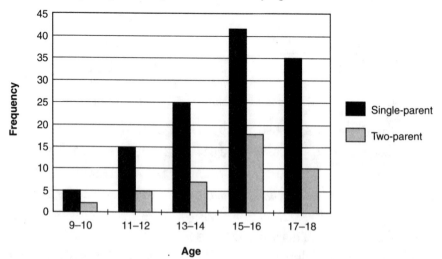

3.6 Problems

1. In the following table, 30 inmates were asked for which crime they currently were incarcerated. Convert the single data distribution into a frequency distribution.

Crime	*Crime*	*Crime*
Robbery	Assault	Theft
Burglary	Theft	Theft
Theft	Assault	Robbery
Theft	Assault	Theft
Burglary	Burglary	Theft
Robbery	Burglary	Burglary
Robbery	Theft	Burglary
Theft	Theft	Theft
Burglary	Assault	Robbery
Robbery	Burglary	Theft

2. Using the frequency distribution created in problem 1, calculate the proportion and percentage of inmates who committed each of the four crimes.

3. Using the table in problem 1, combine robbery and assault into one category, labeled "violent," and theft and burglary into another category, labeled "property," and create a frequency distribution of violent and property offenders. Calculate the ratio of property offenders to violent offenders.

4. A researcher hypothesizes that drug counseling has an effect on the outcome of probation. Using the following data, calculate the percentage of successful probationers who received drug counseling versus the percentage of successful probationers who did not receive drug counseling.

	Drug Counseling		
Probation Outcome	Yes	No	Total
Success	294	395	689
Failure	86	187	273
Total	380	582	962

5. In the preceding table, identify the independent and dependent variable.

6. Among those who did not receive drug counseling, calculate the percentage who succeeded versus the percentage that failed.

7. According to the Bureau of Justice Statistics (1998), 38,419 offenders were sentenced to a term of imprisonment in U.S. district courts in 1997. Using the following data, calculate the percentage, cumulative frequency, and cumulative percentage for the frequency distribution.

Sentence Length	Frequency
1–12 months	9,086
13–35 months	11,054
36–60 months	7,547
Over 60 months	10,732

8. Using Excel, calculate the following crime rates per 1,000 persons—crime index, violent crime, and property crime—for each city listed in the table.

City	Population	Crime Index	Violent Crime	Property Crime
Topeka, KS	121,495	15,394	1,502	13,892
Vallejo, CA	113,069	8,996	1,564	7,432
Waco, TX	110,213	11,553	1,352	10,201
Salem, OR	119,822	10,732	394	10,338
Macon, GA	113,802	14,011	924	13,087
Lansing, MI	120,821	9,744	1,649	8,095

Source: Bureau of Justice Statistics (1998). *Sourcebook of Criminal Justice Statistics* (Washington, DC: U.S. Government Printing Office).

9. In studying the amount of good-time days a sample of offenders lost in a given year, a researcher constructed a frequency distribution to describe his data. Convert the following frequency distribution into a grouped frequency distribution using six intervals.

Lost Days	Frequency	Lost Days	Frequency	Lost Days	Frequency
30	5	18	4	7	9
27	7	17	7	6	12
25	3	15	5	5	8
22	12	11	21	4	17
20	2	9	13	0	32

10. Construct a frequency and percentage bar graph for the sample of 100 convicted defendants who received the following sentences:

Sentence	Frequency
Fine	42
Probation	25
House arrest	16
Community service	12
Prison	5

11. Construct a line chart for the number of prior DUI (driving under the influence) arrests received by a sample of jail inmates currently incarcerated for drunk driving.

Prior DUI arrests	Frequency
12	6
9	11
5	18
4	21
2	19
1	45

12. Enter the following data into an Excel spreadsheet and calculate the proportion and percentage for each attribute. In addition, calculate the ratio of truancy to runaway and the ratio of curfew to incorrigibility.

Status Offense	Frequency
Runaway	5
Truancy	21
Curfew	52
Incorrigibility	18

13. Enter the following data into an Excel spreadsheet and calculate the expulsion rate and disciplinary hearing rate per 100 juveniles for each high school. Additionally, calculate the ratio of disciplinary to expulsion hearings for each school.

High School	Population	Expulsions	Disciplinary Hearings
Sammamish	1,400	5	20
Hudson	800	4	18
Penn	3,000	8	28
Westfield	1,300	4	35
Inglemoore	950	3	42

14. In a survey of criminal justice research methods classes at an eastern college, students were asked to describe their future professional objective. Using the following data, construct a pie chart that represents the data from the survey.

Career Objective	Percentage
Law enforcement	59.26
Corrections	11.11
Graduate school	20.37
Law school	1.85
Other	7.41

Measures of Central Tendency

ExploreIT!

As the chief training officer at the police academy, you have been asked by the director of the academy to provide a report to the police commission concerning the recruitment of police officers. The police commission is particularly interested in knowing how well new recruits performed on the police officer entrance exam. You have the test scores of the 125 recruits. How would you use these scores to provide the police commission with a report on the recruits' test performance? In this case, you would provide descriptive statistics known as measures of central tendency. The three measures of central tendency are the mode, median, and mean.

Descriptive statistics describe or summarize a set of data in order to make numbers understandable. Using a few summary measures enables us to provide accurate descriptions of a group of scores without having to provide the entire set of scores or observations. Characteristics of a data set are commonly described using **measures of central tendency**, *a group of indexes that describe how scores of observations in a distribution tend to cluster*. Put another way, these measures attempt to identify the score(s) that best represent the data distribution. The three measures of central tendency are the mode, median, and mean.

measures of central tendency

4.1 Single Data Distribution

Mode

mode

The **mode** (symbolized as Mo) is defined as *the most frequently occurring score in a group of scores*. More specifically, it is the score in a given data set that occurs more than any other score. Figure 4.1 provides two data sets, of 11 and 10 jail inmates, respectively, containing the number of prior arrests. To determine the mode, we need only to count the number of times each score occurs. In data set A, we can see that one offender had six prior arrests, three offenders had four prior arrests, two offenders had three prior arrests, and so on. The mode for data set A is 4, because that number occurred

FIGURE 4.1 Unimodal and bimodal distributions for prior arrest

Data Set A	Data Set B
Prior Arrests (n = 11)	Prior Arrests (n = 10)
6	6
4	4
4	4
4	4
3	3
3	2
2	2
2	2
1	1
0	0
0	

three times—more than any other number. That is, three offenders had four prior arrests, which was the most frequently occurring score for this group of offenders.

unimodal distribution

In cases where there is only one mode, the distribution is said to be unimodal. A **unimodal** data **distribution** is defined as a data distribution *characterized by only one mode*; that is, one score occurs more frequently than any other score. Data set B, by contrast, is defined as bimodal, because there are two scores that occur most frequently. Thus, a **bimodal distribution** is defined as a data distribution *characterized by two modes*. That is, three offenders had four prior arrests and three offenders had two prior arrests. A distribution *with more than two modes* is defined as a **multimodal distribution**.

bimodal distribution

multimodal distribution

Median

median

The **median** (symbolized as Md) is defined as *the middle score in a data set*. It is the score that falls at the 50th percentile, resulting in an equal number of scores above and below it. To find the median, it is necessary to arrange the data in descending order (highest to lowest score) or ascending order (lowest to highest score). Data set A in Figure 4.1 is arranged in descending order. As there are 11 scores, we know that the middle score will be the score that has five scores above and five scores below the median value. Counting down from the top of the data set the fifth score is a 3, and counting up from the bottom the fifth score is a 2. The score that falls between the 3 and the 2 is a 3. The median value for data set A is 3.

For data sets that have an even number of scores, the median is calculated in much the same way, except we need to take the average of the two middle scores. Because there are ten scores in data set B, the middle score will be the fifth score ($10 / 2 = 5$). Counting from the top down the fifth score is 3, and counting from the bottom up the fifth score is 2. We then need to add these two scores together and divide by 2 to obtain the average of the two scores, which in this case equals 2.5. The median value is therefore 2.5. This represents the middle score for the group of values. It should be noted that 2.5 is the median value, even though no inmate actually had 2.5 arrests.

Mean

mean

The mean for a sample is symbolized as $\bar{X}$ (pronounced *X* bar), and the mean for a population is symbolized as μ (Greek letter mu, pronounced "myoo"). The **mean** is defined as *the average score among a group of scores in a data distribution*. In criminal justice research, the mean is the most common measure of central tendency. The mean is calculated by adding the scores in a distribution and dividing by the total number of scores. The following formulas are used in calculating the mean for a distribution of scores for a sample and a population:

Sample: **Population:**

$$\bar{X} = \frac{\Sigma X}{n} \qquad\qquad \mu = \frac{\Sigma X}{N}$$

Σ = sum
X = each score or observation in the distribution
N = the total number of scores or observations for a population
n = the total number of scores or observations for a sample

Returning to our example of 11 prisoners and the number of prior arrests, we calculate the mean for the data in Figure 4.2 by adding the 11 scores for prior arrests (each score represents one X value), then dividing by the total number of scores in the distribution.

FIGURE 4.2 Calculating the mean for a single data distribution

Prior Arrests (X)
6
4
4
4
3
3
2
2
1
0
0

$\Sigma X =$ 29
n = 11 scores
$\bar{X}$ = 29/11 = 2.64

You are now ready to calculate the three measures of central tendency for a single data distribution. Take the time to complete TryIT! Box 4.1.

TryIT!

BOX **4.1**

Consider the number of campus parking tickets received by a sample of eight faculty members. Calculate the mode, median, and mean for the single data distribution below.

Parking Tickets (X)
5
3
0
1
0
3
3
1

4.2 Frequency Distribution

Up to this point, the methods for obtaining measures of central tendency have been calculated for single data. That is, each score in the distribution corresponds to a single individual or case. In many cases, especially when the sample size is large, it is more efficient to use a frequency distribution rather than listing each individual score. Figure 4.3 illustrates a frequency distribution for a sample of 100 parolees (n = sum of f column). Each number under the variable "technical violations" represents the score for our X variable, whereas the corresponding number under f represents the frequency or number of parolees who had that many violations. For example, 9 parolees had five violations, 14 parolees had four violations, and so on.

FIGURE 4.3 Frequency distribution for technical violations

Technical Violations (X)	Frequency (f)
5	9
4	14
3	26
2	11
1	10
0	30

Mode

In a single data distribution, the calculation of the mode consists of counting each score to determine which score occurred most frequently. In a frequency distribution, the *f* column represents the number of subjects that received each score on our variable. Therefore, to calculate the mode, we need only look at the *f* column to find the highest number of respondents and its corresponding *X* value. In the preceding example, 30 respondents had zero violations, meaning that zero is the most frequently occurring score. Thus, the mode for this data set is zero.

Median

To calculate the median for a frequency distribution, we need to find the middle score. Recall that the median is that score in the distribution that has an equal number of scores above and below it. You can see when you look at the distribution that we have six *X* scores. Because our sample size (*n*) is 100, however, and we are dealing with a frequency distribution, we really have 100 scores. Therefore, the median is going to be the 50th score (100/2 = 50). Using the *f* column, we need to count down 50 scores from the top and count up 50 scores from the bottom. The first 9 scores from the top correspond with 5 technical violations. Scores 10 through 23 correspond with 4 technical violations, scores 24 through 49 with 3, and scores 50 through 60 with 2 technical violations. Thus, the 50th score down from the top has a value of 2 technical violations. We can repeat this process, counting up from the bottom. Scores one through 30 had zero violations, scores 31 through 40 had one violation, and scores 41 through 51 had two violations. The 50th score from the bottom also corresponds with two technical violations. This is the resulting median for this data set.

Mean

Calculating the mean for a frequency distribution requires us to use the following formula:

$$\overline{X} = \frac{\Sigma fX}{n}$$

Σ = sum
f = frequency of *X* score
X = each score or observation in the distribution
n = total number of scores or observations (sum of the *f* column)

Unlike a single data distribution, where we simply summed the *X* scores and divided by the total number of scores, a frequency distribution requires an additional step—we must take into account the frequency of each *X* score. Thus, each value of *X* must be multiplied by its corresponding frequency. To simplify the calculation of the mean, we recommend creating a third column labeled fX, in which you multiply each X score by its corresponding frequency (Figure 4.4)—for example, $5 \times 9 = 45$, $4 \times 14 = 56$—continuing to the end of the distribution. Once the fX column is completed, simply sum the column and divide by the sample size. It is important to remember when using a frequency distribution that the sample size is determined by summing the f column, not the number of X scores. In the preceding example, the sample size is 100. Plugging the numbers into our formula, we have a numerator of 211 ($\Sigma fX = 211$) divided by a denominator of 100 ($\Sigma f = 100$), resulting in a mean of 2.11.

FIGURE 4.4 Calculating the mean for a frequency distribution

Technical Violations (X)	f	fX
5	9	45
4	14	56
3	26	78
2	11	22
1	10	10
0	30	0
	$n = 100$	$\Sigma fX = 211$

$\bar{X} = 211/100 = 2.11$

Complete TryIT! Box 4.2 by calculating the mode, median, and mean for a frequency distribution.

TryIT!   BOX **4.2**

In review, let's consider the following number of delinquent acts committed by a sample of 20 junior high school students. Using what you have learned about measures of central tendency for a frequency distribution, calculate the mode, median, and mean.

Delinquent Acts (X)	Frequency (f)
5	3
4	6
2	9
0	2

4.3 Grouped Data Distribution

There are situations in which data may be presented in such a way that it is not possible to determine the exact score that a respondent obtained on a specific variable. This is particularly likely to be the case when data is presented in a grouped frequency distribution. Figure 4.5 illustrates a distribution of grouped data involving a sample of 100 police recruits and their scores on an officer entrance exam. Grouped data, in similar fashion to a frequency distribution, also uses a frequency column to identify the number of respondents who received a particular value on a variable. With grouped data, however, we do not have the exact score but, rather, a range of values in which each subject scored.

Looking at the first row, we know that 13 respondents scored between 90 and 100. It is possible that all 13 officers scored 100 or that the scores are evenly distributed throughout the range. Simply put, we do not know how the scores fall within the range—only that they are between the two values that mark the low and high ends of the range. To calculate measures of central tendency with grouped data, we need to reduce the range of values to a single value. Our goal is to select the best score in the range, one that would be an accurate reflection of most of the scores falling within the range. Therefore, we select a value that represents the midpoint—the median value—of the range of values. To calculate the midpoint, we need only to add the highest and lowest values of the range and divide by 2. For example, in row 1, we would add 90 (low range) to 100 (high range), which equals 190 divided by 2, resulting in a midpoint of 95. The midpoint for row 2 is 84.50 (80 + 89 = 169/2 = 84.50). As shown in Figure 4.50, we recommend creating a third column, labeled *m*, which represents the midpoint of each range of *X* scores.

FIGURE 4.5 Grouped frequency distribution for officer's exam scores

Exam Score (X)	f	m
90–100	13	95
80–89	21	84.50
70–79	38	74.50
60–69	17	64.50
50–59	11	54.50

Mode

To determine the mode for grouped data, we use the same procedure used for a frequency distribution. We need to identify the *X* score that was obtained by the highest number of individuals. Looking at the frequency column (*f*), we find that 38 recruits scored in the 70–79 range, more than in any other range. Because we want a single score to represent the mode, we simply select the midpoint that corresponds with the selected range. In this case, the mode is identified as 74.50, the midpoint of the 70–79 range.

Median

Determining the median for grouped data is somewhat more complex than the methods we have used for single data and frequency distributions. The following formula is used for locating the median value for grouped data:

$$Md = \begin{array}{c} \text{Lower limit of} \\ \text{Md interval} \end{array} + \frac{\dfrac{n}{2} - \begin{array}{c}cf \text{ below} \\ \text{lower limit} \\ \text{of Md interval}\end{array}}{\text{Frequency in Md interval}} \times \begin{array}{c}\text{Size of the} \\ \text{Md interval}\end{array}$$

The first step in the process is to create a cumulative frequency column (cf). As discussed in Chapter 2, the cumulative frequency is constructed by summing the f column in successive steps. Each f value is added to the cf value to form a running total (see Figure 4.6). The second step is to determine where the middle score falls. As we have 100 scores (total of cf column), the middle score is the 50th score (100/2 = 50). Going up the cf column, we find that the 50th score falls in the 70–79 range. More specifically, scores 1 through 11 fall in the 50–59 range, scores 12 through 28 fall in the 60–69 range, and scores 29 through 66 fall within the 70–79 range (this includes the 50th score). Because we know that the median value falls in the 70–79 interval, we can plug the appropriate numbers into the formula. The lower limit of the median interval is the score that occurs just above the next lowest score and yet is within the 70–79 interval. The next lowest score from 70 is 69, which puts us into the 60–69 interval. Taking into account our rules for rounding numbers, the lowest score possible in the 70–79 interval that is just above the next lowest score of 69 is 69.50, which is the lower limit of the median interval.

FIGURE 4.6 Calculating the cumulative frequency (*cf*) for a grouped frequency distribution

Exam Score (X)	f	m	cf
90–100	13	95	100 (13+21+38+17+11)
80–89	21	84.5	87 (21+38+17+11)
70–79	38	74.5	66 (38+17+11)
60–69	17	64.5	28 (17+11)
50–59	11	54.5	11 (11+0)

The *cf* below the lower limit of the Md level is 28 (column 4), because that is the value of the cumulative frequency for the next lowest interval of 60–69. The frequency in the Md level is found in column 2. It refers to the number of subjects falling within the 70–79 interval, which in this case equals 38. The size of the interval is found in column 1 and represents the total number of scores within the interval. The interval has a range of 70 to 79, which represents a total of 10 possible scores (e.g., 70, 71 . . . 79). Thus, the median is calculated by placing the appropriate values into the formula and solving as follows:

$$Md = 69.50 + \frac{\frac{100}{2} - 28}{38} \times 10$$

$$69.50 + \frac{(50 - 28)}{38} \times 10$$

$$69.50 + \left[(.58)10 \right]$$

$$69.50 + 5.8$$

$$Md = 75.30$$

Mean

We will now return to our example of police recruits and their performance on a police officer entrance exam. We want to know the average exam score for the sample of 100 recruits. The process is similar to that used for determining the mean for a frequency distribution, whereby we multiplied each score by its corresponding frequency. The only difference here is that we replace the exact score used in a frequency distribution with *m*, the midpoint for the range of values used in a grouped data distribution. For grouped data, we multiply each midpoint by its corresponding frequency, as the midpoint represents the best single value for the range of scores. The formula is written as follows:

$$\bar{X} = \frac{\Sigma fm}{n}$$

As shown in Figure 4.7, we recommend creating a fourth column labeled *fm*, which represents each midpoint multiplied by its corresponding frequency. Once the *fm* column is completed, we sum the column and divide by the total sample size (sum of *f* column). This results in a mean of 75.37.

By now you should have a good understanding of how measures of central tendency are calculated for single, frequency, and grouped data distributions. Once again, we recommend that you complete the following TryIT! exercise (Box 4.3) before moving on to the next section.

FIGURE 4.7 Calculating the mean for a grouped frequency distribution

Exam Score (X)	f	m	fm
90–100	13	95	1235
80–89	21	84.50	1774.50
70–79	38	74.50	2831
60–69	17	64.50	1096.50
50–59	11	54.50	599.50
	$\Sigma f = 100$		$\Sigma fm = 7536.50$

$\bar{X} = 7536.50/100 = 75.37$

TryIT!   BOX 4.3

Consider the number of hours worked in a typical week by a sample of 100 inmates at a local jail. Calculate the mode, median, and mean for the grouped data distribution below.

Hours Worked (X)	Frequency (f)
30–40	15
20–29	30
15–19	8
10–14	5
0–9	42

You have now mastered the calculations for measures of central tendency by hand for the three different types of data distributions—single, frequency, and grouped. Next, we turn to the use of computer technology to simplify our calculations and organize our data more effectively.

4.4 Using Excel to Compute Measures of Central Tendency

This section provides a demonstration on the calculation of measures of central tendency using Excel. We assume that the data has already been entered into the spreadsheet. We now proceed with step-by-step instructions for performing the statistical calculations.

Single Data Distribution

Recall that single data consists of one column of values that represents scores or observations on a single variable. Let's assume the police chief of a large urban department wants to know some descriptive information about citizens' complaints against the department. The chief selects a sample of 12 police officers and counts the number of complaints (variable X) each officer received in the past year. The data is presented in Table 4.1. Once the data has been entered into Excel, the following steps are necessary to calculate the mode, median, and mean.

Mode

Step 1: Place the cursor in cell b15 and click on the paste function box (also known as "function wizard").

Step 2: Click on the function category called **statistical**.

Step 3: Click on the name category called **mode**.

Step 4: Click **next** and a box will appear that will ask for the range of scores for which you want to calculate the mode. Type in the range of cells within which the X values lie (b3:b14) and click **finish**; or highlight the range by selecting cell b3 and dragging down through cell b14, then click **finish**. The resulting mode is equal to 2.

Median

Steps 1 and 2: Place the cursor in cell b16 and repeat steps 1 and 2, as shown above.

Step 3: Click on name category called **median**.

Step 4: Same as above.

This results in a median of 2.

Mean

Steps 1 and 2: Place the cursor in cell b17 and repeat steps 1 and 2 as shown above.

Step 3: Click on name category called **average**.

Step 4: Same as above.

The mean for this data is 2.25.

Computing measures of central tendency for single data is relatively easy with the use of the paste function. Additionally, when calculating the median for single data, it is not necessary to reorder the data as it is when performing calculations by hand. Computing these measures for frequency and grouped data distributions requires a bit more work; however, with a little practice, you will find that using a spreadsheet is superior to working with hand calculations.

TABLE 4.1 Calculating Measures of Central Tendency with Single Data

	A	B
1	TABLE 4.1 Calculating Measues of Central Tendency with Single Data	
2		Complaints (X)
3		3
4		2
5		4
6		0
7		0
8		4
9		1
10		3
11		2
12		1
13		5
14		2
15	Mode	2
16	Median	2
17	Mean	2.25

(handwritten annotations:) $(1+3)/2 = 2$ median

– The most frequent score

– sum of scores (27) / total # of sample (12)

Frequency Distribution

Using the previous example of police officer complaints, we can change the data slightly to include more officers into a frequency distribution. Anytime we write formulas in Excel, we must begin with an equals sign (=), as that will tell the program that we want to do a calculation. Once again, we want to know the mode, median, and mean number of citizens' complaints against a sample of police officers from an urban police department. The data is presented in Table 4.2.

Mode

We can determine the mode simply by looking at the frequency column (f) to find where the largest number of officers fall. In our example, 47 officers had zero complaints, which was more than any of the other values of X; therefore, the mode for this sample is zero. This value is typed directly into the spreadsheet (cell b10) as shown in Table 4.2.

Median

We must look at the distribution to determine where the middle score falls when calculating the median. As we have 100 scores, the middle score is the 50th score. Therefore, counting up 50 scores in the *f* column corresponds with an *X* value of 1 complaint and counting down 50 scores also corresponds with 1 complaint. Thus, the median value equals 1. This value is typed directly into the spreadsheet (cell b11) in Table 4.2.

Mean

Our formula for calculating the mean is given as:

$$\bar{X} = \frac{\Sigma fX}{n}$$

Step 1: Create an *fX* column by multiplying each *X* value with its corresponding frequency (*f*). Place the cursor in cell d3 and write: =b3*c3.

b3 is the cell location for 5 complaints.
c3 is the cell location for the frequency 7.
* is the symbol for multiplication.

Step 2: Click on the lower right-hand corner of the cell containing the row 1 *fX* value (cell d3) and drag the cursor down to the last row of values (cell d8). This will automatically create the *fX* column for each row.

Step 3: Place the cursor in the next cell below the last row of the *fX* column (cell d9). Then click on the **autosum** button on the Excel menu.

The *fX* column will be highlighted with a moving dotted line. Hit the return key and the *fX* column will be summed. You should repeat this step for the frequency column in order to obtain the sample size.

Step 4: Divide the sum of *fX* by the sum of *f* to get the mean. Place the cursor in cell b12 and write: =d9/c9. The mean value for this example is 1.36.

d9 cell location for sum of *fx*.
c9 cell location for sum of *f*(*n*).
/ is the symbol for division.

TABLE 4.2 Calculating Measures of Central Tendency for Frequency Distribution Data

	A	B	C	D
1	Table 4.2 Calculating Measues of Central Tendency for Frequency Distribution Data			
2		Complaints (X)	Frequency (f)	fX
3		5	7	35
4		4	6	24
5		3	12	36
6		2	13	26
7		1	15	15
8		0	47	0
9	Sum		100	136
10	Mode	0		
11	Median	1		
12	Mean	1.36		

Grouped Data Distribution

Let's assume that a sample of 75 jail inmates were surveyed on the number of times they used illegal drugs in the past 12 months. The jail superintendent would like to know the mode, median, and mean for the data located in Table 4.3.

Mode

Step 1: Create a midpoint (m) column by adding the lowest number to the highest number and dividing by 2 for each range of X scores. As shown in Table 4.3, for the first range of scores (11–20), place the cursor in cell d3 and write the formula: =(11+20)/2; for the second range of scores, place the cursor in cell d4 and write: =(7+10)/2. Continue on down through the last range of scores (row 6).

Step 2: To determine the mode, simply look at the frequency column to find where the largest number of jail inmates fall in relation to the amount of drug usage (X scores). In the example in Table 4.3, 25 inmates indicated they had used illegal drugs 11 to 20 times in the past year. Because we are using a range of scores, the mode will be the midpoint of the range in which the largest number of respondents fall. Thus, the mode is the midpoint of the 11–20 range, which equals 15.50.

Median

You will recall that finding the median for grouped data requires us to use the following formula:

$$Md = \frac{\text{Lower limit of}}{\text{Md interval}} + \frac{\dfrac{n}{2} - \begin{array}{c}\textit{cf} \text{ below} \\ \text{lower limit} \\ \text{of Md interval}\end{array}}{\text{Frequency in Md interval}} \times \begin{array}{c}\text{Size of the} \\ \text{Md interval}\end{array}$$

Step 1: Create a cumulative frequency column (*cf*) by adding the values of the frequency column up as you move up the rows. In cell f6, type in the value 18. Move up to cell f5 and type in the formula: =f6+c5.

f6 is the cell location of the cumulative frequency for row 6.
c5 is the cell location of the frequency for row 5.

Adding the row 5 frequency to the row 6 cumulative frequency will generate a cumulative frequency for rows 5 and 6.

Step 2: Click on the square in the lower right-hand corner of cell f5 and drag the cursor up to cell f3. This will automatically create the *cf* column for each row.

Step 3: Place the cursor in cell b9 and write the following formula: = 6.5+(((75/2)−33)/17)*4.

6.5 is the lower limit of the median value.
75 is the sample size.
33 is the *cf* below the lower limit of the median level.
17 is the frequency in the median level.
4 is the size of the median interval.

Although we have recommended using cell locations instead of actual values, with this formula it is easier to use the actual values, because the lower limit of the median level and the size of the median interval are not readily defined by cell locations. That is, the values are determined by looking at the distribution and not by the use of a formula. The median for this example is 7.56.

Mean

We use the following formula to calculate the mean for a grouped data distribution:

$$\bar{X} = \frac{\Sigma fm}{n}$$

Step 1: Create a *fm* column by multiplying each midpoint with its corresponding frequency (column E). Place the cursor in cell e3 and write: =c3*d3.

c3 is the cell location for the frequency of 25.
d3 is the cell location for the midpoint of 11–20.
* is the symbol for multiplication.

Step 2: Click on the square in the lower right-hand corner of cell e3 and drag the cursor down to cell e6. This will automatically create the remainder of the *fm* column.

Step 3: Place the cursor in cell e7 and click on the autosum button on the Excel menu. The *fm* column will be highlighted with a moving dotted line. Hit the return key and the *fm* column will be summed. You should repeat this step for the *f* column in order to get the sample size.

Step 4: Place the cursor in cell b10 and divide the sum of *fm* by the sum of *f* (sample size). For our example, the formula is written as: =e7/c7. The mean for this example is 8.57.

e7 is the cell location for the sum of *fm*.
c7 is the cell location for the sum of *f* (sample size).
/ is the symbol for division.

TABLE 4.3 Calculating Measures of Central Tendency for Grouped Data Distribution

	A	B	C	D	E	F
1	TABLE 4.3 Calculating Central Measures of Tendency for Grouped Data Distribution					
2		Drug Use (X)	Frequency (f)	Midpoint (m)	fm	cf
3		11–20	25	15.50	387.50	75
4		7–10	17	8.50	144.50	50
5		4–6	15	5	75	33
6		1–3	18	2	36	18
7	Sum		75		643	
8	Mode	15.50				
9	Median	7.56				
10	Mean	8.57				

4.5 Selecting a Measure of Central Tendency

Criminal justice researchers must confront the issue of determining which measure(s) of central tendency to report. Selecting the appropriate measure of central tendency is dependent on two major factors: (a) the level of measurement and (b) the shape of the distribution.

Level of Measurement

Although we described different levels of measurement in Chapter 2, it still is important to keep in mind that how a variable is measured will determine the measure of central tendency most appropriate for describing a particular data distribution. If a variable is measured at the nominal level, such that the attributes represent different categories, the only measure of central tendency that is appropriate is the mode. For example, if we surveyed 60 prison inmates and classified them into offense categories, we might get a distribution that looks like the following:

FIGURE 4.8 Frequency distribution for inmate offense

Offense	Frequency
Murder	3
Robbery	8
Arson	7
Assault	17
Larceny	25

We can report that the most frequent offense for which this sample of inmates is incarcerated is the crime of larceny (Mo = Larceny). We cannot, however, report the median or the mean for this data, because offenses are simply unordered categories with no numerical values.

The median is commonly used as a measure of central tendency for ordinal-level data in which values represent more or less of an attribute. Let's assume a researcher conducted a study of fear of crime among 100 residents in a small city. The researcher used the following question as a measure of fear: "On a scale of 1 to 5 with 1 being not at all fearful and 5 being very fearful, how fearful are you of going out of your home at night?" This represents ordinal-level data, in that respondents fall into varying degrees of fear ordered from less fear (1) to more fear (5). The median would be that value of fear representing the middle score, with half of the respondents above and half below the median value.

All three measures of central tendency may be used with data consisting of numerical values measured at the interval or ratio level. The most common measure used, however, is the mean, because it provides information on the entire distribution of scores (e.g., actual values) more so than either the median or the mode. Put another way, the mean is calculated by summing all of the scores in the distribution and then dividing by the total number of scores. The mode only reports that value with the largest frequency, whereas the median reports the middle value without considering the actual values. This does not imply that the mean is always the best measure for interval- or ratio-level data.

Shape of Distribution

The second factor that must be considered is the shape of the distribution. The shape of the distribution refers to a graphical representation of the data. A distribution is said to be symmetrical when the mode, median, and mean are all equal. Figure 4.9 is characteristic of a bell-shaped curve (e.g., symmetrical distribution) in which the top of the curve represents the most frequent score (mode), the middle score with an equal number of scores on both sides of the vertical line (median), and the average of all of the scores in the distribution (mean). With interval- or ratio-level data and a symmetrical distribution, the mean would be the measure of choice in terms of using a single measure of central tendency to represent the data.

positively skewed distribution

In cases in which the distribution is not symmetrical, the distribution is characterized as either positively or negatively skewed. A **positively skewed distribution** *is one in which the majority of scores cluster around the middle of the distribution, with the remaining scores falling into the right tail of the distribution*. Extremely high values will draw the mean upward to the right of the median, which creates a positively skewed distribution in which the tail of the distribution stretches to the right (positive

FIGURE 4.9 Bell-shaped curve is a symmetrical distribution as the mode, median, and mean are equal.

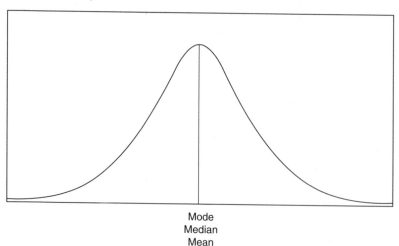

Mode
Median
Mean

negatively skewed distribution side) of the median. By contrast, a **negatively skewed distribution** *is one in which the majority of scores cluster around the middle of the distribution, with the remaining scores falling into the left tail of the distribution.* This type of distribution is created when there are some extremely low scores in the data. This results in the tail of the distribution being stretched to the left (negative side) of the median. In both types of distributions, the mode, median, and mean are not equal as they would be in a symmetrical distribution. Therefore, using the mean as the single best measure of central tendency may not be warranted. We illustrate both types of skewed distributions in Figures 4.10a and 4.10b. As we stated earlier, the mean takes into account all of the

FIGURE 4.10a A positively skewed distribution means that the majority of scores cluster around the middle of the distribution, with the remaining scores falling into the right tail of the distribution.

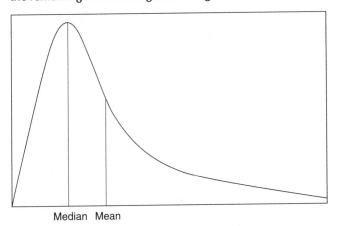

Median Mean

FIGURE 4.10b A negatively skewed distribution means that the majority of scores cluster around the middle of the distribution, with the remaining scores falling into the left tail of the distribution.

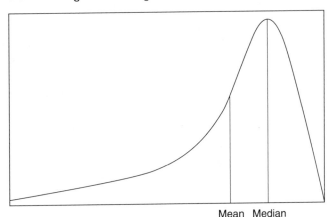

Mean Median

TABLE 4.4 Symmetrical and Positively Skewed Distributions

TABLE 4.4 Symmetrical and Positively Skewed Distributions

	Sample 1 MRs (X)	Sample 2 MRs (X)		
	0	3		
	1	3		
	5	5		
	5	5		
	5	5		
	5	5		
	6	6		
	7	11		
	8	12		
	8	15		
Mode	5	5		
Median	5	5		
Mean	5	7		
	Symmetrical	Positively Skewed		

actual values of the variable, whereas the median relates to the frequency of the values. Because of this characteristic of the mean, it is therefore sensitive to extreme values that may result in a skewed distribution.

To illustrate this point further, consider the hypothetical data presented in Table 4.4. A sample of 10 offenders from a federal penitentiary were measured on the number of misconduct reports. Looking at sample 1, we can see that the distribution of misconduct reports for this sample of offenders is symmetrical. That is, the mode, median, and mean all equal 5. In sample 2, we find that most of the values cluster around the median value of 5. Three of the ten scores, however, are significantly higher compared to the majority of scores in the distribution. The effect of these three values (11, 12, and 15) on the mean is to increase it by 2 points, from 5 to 7, whereas the median and mode remain unchanged. Therefore, depending on the level of skewness, the median may be a more appropriate measure of central tendency than the mean.

4.6 Comparison of the Mode, Median, and Mean

Each measure of central tendency has advantages and disadvantages when compared to the other measures. The mode is by far the easiest to calculate, as we need only look at the data distribution to determine which score or attribute occurs most frequently. Second, as already stated, the mode is an important measure of central tendency in that it is the only measure that can be used for nominal-level variables. Although the mode also can be used for ordinal-, interval-, and ratio-level variables, its utility is limited. Thus, the disadvantage of the mode is that it is not an accurate descriptor of *all* the values in a data set but, rather, describes only the most frequent value. For example, assume we measured the number of citizen complaints against a sample of 25 police officers and found the following data distribution:

Complaints	Frequency
7	4
5	4
4	3
3	1
0	13 (Mo = 0)

If we knew only that the mode for our variable is zero, we might assume that this group of police officers has few citizens' complaints against them. Looking at the data distribution, however, we easily can see that the other 12 officers received anywhere from three to seven complaints. Thus, our original conclusion would be incorrect, simply because the mode only considers the most frequently occurring value or score. Based on the other data values in the distribution, we would conclude that there is a problem with complaints against this group of police officers.

Compared to the mode, the median is considered a more accurate descriptor of the data points, because it represents the score that occurs in the middle of the distribution. More specifically, the median provides more information about the distribution of values than does the mode. If we know the median value for a distribution of scores, then we know something about the other values in the data set without actually having to observe those values. For example, if the median value for a distribution is ten, then we know that half of the data values are greater than ten and half of the values are less than ten. A second advantage of the median is that it is not sensitive to extreme values. Because the median represents the position of the middle score, the actual values of the scores have no influence on the median. For example, consider the cost of prison construction for five prisons, as follows:

Prison	Costs
A	$2,500,000
B	2,100,000
C	2,000,000 (Md = $2,000,000)
D	1,400,000
E	1,200,000

The median value for prison construction for these five prisons is $2,000,000. Two of the five prisons cost more than $2,000,000 and two of the five prisons cost less than $2,000,000. Suppose that the construction of prison A was plagued by severe cost overruns and really cost $10,000,000. What effect does this new value have on the median? The answer is none. We still have two prisons costing more than $2,000,000 and two prisons costing less than $2,000,000. Thus, the median is unaffected by extreme values, whether those values are high or low.

Because the median refers to the position of the middle score and does not take into account the actual values of the distribution, it, too, is limited in its description of the data points. If we examine the number of complaints, we can see that the median is equal to one. The median in this example informs us that 12 officers (50%) had more than one complaint and 12 officers (50%) had one or fewer complaints. The median does not inform us, however, about the distribution of the scores above or below the median value. That is, unless we examine the distribution of scores, we have no way of knowing how many complaints above the median value each officer had.

Complaints (X)	Frequency (f)
7	4
5	4
4	4
1	10 (Md = 1)
0	3

Compared to the mode and the median, the primary advantage of the mean is that it takes into account the actual values of *all* the data points in the distribution. Thus, we get a measure that informs us about the average score over the entire range of scores. A second advantage of the mean is that the majority of statistical techniques discussed in this text—and commonly used in criminal justice research—are based on the mean. More specifically, statistics typically involve the calculation of means and deviations from the mean in analyzing group differences and relationships among interval- and ratio-level variables.

Although we have already stated that an advantage of the mean is that it is based on the actual values of the data points, this also becomes a disadvantage. Unlike the median, the mean is sensitive to extreme scores. When a data set has either extremely high or low values, the mean will be adversely affected, resulting in a skewed distribution. If we return to our example of prison construction costs, we find that the mean cost for the five prisons is $1,840,000, which is the same value of the median. If as before, however, the actual cost for prison A was $10,000,000, then the average cost of prison construction for these five prisons becomes $3,340,000. The median value does not change; it is still $2,000,000. The effect of the extreme value for prison A, however, has distorted the mean, resulting in a value that is an inaccurate descriptor of our data distribution.

Prison	Costs	Prison	Costs
A	$2,500,000	A	$10,000,000
B	2,100,000	B	2,100,000
C	2,000,000	C	2,000,000
D	1,400,000	D	1,400,000
E	1,200,000	E	1,200,000
$\bar{X} =$ 1,840,000		$\bar{X} =$ 3,340,000	
Md = $2,000,000		Md = $2,000,000	

It is essential in statistics to evaluate the relationship among the mode, median, and the mean. If we determine that the mean is an accurate measure of central tendency by way of its equality with the mode and median, then we can proceed with those parametric statistical techniques that use the mean in their calculations. If, however, the mean is not relatively equal to the mode and the median (skewed distribution), then we must proceed with nonparametric alternatives that use either the mode or the median as their basis for comparison.

4.7 Summary

This chapter has introduced a set of descriptive statistics known as measures of central tendency. The three measures of central tendency are the mode, median, and mean. These measures are used to describe the characteristics of a set of observations.

The mode is defined as the most frequently occurring score among a set of scores. If there is only one mode, then the distribution of scores is unimodal. A distribution that has two scores that occur more than any of the other scores is defined as bimodal. Three or more modes is known as multimodal. Calculating the mode requires us to look at the distribution of scores to determine which score has the highest frequency. Whereas the mode is the only measure of central tendency available for nominal-level data, it also may be used for the other levels of measurement. The mode is the least informative of the three measures, however, as it tells us only which score occurred the most.

The median is defined as the middle score in a distribution that has an equal number of scores above and below it. To determine the median value, the scores must be arranged in an ordered array—either ascending or descending. To determine the median, we must divide the sample size by two to find the value that corresponds with the middle score. The median often is the measure of choice for ordinal-level data as well as for interval- and ratio-level data in which the distribution is skewed.

The mean is the average of all of the scores in a distribution. It is calculated by summing the scores and dividing by the total number of scores. The mean is usually considered the best measure of central tendency for interval- and ratio-level data, because its value is a function of all of the values in the distribution. Because the mean takes into account all of the scores, however, it also is influenced by extreme values that may render a biased average that is not a good representation of the data.

This chapter also has demonstrated how to calculate measures of central tendency by hand (with a calculator) and by using a spreadsheet (Excel). Although using a spreadsheet may seem difficult at first, we are confident that once you have command of some basic functions you will find it far more useful than hand calculations.

Key Terms

measures of central tendency   median

mode   mean

unimodal distribution   positively skewed distribution

bimodal distribution   negatively skewed distribution

multimodal distribution

TryIT! Answers

Box 4.1

Mode = 3

Median = 2

Mean = 2

Box 4.2

Mode = 2

Median = 2

Mean = 2.85

Box 4.3

Mode = 4.50

Median = 16.38

Mean = 16.45

4.8 Problems

1. Fifteen correctional officers were asked the following question: "How many times in the past year have you violated institutional rules by bringing reading materials into a tower post?" Calculate the (a) mode, (b) median, and (c) mean for the data presented below:

Officer #	Rule Violations (X)	Officer #	Rule Violations (X)
1	11	8	10
2	11	9	1
3	5	10	9
4	0	11	0
5	2	12	2
6	5	13	0
7	0	14	1
		15	13

2. The police chief of a major metropolitan police department wants to know how well a new recruit class did on a weapons qualification test. The class consists of 150 students, with 15 being the highest possible score. Calculate the (a) mode, (b) median, and (c) mean.

Weapons Score (X)	Frequency (f)
15	37
14	28
13	42
12	22
11	15
10	6

3. The director of corrections would like to know some descriptive information concerning the scores on the correctional officer entrance exam over the past year. Three hundred seventy persons took the exam and their scores are listed below in a grouped frequency distribution. Enter the data into Excel and calculate the (a) mode, (b) median, and (c) mean.

Exam Score (X)	Frequency (f)
90–100	132
80–89	109
70–79	76
60–69	34
50–59	19

4. As a national researcher on correctional institutions, you have been hired to provide some descriptive information on correctional overcrowding in the western United States. The Bureau of Justice Statistics (1996) provides the percentage of design capacity occupied by inmates during 1995. For the 13 states in the western region, calculate the (a) mode, (b) median, and (c) mean.

State	Percent Occupied (X)
Alaska	100
Arizona	107
California	161
Colorado	122
Hawaii	189
Idaho	137
Montana	132
Nevada	137
New Mexico	104
Oregon	124
Utah	102
Washington	100
Wyoming	115

5. In a study of parole board decision making in a midwestern state, offenders were measured on the number of previous incarcerations (Proctor, 1999). Enter the following data into Excel and calculate the (a) mode, (b) median, and (c) mean for the following data set:

Prior Incarcerations (X)	Frequency (f)
6	1
5	2
4	2
3	15
2	35
1	85
0	312

6. In a study of goal orientation among employees of a state probation department, Ellsworth (1990) found that employees' probation experience ranged from 0 to 25 years. Calculate the (a) mode, (b) median, and (c) mean for the following data set:

Years of Experience (X)	Frequency (f)
16–25	6
9–15	35
3–8	87
0–2	116

7. One hundred high school seniors were asked what type of illegal drugs they had used in the past year. The following responses were received: marijuana, cocaine, heroin, and crack. Based on this information, which measure of central tendency would be most appropriate for describing this data?

8. A survey of 65 students registered for a criminal justice statistics course revealed the following grouped data distribution for the variable GPA (grade point average). Calculate the (a) mode, (b) median, and (c) mean. Also, (d) What is the shape of the distribution?

GPA (X)	Frequency (f)
3.50–4.00	9
3.00–3.49	10
2.50–2.99	25
2.00–2.49	18
1.00–1.99	3

9. A study of police contacts among a sample of 15 juvenile offenders resulted in the following measures of central tendency: mode = 2, median = 2, mean = 2.25. What is the shape of the distribution?

10. A survey of alcohol usage among 10 college students reveals the number of times each student has driven an automobile while under the influence of alcohol. Enter the data below into Excel and calculate the (a) mode, (b) median, and (c) mean.

Student #	# Times DUI (X)
1	0
2	1
3	1
4	0
5	2
6	1
7	0
8	3
9	1
10	12

11. Identify the most appropriate measures of central tendency for each measurement level:

    a. The variable is measured at the nominal level.
    b. The variable is measured at the interval or ratio level.
    c. The variable is measured at the ordinal level.

12. A researcher collected data on the number of lawsuits filed against the state by a sample of inmates from a midwestern penitentiary. Identify the shape of the distribution for the "number of lawsuits" for each of the following situations listed below:

    a. mode = 5, median = 5, mean = 25
    b. mode = 7, median = 7.5, mean = 1.2
    c. mode = 1, median = 1.5, mean = 1.3

Measures of Dispersion

ExploreIT!

Consider an inmate who has been found guilty of manufacturing weapons by the prison disciplinary board. The standard penalty for this offense is segregation. The number of days to be spent in segregation can be decided either by the prison disciplinary board or by the warden. The issue of concern for the offender is deciding which entity is more lenient. As his advisor, you have in your possession some descriptive statistics concerning the practices of the disciplinary board and the warden in terms of dispensing days in segregation. For example, the warden gives an average of 115 days, whereas the disciplinary board gives an average of 100 days. How would you use this information to help the offender make a decision? On the surface, it would appear that the disciplinary board is the best choice given the lower average. Segregation days will deviate, however—both higher and lower—from the average. As his advisor, you will want some additional descriptive information, known as measures of dispersion. The three measures of dispersion are the range, variance, and standard deviation.

Measures of dispersion (also known as measures of variability) are a category of descriptive statistics that provide information concerning the range of variation of a given variable. A distribution of scores that has a small range of variation will consist of scores clustered around each other, that is, the values of the scores will be similar. By contrast, a distribution with a large range of variation will consist of scores that are dissimilar and spread out over the distribution. The term **measures of dispersion** *refers to a group of indexes describing the typical range of values for a distribution of scores.* The three measures of dispersion are the range, variance, and standard deviation.

measures of dispersion

5.1 Single Data Distribution

Range

range

The **range** *is defined as the difference between the highest and lowest score in a distribution of scores.* For example, if a group of 30 state police officers took a promotional exam, there would be a distribution of 30 exam scores. Within that distribution, there would be a high score and a low score. Let's assume that the high score was 98 and the low score was 45; therefore, the range would be the difference between these two scores—a value of 53. It is possible that several officers scored 98 and several scored 45. The number of subjects possessing the high and low values has no bearing on the calculation of the range. It simply is defined as the difference between the highest and lowest value.

The range has a very distinguishing feature in that it is easily calculated by comparing only two scores regardless of the number of scores in the distribution. Unfortunately, this feature of comparing only two scores gives the range a major disadvantage as a measure of dispersion. Consider the data presented in Figure 5.1 for a sample of 12 state police officers who took a promotional exam. Ten of the twelve officers scored 90 or better on the exam. As one officer scored a 65, however, the range for this distribution is 33 (98 − 65), which is not a very accurate picture of the range of values for the exam. Thus, the range is a simple yet limited measure of dispersion.

interquartile range

An alternative range that is typically used and that does not rely on the highest and lowest scores is the **interquartile range**. This is the *difference between the scores falling at the third quartile and the first quartile.* A distribution of scores consists of four quartiles, with the first quartile corresponding to the score that falls at the 25th percentile (25% of the scores are below it), the second quartile equals the 50th percentile, the third quartile equals the 75th percentile, and the fourth quartile is equal to the score falling at the 100th percentile. The interquartile range is a measure of variation among the middle 50% of the scores in a distribution and is, therefore, not nearly as affected by extreme scores as is the range. The formula for the interquartile range is:

Interquartile range = $Q_3 - Q_1$

FIGURE 5.1 Range of values on promotional exam

Promotional Exam (X)

98
97
97
96
95
94
92
92
90
90
88
65

To illustrate this point further, let's return to the data on the police officer promotional exam presented in Figure 5.1. To calculate the interquartile range, we must first identify the scores that fall at the first and third quartiles or the 25th and 75th percentiles. To determine the value of the 25th percentile, we need only multiply the total number of scores by .25. Likewise, the value of the 75th percentile is determined by multiplying the total number of scores by .75. Given that in this example there are 12 scores, the first quartile would be the third lowest value (12 × .25 = 3), which is 90. The third quartile would be the ninth value (12 × .75 = 9), which is 96. Therefore, the interquartile range is 6 (96 − 90).

Variance

variance   The **variance** is defined as *the average of the squared deviation scores*. More precisely, the variance measures how much on average the individual scores in a distribution deviate from the mean of the distribution. The variance is a measure of variability that takes into account each score in the distribution and its deviation (actual distance in numerical value) from the mean. Keeping in mind that some scores in a distribution will be higher than the mean and some will be lower than the mean, the purpose of the variance is to determine how much the individual scores deviate or vary from the mean. The variance is symbolized as σ^2 (sigma squared) for a population and s^2 for a sample. The following formulas are used in calculating the variance for a distribution of scores for a population and a sample:

Sample	Population

$$s^2 = \frac{\Sigma\left(X - \bar{X}\right)^2}{n-1} \qquad\qquad \sigma^2 = \frac{\Sigma\left(X - \bar{X}\right)^2}{N}$$

The two formulas are identical with the exception of the value of the denominator. For the population variance, we divide the numerator by the total number of scores in the distribution. The denominator is slightly modified when calculating a sample variance. For a sample, the denominator becomes the total number of scores in the distribution minus one. The question that needs to be answered is, Why the modification? This is because our goal is to obtain sample values that are good estimators of the population values. Specifically, the sample variance should accurately portray the population variance. Thus, an important characteristic of a good estimator is that it is unbiased. An **unbiased** **unbiased estimator** *is a statistic whose average over all possible random samples is equal* **estimator** *to the population value.* For example, if we selected 1,000 random samples and calculated the variance for each of those samples, the average variance of those 1,000 samples would equal the population variance from which the samples were drawn. Statisticians have discovered that using n in the denominator results in a biased estimator that underestimates the population variance. To obtain an unbiased estimator of the population variance we simply use $n - 1$ in the denominator, which increases the size of the variance and, therefore, corrects the underestimation effect caused by using only n in the denominator. Because most criminal justice research involves working with samples and not with total populations, the analysis in this book will be based on sample formulas unless otherwise noted. In order to calculate the variance, we must first calculate the mean. Once the mean has been determined, the formula requires us to subtract the mean from each X score, square the values, sum (numerator), then divide by the sample size minus one (denominator).

Consider the data in Figure 5.2, which consists of seven police officers and their scores on a 10-point weapons exam. The mean score on the exam is 6. The easiest way to figure the variance is to create two additional columns, in which we do the calculations in steps. The first step is to subtract the mean of 6 from each X score. The values in the second column are the deviation scores from the mean. Each score gives two pieces of information. First, the value of the deviation score represents the distance the score falls from the mean. Second, the sign indicates whether the score is above (+ positive) or below (– negative) the mean. The second step is to square each deviation score and place that value in the third column. The third step is to sum the squared deviation scores. The final step is to divide the sum of the squared deviation scores by the sample size minus one. Following these steps results in a variance of 4.

There is an interpretation problem—not obvious in the example—when using the variance as a measure of dispersion for a distribution of scores. Because each deviation score is squared, the value of the variance is not on the same scale as the value of the mean or the individual scores. To demonstrate this point, we change the value of the

FIGURE 5.2 Calculating the variance for a single data distribution

Weapons Exam (X)	(X − X̄)	(X − X̄)²
8	2	4
8	2	4
7	1	1
7	1	1
5	−1	1
4	−2	4
3	−3	9
$n = 7$		$\Sigma = 24$

$s^2 = 24/6 = 4$

last two scores in Figure 5.2 from 4 and 3 to 1, and then recalculate the mean and variance as illustrated in Figure 5.3. The mean for the new sample is 5.29 and the variance is 9.57. This would seem to suggest that the weapons scores for the sample of officers deviates from the mean by an average of 9.57 points. Such an interpretation, however, is incorrect. Looking at the distribution and the value of the mean, we can clearly see that no score deviates from the mean by more than 4 points. Because the scores are squared, the scale of measurement changes, thus resulting in a variance value that is a measure of the squared deviation scores. A more common measure of dispersion, known as the standard deviation, is used to convert the variance back to the original scale of measurement.

FIGURE 5.3 Comparison of variances for single data distributions presented in Figure 5.2

Weapons Exam (X)	(X − X̄)	(X − X̄)²
8	2.71	7.37
8	2.71	7.37
7	1.71	2.94
7	1.71	2.94
5	− .29	.08
1	−4.29	18.37
1	−4.29	18.37
$n = 7$		$\Sigma = 57.44$

$s^2 = 57.44/6 = 9.57$

Standard Deviation

standard
deviation
The **standard deviation** *is defined as the square root of the average squared deviation scores.* More simply, it is the square root of the variance. The computational formula for the standard deviation is exactly the same as that for the variance, with the exception of taking the square root of the value of the variance. The following formulas demonstrate the standard deviation for a sample (symbolized as lowercase *s*) and population (lowercase sigma σ):

Sample

$$s = \sqrt{\frac{\Sigma\left(X - \overline{X}\right)^2}{n-1}}$$

Population

$$\sigma = \sqrt{\frac{\Sigma\left(X - \overline{X}\right)^2}{N}}$$

X = individual X values
$\overline{X}$ = mean
Σ = sum
n = sample size
N = population size

Using the problem presented in Figure 5.3, once we have the variance we need only to take the square root of that value (9.57) to obtain the standard deviation, which equals 3.09. This value makes much more sense. We are saying that on average the scores in the distribution deviate from the mean by 3.09 points. By taking the square root of the variance, the standard deviation essentially changes the scale of measurement from the average of the squared deviation scores to simply the average of the deviation scores. The standard deviation is, therefore, on the same scale of measurement as the individual values for X and the mean.

You are now ready to try calculating the range, variance, and standard deviation for a single-data distribution. Complete TryIT! Box 5.1 before moving on to the next section.

TryIT!
BOX **5.1**

Consider a sample of eight retail stores and the amount of financial loss due to theft during a one-week period. Calculate the range, variance, and standard deviation for the following data. The average amount of loss for the sample of stores is $123.50.

Store #	Lost Revenue (X)
1	$180.00
2	125.00
3	145.00
4	97.00
5	56.00

6	$125.00
7	170.00
8	90.00

5.2 Frequency Distribution

Measures of dispersion are also readily obtainable when data is organized in a frequency distribution. Let's return to the example in Chapter 4, in which 100 parolees were measured on the number of technical violations. The mean for this data is 2.11. Using the data in Figure 5.4, we now want to calculate the range, variance, and standard deviation.

Range

As the range is the difference between the highest and lowest values, we first need to determine what these two values are. We can see that the highest value of technical violations is 5 and the lowest value is 0. Subtracting 0 from 5 gives us a range of 5. Calculating the range for a frequency distribution is exactly the same as for a single data distribution.

Variance

Unlike the range, calculating the variance must take into account the frequency of the scores in the distribution. The variance formula for a frequency distribution is:

$$s^2 = \frac{\Sigma f\left(X - \overline{X}\right)^2}{n-1}$$

X = individual X values
$\overline{X}$ = mean
f = frequency
Σ = sum
n = sample size

The formula is the same as that for a distribution of single scores, with the addition of multiplying the squared deviation scores by their corresponding frequency (f). The first step requires us to create a third column of deviation scores in which we subtract the mean from each X score. It is important to remember that each score refers to the value in the X column (e.g., technical violations) and not to the values in the frequency column—for example, 5 − 2.11 = 2.89, 4 − 2.11 = 1.89—continuing down through the

FIGURE 5.4 Calculating the variance for a frequency distribution

Technical Violations (X)	Frequency (f)	(X − X̄)	(X − X̄)²	f(X − X̄)²
5	9	2.89	8.35	75.17
4	14	1.89	3.57	50.01
3	26	.89	.79	20.59
2	11	− .11	.01	.13
1	10	−1.11	1.23	12.32
0	30	−2.11	4.45	133.56
	n = 100			Σ = 291.78

$s^2 = 291.78 / 99 = 2.95$

last X score. The second step involves creating a fourth column in which we square each of the deviation scores. Once we have completed step 2, we are now ready to use the frequency of the scores. For the third step, we recommend creating a fifth column labeled $f(X - \bar{X})^2$, in which each of the squared deviation scores is multiplied by its corresponding frequency. The final step requires us to sum the fifth column and divide by the sample size minus one. It is important to remember that in a frequency distribution, the sample size (n) is determined by summing the frequency column. Thus, the sum of the $f(X - \bar{X})^2$ column equals 291.79 (numerator), which is divided by the sample size minus one (100 − 1 = 99) resulting in a variance of 2.95. We conclude that the average of the squared deviation scores is 2.95 points.

Standard Deviation

Because the standard deviation is defined as the square root of the variance, it is not necessary for us to repeat the steps outlined above in regard to calculating the standard deviation. To obtain the standard deviation, we need only to compute the square root of the variance. The variance in the above example is 2.95. Computing the square root of this value results in a standard deviation of 1.72.

Try calculating the range, variance, and standard deviation for a frequency distribution by completing TryIT! Box 5.2.

TryIT!   BOX 5.2

A sample of 110 juveniles were asked, "How many days have you skipped school in the past month?" For the following data, calculate the range, variance, and standard deviation. The mean number of days skipped for the sample is equal to .82.

Days Skipped (X)	Frequency (f)
12	2
10	1
8	3
5	1
4	1
2	4
1	15
0	83

5.3 Grouped Data Distribution

To calculate the variance and standard deviation for grouped data, we once again need to select a single score that adequately represents the typical score in each range of scores. As with measures of central tendency, measures of dispersion also make use of the midpoint as the typical score. The midpoint of a range of scores is calculated by adding the lowest and highest value of the range and dividing by 2. For example, if one range of scores is 40 to 50, then the midpoint is 45 ([40 + 50] /2). Similarly, if a range of scores is 75 to 90, then the midpoint is 82.50 ([75 + 90] /2). By using the midpoint, we reduce the entire range of scores to a single value, which enables us to compute the variance and standard deviation.

Variance

The formula for the variance is similar to that used for a frequency distribution, with the exception of replacing the exact value of X with the midpoint value for the range of X.

$$s^2 = \frac{\Sigma f\left(m - \overline{X}\right)^2}{n - 1}$$

m = midpoint for range of X values
$\overline{X}$ = mean
f = frequency
Σ = sum
n = sample size

We will now return to the example of 100 police recruits and their scores on a police officer entrance exam. The distribution of exam scores is shown in Figure 5.5. With one exception, the process for determining the variance for grouped data is the same as that

FIGURE 5.5 Calculating the variance for a grouped data distribution

Exam Score (X)	m	f	$(m - \bar{X})$	$(m - \bar{X})^2$	$f(m - \bar{X})^2$
90–100	95	13	19.63	385.34	5009.38
80–89	84.50	21	9.13	83.36	1750.49
70–79	74.50	38	– .87	.76	28.76
60–69	64.50	17	–10.87	118.16	2008.67
50–59	54.50	11	–20.87	435.56	4791.13
		$\Sigma = 100$			$\Sigma = 13588.43$

$s^2 = 13588.43/99 = 137.26$

used for a frequency distribution. As a first step, we suggest that you create a midpoint (*m*) column in which each range of scores is defined by a single score. The second step requires us to determine the mean for the distribution of scores (recall that the mean equals 75.37, as reported in Chapter 4). Next, we must subtract the mean of $(\bar{X})$ from each midpoint (*m*). Fourth, we square the difference or deviation score between the mean and the midpoint for each range of scores. Fifth, we sum the squared deviation scores. The final step is to divide the sum of the squared deviation scores by the sample size minus one. The resulting variance is equal to 137.26.

Standard Deviation

As is the case with a frequency distribution and single data, the standard deviation is determined by merely taking the square root of the variance. For the above example, the standard deviation is 11.72. In formula notation, the standard deviation is written as:

$$s = \sqrt{\frac{\Sigma f\left(m - \bar{X}\right)^2}{n-1}}$$

You can see that calculating measures of dispersion requires a bit more work than calculating measures of central tendency. It should be noted that the variance and standard deviation are applicable only for interval- and ratio-level data, as we not only use the mean in determining these values but, more specifically, we are interested in the average amount of deviations from the mean.

Now that you understand the formulas and are able to calculate measures of dispersion with the assistance of a hand calculator, let's turn our attention to using Excel to compute measures of dispersion. Before doing so, take a few minutes to practice calculating these measures for a grouped frequency distribution by completing TryIT! Box 5.3.

TryIT!   BOX **5.3**

In review, let's consider the length of prison sentence (in months) received by a sample of 75 inmates for the crime of robbery. The mean sentence length is 52.45. Using what you have learned about measures of dispersion, calculate the variance and standard deviation.

Sentence (X)	Midpoint (m)	Frequency (f)
60–72	66	34
48–59	53.5	18
36–47	41.5	10
24–35	29.5	7
12–23	17.5	6

5.4 Using Excel to Compute Measures of Dispersion

The format for outlining the steps in calculating measures of dispersion will be the same as that used in Chapter 4 to discuss the steps for calculating measures of central tendency. We will begin with a sample problem and proceed with step-by-step procedures for calculating measures of dispersion for each of the three different types of data distributions. The examples we use for each type of distribution are the same examples used in Chapter 4. Therefore, we begin each example with the assumption that the data has been entered into Excel and that the mean has been calculated already.

Single Data Distribution

Using the example from Chapter 4 of a police chief wanting some descriptive information about citizens' complaints against the department, we discovered that the mean number of complaints for the sample of 12 officers was 2.25 (see Table 4.1). Now the chief is interested in knowing how much variation there is in the number of complaints. Therefore, we need to calculate the range, variance, and standard deviation for the data presented in Table 5.1. Because the range and interquartile range are used infrequently in research articles, we present their calculations only for a single data distribution.

Range

Small data sets

Step 1: For small data sets, we recommend looking at the distribution to determine the cell locations of the smallest and largest values.

Step 2: Subtract the lowest value (0) from the highest value (5) to get the range, written as: =b13-b6. The range for this data is 5.

b13 is the cell location for the highest value (5).
b6 is the cell location for the lowest value (0).
- is the symbol for subtraction.

Large data sets

Step 1: For larger data sets, the simplest method is to click on the paste function box (also known as the "function wizard"):

Step 2: Click on the function category called **statistical**.
Step 3: Click on **max**.
Step 4: Type in the range of cells within which the *X* values lie, or highlight the range of cells (b3 through b14), then click **finish**. This will give you the maximum or largest value for the distribution.
Step 5: Repeat steps 1 and 2.
Step 6: Click on **min**.
Step 7: Type in the range of cells within which the *X* values lie, or highlight the range of cells (b3 through b14), then click **finish**. This will give you the minimum or lowest value for the distribution.
Step 8: We recommend subtracting the actual lowest value from the actual highest value unless you know the cell locations of the values. The **max** and **min** functions return only the maximum and minimum values, not the cell locations of those values.

Interquartile Range

Step 1: Click on the paste function box:

Step 2: Click on the function category called **statistical**.
Step 3: Click on the name category called **quartile**.
Step 4: Either highlight the range of *X* values or type in the range of cells that contain the values of *X* (b3:b14) in the box labeled **Array**.
Step 5: Type in 1 in the box labeled **Quart** and then click **finish**. The resulting value will be the score that defines the first quartile (25th percentile).
Step 6: Repeat steps 1 through 4.
Step 7: Type in 3 in the box labeled **Quart** and then click **finish**. The resulting value will be the score that defines the third quartile (75th percentile).

Step 8: Apply the range formula Q3 – Q1. Place the cursor in cell b19 and write: =b18-b17.

> **b18 is the cell location for 3rd quartile.**
> **b17 is the cell location for 1st quartile.**

The resulting value for the interquartile range is 2.25.

Variance

Step 1: Place the cursor in cell b20 and click on the paste function box:

Step 2: Click on the function category called **statistical**.

Step 3: Click on the function name called **VAR** (symbol for sample variance).

Step 4: Click **ok** and a box will appear that will ask for the range of scores for which you want to calculate the variance. Either highlight the range of scores or type in the range of cells within which the X values lie (b3:b14) in the box labeled **Number 1**.

Step 5: Click **ok**. The resulting value of 2.57 is the variance.

Standard Deviation

Step 1: Place the cursor in cell b21 and click on the paste function box:

Step 2: Click on the function category called **statistical**.

Step 3: Click on the function name called **STDEV** (symbol for sample standard deviation).

Step 4: Click **ok**. A box will appear that will ask for the range of scores for which you want to calculate the standard deviation. Either highlight the range of scores or type in the range of cells within which the X values lie (b3:b14) in the box labeled **Number 1**.

Step 6: Click **ok**. The resulting value of 1.60 is the standard deviation.

Because the standard deviation is the square root of the variance, we can bypass the foregoing steps by placing the cursor in cell b21 and writing the following formula: =sqrt(b20).

> **sqrt is the symbol for square root.**
> **b20 is the cell location for the variance.**

TABLE 5.1 Calculating Measures of Dispersion for a Single Data Distribution

	A	B
1	TABLE 5.1 Calculating Measures of Dispersion for a Single Data Distribution	
2		Complaints (X)
3		3
4		2
5		4
6		0
7		0
8		4
9		1
10		3
11		2
12		1
13		5
14		2
15	Mean	2.25
16	Range	5
17	First quartile	1.00
18	Third quartile	3.25
19	Interquartile range	2.25
20	Variance	2.57
21	Standard deviation	1.60

As you may have seen in the function name box in Excel, there are four different formulas for calculating the variance and standard deviation. As explained previously, the VAR and STDEV are the correct formulas for samples. VARP and STDEVP are the formulas to use for calculating the measures for populations. Additional formulas include VARA, VARPA, STDEVA, and STDEVPA. These formulas are for both samples and populations in which logical values and text are included in the cell ranges. For a description of these formulas, you can click on the Excel help function. For the purposes of this book, we will ignore these additional formulas.

As with measures of central tendency, calculating measures of dispersion with the paste function is relatively easy. Calculating the variance and standard deviation for frequency and grouped data distribution requires us to write our own formulas. The methods for computing statistics using Excel will become easier as we progress through this book.

Frequency Distribution

We can change our example of police officer complaints from a sample of 12 officers using a single data distribution to a sample of 100 officers using a frequency distribution. The data is presented in Table 5.2. In Chapter 4, the mean for this data was determined to be 1.36 (see Table 4.2). Our formula for the variance using a frequency distribution is given as:

$$s^2 = \frac{\Sigma f\left(X - \bar{X}\right)^2}{n-1}$$

Variance

Step 1: Create a deviation score column labeled $(X - \bar{X})$ by subtracting the mean from each X score. Place the cursor in cell d3 and write the following formula: =b3b10.

> **b3 is the cell location for 5 complaints.**
> **b10 is the cell location for the mean.**
> **$ holds the column (b) and row (10) constant.**

Step 2: Click on the square on the lower right-hand corner of cell d3 and drag the cursor down to cell d8. This will automatically create the rest of the $(X - \bar{X})$ column.

Step 3: Create a squared deviation score column labeled $(X - \bar{X})^2$ by multiplying each deviation score by itself. Place the cursor in cell e3 and write: =d3^2.

> **d3 is the cell location for the deviation score of 5 complaints minus the mean of 1.36.**
> **^2 is the symbol used to square a value.**

Step 4: Click on the square on the lower right-hand corner of cell e3 and drag the cursor down to cell e8. This will automatically create the rest of the squared deviation score $(X - \bar{X})^2$ column.

Step 5: Create a frequency times squared deviation score column labeled $f(X - \bar{X})^2$ by multiplying each squared deviation score by its corresponding frequency. Place the cursor in cell f3 and write: =c3*e3.

c3 is the cell location for the frequency of 5 complaints.
e3 is the cell location for the squared deviation score of 5 complaints.

Step 6: Click on the square on the lower right-hand corner of cell f3 and drag the cursor down to cell f8. This will automatically create the rest of the $f(X - \bar{X})^2$ column.

Step 7: Place the cursor in cell f9, click on the **autosum** button on the Excel menu, and hit the return key. This will automatically sum the $f(X - \bar{X})^2$. You should repeat this step for the frequency column, to obtain the sample size:

Step 8: Divide the sum of $f(X - \bar{X})^2$ (numerator) by $n - 1$ (denominator). Place the cursor in cell b11 and write: =f9/(c9-1). The variance is equal to 2.64.

f9 is the cell location for the numerator.
c9 is the cell location for the sample size.

Standard Deviation

Once the variance has been determined, calculating the standard deviation is as simple as taking the square root of the variance. In the foregoing example, place the cursor in cell b12 and write the following: =sqrt(b11). Performing this calculation results in a standard deviation of 1.62.

sqrt is the symbol for square root.
b11 is the cell location for the variance.

TABLE 5.2 Calculating Measures of Dispersion for a Frequency Distribution

	A	B	C	D	E	F
1	TABLE 5.2 **Calculating Measures of Dispersion for a Frequency Distribution**					
2		Complaints (X)	Frequency (f)	($X - \bar{X}$)	($X - \bar{X}$)²	$f(X - \bar{X}$)²
3		5	7	3.64	13.25	92.75
4		4	6	2.64	6.97	41.82
5		3	12	1.64	2.69	32.28
6		2	13	0.64	0.41	5.32
7		1	15	-0.36	0.13	1.94
8		0	47	-1.36	1.85	86.93
9	Sum		100			261.04
10	Mean	1.36				
11	Variance	2.64				
12	Standard deviation	1.62				

Grouped Data Distribution

In Chapter 4, we were interested in knowing some descriptive information about a sample of 75 inmates' use of illegal drugs. The average number of times that this sample of offenders had used drugs in the past 12 months was determined to be 8.57. The data is presented in Table 5.3. We use the following formula for the variance:

$$s^2 = \frac{\Sigma f\left(m - \bar{X}\right)^2}{n-1}$$

Variance

Step 1: Create a midpoint (m) column by adding the lowest and highest number of each interval and dividing by 2 for each range of X scores. For example, place the cursor in cell d3 and write: =(11+20)/2. The resulting value of 15.50 is the midpoint for the first range of X scores.

Step 2: Create a deviation score column labeled ($m - \bar{X}$) by subtracting the mean from each midpoint. Place the cursor in cell e3 and write: =d3-b8.

d3 is the cell location for the midpoint for the first range of X scores (11–20).
b8 is the cell location for the mean.
$ holds the column (b) and row (8) constant.

Step 3: Click on the lower right-hand corner of cell e3 and drag the cursor down to cell e6. This automatically creates the remainder of the $(m - \bar{X})$ column.

Step 4: Create a squared deviation score column labeled $(m - \bar{X})^2$ by multiplying each deviation score by itself. Place the cursor in cell f3 and write: =e3^2.

e3 is the cell location for the first deviation score.
^2 is the symbol for squaring a value.

Step 5: Click on the lower right-hand corner of cell f3 and drag the cursor down to cell f6. This will automatically create the rest of the $(m - \bar{X})^2$ column.

Step 6: Create a frequency times squared deviation score column labeled $f(m - \bar{X})^2$ by multiplying each squared deviation score by its corresponding frequency. Place the cursor in cell g3 and write: =c3*f3.

c3 is the cell location for the frequency for the 11–20 midpoint.
f3 is the cell location for the squared deviation score for the 11–20 midpoint.

Step 7: Click on the lower right-hand corner of cell g3 and drag the cursor down to cell g6. The rest of the $f(m - \bar{X})^2$ will automatically be created.

Step 8: Place the cursor in cell g7, click on the **autosum** button on the Excel menu, and hit the return key. This will automatically sum the $f(m - \bar{X})^2$ column. Repeat this step for the frequency column to obtain the sample size.

Step 9: Divide the sum of $f(m - \bar{X})^2$ (numerator) by $n - 1$ (denominator). Place the cursor in cell b9 and write: =g7/(c7-1). The resulting variance equals 29.31.

g7 is the cell location for the numerator.
c7 is the cell location for the sample size.

Standard Deviation

Once again, we need only take the square root of the variance to determine the standard deviation. Therefore, place the cursor in cell b10 and write: =sqrt(b9). The standard deviation is equal to 5.41.

sqrt is the symbol for the square root.
b8 is the cell location for the variance.

As you have probably noticed, the steps for calculating the variance for a grouped data distribution are nearly identical to those used for a frequency distribution, with one exception. We need to perform an additional step in which we reduce our range of scores to a single value by computing the midpoint (see step 1). The midpoint value is then used in place of the exact X value in carrying out the calculations. Other than this additional step, the process is the same for both types of distributions.

TABLE 5.3 Calculating Measures of Dispersion for a Grouped Data Distribution

	A	B	C	D	E	F	G
1	TABLE 5.3 Calculating Measures of Dispersion for a Grouped Data Distribution						
2		Drug Use (X)	Frequency (f)	Midpoint (m)	($m - \bar{X}$)	($m - \bar{X}$)^2	$f(m - \bar{X})^2$
3		11–20	25	15.50	6.93	48.02	1200.62
4		7–10	17	8.50	-0.07	0.00	0.08
5		4–6	15	5	-3.57	12.74	191.17
6		1–3	18	2	-6.57	43.16	776.97
7	Sum		75				2168.85
8	Mean	8.57					
9	Variance	29.31					
10	Standard deviation	5.41					

Up to this point, we have computed the variance using step-by-step procedures, in which we have added columns for each additional step of the process. With Excel, it is possible to reduce the number of columns by combining several steps into one step. For instance, in the previous example, we created three columns that represented three steps in the process of calculating the variance. We can see that in column E of Table 5.3 we subtracted the mean from each midpoint, in column F we squared the difference scores, and in column G we multiplied the squared difference scores by their corresponding frequencies. We could have easily combined these three steps into one step labeled $f(m - \bar{X})^2$.

As shown in column E of Table 5.4, we have successfully eliminated columns F and G (found in Table 5.3) by combining the previously mentioned three steps into one step. Anytime we combine several steps using Excel, the formulas we use to perform the necessary calculations become more complex. In cell e3 of Table 5.4, the following formula was written: =((d3-b8)^2)*c3. The order of operations is the same as shown in Table 5.3. The mean is subtracted from the midpoint (**d3 – b8**), the deviation score is then squared (**^2**), then the squared deviation score is multiplied by its corresponding frequency (***c3**).

TABLE 5.4 Step Reduction in Calculating Measures of Dispersion

	A	B	C	D	E
1	TABLE 5.4 Step Reduction in Calculating Measures of Dispersion				
2		Drug Use (X)	Frequency (f)	Midpoint (m)	$f(m - \bar{X})^2$
3		11–20	25	15.5	1200.62
4		7–10	17	8.5	0.08
5		4–6	15	5	191.17
6		1–3	18	2	776.97
7	Sum		75		2168.84
8	Mean	8.57			
9	Variance	29.31			
10	Standard deviation	5.41			

It will take some practice before you become comfortable using Excel to calculate statistics such as measures of dispersion. We believe, however, that you will find the time well spent. It is very common in research studies to report both measures of central tendency and measures of dispersion. We now turn to the standard deviation, a particularly useful measure and the most common measure of dispersion reported in journal articles.

5.5 Usefulness of the Standard Deviation

The standard deviation is a much better measure of dispersion than is either the range or the variance. The range uses only two values (lowest and highest) in determining the amount of variation in a group of scores. Because of this characteristic, the range is a crude measure of how much the scores vary. The variance, by contrast, uses all of the scores in measuring the amount of dispersion; however, because the variance uses squared deviation scores, it is not on the same scale of measurement as the original X values or the mean. Thus, the interpretation of the variance is difficult. The standard deviation not only uses all of the scores in its calculations but also is measured on the original scale of measurement.

Characteristics of the Standard Deviation

There are some important characteristics of the standard deviation that are worth noting (Agresti and Finlay, 1997):

- The standard deviation equals zero when all of the scores are the same. This characteristic does not imply that all of the scores must equal zero, only that the scores all have the same value. If all five inmates in our sample had the same number of prior arrests—2, 2, 2, 2, 2—then the mean for this sample would be 2, with a standard deviation of 0. The standard deviation is zero because none of the scores deviate from the mean. That is, there is no variation within the set of scores.
- When the scores of a distribution are not all equal, then the standard deviation is always larger than 0. There is never a negative standard deviation. The process of squaring each deviation score eliminates negative values. Squaring a negative value yields a positive value and squaring a positive value yields a positive value. Thus, the standard deviation is always expressed as a positive number.
- The greater the scores vary from the mean, the larger the standard deviation. For example, the following five scores—2, 2, 3, 4, 4—results in a mean of 3. We can see that the greatest amount of variation for any one score from the mean is 1. The standard deviation for these scores is minimal ($s = 1$). In comparison, consider the following scores that also have a mean of 3—1, 1, 1, 6, 6. Because these scores have a larger amount of variation from the mean (the score of 1 is 2 points and the score of 6 is 3 points from the mean) than the scores in the previous example, we would expect the standard deviation to be larger. The standard deviation for the second set of scores is 2.74.
- Transforming the scale of scores through addition or subtraction will not change the standard deviation. For example, let's consider the same five scores above—2, 2, 3, 4, 4—with a mean of 3 and a standard deviation of 1. If we add a constant value of 3 to each score, our new scores are 5, 5, 6, 7, 7. The mean is now 6, but the standard deviation remains 1. The standard deviation remains unchanged because the relative distance between each score and the mean remains the same.
- Changing the scale of scores through the process of multiplication will change the standard deviation by the value of the constant that each score was multiplied by. For example, let's look at the scores—5, 5, 6, 7, 7. If we multiply each of the scores by a constant value of 3, the resulting standard deviation will change by a multiplication of 3. The new scores are now 15, 15, 18, 21, 21, with a mean

standard deviation of 3. The process of multiplication causes the distance between values to change such that the distance between the old values of 5 and 7 is 2, whereas the distance between the new values of 15 and 21 is 6 (the value of the old distance 2 times the value of the constant 3). This, in turn, changes both the mean and standard deviation by the value of the constant (old mean = 6, new mean = 18; old $s = 1$, new $s = 3$).

Interpreting the Standard Deviation

We now will turn to the interpretation of the standard deviation and its relevance for statistics. For interval- and ratio-level variables, it is common in research articles to report the mean and standard deviation. Knowing the value of these two statistics tells us about the distribution of scores without actually looking at the entire distribution of scores.

In order to understand how the standard deviation provides us with important information about a distribution, we need to make use of what is called the normal curve. The normal curve is characterized as having a standardized unit of measurement with a mean of 0 and standard deviation of 1. The relationship between the standard deviation and the normal curve is such that we can approximate how the scores in a distribution will fall if the distribution is symmetrical or normal. In a symmetrical distribution (Figure 5.6), scores will be distributed in the following manner:

- Approximately 68% of the scores will fall between $-1s$ and $+1s$.
- Approximately 95% of the scores will fall between $-2s$ and $+2s$.
- Approximately 100% of the scores will fall between $-3s$ and $+3s$.

To further illustrate this point, let's assume that a sample of 100 inmates was measured as to the number of times each inmate skipped an educational program in the past month. Furthermore, let's assume that the mean for this sample is 3.5 with a standard deviation of 1.5. Using our sample mean of 3.5, we subtract 1.5 (-1 standard deviation) and add 1.5 ($+1$ standard deviation) to determine the range of scores within which 68% of the sample fall. As demonstrated in Figure 5.6, we would expect 68 inmates to have skipped class between 2 and 5 times. To determine the range of values in which 95% of the sample fall, we need to subtract two standard deviations from the mean ($-2s$) and add two standard deviations to the mean ($+2s$). The results indicate that 95% (95 out of 100) of the inmates skipped class between .5 and 6.5 times.

It is important for us to reiterate that knowing the mean and standard deviation provides detailed information about the distribution of a variable such as whether the shape of the distribution is symmetrical or skewed. In the above example, we know that the variable is from a normal distribution, because 95% of the cases fall between two real values—.5 and 6.5. We may need to go three standard deviations to get the other 5% of the cases, which in this example would give us a range of -1 ($-3s$) and 8 ($+3s$).

FIGURE 5.6 Symmetrical distribution characterized as having a standardized unit of measurement with a mean of 0 and a standard deviation of 1

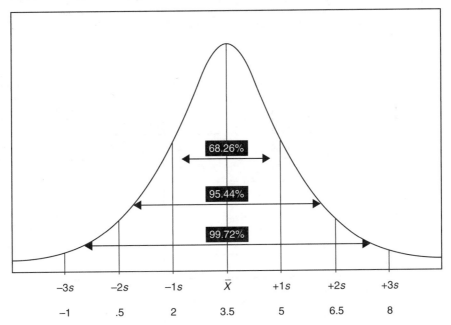

	–3s	–2s	–1s	X̄	+1s	+2s	+3s
	–1	.5	2	3.5	5	6.5	8

The lowest possible value that any inmate could have for the number of days they skipped class is 0, whereas the highest would be around 25 (assuming the class was offered five days per week). Given that the magnitude of s is small (1.5), in relation to the mean, we know that it would be very unlikely that a case would be greater than 8, as 99.72% of the cases fall within 3 standard deviations of the mean. In addition, only a small number of cases (roughly 5%) are likely to be less than .5 or greater than 6.5.

To explain this further, let's assume we drew two samples of eight police officers and measured the number of complaints each officer had. As shown in Table 5.5, both samples have an average of 3.63 complaints. Sample one, however, has much less variation in the number of complaints ($s = 1.30$) than does sample two ($s = 3.54$). The one extreme value of 12 in sample two is the reason for this disparity in the standard deviation. The mean and standard deviation of sample one inform us that the variable is from a normal distribution like the one shown in Figure 5.6. In this particular example, 100% of the officers fall within 2 standard deviations above (3.63 + 1.30 + 1.30 = 6.23) and below (3.63 – 1.30 – 1.30 = 1.03) the mean. The mean and standard deviation of sample two inform us that the variable is not from a normal distribution. Moving 1 standard deviation below and above the mean gives us a range of values between .09 and 7.19. Seven out of the eight officers fall within this range. Because of the one extreme value (12), however, we need to go out 3 standard deviations above the mean to get this value under the curve. The extremely high value of 12 causes the distribution

TABLE 5.5 Symmetrical and Positively Skewed Distributions

	A	B	C
1	TABLE 5.5 Symmetrical and Positively Skewed Distributions		
2		Sample 1	Sample 2
3		Complaints (X)	Complaints (X)
4		2	1
5		2	1
6		3	2
7		3	3
8		4	3
9		5	3
10		5	4
11		5	12
12	**Mean**	**3.63**	**3.63**
13	**Standard deviation**	**1.30**	**3.54**
14		**Symmetrical**	**Positively skewed**

to be nonnormal, otherwise known as positively skewed. We can not go 3 standard deviations below the mean, because we are already at the minimum value of complaints at 1 standard deviation. An illustration of how the curve would look given the data in sample two is shown in Figure 5.7.

Let's return to the scenario at the beginning of the chapter. Recall that an offender has been found guilty by the prison disciplinary board of manufacturing weapons. The offender has asked you to advise him in terms of obtaining the fewest number of days in segregation. He has the option of being sentenced by the warden or by the prison disciplinary board. The warden gives an average sentence of 115 days in segregation for this type of offense, with a standard deviation of 5. The prison disciplinary board gives an average sentence of 100 days, with a standard deviation of 25. Using what you have learned about measures of dispersion, which entity would you recommend to the offender? Although the warden sentences offenders to an average of 15 days longer than the disciplinary board, the warden has much less variability in the sentences handed down. Nearly 100% of the time, the warden sentences an offender to anywhere from 100 (–3s) to 130 (+3s) days in segregation. In comparison, the disciplinary board sentences offenders to a range of 25 (–3s) to 175 (+3s) days in segregation. The warden deviates from the mean, on average, by five days, compared to the disciplinary board, which

FIGURE 5.7 Positively skewed distribution

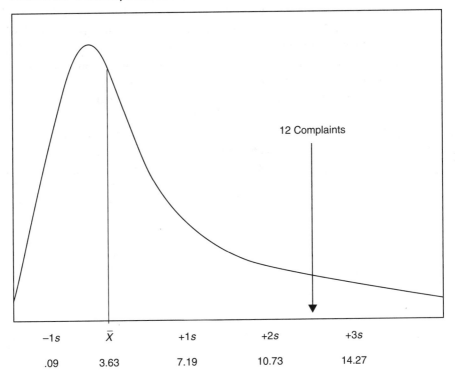

deviates from the mean by 25 days. If the offender chooses the disciplinary board, there is a chance that he could get much less time than he would get from the warden. Unfortunately, it is equally as likely that the offender could get more time. All the offender knows for sure is that he will most likely be sentenced to anywhere from 25 to 175 days. We would advise the offender to be sentenced by the warden, because the warden does not vary considerably from the mean. The offender knows that he will spend between 100 and 130 days in segregation and will avoid the possibility of extended time that he might be given by the disciplinary board.

5.6 Summary

In this chapter, we have discussed a set of descriptive statistics known as measures of dispersion. The three measures of dispersion are the range, variance, and standard deviation. These measures are used to describe the amount of variation among a set of scores or observations of a given variable.

The range is the difference between the highest and lowest score in a distribution. Because the range is calculated using the two extreme scores, it is not recommended as an adequate measure of variability. An alternative to the range is the interquartile range. This is defined as the difference between the scores occurring at the 1st and 3rd quartiles. The resulting value is the amount of variation among the middle 50% of the scores. This measure is an improvement over the range; however, once again it is still only a crude measure of variation because of its reliance on only two values.

The variance is the average of the squared deviation scores. The mean is subtracted from each score and then squared. The sum of the squared scores is then divided by the total number of scores minus one to determine the average amount of variation among the distribution. Recall, however, that the process of squaring the deviation scores changes the scale of measurement, rendering the interpretation of the variance problematic. To resolve this problem, we take the square root of the variance, which is called the standard deviation. This process returns the measure of dispersion back to its original scale, which is the same scale. Thus, the standard deviation eliminates the interpretation problem associated with the variance. Several characteristics of the standard deviation have been identified, as well as its relationship to the normal curve. The standard deviation is the most appropriate measure of dispersion for interval- and ratio-level data. It should be reported anytime that the mean is used as the measure of central tendency.

Key Terms

measures of dispersion	variance
range	unbiased estimator
interquartile range	standard deviation

TryIT! Answers

Box 5.1

Range = $124.00   Standard Deviation = $41.75

Variance = $1743.14

Box 5.2

Range = 12   Standard Deviation = 2.30

Variance = 5.31

Box 5.3

Variance = 249.69   Standard Deviation = 15.80

5.7 Problems

1. A sample of 12 inmates at a local jail reported the number of crimes they committed in the past five years. Calculate the (a) range, (b) interquartile range, (c) variance, and (d) standard deviation for the following data:

Offender #	Crimes (X)
1	5
2	2
3	1
4	1
5	7
6	12
7	1
8	3
9	2
10	2
11	1
12	8

2. An appellate court wants to know the amount of variation in determinate prison sentences handed down by a district court judge for the crime of burglary. Calculate the (a) range, (b) variance, and (c) standard deviation for the following data:

Sentence in Months (X)	Frequency (f)
60	42
48	38
36	35
24	15
18	7
12	5

3. The jail superintendent is interested in knowing some information about how much time pre-trial defendants actually spend in jail. Enter the data into Excel and calculate the (a) variance and (b) standard deviation.

Days in Jail (X)	Frequency (f)
61–100	5
46–60	23
31–45	32
15–30	70
8–15	45
1–7	25

4. In Chapter 4, you calculated the mean, median, and mode for the following data on prison overcrowding (Bureau of Justice Statistics, 1996, p. 84). We now want some information on the amount of variation in prison crowding. Enter the data into Excel and calculate the (a) range, (b) interquartile range, (c) variance, and (d) standard deviation.

State	Percent Occupied (X)
Alaska	100
Arizona	107
California	161
Colorado	122
Hawaii	189
Idaho	137
Montana	132
Nevada	137
New Mexico	104
Oregon	124
Utah	102
Washington	100
Wyoming	115

5. In a study of parole board decision making in a midwestern state, offenders were measured on the number of prior incarcerations (Proctor, 1999). Calculate the (a) range, (b) variance, and (c) standard deviation for the following data distribution:

Prior Incarcerations (X)	Frequency (f)
6	1
5	2
4	2
3	15
2	35
1	85
0	312

6. In a study of the deterrent effects of Driving Under the Influence (DUI) legislation on DUI recidivism, Kingsnorth, Alvis, and Gavia (1993) reported the following blood alcohol consumption levels (BAC) for a sample of 602 DUI defendants:

BAC Level (X)	Frequency (f)
.25–.29	46
.20–.24	135
.15–.19	215
.10–.14	184
.05–.09	22

Calculate the (a) variance and (b) standard deviation for this data.

7. Which of the following measures of dispersion—range, variance, standard deviation—provides the least amount of information about the variability of the values of a given variable?

8. A study of probation violations among a sample of probationers found that the average number of violations within the last 30 days was 3.2, with a standard deviation of 4.5. Based on this information, what is the shape of the distribution?

9. Approximately what percentage of the values of a variable fall within two standard deviations above and below the mean?

10. The results from a 100-point final exam in a criminal justice statistics course revealed an average score of 85, with a standard deviation of 15. Describe the shape of the distribution for the variable "Exam Score."

11. A researcher finds that a sample of ten juveniles who participated in a delinquency prevention program each had two police contacts within five months after the program ended. What is the standard deviation for the variable "Police Contacts"?

12. Fill in the missing value for either the variance or the standard deviation:

	Variance	Standard Deviation
a.	3.45	
b.		5.45
c.	1.22	
d.		.89
e.	10.56	
f.		1.25

13. Fourteen victims of burglary reported the amount of monetary loss due to the crime. Enter the data into Excel and calculate the (a) range, (b) variance, and (c) standard deviation. Based on the value of the mean and standard deviation, what would you conclude about the shape of the distribution for the variable "Monetary Loss"?

$500.00	$1,200.00	$850.00	$45.00	$30.00	$580.00
$450.00	$575.00	$1,250.00	$1,000.00	$1,200.00	$900.00
$1,000.00	$1,000.00				

14. A survey of 65 students registered for a criminal justice statistics course revealed the following grouped data distribution for the variable "GPA." Calculate the (a) variance and (b) standard deviation for both males and females.

Males		Females	
GPA (X)	Frequency (f)	GPA (X)	Frequency (f)
3.50–4.00	6	3.50–4.00	3
3.00–3.49	2	3.00–3.49	8
2.50–2.99	21	2.50–2.99	4
2.00–2.49	15	2.00–2.49	3
1.00–1.99	3	1.00–1.99	0

Probability Theory

ExploreIT!

As a defense attorney, you need to determine whether a particular plea bargain offered to your client should be accepted or rejected. The defendant is charged with armed robbery and either can accept the plea bargain or can take his chances by going to trial. The district attorney (DA) wants the defendant to plead guilty to armed robbery in exchange for nine years in prison—what the DA calls a reduced sentence. The DA has stated that she will argue for the maximum sentence of 18 years if the defendant elects to go to trial and is convicted. How do you know whether pleading guilty to armed robbery and receiving nine years in prison is a good deal and should be accepted? To answer this question, you need to know the population mean and standard deviation for the length of sentence given for armed robbery. With this additional information, you will be able to create a z-score to determine how a sentence of nine years compares to sentences among the population of individuals who have pleaded guilty to robbery.

In the previous chapters, we focused on laying the foundational blocks of criminal justice research. We examined the process of describing variables and attributes through the use of descriptive statistics. We also discussed various methods for describing our variables, including percentages, rates, measures of central tendency, and dispersion. Furthermore, we analyzed a variety of graphical techniques commonly used to make the representation of our data more meaningful and understandable.

We now want to turn our attention away from descriptive statistics, in which we describe our sample observations, to inferential statistics. You will recall from Chapter 1 that inferential statistics involve drawing conclusions about a population based on observations from a sample. For instance, inferential statistics allow us to argue that U.S. citizens favor tougher sentences for criminals, on the basis of a sample of all U.S. citizens. To move into inferential statistics, we must have a basic understanding of probability theory. In essence, probability theory allows us to make inferences about populations.

This chapter will focus on several aspects of probability including basic concepts, probability distributions, the normal curve, and standardized scores. In Chapter 7, we extend the discussion of probability to the use of probability sampling.

6.1 Basic Concepts of Probability Theory

probability **Probability** is best defined as *the number of times that a particular event or outcome can occur divided by the number of times any event or outcome can occur*. The probability of an event or outcome is expressed in terms of a proportion. In notational form, this looks like the following:

$$\text{Probability of outcome 1} = \frac{\text{Number of times outcome 1 can occur}}{\text{Number of times any outcome can occur}}$$

The probability that if we flip a coin we will get a tail is determined by dividing the number of times a tail could occur on a single flip of the coin by the number of times that any outcome could occur on a single flip. Thus, the number of times a tail could occur is one; the number of times any outcome—heads or tails—could occur is two. The probability of a coin flip resulting in a tail is expressed as:

$$P(\text{tail}) = \frac{1}{2} = .50$$

Suppose that a newly incarcerated offender has been cleared by the warden to receive a job in the institution. Let's further assume that job assignments are randomly assigned to inmates by the warden, regardless of the skills or desires of the offender, and that an equal number of inmates is assigned to each task. Furthermore, suppose that newly admitted inmates are allowed to work in one of the following five areas: a) kitchen, b) laundry, c) maintenance, d) wood shop, or e) yard crew. What is the probability that offender A will be working in the kitchen? Again, to calculate the probability, we need only to divide the number of times the outcome can occur by the total number of times that any equally likely outcome can occur. The formula and resulting probability are:

$$P(\text{kitchen}) = \frac{1}{5} = .20$$

Two important points are worth mentioning. First, although probabilities are typically stated in terms of proportions, we can easily state a probability as a percentage by multiplying the proportion by 100. Thus, offender A has a 20% chance of working in the kitchen, which is the same as saying that the probability that the offender will be working in the kitchen is .20. The second point to consider is that the probability of an outcome occurring ranges between 0 and 1.0. The closer the probability of an outcome is to zero, the less likely that outcome will occur. In contrast, the closer the probability of an outcome is to 1.0, the more likely that outcome will occur. If an outcome has a probability of 0, that means it will never occur, whereas an outcome with a probability of 1.0 means it will always occur.

Using the preceding example, we will now discuss two associated characteristics of probability theory. Instead of merely asking about the probability of receiving any one particular job, a more appropriate question for the offender might be, "What is the probability of receiving any job other than yard crew?" To determine the overall probability that the offender will receive a job other than yard crew, we must sum the probabilities of all of the outcomes except yard crew. This is known as the addition rule of probability.

addition rule

The **addition rule** states that *the probability of any number of outcomes occurring is equal to the sum of the separate probabilities of the number of outcomes.* In our example, the probability of offender A receiving any one of four possible jobs other than yard crew is equal to the sum of the separate probabilities of each of the four jobs. As shown in Table 6.1, the offender has a .20 probability of receiving any one of the five jobs. Therefore, the probability that the offender will receive a job other than yard crew is calculated by summing the probabilities of the other four jobs (kitchen .20 + laundry .20 + maintenance .20 + wood shop .20 = .80), which is equal to .80. Thus, offender A has an 80% chance of having a job other than yard crew.

mutually exclusive

The addition rule applies only to those outcomes that are mutually exclusive. **Mutually exclusive** means *that no more than one outcome can occur at a given time.* On a single flip of a coin, it is impossible to obtain a head *and* a tail at the same time. The probability, however, of obtaining a head *or* a tail is the sum of the probability of each outcome ($P[\text{head}] = .50 + P[\text{tail}] = .50 = 1.0$). There is a 100% chance that we will obtain a head or a tail on a single flip of the coin; there can be no other outcome. If we

TABLE 6.1 Probability of Receiving a Job

Job	Probability
Kitchen	.20
Laundry	.20
Maintenance	.20
Wood shop	.20
Yard crew	.20

assume that our offender can have only *one* of the five jobs listed, then he has a 100% chance of working either in the kitchen, laundry, maintenance, wood shop, or yard crew.

multiplica-tion rule A second important characteristic of probability is the multiplication rule. The **multiplication rule** states that *the probability of obtaining two or more outcomes simultaneously is equal to the product of their separate probabilities.* Let's assume that offender A can have more than one job. Instead of asking about the probability of receiving any job other than yard crew, the offender may want to ask, "What is the probability of working in the kitchen *and* the laundry?" To determine the probability of working in the kitchen *and* working in the laundry, we need to multiply the separate probabilities of both outcomes (kitchen .20 × laundry .20 = .04). In this case, the offender has a 4% chance of having a job in both the kitchen and the laundry.

indepen-dence An important feature of the multiplication rule is that the outcomes must be independent. We define **independence** as meaning that *the occurrence of one outcome does not affect the likelihood of the occurrence of any other outcome.* For example, if we flipped a coin 10 times, and it landed on tails all 10 times, the probability that the coin will land on tails with the 11th flip is still .50. The fact that it landed on tails 10 times in a row does not alter the probability that it will land on tails on the 11th flip.

These basic concepts are relevant to understanding the usefulness of the probability distribution. The core of inferential statistics involves comparing a test statistic against a probability distribution to determine whether observed differences are the result of actual differences in the population or due to sampling error.

6.2 Probability Distribution

probability distribu-tion A probability distribution is similar to a frequency distribution; however, a **probability distribution** is *based on theoretical assumptions of what outcome would be expected rather than what outcome actually is observed.* A probability distribution is used to determine the associated probability or likelihood of obtaining a particular outcome.

Let's assume that we have ten marbles in a paper bag and that five of the marbles are green and five are red. We ask the following question, "What is the probability of randomly selecting a green marble on two consecutive picks?" The probability of randomly selecting a green marble on the first pick *and* the second pick requires us to use the multiplication rule to determine the probability. The probability of selecting a green marble on two consecutive picks is given as:

$$P(\text{two green marbles}) =$$

$$P(\text{green — pick 1}) = \frac{5}{10} = .50$$

$$P(\text{green — pick 2}) = \frac{5}{10} = .50$$

$$(.50) \times (.50) = .25$$

The probability of selecting two green marbles on consecutive picks is .25. That is, the probability of selecting a green marble on the second pick is equal to the probability of selecting a green marble on the first pick (.50), as long as there are the same number of green and red marbles in the bag during both selections. This is known as sampling with replacement.

sampling with replacement   **Sampling with replacement** involves *replacing a selected sample element back into the population*. If we selected a green marble on the first pick and did not replace that green marble back into the bag, the probability of selecting a green marble on the second pick would not be equal to the probability of its selection for the first pick. We now have only four green marbles in a population of nine total marbles. Thus, the probability of selecting a green marble on the second pick is now 4/9, or .44. In turn, this changes the probability of selecting two green marbles on two consecutive picks (.50 × .44 = .22).

The probability of selecting zero green marbles—that is, selecting two red marbles on two consecutive picks—is the same as the probability of selecting two green marbles. Once again, the probability of selection is determined by:

$$P(\text{zero green marbles}) =$$

$$P(\text{red — pick 1}) = \frac{5}{10} = .50$$

$$P(\text{red — pick 2}) = \frac{5}{10} = .50$$

$$(.50) \times (.50) = .25$$

Because we are trying to determine the probability of not selecting a green marble on the first pick *and* not selecting a green marble on the second pick, we need to multiply their respective probabilities together to determine the probability of obtaining zero green marbles.

To determine the probability of selecting only one green marble, we need to determine the probability of selecting a green marble on either the first or second pick and then sum the separate probabilities. In order to do this, we must recognize that it is possible to select a green marble on pick one and a red marble on pick two, or a red marble on pick one and a green marble on pick two. Thus, the probability of selecting only one green marble is determined by adding the probability of selecting a green marble first and a red marble second to the probability of selecting a red marble first and a green marble second. In notational form, the probability is determined as follows:

$$P(\text{green} / \text{red}) + P(\text{red} / \text{green}) =$$
$$(.50)(.50) + (.50)(.50) = .25 + .25 = .50$$

The probability distribution based on this hypothetical example of selecting two marbles should look like the distribution shown in Figure 6.1a. The probability distribution is characterized as being *symmetrical,* meaning that there is an equal proportion of probabilities on both sides of the curve. Specifically, the probability of obtaining two green marbles (.25) is exactly the same as the probability of obtaining zero green marbles (.25).

Now, let's assume that we actually conducted an experiment in which we selected twenty different samples of two marbles by randomly picking a marble, on two consecutive tries, from a bag of ten marbles. Suppose that we picked zero green marbles eight times (40%), one green marble nine times (45%), and two green marbles three times (15%). We can report these results in a frequency distribution, as shown in Figure 6.1b.

Remember, the probability distribution (Figure 6.1a) is theoretical. That is, the distribution shows us what our results are expected to look like given the random process of selecting a single marble on two consecutive picks from a bag of ten marbles. The frequency distribution (Figure 6.1b), by contrast, is what was actually observed in drawing the different samples. Probability theory tells us that we would expect our frequency distribution to model the probability distribution. A comparison of the two distributions reveals a marked discrepancy between our expectation of what should occur and what actually occurred under our observation. The question is why. The answer lies in the number of samples that we drew. Our frequency distribution is based on only 20 samples—a very small number of samples. Therefore, it is likely that a skewed distribution, such as that shown in Figure 6.1b, would occur simply because a series of zero green marbles and very few samples of two green marbles were selected.

As we increase the number of samples drawn, the more likely the frequency distribution is to approximate the probability distribution. For example, if we were to select five hundred samples of two marbles, we would likely get a frequency distribution like that shown in Figure 6.2. Using this hypothetical data, we selected zero green marbles 27% of the time (133), one green marble 49% of the time (247), and two green marbles 24% of the time (120). You will notice that although these percentages do not equal the

FIGURE 6.1a Probability distribution of selecting 0, 1, and 2 green marbles

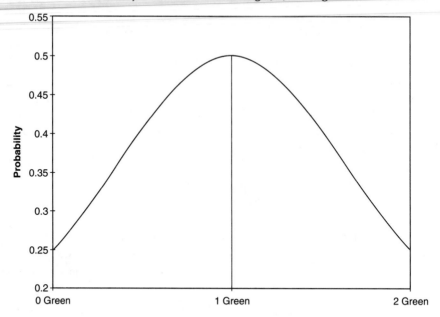

FIGURE 6.1b Frequency distribution of selecting 20 samples of 0, 1, and 2 green marbles

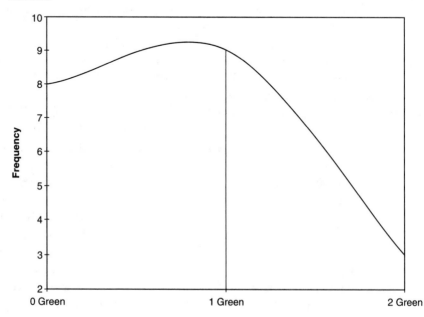

FIGURE 6.2 Frequency distribution of selecting 500 samples of 0, 1, and 2 green marbles

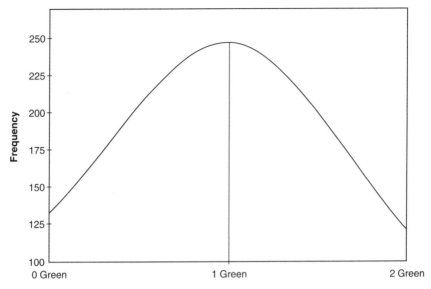

probabilities exactly as shown in Figure 6.1a, they are, however, much closer than the percentages given for only 20 samples. If we increased the number of samples to 1,000, the discrepancy between our frequency distribution and the probability distribution would be further minimized. This effect, known as the **law of large numbers**, *implies that as the number of samples increases, the frequency distribution will more closely approximate the probability distribution.*

law of large numbers

This brings us to a very important point concerning the probability distribution. Probability theory informs us that for an infinite number of randomly selected samples, we would obtain a frequency distribution that is symmetrical—such as the probability distribution shown in Figure 6.1a. More specifically, the frequency distribution for our samples of marbles would model the probability distribution if we randomly selected an infinite number of samples of two marbles. Once again, we must reiterate that the probability distribution is theoretical, identifying what should occur based on an infinite number of randomly selected samples.

6.3 The Normal Curve

We now turn our attention to a particular type of probability distribution known as the normal curve. We first introduced the concept of the normal curve in Chapter 5, when discussing the usefulness of the standard deviation. The exact shape of the normal curve is determined by the population mean (μ) and the population standard deviation (σ). The **normal curve** is *a type of probability distribution mathematically defined as being unimodal, symmetrical, and asymptotic.*

normal curve

FIGURE 6.3 Normal curve

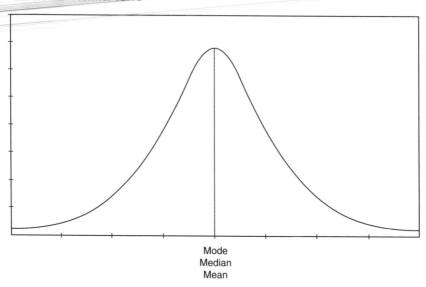

Mode
Median
Mean

Properties of the Normal Curve

Several properties characterize the normal curve. First, the normal curve is commonly referred to as a *bell-shaped* curve because of its resemblance to a bell. A second property of the normal curve is that it is *unimodal.* You will recall from our discussion on measures of central tendency that a distribution is characterized as unimodal if the distribution has only one mode—that is, if only one value occurs most frequently in the distribution. The normal curve is further characterized as being *symmetrical.* A symmetrical distribution occurs when the values of the mode, median, and mean are all equal. The normal curve can be split into two equal halves, with a vertical line at its highest point—where the mode, median, and mean occur. An equal proportion of cases will occur above and below the vertical line, as shown in Figure 6.3. Finally, the normal curve is *asymptotic.* That is, the tails of the curve never touch the horizontal axis even as they move further and further away from the midpoint of the distribution.

Area Under the Normal Curve

In Chapter 5, we noted that the normal curve is defined as having a standardized unit of measurement, with a mean of zero and a standard deviation of one. When we add the properties of being unimodal, symmetrical, and asymptotic, the normal curve allows us to measure the distance between any given score or value and its mean.

Let's return to this concept of standardized units of measurement. Figure 6.4 illustrates the percentage of cases falling within standard units of measurement from the

FIGURE 6.4 Area under the normal curve

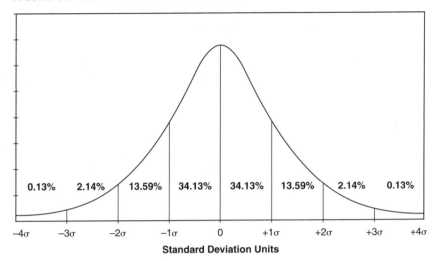

mean. We use σ (sigma) to represent the standard deviation of the population. For any given variable, we find that 100% of the values or cases for the variable lie under the curve.

One of the properties of the normal curve is that it is symmetrical. In Figure 6.4, we see that 34.13% of the cases fall between the mean and +1σ, which is exactly the same percentage of cases falling between the mean and –1σ (34.13%). The percentage of cases occurring between the mean and each standard deviation unit is the same for both positive and negative values. Thus, the total percentage of cases falling above the mean is 50%, and the total percentage of cases falling below the mean is also 50%. This property allows us to determine the percentage of cases falling within a specified distance of the mean by summing the percentage of cases occurring between the mean and the standard deviation unit above and below the mean. For example, by adding the percentage of cases falling between the mean and +1σ (34.13%) with the percentage of cases falling between the mean and –1σ (34.13%), we say that 68.26% of the cases lie within *plus* or *minus* 1 standard deviation unit (±1σ) of the mean. The percentage of cases falling within 2 standard deviation units (±2σ) of the mean is 95.44%, and 99.72% of the cases lie within 3 standard deviation units (±3σ) of the mean. It should be noted that although the normal curve extends out 4 standard deviation units from the mean to capture 100% of the cases under the curve, the percentage of cases less than –3σ or greater than +3σ is exceedingly small (.26%).

We say that the probability that any one score will fall within *plus* or *minus* 1 standard deviation unit of the mean is approximately .68. Put another way, the probability is 68 in 100 that any single score will fall between –1σ and +1σ. The probability of any score falling within *plus* or *minus* 2 standard deviation units of the mean is .95 or 95 in 100, and .99 for 3 standard deviation units from the mean or 99 in 100.

6.4 Standardized Scores (z)

**standard-
ized scores
(z)**

Because the normal curve is a probability distribution with a mean of zero and a standard deviation of one, we can use this distribution to create scores that are based on this standardized unit of measurement. The **standardized scores** that we create, known as *z-scores, indicate the direction and degree a raw score deviates from its mean in standard deviation units.* As shown in Figure 6.5, the z distribution is the same as the normal curve having a mean of zero and a standard deviation of one. Although we report the percentage of cases that fall within specified distances from the mean, it is important to remember that these percentages are also proportions. Thus, the proportion of cases that lie between the mean and plus 1 standard deviation is .3413. Converting raw scores into z-scores enable us to make meaningful comparisons among the scores in a distribution. To convert any raw score into a z-score, we use the following formula:

$$z = \frac{X - \mu}{\sigma}$$

X = value of raw score
μ = population mean
σ = population standard deviation

Let's assume that an incarcerated offender accumulated 12 misconduct reports over the course of one year. We might be tempted to say that the offender's disciplinary record is good, given the fact that he averaged only one report per month. In order to make a statement about the offender's disciplinary record as being good or bad, we must have some additional information concerning misconduct in the population. Assume that

FIGURE 6.5 Area under the normal curve and z-scores

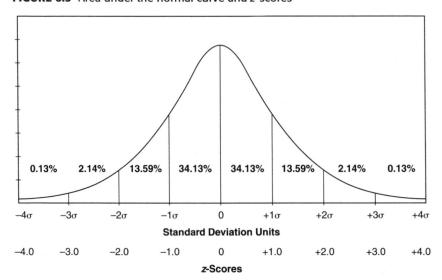

the mean number of misconduct reports for the prison population during the same time period is 7.50, with a standard deviation of 3. To convert our raw score of 12 into a z-score, we merely place the appropriate values into the formula:

$$z = \frac{12 - 7.5}{3} = 1.50$$

Our offender has a z-score of 1.50. What does this score mean? At first glance, we know that the offender did worse than average, because he has a positive z-score. This indicates that his score is above the mean of zero (in standardized units). To fully interpret the meaning of the z-score, however, we need to make use of the z distribution table. Table 6.2 provides a sample portion of the z distribution table with the full z distribution located in Table A, Appendix A.

The z table provides three pieces of information—the z-score, the proportion of cases falling between the mean and the z-score, and the proportion of cases falling beyond the z-score. In order to interpret the meaning of our z-score, we must introduce **percentile rank** another term—the percentile rank. The **percentile rank** is a *value that indicates the percentage of cases in a distribution falling below a particular z-score*. Each z-score has a percentile rank associated with it. For example, a z-score of 0 has a percentile rank of 50%, because zero is equal to the mean of the distribution. That is, 50% of the scores in the distribution fall below the z-score of zero.

To use the z distribution table, we must first locate the z-score in column A of the z table. Once we have located our score (1.50), we then look at column B to find the area between the mean and z. For our example, this value equals .4332, which represents the proportion of cases falling between the mean of zero and the z-score of 1.5. Put another way, our z-score is 1.50 standard deviation units above the mean. You have probably noticed that the z table reports proportions instead of percentages. We feel that the

TABLE 6.2 Sample z Distribution Table

Column A	Column B	Column C
	Area between	
z-score	mean and z	Area beyond z
1.46	0.4279	0.0721
1.47	0.4292	0.0708
1.48	0.4306	0.0694
1.49	0.4319	0.0681
1.50	0.4332	0.0668
1.51	0.4345	0.0655
1.52	0.4357	0.0643
1.53	0.4370	0.0630
1.54	0.4382	0.0618

interpretation of the scores is simplified by using percentages; therefore, we recommend reporting the percentage instead of the proportion. This is easily accomplished by multiplying the proportion by 100, or simply by moving the decimal point two places to the right. Thus, our proportion of .4332 becomes a percentage of 43.32%.

It is important to remember that the *z* distribution table is in standardized units. This means that an offender with a *z*-score of zero does not actually have a value of zero misconduct reports but, rather, has 7.50 misconduct reports, which, when converted to a *z*-score, results in a score of zero. Therefore, to determine the percentile rank of the offender with 12 misconduct reports, calculate the proportion of cases falling below the *z*-score of 1.50. To do this, we simply add 43.32%—the area between the mean and *z*—and the percentage of cases falling below the mean, equal to 50%. Thus, our offender ranks in the 93rd percentile among the population of offenders. Simply put, this means that this offender received more misconduct reports than 93% (rounded) of the inmate population (43.32% + 50% = 93.32%). This example is further illustrated in Figure 6.6.

We can also use column C, the area beyond the *z*, to calculate the offenders' percentile rank. Since we know that 100% of the cases fall under the curve, we need only to subtract the area beyond the *z* from 1.00 (1.00 – .0668 = .9332, or 93% rounded). We are able to conclude that, based on our *z*-score, the disciplinary record of our offender is less than admirable.

Let's assume an inmate had a *z*-score of –1.47. You have probably already noticed that there are no negative values in the *z* distribution table. This is because the normal curve is symmetrical such that the areas between the mean and *z* and beyond the *z*

FIGURE 6.6 Probability and the *z* distribution

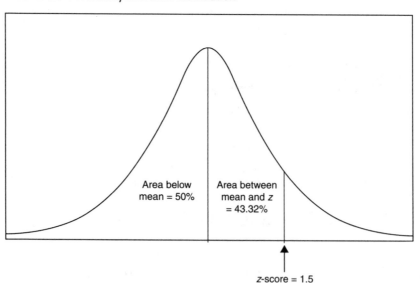

are exactly the same, regardless of whether the *z*-score is negative or positive. To determine the percentile rank for a negative *z*-score, we simply ignore the sign (which informs us in which half of the distribution our *z*-score is located), and find the absolute value of *z*, which is equal to 1.47. We then look at column C in Table 6.2—the area beyond the *z*—where we find the value of .0708. This is the percentile rank for −1.47, because the area beyond the *z* accounts for those scores below the *z*-score, as illustrated in Figure 6.7.

Suppose we wanted to know the percentage of offenders who had between five and ten misconduct reports. In order to determine this, we first need to convert each of the raw scores to *z*-scores. Thus, our raw scores are converted by way of the following formulas:

$$z = \frac{5 - 7.50}{3} = -.83 \qquad\qquad z = \frac{10 - 7.50}{3} = .83$$

We now proceed to our *z* table to find the percentage of cases falling between the mean and *z*. According to the *z* distribution table in Appendix A, 29.67% of the cases are located between the mean and *z* of .83. As 29.67% of the cases fall between the mean and positive *z* of .83, then 29.67% of the cases will also occur between the mean and a negative *z* of .83. To determine the percentage of cases falling between −.83 and +.83, we simply sum the two percentages (29.67 + 29.67 = 59.34), and conclude that 59.34% of the offenders had between five and ten misconduct reports.

Take some time to practice determining the area between the mean and *z* and the area beyond *z* by completing TryIT! Box 6.1.

FIGURE 6.7 Probability and the *z* distribution for a negative *z*-score

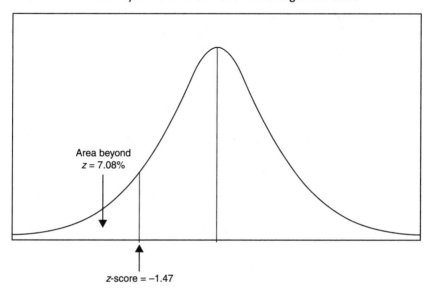

TryIT! BOX **6.1**

Using the *z* distribution, Table A in Appendix A, determine the area between the mean and *z* and the area beyond the *z* for each of the *z*-scores listed below.

z-score	Area between Mean and z	Area beyond z
−2.31	48.96%	0.04
1.21	38.69	1.31
1.91		
3.04		
−.56	21.23	28.77
.12		
−1.39		

Probability and the Normal Curve

With the normal curve, we can answer several questions regarding probabilities. For example, what is the probability of randomly selecting an offender from the population who has 12 or more misconduct reports $P(X \geq 12)$? We already determined that the *z*-score for 12 misconduct reports was 1.50. Because we want to know the probability of selecting an offender who has a *z*-score equal to or higher than 1.50, we need to look at column C in the *z* table, where we find the proportion of cases equal to .0668. Thus, the probability of randomly selecting an offender who has 12 or more misconduct reports is roughly 7% (rounded).

We can also apply the addition and multiplication rules for figuring probabilities that were learned earlier. What is the probability of randomly selecting an offender who has 1 or fewer misconduct reports or 15 or more misconduct reports? Once again, we need to convert the raw scores to *z*-scores in the following manner:

$$p(x \geq 15) \quad z = \frac{15 - 7.50}{3} = 2.50 \qquad p(x \leq 1) \quad z = \frac{1 - 7.50}{3} = -2.17$$

Consulting column C (area beyond *z*) in the *z* distribution table, we find that a *z*-score of 2.50 corresponds with .0062, while a *z*-score of −2.17 corresponds with .0150. To determine the probability of randomly selecting one *or* the other, we simply add the two probabilities (.0062 + .0150 = .0212). Thus, we have a 2% chance of randomly selecting an offender who has either 1 or fewer misconduct reports or 15 or more misconduct reports. Conversely, we have a 98% chance of selecting an offender who has between 1 and 15 misconduct reports.

We can arrive at this figure in one of two ways. First, since the proportion of cases falling under the normal curve is equal to 1.00, we can simply subtract the probability of .0212 from 1.00, which is equal to .9788 (rounded to 98%). Second, we can use column B (area between the mean and z) to determine the proportion of cases falling between the mean and each z-score, and then sum the two proportions to determine the probability of selection (.4938 + .4850 = .9788).

What is the probability of randomly selecting 2 offenders in which 1 has 1 or fewer misconduct reports *and* the other has 12 or more misconduct reports? This problem requires the use of the multiplication rule. The associated probability of such an outcome is determined by multiplying their associated probabilities (.0062 × .0150 = .000093). The chance of selecting two offenders having these criteria is extremely small.

There may be instances in which we know the z-scores and yet would like to know the values of the original unstandardized scores. Let's assume that we were given the z-scores for misconduct of five offenders randomly selected from the inmate population. Looking at the data in Figure 6.8, we can easily determine that offender 3 is the worst offender, as his z-score is greater than those of the other four offenders. Furthermore, we can look up his value in the z table, where we find that his percentile rank is 99.73%. This means that this offender is in the top 1% of the inmate population in terms of the number of misconduct reports received.

FIGURE 6.8 z-scores for misconduct of 5 offenders

Offender	z-score
#1	−1.23
#2	.67
#3	2.78
#4	.43
#5	−2.34

We use the following formula to convert a z-score back to its original unstandardized value:

$$X = \mu + z\sigma$$

Remember, the mean for misconduct reports was 7.50, with a standard deviation of 3. We plug these three values into the formula to determine the frequency of misconduct reports for offender 3 as demonstrated:

$$
\begin{aligned}
X &= 7.50 + (2.78)(3) \\
&= 7.50 + 8.34 \\
&= 15.84
\end{aligned}
$$

Thus, offenders that rank in the 99th percentile will have approximately 16 (rounded) misconduct reports.

Practice calculating both z-scores and percentile ranks by completing TryIT! Box 6.2 before moving on to section 6.5.

TryIT!   BOX **6.2**

A sample of seven seventh graders from a local middle school were asked the number of times they vandalized property in the last 12 months. Assume that the mean and the standard deviation for the population of seventh graders in the town where the school is located is 3.30 (μ) and 1.20 (σ). Calculate a z-score and percentile rank for each subject.

Subject #	Vandalism (X)	z-score	Percentile
1	1		
2	6		
3	4		
4	3		
5	1		
6	5		
7	0		

6.5 Using Excel to Calculate z-Scores

By now you are familiar with the advantages of using Excel to calculate descriptive statistics. As we continue to move forward, you will discover that Excel is also a valuable tool for calculating more complicated inferential statistics. In this section, you will learn how to calculate both z-scores and their percentile ranks.

Suppose that a state parole board is considering the cases of 12 parolees with the intention of releasing 5 of the 12 from further parole supervision. The board would like to rank the parolees from best to worst in terms of the number of technical violations each parolee received during the previous six months on parole. Unfortunately, the board cannot construct its ranking by simply counting the number of technical violations, because levels of supervision vary. For example, parolees with high levels of supervision are likely to have more technical violations than parolees with lower levels of supervision, because of the increased number of contacts with parole officers. Therefore, we need to convert the raw scores into z-scores so the parole board can rank the offenders by taking into account the different levels of supervision. The data is presented in Table 6.3. The means and standard deviations are hypothetical for the number of technical violations for the population of offenders in each group.

z-score

Our formula for calculating a z-score is given as:

$$z = \frac{X - \mu}{\sigma}$$

Step 1: Place the cursor in cell c3 and write: =(b3-b7)/b8.

> b3 is the cell location for 3 technical violations for parolee 1.
> b7 is the cell location for the mean number of technical violations for the population of high-supervision parolees.
> b8 is the cell location for the standard deviation of technical violations for the population of high-supervision parolees.
> $ hold the column and row constant.

Step 2: Click on the lower-right hand corner of the cell containing the first z-score (cell c3) and drag the cursor down to the last row of values for the high-supervision group (cell c6). This will automatically create the rest of the z-score column for this group.

Percentile Rank

Step 1: Place the cursor in cell d3 and click on the paste function box:

Step 2: Click on the function category called **statistical**.
Step 3: Click on the name category called **normsdist**.
Step 4: Click **OK**. A box will appear that will ask for z—the value for which you want the distribution. Type in cell c3 and you will get the percentile rank of that parolee's z-score.
Step 5: Click on the lower right-hand corner of the cell containing the first percentile . rank (cell d3), and drag the cursor down to the last row of values for the high supervision group (cell d6). This will automatically create the rest of the percentile rank column for this group.

It is important to remember that the percentile rank values in column D are proportions, not percentages. To convert the values to percentages, simply highlight the values in column D and click on the percentage button on the menu. The resulting values represent the parolees' percentile ranks.

Repeat the foregoing steps for calculating z-scores and percentile ranks for the moderate- and low-supervision groups. For example, for the moderate-supervision group, the formula should be written in cell c10 for parolee 2 as: =(b10-b14)/b15. For the low-supervision group, the formula should be written in cell c17 for parolee 3 as: =(b17-b21)/b22.

TABLE 6.3 Parolee z-Scores and Percentile Ranks

	A	B	C	D
1	Table 6.3 Parolee z-Scores and Percentile Ranks			
2	High-Supervision Parolee #	Technical Violations (X)	z-Score	Percentile Rank
3	1	3	-1.13	0.13
4	4	6	0.75	0.77
5	7	5	0.13	0.55
6	11	2	-1.75	0.04
7	Mean	4.8		
8	Standard deviation	1.6		
9	Moderate-Supervision Parolee #	Technical Violations (X)	z-Score	Percentile Rank
10	2	4	1.25	0.89
11	5	2	-0.42	0.34
12	9	1	-1.25	0.11
13	12	5	2.08	0.98
14	Mean	2.5		
15	Standard deviation	1.2		
16	Low-Supervision Parolee #	Technical Violations (X)	z-Score	Percentile Rank
17	3	3	2.85	1.00
18	6	1	0.07	0.53
19	8	0	-1.32	0.09
20	10	1	0.07	0.53
21	Mean	0.95		
22	Standard deviation	0.72		

The paste function box can also be used to calculate z-scores. Thus, we offer the following demonstration for calculating z-scores using the paste function box.

Step 1: Place the cursor in cell c3 and click on the paste function box:

Step 2: Click on the function category called **statistical**.
Step 3: Click on the name category called **standardize**.
Step 4: Click **OK**. A box will appear that will ask for x—the value you want to standardize (cell b3), mean—the mean of the distribution (cell b7), and standard deviation—the standard deviation of the distribution (cell b8).

x	b3
Mean	b7
Standard_dev	b8

This will create the z-score for parolee 1. To calculate the z-scores for the other three offenders in this group, we must repeat these steps for each offender. Compared to the formula method that enabled us to click and drag to create the rest of our values, the paste function method appears to be more time-consuming, because of repetition of steps. We can eliminate this repetitiveness by placing dollar signs in front of the row and column headings. This will enable us to click and drag to create the rest of our z-scores.

By converting the raw scores to standardized z-scores, we are now able to compare all 12 parolees regarding the number of technical violations received. Table 6.4 provides a comparison ranking of the offenders based on their raw scores and z-scores. If we had ranked the parolees based on the unstandardized (raw score) number of technical violations, parolee 8 would have been the best, because he had zero violations, and parolee 4 would have been the worst, with six violations.

These conclusions, however, would be incorrect, simply because the level of supervision affects the number of violations. Therefore, based on the z-score rankings, we find that parolee 11 was the best with a z-score of −1.75, which places him in the 4th percentile among the high-supervision group (see Table 6.3, row 6). Put another way, parolee 11 had fewer misconduct reports than 96% of the high-supervision population. Parolee 3 was the worst, with a z-score of 2.85, which places him in the 100th percentile among the low-supervision group (see Table 6.3, row 17). To simplify, this parolee had more misconduct reports than the entire population of low-supervision parolees.

The difference in ranking between parolee 11 and parolee 3, based on their raw scores, is a difference of one. When looking at the z-score rankings, however, the difference is more pronounced, simply because we have made all of the scores comparable by taking into account the different levels of supervision through the process of standardization.

TABLE 6.4 Comparison of Raw Score and z-Score Rankings

Rank	Parolee #	Raw Score	Rank	Parolee #	z-Score
1	8	0	1	11	−1.75
2	9	1	2	8	−1.32
2	6	1	3	9	−1.25
2	10	1	4	1	−1.13
3	11	2	5	5	−0.42
3	5	2	6	6	0.07
4	1	3	6	10	0.07
4	3	3	7	7	0.13
5	2	4	8	4	0.75
6	7	5	9	2	1.25
6	12	5	10	12	2.08
7	4	6	11	3	2.85

6.6 Summary

It is important that you have a basic understanding of probability theory, although we do not expect you to be an expert after reading this chapter. You must, however, understand the role of probability in inferential statistics, because it forms the basis of decision making regarding hypothesis testing.

Probability is defined as the number of times that a particular event or outcome can occur divided by the number of times any event or outcome can occur. We demonstrated this concept using coin flips, in which the probability of a tail occurring on a single flip is equal to .50. This was further illustrated using the random selection of green and red marbles from a bag. We also discussed the addition and multiplication rules of probability and how they are used to determine probabilities of multiple outcomes. The addition rule is used to determine the probability of any number of mutually exclusive outcomes occurring, and the multiplication rule is used to determine the probability of two or more outcomes occurring simultaneously.

The relationship between a probability distribution based on theory and a frequency distribution based on observed data was also addressed. The law of large numbers informs us that, as we increase the number of samples, the frequency distribution will more closely approximate the probability distribution. We discussed the normal curve as a probability distribution. A normal probability distribution is characterized as being unimodal, symmetrical, and asymptotic. We also explained the areas under the normal curve and how this information is useful in determining the number of cases or the probability of a single case falling within a particular distance of the mean.

We also focused on the usefulness of standardized scores—known as *z*-scores—and percentile ranks and how we can use these in relation to the normal curve to determine probabilities and make useful comparisons among noncomparable raw scores. Finally, we discussed how to calculate *z*-scores and percentile ranks using Excel.

Key Terms

probability	sampling with replacement
addition rule	law of large numbers
mutually exclusive	normal curve
multiplication rule	standardized scores (*z*)
independence	percentile rank
probability distribution	

"TryIT" Answers

Box 6.1

z-score	Area between Mean and z	Area beyond z
−2.31	.4896	.0104
1.21	.3869	.1131
1.91	.4719	.0281
3.04	.4988	.0012
−.56	.2123	.2877
.12	.0478	.4522
−1.39	.4177	.0823

Box 6.2

Subject	Vandalism (X)	z-score	Percentile
1	1	−1.92	2.74
2	6	2.25	98.78
3	4	.58	71.90
4	3	−.25	40.13

Box 6.2 *(Continued)*

Subject	Vandalism (X)	z-score	Percentile
5	1	−1.92	2.74
6	5	1.42	92.22
7	0	−2.75	.30

6.7 Problems

1. Which measure of central tendency and which measure of dispersion are used to calculate z-scores?

2. A local police department has calculated z-scores for the number of tickets written in the month of January for five officers going for promotion. The departmental average for the month was 17, with a standard deviation of 4. For the following data:

   a. Determine the percentile rank for the set of z-scores listed below.
   b. Determine the raw score equivalent for each z-score.

Officer	z-score
Smith	−1.35
Jones	2.45
Norbert	0
Wright	−.76
Dawn	.34

3. The population of 100 police recruits in 1999 was given a weapons qualification test. The average score on the weapons exam was 12.6, with a standard deviation of 2.9.

   a. What raw score constitutes being in the top 5%?
   b. What is the probability of randomly selecting an officer who scored 10 or less, *or* 15 or more?
   c. What is the probability of randomly selecting two officers, one of whom scored less than 8 *and* the other scored more than 13?
   d. What percentage of officers scored between 12 and 18?

4. In a criminal justice statistics class, there are 34 students. Of these students, there are 14 males, 4 of whom are criminal justice majors. The other 10 are psychology majors. Among the 20 females, 13 are criminal justice majors and 7 are psychology majors.

   a. What is the probability of randomly selecting a female?
   b. What is the probability of randomly selecting a criminal justice major?
   c. What is the probability of randomly selecting a male psychology major?

d. What is the probability of randomly selecting a male criminal justice major *or* a female psychology major?

e. What is the probability of randomly selecting a male criminal justice major *and* a male psychology major on two consecutive picks without sampling with replacement?

5. Among the population of criminal justice students at a state university, the average score on the final exam in research methods during the spring semester was 74, with a standard deviation of 11.6.

   a. What percentage of students scored between 80 and 90 during the fall semester?
   b. What percentage of students failed the exam during the fall semester (assume a failing score is 59 or below)?
   c. What is the probability of randomly selecting a student who earned an A (90 or better)?
   d. What proportion of students scored between 60 and 80?

6. What is the difference between a frequency distribution and a probability distribution?

7. List and define the properties of the normal curve.

8. For a distribution of scores that has a mean of 83 and a standard deviation of 6.4, find the following probabilities:

   a. $P(X \geq 90)$
   b. $P(X \leq 70)$
   c. $P(70 \leq X \leq 90)$

9. What is the probability of any given score falling within the following range?

   a. $\pm 1\sigma$ from the mean
   b. $\pm 2\sigma$ from the mean
   c. $\pm 3\sigma$ from the mean

10. The average number of complaints against police officers in a large urban department during 1998 was 4.7, with a standard deviation of 1.1. Find the following z-scores and percentile ranks:

    a. $X = 2$
    b. $X = 6$
    c. $X = 1$
    d. $X = 3$

11. What percentage of officers in the population had six or more complaints?

12. What percentage of officers in the population had three or fewer complaints?

13. A student scored an 83 on a criminal justice statistics exam in which the class average was 76 with a standard deviation of 5. The same student scored an 89 on a psychology statistics exam in which the class average was 81 with a standard deviation of 11. In which class did the student perform better?

14. A researcher found that the rate of violent confrontations among the population of county jails is equal to 5.7 per 100 prisoners, with a standard deviation of 2.9. Enter the following data into Excel, and calculate the z-score and percentile rank for violent confrontations for each of the jails listed below.

Jail	Violent	Confrontations
A	6.5	
B	10.2	
C	2.9	
D	1.7	
E	5.9	

15. Enter the following cities and their corresponding crime rates into Excel. Assume that the average crime rate for the population of cities similar in size is 105.67, with a standard deviation of 39.56. For each city, calculate the z-score and percentile rank for the variable crime rate.

City	Crime Rate
Ellensburg	123.45
Whitewater	145.65
Kalamazoo	110.56
Agawam	106.57
Beaverton	98.43
Beatrice	101.45
Buckley	87.65
Juniper	99.01
Custer	105.31
Blaine	100.21

Sample Statistics to Population Parameters

ExploreIT!

The National Rifle Association (NRA) is interested in knowing what percentage of its members used a gun for self-defense purposes in 1999. Additionally, the NRA would like to know the average number of hours per month members spend on target practice. You have been hired by the NRA as an independent research analyst to answer these two research questions. You have decided to conduct a survey with NRA members in which you ask the following two questions: (a) Did you use a gun for self-defense purposes at any time during the year 1999—yes or no? (b) Approximately how many hours per month do you spend on target practice? As the NRA has several million members, it is not possible for you to give your survey to the entire population of members. Therefore, you will need to obtain a list of all members and select a probability sample from the population. This will enable you to estimate the true values in the population based on the values obtained from the sample. You will make these population estimates by calculating the amount of error in your sample and using this information to construct confidence intervals at various confidence levels.

As discussed in Chapter 1, a sample is a subset of people or objects that is drawn from and representing the larger population. In criminal justice research, we collect and analyze information obtained from a sample with the goal of making inferences or generalizations to the larger population. For example, we might ask a sample of 200 college students, "Are you afraid of being a victim of crime on campus?," and find that 27% of our sample said Yes. We are not so much interested in the percentage of the *sample* that said yes as in the percentage of the *population*—all students on campus—that would say Yes. What if we wanted to know how supportive Massachusetts residents are of Megan's Law? We would draw a sample of citizens living in Massachusetts from the population of all adult citizens, 18 years old and older, living in Massachusetts. We would then ask the subjects in our sample to indicate their level of support on a scale of 1 to 10, with 1 being not supportive and 10 being very supportive.

In both of these examples, we are obtaining information based on a small group of individuals (sample) with the goal of generalizing our findings to the whole group of individuals (population). At this point, you might wonder why we don't just use the whole population, instead of a sample. It seems that our findings would be more accurate if we asked all students on campus whether they are afraid of being victims of crime or if we asked all Massachusetts residents how supportive they are of Megan's Law. Our findings would be more accurate based on the entire population of individuals instead of a sample. But researchers rarely have the time or the financial resources to study entire populations. Imagine if the population of students on campus was 12,000 and our study consisted of a four-page self-administered questionnaire. It would take not only a substantial amount of time to conduct surveys with a group this large, but a considerable amount of money in printing and mailing costs as well. The same would be true if we elected to survey the entire population of 6 million Massachusetts residents rather than a sample of 400 residents. Although sampling may result in a somewhat less accurate result, the increased efficiency in terms of time and resources makes sampling most often the method of choice for conducting criminal justice research.

In rare instances, we may elect to study the entire population. Let's say that we want to conduct our fear-of-crime study on a campus that has only 400 students. Although we could certainly elect to draw a sample from this population, it might be feasible to study the population in its entirety. But criminal justice research commonly involves large populations, thus requiring researchers to collect observations from a sample in order to make generalizations about the population.

Our goal in this chapter is to demonstrate how researchers make inferences or generalizations about a population based on observations from a sample. You will learn that through the process of probability sampling, in conjunction with probability theory, we can generalize our findings from a sample to the larger population with a high degree of accuracy. The methods used for estimating population values based on sample observations are dependent on the level of measurement of the variable, the sample size, and the use of probability sampling. With this information, we can determine the amount of error in our sample and proceed to estimate the value of the population parameter.

7.1 Sample Statistics and Population Parameters

statistic   It is important to make a distinction between values obtained from a sample and those from a population. A **statistic** is *the value of a given variable in a sample*. If we asked 200 college students, "Are you afraid of being a victim of crime on campus?," and 27% of the students said Yes, this value is the statistic for the variable "fear of victimization." It should also be noted that 73% of the students said No; this also is a statistic for the variable "fear of victimization." The percentage associated with each of the attributes of our variable is known as a statistic.

parameter   In contrast, a **parameter** is *the value of a given variable in a population*. Assume that our sample of 200 college students comes from an institution with 12,000 students. The parameter for our variable "fear of victimization" would be the percentage of all 12,000 students who said Yes or No. Thus, if we surveyed all 12,000 students about fear of victimization, a certain percentage would say Yes and a certain percentage would say No. These values would be known as parameters, because the percentages are the true values that exist in the population. We could obtain these values by surveying the entire population. Because we usually collect observations from a sample and not a population, parameters typically are unknown. Our goal is to make inferences or generalizations about a population based on observations obtained from a sample. We there-

statistical   fore make use of **statistical inference**, which is defined as *the process of using sample*
inference   *statistics to estimate population parameters* (Williams, 1979).

The question we must ask now is, "What is the probability that our sample statistic is an accurate estimate of the population parameter?" More precisely, this question should be, "How closely does the value of our sample statistic approximate the value of the population parameter?" Probability theory allows us to answer this question.

7.2 Probability Sampling

The relationship between probability theory and sampling is complex. Remember, our goal is to estimate population parameters on the basis of sample statistics. Thus, we want to select a sample in such a way that the statistics from our sample approximate the population parameters. We do this through the process of probability sampling.

probability   **Probability sampling** is *a random method of selection in which every member in the*
sampling   *population has an equal and known probability of selection*. The key to this process is random selection, in which the probability of an individual being selected from the population into the sample is the same for the entire population of individuals. We want to select a sample that is representative of the population. That is, the characteristics of our sample should closely resemble the characteristics of the population. To explain this further, we need to return to the concept of probability as discussed in Chapter 6.

You will recall that the probability of an outcome is determined by the following formula:

$$\text{Probability of outcome 1} = \frac{\text{Number of times outcome 1 can occur}}{\text{Number of times any outcome can occur}}$$

Returning to the example of "fear of crime victimization" on a college campus, we can determine the probability of being selected into the sample by calculating the probability of any one particular individual being selected from the population into the sample. As the process of selection is random, every individual will have an equal and known probability of selection, determined by using the above formula. Thus, the probability of selection into the sample is:

$$P(\text{selection}) = \frac{1}{12,000} = .000083$$

The numerator is the number of times that one specific person can be selected, and the denominator is the number of times that *any* person can be selected, equal to the population. All of the college students at this particular campus have an equal probability (.000083) of being selected into the sample.

In our previous discussion of probability in which we selected marbles from a bag (Chapter 6), we stressed the importance of sampling with replacement. If we did not replace a marble after one was selected, the probability of the next selection was significantly altered. This was true for the marble example simply because the population of marbles was so small ($N = 10$). Our current example—as actually occurs in most **sampling without replacement** criminal justice research—is **sampling without replacement**, which involves *selecting sample elements from the population without replacing those elements back into the population*. When the population is large, such as the number of college students on campus ($N = 12,000$), the changes in the probability of selection are very small. For example, if we select a sample of 200 students, the probability for selection for the first student in the sample was given as .000083. The population of students changes after the selection of a student into the sample. Thus, the probability of selection for the 200th student after 199 students had been selected already would be given as:

$$P(\text{selection}) \frac{1}{11,801} = .000085$$

Notice that the difference in the probability of selection between the first and the 200th student is nearly identical. Another reason that sampling without replacement is the more common approach is that in many instances it is impossible to replace elements of the population. In our example, the number of college students is fixed at 12,000.

After a student is selected into the sample, the population of students available to be selected into the sample is reduced by one; replacement is not possible. That is, there are now 11,999 students in the population from whom to select the next student into the sample.

Types of Probability Samples

There are several types of probability samples that are commonly used in criminal justice research. The first type of sample is known as a **simple random sample** (SRS), *a type of probability sample in which subjects are randomly selected from a list of all members of the population.* This type of design requires us to have a list of the elements (subjects) in the population. We then randomly select subjects from the list until we have reached our desired sample size. How do we randomly select names from a list? The common approach is to number each element or subject on the list and then use a random-numbers table to select subjects. For example, if we wanted to select a sample of 200 college students from a population of 12,000 students, we would need to obtain a list of names of all 12,000 college students and number them from 00001 to 12,000. Since every student has a five-digit number, we will need to use five-digit numbers from the random-numbers table to select our sample. Table 7.1 illustrates a portion of a random-numbers table. To select our sample, we simply select a random starting point on the table and determine if that number corresponds with a subject in the population. If so, then that subject is selected into the sample. We then proceed to the next number, moving either down the columns or across the rows. For example, in

simple random sample

TABLE 7.1 Random Numbers

	A	B	C
1	TABLE 7.1 Random Numbers		
2	03528	28071	97041
3	49761	39465	52683
4	80219	29485	85093
5	43657	70361	24176
6	36524	07561	67820
7	97801	98234	13459
8	56913	06289	64527
9	84027	51734	80193
10	70523	83297	81239
11	68194	60541	06745

cell a2, we see that the number is 03528. This is a legitimate number assigned to a student in the population. The individual with this number is selected into the sample. Proceeding down the column to the next cell (a3), we find the number 49761. Since there are only 12,000 students in the population, this number is not assigned to a student. We continue this process through the random-numbers table until we have selected a sample of 200 students. This can be quite labor-intensive: You realize that you need to examine a lot of numbers before you get 200 legitimate numbers for your sample. As indicated in Table 7.1, we get only four legitimate numbers (03528, 07561, 06289, 06745) among 30 numbers listed in the table.

systematic sample   A second type of probability sample is the **systematic sample**, which is *a type of probability sample in which every kth element from the population list is selected into the study*. Again, we must have a list of the elements in the population from which to draw a sample. The *k*th element refers to a number determined by the sampling interval, which is calculated as:

$$\text{Sampling interval} = \frac{N}{n}$$

We simply divide the population by the desired sample size. Let's say that we wanted to select a sample of 10 people from a population of 100 workers at a local factory to sit as a jury during a mock civil trial concerning air pollution. We determine that the sampling interval is equal to 10 (100/10 = 10). Assume that each number in Table 7.2 has a corresponding name of a factory worker attached to it. After selecting a random place to start (close your eyes and pick a number), move through the list in an orderly fashion, selecting every tenth name until you have selected a sample of ten subjects. In this example, we randomly selected subject 22 as our starting point; the tenth subject after 22 is subject 32, and the tenth subject after 32 is subject 42, and so on. If we get to the end of the list and have not selected ten subjects, we simply continue counting back up through the beginning of the list and go through it again. As shown in Table 7.2, subjects selected during the first run through the list are marked in light gray, while subjects selected during the second run are marked in dark gray.

stratified sample   A third type of probability sample is known as a **stratified sample**, which is *a probability sample that categorizes a population in terms of a specific characteristic and then randomly selects subjects from the population for entry into the study*. Stratification is a method by which researchers can ensure that an underrepresented characteristic or group will be adequately represented in the sample. To illustrate, suppose we want to select a sample of 100 criminal justice majors from a population of 500 criminal justice majors. At this particular college, males account for 80% of the majors and females for 20%. We would expect a simple random or systematic sample to result in the same percentages of males and females in our sample as in the population—that is, about 80 males and 20 females. It is possible, however, that our sample may not adequately represent the population of criminal justice majors. Because of unwillingness to participate and chance variations, our sample could conceivably consist of almost all males.

TABLE 7.2 Population List of Names As Numbers

	A	B	C	D	E	F	G
1	TABLE 7.2 Population List of Names As Numbers						
2	1	16	31	46	61	76	91
3	2	17	32	47	62	77	92
4	3	18	33	48	63	78	93
5	4	19	34	49	64	79	94
6	5	20	35	50	65	80	95
7	6	21	36	51	66	81	96
8	7	22	37	52	67	82	97
9	8	23	38	53	68	83	98
10	9	24	39	54	69	84	99
11	10	25	40	55	70	85	100
12	11	26	41	56	71	86	
13	12	27	42	57	72	87	
14	13	28	43	58	73	88	
15	14	29	44	59	74	89	
16	15	30	45	60	75	90	

To ensure equal representation in the sample, we can use a stratification procedure in which we construct two lists of the population and then proceed to use either a simple or a systematic sampling strategy from each list. In our example, we would construct a population list of male students ($N = 400$) and a population list of female students ($N = 100$). Because we want a sample of 100 students of which 80% ($n = 80$) should be male and 20% ($n = 20$) should be female, we can calculate a sampling interval for each list and then select the subjects for our sample. For the males, we would select every fifth element (400/80 = 5) from the population list of male criminal justice students; for females, we would select every fifth element (100/20 = 5) from the population list of female criminal justice students. Stratified sampling is a method to be used in conjunction with simple or systematic sampling to ensure that the characteristics of the sample adequately represent those of the population.

multistage cluster sample   A final type of probability sample is the **multistage cluster sample**, which is *a procedure that involves randomly selecting two or more clusters and then selecting subjects randomly from the initial sample of clusters.* Up to this point, we have always assumed that we had a list of elements or subjects in the population from which to draw a sample.

The multistage cluster sample is particularly useful for research situations in which no list of elements exists. For example, suppose we want to study stress among state correctional officers in the United States. It is highly unlikely that a list of all correctional officers in the country exists, but what does exist are 50 separate state lists of correctional officers employed within each state.

To get to the list of actual officers from which to draw a sample, we first construct a list of all 50 state correctional departments. These departments form clusters, known as primary sampling units (initial clusters), from which we select a random sample of departments from the population of 50 state departments. Once we have selected a sample of, say, 15 state correctional departments, we would then get lists of the population of officers employed in the 15 state departments. These lists then become the final sampling units from which we actually select subjects into our sample by means of a simple or systematic sampling design.

Although our discussion of the various types of probability samples has been brief, it is important to recognize that sampling can be a straightforward process, as is the case with a simple random sample, or it can be a highly complex process, such as that using a multistage cluster sample with stratification. The basic premise of probability sampling is the same regardless of which design is employed. Probability sampling relies on the process of random selection. That is, elements or subjects within the population must have an equal and known probability of being selected into the sample. This allows researchers to determine how closely a sample statistic approximates a population parameter.

Sampling Error

It is important to understand that a sample statistic will rarely equal the population parameter. Even in the most carefully thought out and well-executed sampling design, we should expect a degree of difference between the statistic and parameter. This difference between the value of a statistic and the value of the population parameter is known **sampling** as **sampling error**. Specifically, sampling error is *the estimated difference between a* **error** *sample statistic and a population parameter.*

To illustrate this concept, let's return to our example of surveying Massachusetts residents to find out their level of support for Megan's Law. Assume that the mean level of support for the population (population parameter symbolized by μ) is 7.50 and the mean level of support for our sample (symbolized as $\bar{X}$) is 7.90. The difference between the population μ and the sample $\bar{X}$ is .40. This is referred to as the amount of error in our sample. In this example, we can conclude that our sample statistic closely approximates the population parameter. Unfortunately, in criminal justice research, we rarely know the value of the population parameter. Remember, we are using a sample statistic as an estimate of the population parameter (true value for the entire population). If we knew the value of the population parameter, there would be no reason to obtain a sample statistic in order to estimate the parameter.

How, then, do we know if our statistic is an accurate estimate of the parameter? We now turn our attention to the use of a sampling distribution to estimate how much error exists in our sample—that is, how closely our sample statistic represents the population parameter.

Sampling Distribution

Let's assume that we drew a sample of 200 Massachusetts residents and calculated the mean level of support for Megan's Law. Based on our sample characteristics, we find the mean for our first sample ($\bar{X}_1$) is equal to 7.90. Suppose we drew four more random samples from the same population and obtained the following means: $\bar{X}_2 = 6.50$, $\bar{X}_3 = 7.70$, $\bar{X}_4 = 8.10$, $\bar{X}_5 = 6.80$. You can see that the five means are different from each **sampling** other, primarily as a result of sampling variation. **Sampling variation** is defined as *the* **variation** *difference between sample statistics as a result of differing sample characteristics.* That is, there are 200 different people within each sample, which is likely to result in different levels of support among the samples.

Notice that the values of these five means are different in two ways. First, each sample mean is different from the population mean of 7.50. This is the result of sampling error. Second, each sample mean is different from the other sample means. This is due to sampling variation. Figure 7.1 provides an illustration of both sampling variation and sampling error. Remember, differences among the sample statistics are the result of sampling variation, whereas differences between the population parameter and the sample statistics result from sampling error.

FIGURE 7.1 Sampling variation and sampling error

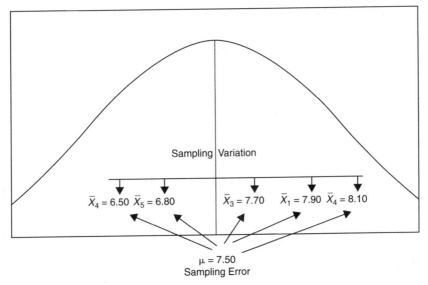

On the basis of the values of these five sample means, we can calculate a *mean of means*. In this example, the mean of the five sample means is equal to 7.40. Notice that the mean of means (7.40) is closer to the population parameter of 7.50 than any one of the five sample means taken by itself. Now, imagine if we selected an infinite number of samples and calculated the mean for each of those samples. Remember, the characteristics of the samples will differ, thus resulting in differences among the means. This is not to say that none of the sample means will be equal, only that there will be many different mean values. The result of these differing values produces a sampling distribution of means characterized by a mean and standard deviation. More specifically, the mean of means forms a sampling distribution that, according to probability theory, will be

sampling distribution of means

distributed around the population parameter in a known way. We define the **sampling distribution of means** as *a probability distribution of a statistic based on an infinite number of samples randomly selected from a given population*. It is important to remember that the sampling distribution is theoretical and is derived from the basic tenets of probability theory. Therefore, the sampling distribution of means has certain characteristics, which include the following:

- *The sample statistics cluster around the population parameter.* The sample means will be different from the population mean (sampling error) and from each other (sampling variation). The majority of sample means will occur, however, right around the population mean, because our samples are representative of the population through the process of random selection.
- *The mean of the sampling distribution is equal to the population mean.* The calculated mean for an infinite number of sample means is equal to the true population mean.
- *The standard deviation of the sampling distribution is smaller than the population standard deviation.* As we increase the sample size for each of our randomly selected samples, the magnitude of difference among our sample means decreases. That is, larger sample sizes result in less variation among the sample means as the sample means cluster ever more narrowly around the true population mean.
- *The sampling distribution approximates the normal curve.* If the shape of the population distribution is normal, then the shape of the sampling distribution of means will also be normal. Even if a population distribution is skewed, the sampling distribution will approximate normality as long as the sample size is sufficiently large (usually 30 or more).

central limit theorem

This last characteristic is based on a statistical concept known as the central limit theorem. According to the **central limit theorem** for sufficiently large samples, *the sampling distribution of a statistic will be normally distributed regardless of the shape of the population distribution*. More specifically, the larger the sample size, the more likely the sampling distribution of our statistic will approximate the normal curve. The importance of a statistic being normally distributed is one of the primary assumptions for many of the inferential statistics (we will discuss this in later chapters).

To clarify these characteristics further, let's assume that we drew 100 samples of 200 inmates from a population of 10,000 inmates housed in a federal penitentiary. Of interest to us is the average number of prior convictions for the population of inmates. Thus, there is a value for the population parameter; however, this value is unknown to us and must be estimated using our sample statistics. For each of our 100 samples, we will calculate a statistic—mean number of prior convictions and plot these statistics on a graph—that will form the sampling distribution of means. As illustrated in Figure 7.2, each *x* represents a single statistic. Notice that our sampling distribution of means approximates the normal curve with the bulk of the statistics (sample means) clustered around the population parameter. The area under the normal curve is measured in standard deviation units, with a mean of zero and a standard deviation of 1. Previously, we used this information to determine the probability of a particular value or case falling within a specified distance from the mean. We use the same logic here to conclude that 68.26% of the sample means (statistics) will fall within 1 standard deviation of the true population mean (parameter). Approximately 95.44% of the sample means will fall within 2 standard deviation units of the population mean, and 99.72% will fall within 3 standard deviation units of the population mean.

By now, you understand that researchers never select an infinite number of samples but, rather, only one sample. That single sample statistic is used to estimate the population parameter. Thus, we use our knowledge about the sampling distribution of means

FIGURE 7.2 Sampling distribution of means approximating the normal curve

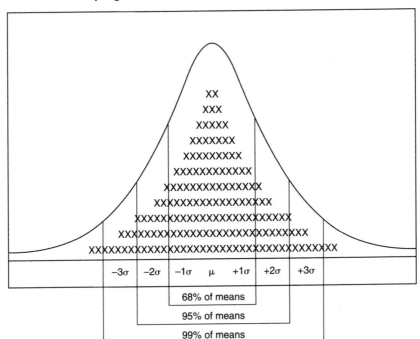

and the normal curve to say that for any single random sample drawn, there is a 68.26% chance that the sample statistic will fall within one standard deviation unit of the population parameter. The chance that our sample statistic will fall within two standard deviation units of the population parameter is 95.44%, and there is a 99.72% chance the sample statistic will fall within three standard deviation units of the parameter.

It is essential that you have a basic understanding of probability sampling in order to understand the process of statistical inference—making generalizations about a population based on observations from a sample. We now turn our attention to the methods by which we use sample statistics to estimate population parameters.

7.3 Estimating a Population Mean (μ) Using the z Distribution

To determine how accurately a sample statistic estimates a population parameter, we need to calculate the probability that the parameter lies within a given distance of the statistic. Put another way, we can measure the standard distance between the sample mean ($\bar{X}$) and the population mean (μ) by calculating the standard error of the mean. **standard error of the mean** The **standard error of the mean** is *the standard deviation of the sampling distribution of means*, and is determined by the following formula:

$$s_{\bar{x}} = \frac{s}{\sqrt{n-1}}$$

We simply divide the standard deviation by the square root of the sample size minus one. We use $n-1$ in the denominator to correct for bias in the numerator, because we are using the sample standard deviation (s) as an estimate of the population standard deviation (σ).

An important feature of this formula is that as the sample size increases, the standard error decreases. For example, suppose we sampled 50 police officers and asked them to rate their level of stress from 1 to 100. Assume that the mean level of stress for our sample was 76.5, with a sample standard deviation of 8.7. Placing these values into the formula

$$s_{\bar{x}} = \frac{8.7}{\sqrt{50-1}} = 1.24$$

results in a standard error of 1.24. Increasing our sample size to 100 police officers results in a standard error of .87. The smaller the standard error, the more closely our sample statistic will approximate the population parameter. This is true because larger samples will have less variation (smaller standard deviation), which in turn results in less variability in the sampling distribution. That is, the means from the different samples will be less variable. As a result, we can be more confident that any one sample statistic will more accurately estimate the population parameter.

How does knowing the standard deviation of the sampling distribution (standard error of the mean) inform us of the value of the population parameter? We must combine our knowledge of the normal probability curve and the sampling distribution of means in order to estimate the amount of sampling error occurring within our sample. Two related concepts that need to be discussed are confidence levels and confidence intervals.

Take some time to practice calculating the standard error of the mean by completing TryIT! Box 7.1.

TryIT!   BOX **7.1**

For each example listed below, calculate the standard error of the mean using the following formula:

$$s_{\bar{x}} = \frac{s}{\sqrt{n-1}}$$

	Standard Deviation (s)	*Sample Size (n)*
A.	5.91	150
B.	2.73	230
C.	.97	450
D.	10.54	75
E.	1.59	50
F.	8.41	1000

Confidence Levels

confidence level The **confidence level** (CL) is *the probability that a population parameter lies within a given confidence interval.* The probability of a single sample mean falling within one standard error above or below the true population mean is .6826. Put another way, there is a 68.26% chance that a single sample mean will produce a value that is within one standard error, either above or below, the true population mean. Researchers commonly round these percentages to whole numbers such that the three confidence levels typically discussed are the 68%, 95%, and 99% levels. Each of these confidence levels has a standard error and z-score associated with it, as shown in Figure 7.3. We further illustrate this in Figure 7.4 using the normal curve. Each standard error unit on the normal curve has a z-score associated with it as well as a confidence level. Thus, the 95% confidence level is characterized as two standard errors above and below the mean, with a z-score of 1.96.

FIGURE 7.3 Typical confidence level and associated standard error and z-score

Confidence Level	Standard Error	z-score
68%	$\pm 1 s_{\bar{x}}$	1.00
95%	$\pm 2 s_{\bar{x}}$	1.96
99%	$\pm 3 s_{\bar{x}}$	2.58

FIGURE 7.4 Normal curve with standard error units and z-scores

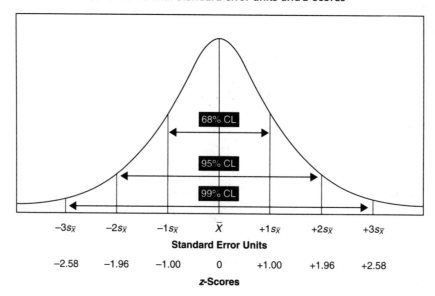

Confidence Intervals

confidence   The **confidence interval** (CI) is *the range of values in which the population parameter*
interval   *is estimated to fall.* It is important to remember that our statistic is an estimate of the
parameter and will rarely equal the parameter exactly. This is due to sampling error.
Therefore, we need to calculate a range of values in which the population parameter is
likely to fall.

To calculate the confidence interval for the 68% confidence level, we simply subtract
one standard error from the sample mean and add one standard error to the sample
mean. The formula is given as:

68% Confidence Level

$$\bar{X} - 1 s_{\bar{x}}$$
$$\bar{X} + 1 s_{\bar{x}}$$

In our example of police officer stress, the mean rating of stress for the sample of 50 officers was 76.50, with a standard error of 1.24. Using our sample statistic and the standard error of the mean, we can calculate the confidence interval. This will provide us with a range of values in which the population parameter is likely to fall at a given level of probability, which in our example is .68. Thus, the confidence interval is determined by the following:

$$76.50 - 1.24 = 75.26$$
$$76.50 + 1.24 = 77.74$$

We are 68% confident that the mean stress rating among the population of police officers from which the sample was drawn is between 75.26 and 77.74. In other words, there is a 68% chance that the population parameter (population mean) falls between 75.26 and 77.74. A 68% confidence level is not very good, because there is a 32% chance that the actual population mean is either higher than 77.74 or lower than 75.26. Hence, the 95% level of confidence is most commonly used in criminal justice and criminological research.

To calculate the confidence interval for the 95% confidence level, we might be tempted to simply subtract and add the standard error twice from the sample mean. Although we could do this, the resulting confidence interval would be somewhat larger than necessary, because 95.44% of the sample means fall between $-2s_{\bar{x}}$ and $+2s_{\bar{x}}$ of the sample mean. If we multiply the standard error by 2 ($1.24 \times 2 = 2.48$) and then subtract and add that value to the sample mean ($76.50 - 2.48 = 74.02$; $76.50 + 2.48 = 78.98$), we get a resulting confidence interval of 74.02–78.98 at the 95.44% confidence level. Because we want to be at the 95% confidence level and not 95.44%, however, we need to multiply the standard error by the z-score associated with the 95% confidence level. Thus, our formula for obtaining the confidence interval for the 95% confidence level is written as:

95% Confidence Level
$$\bar{X} - 1.96s_{\bar{x}}$$
$$\bar{X} + 1.96s_{\bar{x}}$$

In our example of police officer stress, we want to know the confidence interval in which there is a .95 level of probability in which the population parameter is likely to fall. We calculate this as:

$$76.50 - 1.96(1.24) = 76.5 - 2.43 = 74.07$$
$$76.50 + 1.96(1.24) = 76.5 + 2.43 = 78.93$$

Thus, we are 95% confident that the mean level of stress among the population of police officers from which the sample was drawn is between 74.07 and 78.93. There is still a chance that the value of the population parameter could be outside of the confidence interval; however, the chance of that occurring is only 5 out of 100. Put another way, if we were to draw 100 samples and calculate a mean stress level for each sample, we would expect 95 of those sample means to be between 74.07 and 78.93. Thus, the probability that any one sample mean will fall between 74.07 and 78.93 is .95.

If we want to be even more confident about our sample mean, then we can construct a confidence interval for the 99% confidence level. The formula is written as:

99% Confidence Level
$$\bar{X} - 2.58s_{\bar{x}}$$
$$\bar{X} + 2.58s_{\bar{x}}$$

Again, the process involves multiplying the standard error by the *z*-score that corresponds to the appropriate confidence level and then subtracting and adding that value to the sample mean. The confidence interval for the 99% confidence level is:

$$76.50 - 2.58(1.24) = 76.50 - 3.20 = 73.30$$
$$76.50 + 2.58(1.24) = 76.50 + 3.20 = 79.70$$

We are now 99% confident that the population parameter is between 73.30 and 79.70. The chance that the population parameter could fall outside of this confidence interval is only 1%. We illustrate the three confidence levels and their corresponding confidence intervals using the normal curve in Figure 7.5.

FIGURE 7.5 Normal curve with standard error units and confidence intervals

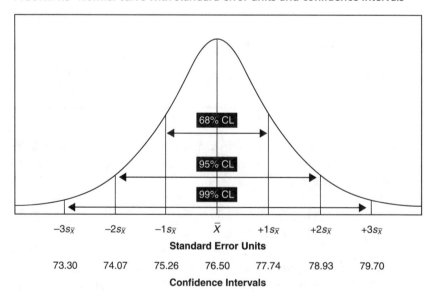

There are some key points to emphasize. First, we can calculate a confidence interval for any level of probability. We need only to determine the z-score that corresponds with a given level of probability. Once we have identified this value, we multiply the standard error by the z-score and then subtract and add that value to the sample mean.

Second, higher levels of confidence result in wider confidence intervals. We have already indicated that the 68% confidence level is rarely used, simply because there is too high a chance that the population parameter could fall outside of the confidence interval. Criminal justice research typically uses either the 95% or 99% confidence levels. Which level is more appropriate? As there is no concrete rule as to which confidence level is more appropriate, this decision must be determined by the individual researcher. Most often, researchers report the confidence interval for the 95% confidence level. The increased width of the confidence interval is rarely worth the increased level of confidence, except in cases where the standard error is extremely small. Our suggestion is to use the 95% confidence level for most research situations.

Third, consider the effect that sample size has on the confidence interval. You will recall that as the sample size increases, the standard error decreases. As the standard error decreases, the confidence interval becomes narrower for each of the three confidence levels. Let's return to our example of police officer stress. The standard error for the sample of 50 police officers was 1.24. On increasing the sample size to 100 officers, our standard error dropped to .87. Using the standard error based on the sample size of 100 officers, we determine the confidence interval for the 95% confidence level as follows:

$$76.50 - 1.96(.87) = 76.50 - 1.71 = 74.79$$
$$76.50 + 1.96(.87) = 76.50 + 1.71 = 78.21$$

There is a 95% probability that the mean level of stress among the population of police officers is between 74.79 and 78.21. Figure 7.6 provides a graphical comparison of the confidence intervals for the two sample sizes. We can readily see that increasing the sample size decreases the standard error, which effectively narrows the confidence interval.

margin of error   Finally, it is common in survey research to use the term **margin of error**, *defined as the difference between the sample mean and the population parameter based on the 95% confidence level*, in place of confidence intervals and confidence levels. For example, we could report the results from our study of 100 police officers by saying that the mean level of stress was 76.50 with a margin of error of ±1.71. It is important to recognize that the value of 1.71 is not the standard error but, rather, the standard error multiplied by a z-score of 1.96. The common practice in social science research in general, and criminal justice research in particular, is to report the results of a study at the 95% confidence level by reporting the margin of error that equals the standard error multiplied by 1.96.

FIGURE 7.6 Confidence intervals of two sample sizes at the 95% confidence level

n = 50	74.07	76.50	78.93
n = 100	74.79	76.50	78.21

You are now ready to estimate the value of a population parameter by constructing confidence intervals. Take a few moments to complete TryIT! Box 7.2 before moving on to section 7.4.

TryIT!   BOX 7.2

The chief probation officer of a large western state wants to know how many undetected probation violations occur within a given week. The research analyst at the central office has decided to conduct a survey with a sample of probationers to answer the chief's question. She selects a probability sample of 100 probationers and asks the following question: "How many times within the past seven days have you violated any condition of your probation?" Results from the survey show that the average $(\bar{X})$ number of violations is 2.6 with a standard deviation (s) of 1.2. Provide an estimate of the average number of violations among the population of probationers by calculating the standard error of the mean and confidence intervals for the 95% and 99% confidence levels. Interpret your findings.

7.4 Estimating a Population Mean (μ) Using the t Distribution

In section 7.3, we discussed using the standard error of the mean along with the normal curve to calculate confidence intervals around a sample mean at various levels of probability or confidence levels. The use of the normal distribution is based on the central limit theorem, in which large samples will produce a normally distributed sampling distribution. That is, with a large sample, we can safely assume that sampling distribution for the statistic will approximate the normal curve. This property allows us to use the *z* distribution to estimate population parameters on the basis of sample statistics.

The question that has yet to be answered is, "How large does a sample need to be to assume that the sampling distribution of a statistic is normally distributed?" The general rule appears to be that at least 30 subjects are needed. As you recall, one of the characteristics of the sampling distribution is that the sampling distribution of a statistic will approximate normality for samples having 30 or more subjects. Given this characteristic, it seems advisable to use the *z* distribution to construct confidence intervals for samples of 30 or larger. A word of caution is warranted, however: Always evaluate the distributional properties of a statistic by comparing the mean with the standard deviation to determine whether the assumption of normality is met. This is especially important for samples containing fewer than 100 subjects. For samples of 100 subjects or more, the assumption of normality is met as indicated by the central limit theorem, and the use of the *z* distribution is preferred.

In cases in which the sample size is small (less than 30), the use of the *z* distribution is unwarranted, because we can no longer assume that the sampling distribution of a statistic is normal. In our discussion of the sampling distribution, we learned that large samples will typically have less variation among the sample means, which allows us to assume that the sampling distribution is normal. Small samples, by contrast, will have more variation among the sample means, which will lead to a nonnormal sampling distribution for a statistic. Thus, for small samples, we need to use an alternative method for computing confidence intervals, as we can no longer assume that the sampling distribution is normal.

The appropriate method for constructing confidence intervals for small samples is to use the *t* distribution. The *t* distribution is characterized as being wider and flatter than the *z* distribution. This is primarily due to the increased amount of variation in the sampling distribution that results from the greater sample-to-sample variation that occurs among small samples. To account for this increased variability, we use the *t* distribution, which results in a wider confidence interval than the *z* distribution. In essence, we are being more conservative with our confidence interval by using a larger number as the multiplier of the standard error. This multiplier is determined by the desired confidence level and the sample size.

The general formula for using *t* to construct confidence intervals is given as:

$$\overline{X} \pm ts_{\overline{x}}$$

As with using *z*, we must multiply the standard error of the mean by the appropriate *t* value and then add and subtract that value from the sample mean to construct the confidence interval. Unlike using *z*, however, determining the correct value of *t* requires a bit more work.

The *t* distribution comprises many different distributions based on a concept known
degrees of as **degrees of freedom**, *the number of values in a data set that are free to vary.* For
freedom instance, if we had 5 values in a data set and we knew that the mean was equal to 12
and also that the values of 4 of the 5 numbers were 12, 15, 8, and 5, then the last value
must be fixed. That is, it is not free to vary, because the 5 values have a mean of 12, so
the last value must equal 20. The degrees of freedom for the *t* distribution are calculated
as *n* − 1: We simply subtract 1 from the total sample size. Thus, all of the values are free
to vary, with the exception of one value. As the sample size and corresponding degrees
of freedom increase, the *t* distribution more closely resembles the *z* distribution. For
samples over 100, the *t* distribution is identical to the *z* distribution.

To determine the appropriate value of *t* by which to multiply the standard error, we
must look at the *t* distribution table (Table B) located in Appendix A. The confidence
levels used for small samples are the same as those used for large samples. That is, we
want to be either 95% or 99% confident that the actual population parameter falls
within a given confidence interval. The use of the *t* distribution requires us to find the
appropriate alpha (α) level. The alpha level represents the area in the tails of the *t* distribution. This is similar to the column of the *z* distribution that defines the area beyond
the *z*. The alpha level for *t* is calculated as:

$$\alpha = 1 - \text{confidence level}$$

If we are interested in constructing a confidence interval for the 95% confidence level,
our alpha will be determined as $1 - .95 = .05$. For the 99% confidence level, the alpha is
determined as $1 - .99 = .01$.

We are now ready to work through an example. Suppose we surveyed a random
sample of 20 criminal justice majors from a large metropolitan college, and asked the
following question: "How many times in the past month have you committed a parking violation on campus?" Let's assume that the mean is equal to 4.80, with a standard
deviation of 4.20. Because the sample size is small, we know that there will be more
variation in the sampling distribution of the statistic, as further supported by the large
standard deviation in relation to the size of the mean (see Chapter 5). Therefore, we
want to use the *t* distribution to construct our confidence intervals. We first need to calculate an estimate of the standard error of the mean ($s_{\bar{x}}$), which is determined by:

$$s_{\bar{x}} = \frac{s}{\sqrt{n-1}}$$

$$s_{\bar{x}} = \frac{4.20}{\sqrt{20-1}} = .96$$

We are now ready to proceed to the *t* distribution table to find the appropriate value
of *t* to plug into the formula. Remember, in order to find the correct value of *t*, we
need to know the degrees of freedom and the desired confidence level. The degrees of

TABLE 7.3 Sample *t* Distribution Table $1 - conf. level$

df	Alpha Levels for Two-Tailed Test		
	0.10	0.05	0.01
15	1.75	2.13	2.95
16	1.75	2.12	2.92
17	1.74	2.11	2.90
18	1.73	2.10	2.88
19	1.73	2.09	2.86
20	1.73	2.09	2.85
21	1.72	2.08	2.83
22	1.72	2.07	2.82
23	1.71	2.07	2.81

n − 1

freedom are determined by subtracting one from the sample size: 20 − 1 = 19. Assuming that we want the 95% confidence level, we simply convert to an alpha level using our formula (1 − confidence level) 1 − .95 = .05. Looking at Table 7.3, we first find the column with an alpha level of .05. We then proceed to the row that has the appropriate degrees of freedom (*df* = 19). The *t* value located at the intersection of the column and the row equals 2.09. This is the value we use in our formula to construct the confidence interval.

Our next step is to place the appropriate values into the following formula and solve:

$$\overline{X} \pm ts_{\overline{x}}$$
$$4.80 - 2.09(.96) = 4.80 - 2.01 = 2.79$$
$$4.80 + 2.09(.96) = 4.80 + 2.01 = 6.81$$

We interpret our results as being 95% confident that the mean level of campus parking violations among the population of criminal justice majors is between 2.79 and 6.81. If we had used the *z* distribution instead of *t*, we would have estimated the mean level of violations to be between 2.92 and 6.68, using the *z* value of 1.96. As stated earlier, the *t* distribution provides a more conservative estimate of the population parameter by expanding the width of the confidence interval. This is illustrated in Figure 7.7.

To calculate the confidence interval at the 99% confidence level, we select the value of *t* that corresponds with the .01 alpha level. As shown in Table 7.3, the new value of *t* is 2.86. Substituting this value into our formula we compute the confidence interval as follows:

$$4.80 - 2.86(.96) = 4.80 - 2.75 = 2.05$$
$$4.80 + 2.86(.96) = 4.80 + 2.75 = 7.55$$

FIGURE 7.7 Confidence intervals for *z* and *t* at the 95% confidence level

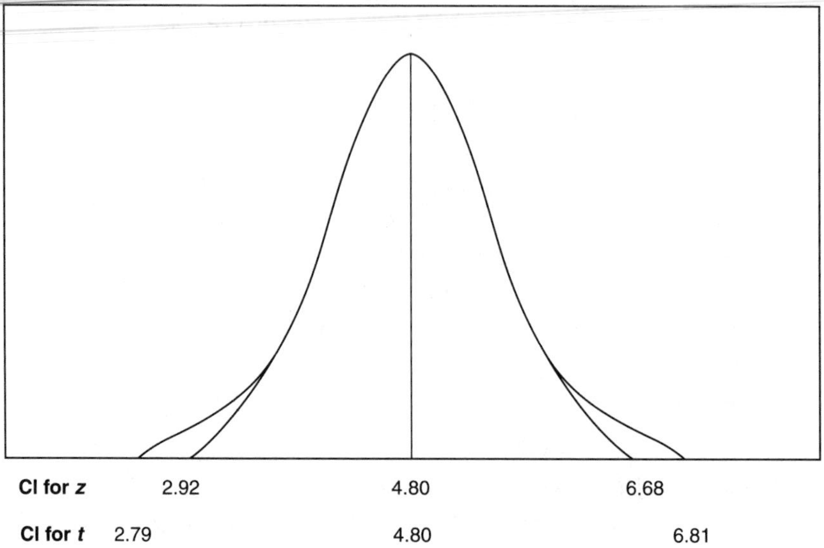

CI for *z*	2.92	4.80	6.68
CI for *t*	2.79	4.80	6.81

We are now 99% confident that the mean level of parking violations among criminal justice majors is between 2.05 and 7.55. As with the *z* distribution, higher levels of confidence result in wider confidence intervals.

Whenever the *t* distribution is used to construct confidence intervals, we must be sure that we are using the two-tailed *t* distribution table to locate the correct value of *t*. This is because we want the *t* value that represents the upper boundary above the mean and the lower boundary below the mean in which 95% of the sample means would fall in the sampling distribution. As the *t* distribution is symmetrical, the value of *t* for the areas above and below the mean are the same. Using the one-tailed *t* distribution table provides us with a *t* value that covers either the area above the mean or the area below the mean, but not both simultaneously. Thus, the one-tailed distribution does not allow us to construct a confidence interval around the population parameter.

Although we use the *t* distribution in place of *z* whenever the normality assumption is violated—as is the case when using small samples—there are some similar characteristics between the two distributions. First, both distributions are characterized as being bell-shaped and symmetrical. That is, the area above the mean is an exact replicate of the area below the mean. Second, both distributions are identical for samples of 100 or more subjects. We recommend using the simpler *z* distribution when dealing with large samples.

You are now ready to calculate confidence intervals for small samples using the *t* distribution. Complete TryIT! Box 7.3 before moving on to the next section.

TryIT! BOX **7.3**

A criminologist is interested in studying school violence. She selects a random sample of 25 adolescents aged 12 to 15 from a local middle school and asks the following question: "How many times within the past school year have you been physically assaulted at school (such as pushed, shoved, hit, or kicked) by another student?" The criminologist calculates some descriptive statistics based on the answers to her survey. She determines that the average ($\bar{X}$) number of assaults is 3.70, with a standard deviation (s) of 3.30. On the basis of this information, provide an estimate of the population parameter (average number of assaults among the population of students) by calculating the standard error of the mean and constructing confidence intervals for the 95% and 99% confidence levels, using the t distribution formula.

7.5   Estimating a Population Proportion (π) Using the z Distribution

We have demonstrated how to estimate a population mean (μ) by constructing a confidence interval around the sample mean ($\bar{X}$). You will recall from Chapter 2 that the mean is the appropriate statistic for a variable measured at the interval or ratio level. In many instances, criminal justice research uses variables measured at the nominal or ordinal level. For these variables, a proportion or percentage—instead of the mean—is the appropriate statistic used to describe the variable. In this section, we extend our discussion to estimating population parameters for proportions. A population proportion is symbolized as π (Greek pi).

At the beginning of this chapter, we introduced a scenario in which a researcher asked 200 college students the following question: "Are you afraid of being a victim of crime on campus?" The responses to this question include only two attributes—Yes or No—indicating that the variable "fear of victimization" is measured at the nominal level. Given this level of measurement, we are unable to calculate a mean level of fear; however, we are able to calculate the proportion of respondents indicating Yes and the proportion indicating No. We can use this information to estimate the standard error of the proportion and then proceed to construct a confidence interval around the sample proportion. Our interpretation of the confidence interval for a proportion is exactly the same as that used for a mean; it is the range of values in which the population parameter is estimated to lie. The only difference is in the type of parameter we are estimating—population mean versus population proportion.

The following formula is used to estimate the standard error of the proportion:

$$s_P = \sqrt{\frac{P(1-P)}{n}}$$

standard error of the proportion We use s_p as the symbol for the **standard error of the proportion**, *which is an estimate of the standard deviation of the sampling distribution of proportions.* Notice that this definition is similar to the definition for the standard error of the mean. The sampling distribution of a proportion, which is similar to the sampling distribution of a mean, also approximates normality with a sufficiently large sample size ($n \geq 30$). The letter P represents the sample proportion of one of the attributes of the variable, which is multiplied by that proportion minus one. Next, we divide by the sample size and then take the square root of that value, which equals the estimated standard error of the proportion.

Returning to our example of fear of victimization among college students, 27% indicated they were afraid of being victimized. To determine the standard error of the proportion, we need only to place the appropriate values into the preceding formula, as shown:

$$s_P = \sqrt{\frac{.27(1-.27)}{200}}$$

$$= \sqrt{\frac{(.27)(.73)}{200}}$$

$$= \sqrt{\frac{.1971}{200}}$$

$$= \sqrt{.0009}$$

$$= .03$$

The standard error of the proportion is equal to .03. We can now construct a confidence interval around the sample proportion. In doing so, we once again make use of the normal z distribution. The formula for the confidence interval at the 95% confidence level is given as:

95% Confidence Level
$$P - 1.96\, s_P$$
$$P + 1.96\, s_P$$

Once we have multiplied the standard error of the proportion (s_p) by 1.96, we need only to subtract and add that value to the sample proportion to complete the confidence interval.

$$.27 - 1.96(.03) = .27 - .06 = .21$$
$$.27 + 1.96(.03) = .27 + .06 = .33$$

The interpretation is the same as when using a mean. We are 95% confident that the actual proportion of students on campus who are afraid of being the victim of crime is between .21 and .33. The more common method of interpretation is to report the percentages in place of the proportions. We need only to multiply the proportions by 100 to obtain the percentages, which results in a confidence interval of 21% to 33%.

To construct a confidence interval at the 99% confidence level, simply change the value of z from 1.96 (95% CL) to 2.58 (99% CL). As before, increasing the level of confidence increases the width of the confidence interval. Additionally, increasing the sample size decreases the standard error of the proportion, which reduces the width of the confidence interval.

It is common to report the margin of error rather than confidence intervals. In our example, we could report that 27% of the students at a particular college indicated they were afraid of being the victim of crime on campus, with the margin of error being ± 6%. There are two important points to remember. First, results are usually reported at the 95% confidence level. Thus, the proportion of .06 is the standard error of the proportion multiplied by 1.96. Second, results are typically reported as percentages, not proportions. We simply multiplied the proportion of .06 by 100 and reported it as a percentage.

Be sure to take a few minutes and try calculating the confidence intervals for a proportion by completing TryIT! Box 7.4.

TryIT!   BOX **7.4**

A criminologist is conducting a study of public perceptions of the likelihood of being given a ticket for the offense of speeding. He selects a probability sample of 450 Indiana automobile drivers and asks the following question: "How likely are you to be given a ticket by the police for the offense of speeding? Would you say that you are Not at all likely, Somewhat likely, or Very likely to receive a ticket?" The following results are reported: 32% said Not at all likely, 59% said Somewhat likely, and 9% said Very likely. Calculate the standard error of the proportion for those who said Not at all likely, and construct confidence intervals for the 95% and 99% confidence levels. Interpret your findings.

7.6 Using Excel to Construct Confidence Intervals

You should have a good understanding of how researchers estimate population parameters using sample statistics. You have also had several opportunities to practice constructing confidence intervals around a mean and a proportion using a hand calculator. We now want to use Excel to assist us in estimating population parameters using sample statistics.

Suppose a researcher was interested in studying alcohol use among high school students in a particular state. The state department of education has provided the researcher with a list of all high school students within the state. This list represents the population from which our researcher will draw a probability sample. The researcher's goal is to make inferences or generalizations about the population based on observations obtained from a sample. The researcher is interested in the following three areas in particular: the average number of drinks per month among those who drink, the average amount of money spent on alcohol per month among those classified as heavy drinkers (having 10 or more drinks per month), and the percentage of students who drink alcohol.

Let's assume that 220 completed surveys were returned to the researcher. Table 7.4 provides data on the number of drinks per month. Each value in the table represents one subject's response to the following question: "How many alcoholic drinks have you had within the past 30 days?" This question was only asked for those students who said they drink alcohol. Thus, the data in Table 7.4 represents about 65% ($n = 144$) of the overall sample of 220. The question of interest to the researcher is, "What is the average number of drinks per month among the population of high school students in the state who drink alcohol?"

Confidence Intervals for a Population Mean (μ) Using z

Because the sample size is sufficiently large ($n = 144$), the researcher can assume the sampling distribution is normal and proceed with the z distribution for constructing the confidence intervals.

Step 1: Calculate the sample mean ($\bar{X}$) by placing the cursor in cell b20 and using the paste function box.

Step 2: Calculate the standard deviation (s) by placing the cursor in cell b21 and using the paste function box.

Step 3: Calculate the standard error of the mean ($s_{\bar{x}}$) using the following formula:

$$s_{\bar{x}} = \frac{s}{\sqrt{n-1}}$$

Place the cursor in cell b22 and write the following: =b21/(sqrt(b19–1)).

b21 is the cell location for the standard deviation.
sqrt is the symbol for square root.
b19 is the cell location for the sample size.

Step 4: Construct the confidence interval for the 95% confidence level.

95% Confidence Level
$$\bar{X} - 1.96s_{\bar{x}}$$
$$\bar{X} + 1.96s_{\bar{x}}$$

TABLE 7.4 Confidence Intervals for Mean Using *z*

	A	B	C	D	E	F	G	H	I	J
1	**TABLE 7.4 Confidence Intervals for Mean Using z**									
2	How many alcoholic drinks have you had in the past 30 days?									
3		9	11	5	2	0	0	5	1	12
4		0	11	5	2	3	4	5	1	0
5		8	10	3	1	1	4	1	7	2
6		8	10	0	1	5	2	0	9	1
7		5	0	6	9	8	1	7	12	0
8		5	9	6	3	5	12	4	12	5
9		5	1	7	8	1	10	4	5	4
10		4	1	7	8	2	11	3	5	0
11		3	1	0	7	8	8	0	12	1
12		5	2	1	6	7	7	5	12	1
13		4	2	1	6	12	7	9	10	2
14		6	9	1	9	11	0	12	11	0
15		4	10	2	0	1	1	1	9	5
16		2	12	3	3	1	2	3	8	5
17		11	10	1	8	2	0	10	7	7
18		9	9	4	7	8	3	10	7	0
19	**Sample size (n)**	144								
20	**Mean ($\bar{X}$)**	5.05								
21	**Standard deviation (s)**	3.80								
22	**Standard error of mean ($s_{\bar{x}}$)**	0.32	95% CL		99%CL					
23	**Confidence intervals (CI)**		4.43	5.67	4.23	5.87				

a. Place the cursor in cell c23 and write: =b20–(1.96*b22).
b. Place the cursor in cell d23 and write: =b20+(1.96*b22).

> b20 is the cell location for the mean.
> – is the symbol for subtraction.
> + is the symbol for addition.
> 1.96 is the value of z for the 95% confidence level.
> * is the symbol for multiplication.
> b22 is the cell location for the standard error of the mean.

We are 95% confident that the average number of drinks per month for the population of high school students who drink alcohol is between 4.43 and 5.67.

Step 5: Construct the confidence interval for the 99% confidence level. We use the same formula as above with the exception of the value of z, which now becomes 2.58. Place the cursor in cell e23 and write: =b20–(2.58*b22); place the cursor in cell f23 and write: =b20+(2.58*b22). The resulting values represent the confidence interval for the 99% confidence level. We are 99% confident that the average number of drinks per month for the population of high school students who drink alcohol is between 4.23 and 5.87.

Confidence Intervals for a Population Mean (μ) Using t

The second area of interest to our researcher concerns the amount of money spent on alcohol per month by heavy drinkers. The data is presented in Table 7.5, in which each value represents one subject's response to the following question: "Approximately how much money did you spend on alcohol in the past 30 days?" Remember, only those individuals who had ten or more drinks in the past 30 days were asked this question. Of the 144 subjects represented in Table 7.4, only 23 were identified as heavy drinkers. In order to construct a confidence interval with such a small sample size, our researcher must use the t distribution in place of the normal z distribution.

Step 1: Calculate the sample mean ($\bar{X}$) by placing the cursor in cell b10 and using the paste function box.

Step 2: Calculate the standard deviation (s) by placing the cursor in cell b11 and using the paste function box.

Step 3: Calculate the standard error of the mean ($s_{\bar{x}}$) by placing the cursor in cell b12 and writing the following: =b11/(sqrt(b9–1)).

> b11 is the cell location for the standard deviation.
> sqrt is the symbol for square root.
> b9 is the cell location for the sample size.

Step 4: Calculate the degrees of freedom (df), place the cursor in cell b13, and write: =b9–1.

Step 5: Construct the confidence interval for the 95% confidence level. You must first locate the appropriate *t* value by consulting the *t* distribution table in Table B (Appendix A) at the .05 alpha level with 22 degrees of freedom (*t* = 2.07).

95% Confidence Level

$$\overline{X} - ts_{\overline{x}}$$
$$\overline{X} + ts_{\overline{x}}$$

a. Place the cursor in cell c14 and write: =b10–(2.07*b12).
b. Place the cursor in cell d14 and write: =b10+(2.07*b12).

b10 is the cell location for the mean.
– is the symbol for subtraction.
+ is the symbol for addition.
2.07 is the *t* value at the .05 alpha level with 22 degrees of freedom.
* is the symbol for multiplication.
b12 is the cell location for the standard error.

TABLE 7.5 Confidence Intervals for Mean Using *t*

	A	B	C	D	E	F
1	TABLE 7.5 Confidence Intervals for Mean Using *t*					
2	How much money did you spend on alcohol during the past 30 days?					
3		$ 15.00	$ 40.00	$ 20.00	$ 25.00	
4		$ 50.00	$ 40.00	$ 15.00	$ 28.00	
5		$ 10.00	$ 38.00	$ 25.00	$ 30.00	
6		$ 12.00	$ 50.00	$ 55.00	$ 25.00	
7		$ 15.00	$ 45.00	$ 45.00	$ 40.00	
8		$ 18.00	$ 20.00	$ 50.00		
9	Sample size (n)	23				
10	Mean ($\overline{X}$)	$ 30.91				
11	Standard deviation (*s*)	$ 14.21				
12	Standard error of mean (s_x)	3.03				
13	Degrees of freedom	22	95% CL		99%CL	
14	Confidence intervals (CI)		$ 24.63	$ 37.20	$ 22.37	$ 39.45

We are 95% confident that the average amount of money spent on alcohol per month among the population of high school students identified as heavy drinkers is between $24.63 and $37.20.

Step 6: Construct the confidence interval for the 99% confidence level. The only change from the above formula is the *t* value, which is multiplied by the standard error. Looking at the *t* distribution table (Table B in Appendix A), we find a *t* value of 2.82 for an alpha of .01 with 22 degrees of freedom. Thus, we write: =b10–(2.82*b12) in cell e14 and =b10+(2.82*b12) in cell f14. We are 99% confident that the average amount of money spent on alcohol per month among the population of high school students identified as heavy drinkers is between $22.37 and $39.45.

Confidence Interval for a Population Proportion (π) Using *z*

Our researcher is also interested in knowing the percentage of high school students who drink alcohol. The data for this question is presented in Table 7.6. Our researcher asked the question: "Do you drink alcohol?" Because our question represents a nominal measure having only two response categories—Yes or No—we must use the proportion formula to construct a confidence interval for the population parameter.

Step 1: Calculate the proportions for the two attributes of the variable by dividing the frequency of each attribute by the total sample size (*f/n*). Place the cursor in cell c4 and write: =b4/b6. This is the proportion of the sample who said Yes. Place the cursor in cell c5 and write: =b5/b6. This is the proportion of the sample who said No.

Step 2: Calculate the standard error of the proportion (s_p) using the following formula:

$$s_p = \sqrt{\frac{P(1-P)}{n}}$$

Place the cursor in cell b8 and write: =sqrt((c4*(c6–c4))/b6).

sqrt is the symbol for square root.
c4 is the cell location for proportion who said Yes.
c6 is the cell location for the total proportion.
b6 is the sample size.

Step 3: Construct the confidence interval for the 95% confidence level:

95% Confidence Level
$$P - 1.96 s_p$$
$$P + 1.96 s_p$$

a. Place the cursor in cell c9 and write: =c4–(1.96*b8).
b. Place the cursor in cell d9 and write: =c4+(1.96*b8).

TABLE 7.6 Confidence Intervals for Proportion

	A	B	C	D	E	F
1	TABLE 7.6 Confidence Intervals for Proportion					
2	Do you drink alcohol?					
3		Frequency	Proportion			
4	Yes	144	0.65			
5	No	76	0.35			
6	Sum	220	1.00			
7						
8	Standard error of proportion (S_p)	0.03	95% CL		99%CL	
9	Confidence intervals (CI)		0.59	0.71	0.57	0.74

c4 is the cell location for the proportion of the sample who said Yes.

1.96 is the value of z for the 95% confidence level.

b8 is the cell location for the standard error of the proportion.

We interpret our findings as being 95% confident that the percentage of high school students in the state who drink alcohol is between 59% and 71%. We want to report the percentages, not the proportions, so we multiply the proportion by 100 to convert it to a percentage. With Excel, simply highlight the four cells (cells c9 through f9) and then click on the **%** button on the menu. This procedure will automatically change the proportions to percentages.

Step 4: Construct the confidence interval for the 99% confidence level. As before, when moving from the 95% confidence level to the 99% confidence level, simply change the value of z from 1.96 to 2.58 and recalculate using the same formula. In cell e9, write: =c4–(2.58*b8), and in cell f9, write: =c4+(2.58*b8). We are now 99% confident that the percentage of high school students in the state who drink alcohol is between 57% and 74%.

7.7 Summary

This chapter has provided an overview of the various methods used for estimating population parameters using sample statistics. This process is known as statistical inference—making inferences or generalizations about a population based on observations from a sample. To use statistical inference, it is imperative to draw a probability sample from the population. We discussed four types of probability samples commonly used in criminal justice research—simple random, systematic, stratified, and multistage cluster samples.

Regardless of the type of probability sampling, there will be a certain amount of error between the value of a sample statistic and a population parameter. Probability theory informs us of the characteristics of the sampling distribution of a statistic, which approximates the normal curve. The properties of the normal curve allow us to determine the amount of sampling error for a statistic by calculating the standard deviation of the sampling distribution, known as the standard error of the mean or the standard error of the proportion. Under the normal curve, we know that 95% of the sample means will fall within two standard errors below and above the mean and that 99% of the sample means will fall within three standard errors below and above the mean. Using this information, we can construct confidence intervals, defined as a range of values in which the population parameter is estimated to lie, for various levels of probability, known as confidence levels.

We demonstrated the construction of confidence intervals using a hand calculator and Excel. Confidence intervals were calculated for a mean using both the *z* distribution (large samples) and *t* distribution (small samples), as well as for a proportion using the *z* distribution. We also explained that research results are commonly reported as percentages at the 95% confidence level using the term margin of error. Thus, the next time the results of a nationwide survey are reported in the media, you will be able to understand that the population parameter is determined by adding and subtracting the margin of error from the sample statistic. For example, if a criminal justice survey reports 83% (±10%) of criminal justice students enjoy statistics, you will know that the percentage of criminal justice students in the population who enjoy statistics is between 73% and 93%.

Key Terms

statistic	**sampling variation**
parameter	**sampling distribution of means**
statistical inference	**central limit theorem**
probability sampling	**standard error of the mean**
sampling without replacement	**confidence level**
simple random sample	**confidence interval**
systematic sample	**margin of error**
stratified sample	**degrees of freedom**
multistage cluster sample	**standard error of the proportion**
sampling error	

TryIT! Answers

Box 7.1

A. .48

B. .18

C. .05

D. 1.23

E. .23

F. .27

Box 7.2

$$s_{\bar{x}} = \frac{1.20}{\sqrt{100-1}} = .12$$

95% Confidence Level

$$2.60 - 1.96(.12) = 2.60 - .24 = 2.36$$
$$2.60 + 1.96(.12) = 2.60 + .24 = 2.84$$

We are 95% confident that the average number of probation violations per week for the population of probationers is between 2.36 and 2.84.

99% Confidence Level

$$2.60 - 2.58(.12) = 2.60 - .31 = 2.29$$
$$2.60 + 2.58(.12) = 2.60 + .31 = 2.91$$

We are 99% confident that the average number of probation violations per week for the population of probationers is between 2.29 and 2.91.

Box 7.3

$$s_{\bar{x}} = \frac{3.30}{\sqrt{25-1}} = .67$$

95% Confidence Level

$$3.70 - 2.06(.67) = 3.70 - 1.38 = 2.32$$
$$3.70 + 2.06(.67) = 3.70 + 1.38 = 5.08$$

We are 95% confident that the average number of assaults for the population of students at the middle school is between 2.32 and 5.08.

99% Confidence Level

$$3.70 - 2.80(.67) = 3.70 - 1.88 = 1.82$$
$$3.70 - 2.80(.67) = 3.70 + 1.88 = 5.58$$

We are 99% confident that the average number of assaults for the population of students at the middle school is between 1.82 and 5.58.

Box 7.4

$$S_p = \sqrt{\frac{.32(1-.32)}{450}} = .02$$

95% Confidence Level

$$.32 - 1.96(.02) = .32 - .04 = .28$$
$$.32 + 1.96(.02) = .32 + .04 = .36$$

We are 95% confident that the percentage of Indiana automobile drivers who believe that they are not at all likely to receive a ticket from the police for speeding is between 28% and 36%. Or 32% (±4%) of Indiana drivers believe that they are not at all likely to receive a ticket for speeding.

99% Confidence Level

$$.32 - 2.58(.02) = .32 - .05 = .27$$
$$.32 + 2.58(.02) = .32 + .05 = .37$$

We are 99% confident that the percentage of Indiana automobile drivers who believe that they are not at all likely to receive a ticket from the police for speeding is between 27% and 37%. Or 32% (±5%) of Indiana drivers believe that they are not at all likely to receive a ticket for speeding.

7.8 Problems

1. A researcher wants to select a probability sample of 350 subjects from a community of 2,500 residents. Determine the probability of selection for the following subjects:

   a. 1st
   b. 50th
   c. 175th
   d. 230th
   e. 350th

2. A researcher wants to draw five systematic samples from five surrounding counties with different sized populations. Calculate the sampling interval to be used for each county.

County	Sample Size (n)	Population Size (N)
A	400	32,000
B	1200	1,500,453
C	220	12,540
D	400	28,500
E	800	654,000

3. Determine the z-score that corresponds with the following probability levels:

Probability	z-score
a. .68	
b. .75	
c. .80	
d. .90	
e. .95	
f. .97	
g. .99	

4. Find the appropriate t values to be used in constructing confidence intervals for small samples for the following alpha levels and degrees of freedom.

Alpha Level	Degrees of Freedom
a. .10	15
b. .10	28
c. .05	20
d. .05	17
e. .01	12
f. .01	26

5. Calculate the standard error for each of the following:

Standard Deviation	Sample Size
a. 2.40	500
b. 3.80	250
c. 5.70	120
d. .85	1000
e. 1.50	50

6. In a study of attitudes toward the police, a researcher finds that the average rating of the police on a scale of 1 to 10, with 10 being excellent and one being very poor, is 5.40, with a standard deviation of 2.30. Construct confidence intervals for the 95% and 99% confidence levels for each of the following sample sizes:

attitude toward police

1-10   95% & 99%

$\bar{X} = 5.40$, $S = 2.30$

a) $n = 100$ (it's >than 30)
      not use t distribution

Sample Size $95\% = \bar{X} \pm (1.96)(S_{\bar{X}})$
a. 100
b. 250   1) $S_{\bar{X}} = \dfrac{S}{\sqrt{n-1}} = \dfrac{2.3}{\sqrt{99}} = \dfrac{2.3}{9.9} = 0.23$
c. 500
d. 1000   2) $95\% = 5.4 \pm (1.96)(0.23) = \boxed{4.95 \big/ 5.35}$ $\begin{array}{c}(-)\ \ to\ (+)\\ \end{array}$ $\begin{array}{c}99\% \to\\ same\end{array}$

7. The results of a nationwide survey show that 57.40% of college students have violated university rules regarding alcohol use. The margin of error for the survey is 2.30%. What does this mean?

8. A university professor draws a random sample of 12 students from an introductory statistics course and determines that the average score on the final exam was 84.20, with a standard deviation of 8.50. What are the confidence intervals for the population of students in the class at both the (a) 95% and (b) 99% confidence levels? $95\% = \bar{X} \pm (t)(S_{\bar{X}})$
    $\alpha = 1 - 0.95;\ 1 - 0.99;\ 12 - 1 = 11 \to$ to find a t.

9. The university administration wants to know how well students are performing in introductory statistics classes across several different departments. Institutional research has selected probability samples from statistics courses in several departments and has calculated the mean and standard deviation of the final exam score for a sample of students. Calculate confidence intervals for the 95% and 99% confidence levels for each department.

Department	Sample	Mean	Standard Deviation
Criminal Justice	15	84.30	8.10
Sociology	12	82.40	7.90
Psychology	17	80.80	7.80

10. In a survey of 225 households in a medium-sized city, respondents were asked the following questions, (1) "Has your home ever been burglarized?," (2) "Do you have a home security system?," and (3) "How safe do you feel in your home at night?" The responses are listed below. Calculate the 95% and 99% confidence intervals for the Yes responses for questions one and two, and for the Not at all safe response for question three. Be sure to construct your confidence intervals using percentages and not proportions.

    a. Has your home ever been burglarized?
        Yes—33%
        No—67%

    b. Do you have a home security system?
        Yes—29%
        No—71%

    c. How safe do you feel in your home at night?
        Very safe—52%
        Somewhat safe—37%
        Not at all safe—11%

11. In a national survey of gun ownership, researchers discovered that 38.40% (± 3.40%) of those surveyed indicated that they own a gun. What does this mean?

12. Enter the following data into Excel and calculate the standard error of the mean and the confidence interval for the 95% confidence level for each of the following examples, using the z distribution.

	Mean	Standard Deviation	Sample Size
a.	2.59	1.34	55
b.	5.92	2.56	125
c.	75.61	11.69	100
d.	150.45	49.31	70

13. Enter the following data into Excel and calculate the standard error of the mean and the confidence interval for the 99% confidence level for each of the following examples, using the t distribution.

	Mean	Standard Deviation	Sample Size
a.	2.56	2.11	12
b.	89.21	25.67	8
c.	10.98	5.45	15
d.	15.32	7	21

14. In a national survey of 800 respondents, a researcher finds that 335 respondents support photo identification cards for gun owners. Using Excel, calculate the standard error of the proportion and construct the confidence interval for the 99% confidence level.

15. Results from a survey of 120 state police officers revealed that 45% of the officers in the sample accept gratuities on a regular basis. Enter the data into Excel and calculate the standard error of the proportion and construct the confidence interval for the 95% confidence level.

7) mean level of of students violating univ. rules is 57.40% with a margin error ±2.30%

Statistical Analysis for a Population Mean and Proportion: z Tests

ExploreIT!

The state legislature is considering adopting sentencing guidelines to govern judicial decision making in felony cases. A number of female judges have voiced support for the guidelines, whereas several male judges have indicated they are opposed to the measure. The legislative committee would like to know whether these voices represent actual differences among male and female judges across the state. As a research consultant for the legislature, you have been given the task of assessing whether male and female judges differ in their level of support for the guidelines. You have decided to select a probability sample of 30 male judges and 30 female judges, and ask them the following question: "Do you support sentencing guidelines for felony cases?" How do you know if the proportion of female judges who support sentencing guidelines is different than the proportion of male judges? You will conduct a z test for proportions to determine if the different levels of support between male and female judges found in the sample is due to sampling error or is the result of an actual difference in the population.

In Chapter 7, we discussed statistical inference—the process by which we estimate population parameters using sample statistics. In the present chapter, we extend the discussion of statistical inference to estimating *differences* among population parameters through the process of hypothesis testing. We first discussed the idea of hypothesis testing in Chapter 2. You will recall that a hypothesis proposes a relationship between two or more variables. Hypothesis testing requires us to rely on the second class of statistical techniques, known as inferential statistics.

As discussed in Chapter 1, inferential statistics are used to make generalizations about a population based on sample observations. Once we have formulated some testable hypotheses and collected sample observations from a population, we can apply inferential statistical techniques to test our hypotheses. Our goal is to determine whether we can accept our hypotheses as supported by the sample observations. For example, we might hypothesize that females are more likely to favor three-strikes legislation than males. Let us assume that our results show that 70% of the female respondents in our sample favor three-strikes legislation, compared to 65% of the males. We need to determine whether the differences found in our sample are the result of sampling error (variation among different samples) or of actual differences among the population parameters. The use of probability theory allows us to determine how likely differences found among sample statistics are the result of sampling error.

This chapter will discuss the logic of hypothesis testing and how inferential statistics, in conjunction with probability theory, enable us to make decisions regarding relationships between population parameters. Furthermore, you will learn how to make decisions concerning a population mean and a population proportion using some fundamental data analysis techniques known as *z*-tests.

8.1 The Logic of Hypothesis Testing

As researchers, we formulate hypotheses because we suspect that a relationship exists between two or more variables in a given population. For instance, we might suggest the following research hypotheses in relation to crime:

Research Hypothesis 1: The number of crimes committed by males and females is different.

Research Hypothesis 2: Lower income and higher income persons differ in the number of serious crimes committed.

Research Hypothesis 3: The frequency of crime is different in inner-city neighborhoods than in suburban neighborhoods.

In each of the above hypotheses, we are making a statement about the effect of an independent variable (sex, income, location) on the dependent variable (crime). These hypotheses are known as research hypotheses and are symbolized as H_1. We define the

research   research hypothesis as *the hypothesized effect of an independent variable on a depend-*
hypothesis *ent variable that we believe to be true in the population.* For example, we believe that
gender, income, and location all have an effect on crime. Research hypotheses are
important, because they provide the impetus for conducting research.

In statistics, however, we do not actually test the research hypothesis but, rather, the
null   null hypothesis, symbolized as H_0. We define the **null hypothesis** as *a statement of no*
hypothesis *difference or no association between an independent variable and a dependent vari-*
able. Thus, we can restate the research hypotheses listed earlier as null hypotheses in the
following manner:

Null Hypothesis 1: There is no difference in the number of crimes committed
between males and females.

Null Hypothesis 2: There is no difference between lower-income and higher-income
persons in regard to the number of serious crimes committed.

Null Hypothesis 3: The frequency of crimes in inner-city neighborhoods is equal to
the frequency of crimes in suburban neighborhoods.

In each of the three null hypotheses, we simply restated our research hypothesis from a
statement about the effect of an independent variable on a dependent variable to a
statement of no effect.

Statistical theory involves testing the assumption of no difference against data
derived from a sample of observations. For example, if the sample data indicates differences in the number of crimes committed between low-income and high-income
individuals, then the null hypothesis of no difference is rejected. Rejecting the null
hypothesis means that we accept the research hypothesis and conclude that the differences observed in our sample data are the result of actual differences in the population.
More specifically, we are saying that the independent variable does affect the dependent
variable as hypothesized. By contrast, if the sample data indicates no differences in the
number of crimes committed between low-income and high-income individuals, then
we fail to reject the null hypothesis. Failing to reject the null hypothesis does not mean
we are accepting the null hypothesis as true but, rather, that our sample observations
have not shown support for the research hypothesis. Statistical analysis requires us
either to reject the null hypothesis and, thus, accept the research hypothesis, or to fail to
reject the null hypothesis and, thus, not accept the research hypothesis. As you can
probably guess, our goal is to reject the null hypothesis. In doing so, we are able to provide support for our research hypothesis.

A criminal trial provides a good analogy to this decision-making process concerning
the null hypothesis. In a criminal trial, a person accused of a crime is presumed to be
innocent (null hypothesis) until proven guilty. The prosecution believes that the person
is guilty (research hypothesis) and proceeds to present evidence to the jury that will
render a decision to convict. The jury must then weigh the evidence presented by the
prosecution against the presumption of innocence. If the evidence outweighs this pre-

sumption, then the person is convicted—the null hypothesis is rejected and the research hypothesis is accepted. If the trial evidence does not outweigh the presumption of innocence, then the jury fails to convict—the null hypothesis is not rejected and the research hypothesis is not supported. This does not mean that the accused is truly innocent—only that the jury failed to convict.

Let's return to our example of gender and crime. Symbolically, we write the research and null hypotheses as:

$$H_1 : \mu_1 \neq \mu_2$$
$$H_0 : \mu_1 = \mu_2$$

Our statistical analysis will involve comparing the mean number of crimes for males (μ_1) versus the mean number of crimes for females (μ_2). Recall that our research hypothesis (H_1) suggests that the mean number of crimes committed by males and females is different, while the null hypothesis (H_0) states that the mean number of crimes is not different. It is important to note that the null hypothesis implies that the two means are not different—that is, they are equal. Technically, this is true. This does not mean, however, that the absolute value of the two means is identical. For example, suppose that the mean number of crimes committed by males is 2.70, and for females, 2.30. Does this indicate that there is a difference in the number of crimes committed by males and females in the population? Not necessarily. The difference may be a product of sampling error. That is, the different mean values more likely can be attributed to sampling variation than to an actual difference in the population.

Our goal in inferential statistics, then, is to determine whether the differences observed in our sample data are the result of sampling error or reflect an actual difference in the population. If they result from sampling error, then we are unable to reject the null hypothesis of no difference. If the results are attributed to population differences, then we reject the null hypothesis of no difference and accept the research hypothesis.

Nondirectional and Directional Hypotheses

It is important to note that in these hypotheses we are not specifying *how* the independent variable affects the dependent variable, only that it does. For example, we are hypothesizing only that there is a difference in the number of crimes committed between males and females; we are not hypothesizing that males commit more crimes than females. The same is true for income and location. Thus, the hypotheses, as stated above, are known as nondirectional hypotheses. A **nondirectional hypothesis** is *a statement about the differences existing in the populations without specifying the direction of the differences.* The alternative to the nondirectional hypothesis is the directional hypothesis. A **directional hypothesis** is *a statement about the direction of the differences existing in the populations.* To change our hypotheses from nondirectional

nondirectional hypothesis

directional hypothesis

to directional, we need only include a statement as to the direction of the differences between the populations. That is, we specify *how* the population parameters are different as demonstrated in the following research hypotheses:

Research Hypothesis 1: Males commit a greater number of crimes than females.

Research Hypothesis 2: Lower-income persons commit more serious crimes than higher-income persons.

Research Hypothesis 3: The frequency of crime is greater in inner-city neighborhoods than in suburban neighborhoods.

Notice that each of these hypotheses specifies "how" the number of crimes are different in the population—males greater than females, lower income greater than higher income, inner-city neighborhoods greater than suburban neighborhoods.

In addition to including a statement about "how" the populations are different, we also must change the symbolic notation we use for a directional hypothesis. For example, our first research hypothesis stated that males commit a greater number of crimes than females. Specifically, we are predicting that the average number of crimes committed among the population of males (μ_1) will be greater than the average number of crimes committed by the population of females (μ_2). Symbolically, we write the research and null hypotheses as:

$$H_1 : \mu_1 > \mu_2$$
$$H_0 : \mu_1 \leq \mu_2$$

It is important to note the differences in notation between a nondirectional and directional hypothesis. With the nondirectional hypothesis, our research hypothesis stated that the mean number of crimes between males and females were not equal, whereas the null hypothesis stated that they were equal. The directional hypothesis states that the mean number of crimes for males is greater than the mean for females; thus, the null hypothesis states that the mean number of crimes is either greater for females than males or that the mean number of crimes is equal between males and females.

As with the nondirectional hypothesis, a directional hypothesis also requires us to make a decision about the null hypothesis. If the average number of crimes is greater for males than females, then we are able to reject the null hypothesis and accept the research hypothesis. By contrast, if the average number of crimes is greater for females or is equal, then we are unable to reject the null hypothesis.

At this point you are probably wondering why would anyone want to specify a directional hypothesis. It may appear that you have a better chance of accepting the research hypothesis with a nondirectional hypothesis, as it does not matter which mean is higher or lower—only that they are different. That is, with a nondirectional hypothesis it does not matter if males have a higher or lower average than females—only that the two averages are different. Accepting our directional research hypothesis, however, requires males to have a higher average than females; if the male average is lower or equal to the female average, we are unable to accept our research hypothesis. Although it may seem easier to accept a nondirectional hypothesis, it may not be to a researcher's advantage to propose such a hypothesis. As you will see shortly, statistical testing takes into account whether the researcher is proposing a directional or nondirectional hypothesis.

Now that you have a good understanding of research and null hypotheses, as well as directional and nondirectional hypotheses, take a few minutes to complete TryIT! Box 8.1.

TryIT!   BOX **8.1**

For each research hypothesis listed below, construct the corresponding null hypothesis. Identify your hypothesis as either directional or nondirectional.

H_1: Probation officers are more satisfied with their careers than are parole officers. *d*

H_2: The frequency of drug use is different for high school dropouts than for high school graduates. *nd*

H_3: The rate of institutional misconduct differs for Latino and Asian inmates. *nd*

H_4: Male police officers have higher rates of job burnout than do female police officers. *d*

H_5: Private attorneys have a higher average number of acquittals than do public defenders. *d*

H_6: The number of misdemeanor offenses committed by rural adolescents is different from the number committed by urban adolescents. *nd*

H_7: Female respondents have higher levels of fear of crime than do male respondents. *d*

H_8: The rate of absenteeism for correctional officers differs from that for police officers. *nd*

Decision Making about the Null Hypothesis

By now you should understand that hypothesis testing requires us to make a decision about the null hypothesis. We either must reject the null hypothesis, allowing us to accept the research hypothesis, or fail to reject the null hypothesis, making us unable to accept the research hypothesis. Inferential statistics involve making decisions about populations based on the analysis of sample observations. Thus, our decision about the null hypothesis involves answering the following question: What is the probability that the difference in our sample observations is a result of an actual difference in the population and not the result of sampling error?

Because the decisions we make about populations are based on sample data, we can never be 100% sure that our decision about the null hypothesis is correct. That is, it is possible that we will make an incorrect decision about the null hypothesis. Let's return to our example of a nondirectional hypothesis in which we stated that the number of crimes committed by males and females is different. If this is true in the population and our sample observations support this, with males having either a higher or a lower average number of crimes than females, then we have made the correct decision by rejecting the null hypothesis. If, however, the number of crimes for males and females in the population is equal, and yet our sample observations indicate that they are different, leading us to reject the null hypothesis, then we have made an incorrect decision regarding our hypothesis.

Type I error

There are two types of incorrect decisions we can make in hypothesis testing. The first is known as a **Type I error**, *defined as rejecting the null hypothesis when the null hypothesis is true*. For instance, we reject the null hypothesis and conclude that the average number of crimes committed is different between males and females based on the analysis of our sample observations, when, in fact, the average number of crimes committed by males and females in the population is equal. A second error that we are

Type II error

susceptible to is known as a **Type II error**, *defined as accepting the null hypothesis when the null hypothesis is false*. In this case, based on our sample observations, we fail to reject the null hypothesis of no difference in the number of crimes committed between males and females, when in fact males and females in the population do differ in the number of crimes committed. We illustrate this decision making dilemma in Figure 8.1. Type I error is known as alpha (α), while Type II error is referred to as beta (β).

Significance Level

Although the possibility of making an incorrect decision regarding the null hypothesis does exist, it is possible for us to determine the probability of making an incorrect

FIGURE 8.1 Reality of research situation

	Null Hypothesis Is True	Null Hypothesis Is False
Fail to Reject the Null Hypothesis	Correct Decision	Type II Error (beta)
Reject the Null Hypothesis	Type I Error (alpha)	Correct Decision

Decision

decision. We do this by determining the probability of making a Type I error (rejecting the null hypothesis when the null hypothesis is true). The chance of making a Type I error is commonly referred to as the significance level or alpha (α). In other words, the

significance level or alpha (α) is *defined as the probability (p) of making a Type I error.*

signifi-cance level (alpha)

We first introduced the term alpha in Chapter 7. You will recall that the alpha level is determined by: 1 – confidence level. Furthermore, we want to be 95% confident that the population parameter falls within a given confidence interval, which is the same as saying there is less than a 5% chance that the parameter falls outside the confidence interval. The same logic applies to hypothesis testing; however, instead of using the confidence level, we use the alpha level. For example, if we reject the null hypothesis at the .05 significance level, we are saying that there is less than a 5% chance that we have made a Type I error. The reverse of this is to say that the probability of the observed difference being attributed to an actual difference in the population is .95 or 95%.

Although it is up to the individual researcher to determine the level of risk in regards to making a Type I error, there are some conventional rules that are commonly followed in criminal justice research. The maximum significance level that is typically accepted is the .05 level. Research articles also may report results at the .01 and .001 levels of significance. A statistic that is significant at the .01 level indicates that there is less than a 1% chance that we have made a Type I error. A statistic that is significant at the .001 level indicates there is less than one chance out of 1,000 that we have made a Type I error.

The question you may be pondering is, "Why not select a stringent level of significance, such as .001, to guard against making a Type I error?" At first glance, this seems reasonable; after all, the chance of making a Type I error would be very small (1 out of 1,000). You must keep in mind, however, that we also run the risk of making a Type II error (failing to reject the null hypothesis when the null hypothesis is false). The more we guard against making a Type I error by decreasing the significance level, the more likely we are to make a Type II error. In criminal justice research, we are more willing to tolerate making a Type II error than a Type I error. That is, finding a guilty person innocent (Type II error) is a less severe error than finding an innocent person guilty (Type I error). To understand this further, we need to examine the next step in the process of hypothesis testing.

Comparing the Test Statistic to the Probability Distribution

Once we have selected a significance level, we can proceed to calculate the test statistic. After calculating the test statistic, we then compare the test statistic with a probability distribution of *what is expected by chance*. If our calculated statistic equals or exceeds the value in the probability distribution at the selected significance level, we reject the null hypothesis and conclude that there is an actual difference among the population parameters. If, however, the calculated statistic is less than the value in the probability distribution, we are unable to reject the null hypothesis and must conclude that the difference is due to sampling error. The value in the probability distribution is often

critical value referred to as the critical value. The **critical value** is *the value in the probability distribution that marks the lower boundary of the critical region.* If our test statistic equals or exceeds the critical value—that is, it falls within the critical region—we reject the null hypothesis and conclude that the difference between the two sample means is statisti-**statistically significant** cally significant. To say that our test statistic is **statistically significant** is *to conclude that the differences observed between our sample statistics are the result of actual differences between the population parameters.*

Let's return to our example of a directional hypothesis, in which we stated that the average number of crimes committed by males is higher than females ($H_1: \mu_1 > \mu_2$). Once we have calculated a test statistic, we need to compare the calculated statistic to the critical value found in the probability distribution table to make a decision about the null hypothesis ($H_0: \mu_1 \leq \mu_2$). Where do we find the probability distribution table with which to compare our test statistic? In our discussion of estimating population parameters using sample statistics, we presented two types of probability distributions known as the z (i.e., normal curve) and the t distribution. A probability distribution is the sampling distribution of a statistic that is derived from probability theory. Thus, every statistical test that we use in criminal justice research has a probability distribution associated with it. The probability distribution tables are located in Appendix A. For example, if we perform a t test, then we want to compare the calculated t statistic with the critical t value found in the t probability distribution or, more simply, the t distribution table.

We illustrate this process of comparing a test statistic with a critical value in Figure 8.2 using the t distribution table (Table B). Assume that our calculated test statistic is equal to 2.08 and the critical value is equal to 1.70. As shown in Figure 8.2, we can readily determine that the calculated test statistic falls within the critical region, as it is

FIGURE 8.2 Comparison of test statistic with critical value using .05 alpha level

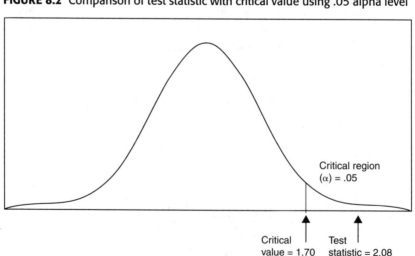

larger than the lower boundary mark of the critical region (2.08 > 1.70). Based on this comparison, we would reject the null hypothesis.

What if we wanted to use a more stringent alpha level to further guard against making a Type I error? Based on conventional rules, we could have selected either the .01 or .001 level of significance. Recall that the more we guard against a Type I error by lowering the alpha level, the more we increase the chance of making a Type II error (failing to reject the null hypothesis when the null hypothesis is false). We illustrate this in Figure 8.3, using the .01 level of significance. Our test statistic is not affected by the change in the significance level; it is still 2.08. What does change, however, is the size of the critical region as reflected by the increased critical value.

In the first example, we rejected the null hypothesis, because the test statistic (2.08) exceeded the critical value of 1.70, even though there exists a 5% chance that we made a Type I error. In this example, we decreased the chance of making a Type I error from 5% to 1%, but now our test statistic no longer falls within the critical region (2.08 < 2.75). The desire to reduce the risk of making a Type I error has resulted in an increased risk of making a Type II error, because the critical value has increased. This makes it more difficult for the test statistic to achieve statistical significance by falling beyond the critical value into the critical region. Based on the comparison between the test statistic and the critical value, we are unable to reject the null hypothesis, and must conclude that the difference between the sample statistics is the result of sampling error.

Here, then, is the dilemma. We can lower the risk of making a Type I error by decreasing the significance level, yet doing so increases the chance of making a Type II error. We can decrease the chance of making a Type II error by increasing the significance level, but this will result in an increased risk of making a Type I error. So what do we do? Although decisions about choosing an appropriate significance level are primarily a function of the research question, for the purposes of this text we recommend relying on the conventional rules regarding significance levels by selecting the .05 alpha level. That is, if your test statistic is equal to or greater than the critical value at the .05 level of significance, you should reject the null hypothesis and conclude that the observed differences are the result of actual differences among the population parameters.

At this point, we return to the question that we raised earlier regarding the use of a directional hypothesis. We asked, "Why would anyone want to specify a directional hypothesis?" If we hypothesize that males commit a greater number of crimes than females, then we can only reject the null hypothesis if males have a higher average. If females have a higher average or the average between males and females is equal, then we cannot reject the null hypothesis. Thus, there is only one condition that allows us to reject the null hypothesis ($\mu_{males} > \mu_{females}$). With a nondirectional hypothesis, there are two conditions that would allow us to reject the null hypothesis ($\mu_{males} > \mu_{females}$) or ($\mu_{males} < \mu_{females}$). So why propose a directional hypothesis?

The benefit of a directional hypothesis is found in the size of the critical region of the probability distribution. For a directional hypothesis, we specify the direction of the difference; therefore, the critical region is located in one tail of the probability distribution.

FIGURE 8.3 Comparison of test statistic with critical value using .01 alpha level

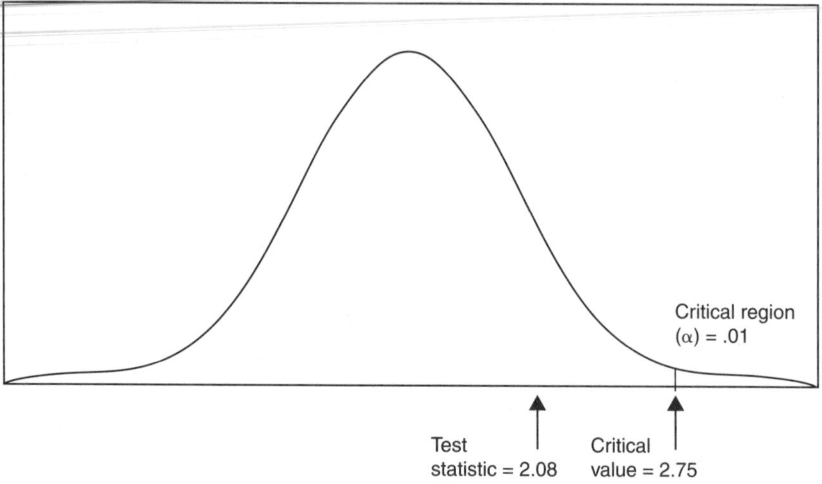

For example, we hypothesized that males commit a greater number of crimes than females. We will only reject the null hypothesis if this one condition is met (μ_{males} > $\mu_{females}$). Let's assume that the data for each group is as follows: μ_{males} = 8.40; $\mu_{females}$ = 6.32. The difference between males and females is 2.08 (8.4 – 6.32), which represents our test statistic. Using the .05 level of significance, we found that the critical value is equal to 1.70 (see Figure 8.2). Based on this information, we would reject the null hypothesis, because the test statistic is greater than the critical value and it is in the direction we hypothesized.

If females had the greater number, our test statistic would be –2.08, which is still greater than the critical value of 1.70 (comparison involves the absolute values); however, the direction of the difference was different from what was hypothesized. Thus, not only does the test statistic have to be greater with a directional hypothesis than the critical value, but it must also be in the hypothesized direction. This type of hypothesis test is known as a one-tailed test. A **one-tailed test** is *used to test a directional hypothesis in which the critical region lies in one tail of the probability distribution.*

one-tailed test

If we had used a nondirectional hypothesis, then we would have conducted a two-tailed test. A **two-tailed test** is *used to test a nondirectional hypothesis in which the critical region lies in both tails of the probability distribution.* A nondirectional test means that we are not hypothesizing that one group committed more or fewer crimes than the other but only that the two groups are not equal. Thus, we will reject the null hypothesis if males have a higher average than females (μ_{males} > $\mu_{females}$) or males have a lower average than females (μ_{males} < $\mu_{females}$). Once again, at first glance this appears to be an advantage. Because either condition may be present, however, we need to have a critical region in both tails of the probability distribution, while at the same time maintaining our alpha level of .05. To accomplish this, we divide the .05 alpha level in half,

two-tailed test

FIGURE 8.4 Comparison of test statistic with critical value for a two-tailed test at the .05 alpha level

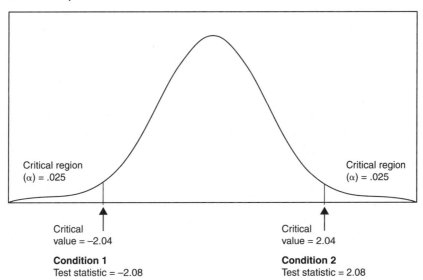

such that each tail of the probability distribution accounts for a critical region of .025. We illustrate this in Figure 8.4.

Notice what happens to the critical value when moving from a one-tailed test to a two-tailed test. The critical value increases as a result of decreasing the critical region from .05 in one tail to .025 in two tails. With a one-tailed test, the critical value was 1.70, because the critical region fell within one tail of the probability distribution. Using a two-tailed test requires us to split the critical region into two tails, which increases the critical value to 2.04. What does this mean? Simply put, it means that we have an increased risk of making a Type II error (failing to reject a false null hypothesis), because our test statistic must now be larger in order to fall within the critical region.

As shown in Figure 8.4, we can conclude from our data that two possible conditions could exist. First, it is possible that females committed a greater number of crimes than males. For example, if the average for males was 6.32 and females was 8.40, we would get a negative test statistic of −2.08 (6.32 − 8.40). If males committed a greater number of crimes than females, then we would get a positive test statistic 2.08 (8.40 − 6.32). The absolute value of the test statistic is the same for both conditions; what changes is the direction of the difference (i.e., which group has the higher average). Regardless of which condition actually emerges, the decision we make regarding the null hypothesis is to reject it, because the test statistic (−2.08 or 2.08) exceeds the critical value of 2.04.

By now, you should understand that there are advantages and disadvantages in conducting one-tailed and two-tailed tests. The advantage of a one-tailed test is that it is easier for the test statistic to exceed the critical value, which translates into a decreased risk of making a Type II error. The disadvantage, however, is that if the difference is not in the hypothesized direction, we are unable to reject the null hypothesis. The most obvious advantage of a two-tailed test is that if the test statistic is equal to or greater than the critical value, we are able to reject the null hypothesis, regardless of the direction of the difference. By contrast, we are more likely to make a Type II error with a two-tailed test, because the critical value that must be equaled or exceeded by the test statistic is larger.

One final point to consider concerning hypothesis testing is the effect of sample size. In Chapter 7, we saw that as the sample size increased, the standard error decreased, leading to a narrower confidence interval. The same principle applies to hypothesis testing. That is, as the sample size increases, the critical value decreases, making it easier for our test statistic to fall within the critical region. This is true for many of the inferential statistics used in this text.

Now that you have a good understanding of hypothesis testing, we now want to turn your attention to hypothesis testing using a set of statistical techniques known as z tests. Although there are a variety of z tests that can be used for testing specific hypotheses, our focus will be on two different types referred to as the one-sample z test and the z test for proportions.

8.2   One-Sample z Test

one-sample z test
{.margin}

The **one-sample z test** is a *statistical technique that is used for testing a hypothesis about the relationship between a known population mean and a sample mean.* Essentially, we are interested in knowing if our hypothesis concerning the population mean is true, based on the observations calculated from a sample. For example, we might hypothesize that the average score on a police officer entrance exam is higher in 1998 than in previous years, because the 1998 recruits took a prep course to prepare for the entrance exam. Thus, we are implying that the sample of police recruits who took the prep course in 1998 is different than the population of recruits in previous years.

To test our hypothesis, we begin by comparing the average exam score from a sample of recruits in 1998 to the average exam score from the population of recruits in the previous years. Once we have calculated our test statistic, we simply compare that value to the critical value in the z distribution table, and make a decision about the null hypothesis. If the calculated z statistic is equal to or larger than the critical z value, then we reject the null hypothesis and conclude that the population parameters are significantly different. If the calculated z statistic is less than the critical z value, we are unable to reject the null hypothesis and must conclude that the difference between the sample mean and population mean is the result of sampling error.

Procedures for Calculating a One-Sample z Test

Let's assume that the average exam score for the population of police recruits is 83.40, with a standard deviation of 6.70, while the average score for the sample of recruits in

1998 is 86.84, with a standard deviation of 7.94. Notice that the two means are not equal, but we are not saying that they are necessarily statistically different. The question is, "Is the difference due to an actual difference between the sample statistic and population parameter or is the difference due to sampling error?" We use the following formula to calculate the one-sample z test:

$$z = \frac{\overline{X} - \mu}{s_{\overline{x}}}$$

$\overline{X}$ = sample mean
μ = population mean
$s_{\overline{x}}$ = standard error of the mean

Step 1: State the research and null hypotheses.
   H_1: The average exam score for the sample of recruits in 1998 is higher than the population average.

   $$\overline{X} > \mu$$

   H_0: The average exam score for the sample of recruits in 1998 is equal to or lower than the population average.

   $$\overline{X} \leq \mu$$

Notice that we have hypothesized a directional hypothesis by stating that the average exam score will be higher for the sample of 1998 recruits ($\overline{X}$) compared to the population of previous recruits (μ).

Step 2: Compute the mean and standard deviation for the sample.

Exam Score (X)	Frequency (f)	fx	f(X − X̄)²
98	7	686	871.82
96	7	672	587.34
94	9	846	461.39
88	17	1496	22.88
85	9	765	30.47
84	11	924	88.72
80	6	480	280.71
78	3	234	234.44
70	4	280	1134.34
65	2	130	953.97
Sum (Σ)	75	6513	4666.08
Mean ($\overline{X}$) 86.84			
Standard Deviation (s) 7.94			

This represents a frequency distribution of the officer entrance exam scores for a sample of 75 1998 recruits who took the entrance exam prep course. The steps illustrated here for calculating the mean and standard deviation using a frequency distribution are precisely the same as those shown in Chapters 4 and 5.

It is important to note that we also need to know the mean exam score for the population of recruits. This is necessary because we are comparing the sample mean of those officers who took the prep course with the population mean comprised of officers who had not taken the prep course.

Step 3: Calculate the standard error of the mean $(s_{\bar{x}})$.

We calculate the standard error of the mean by using the following formula:

$$s_{\bar{x}} = \frac{s}{\sqrt{n-1}}$$

We know that the standard deviation for our sample of 1998 recruits is 7.94 and the sample size is 75. Substituting our data into the above formula, we obtain the following:

$$s_{\bar{x}} = \frac{7.94}{\sqrt{75-1}} = \frac{7.94}{8.60} = .92$$

Step 4: Calculate the z statistic.

In Chapter 6, we learned how to convert a raw score into a standardized score. These standardized values are known as z scores. We use the same logic when applying the one-sample z test. We must convert our sample mean into a z score by way of the following formula:

$$z = \frac{\bar{X} - \mu}{s_{\bar{x}}}$$

We calculate the z score by subtracting the population mean (μ) from the sample mean $(\bar{X})$ and dividing by the standard error of the mean $(s_{\bar{x}})$. Substituting our data into the formula, we obtain:

$$z = \frac{86.84 - 83.40}{.92} = \frac{3.44}{.92} = 3.74$$

The above formula is identical to the formula used in Chapter 6 for converting a single raw score from a distribution into a z score. The calculated z statistic for the one-sample z test is equal to 3.74.

Step 5: Compare the calculated z statistic with the critical z value.

Once we have calculated the z statistic, we then need to find the critical z value in the z distribution table, which represents the critical region at the selected alpha level. Let's assume that we have selected the standard significance level of .05. At this point, it is important to remember that we formulated a directional hypothesis. That is, we hypothesized that the average exam score for the sample of recruits who took the prep course would be higher than the average exam score for the population of recruits from previous years. Because our hypothesis is directional, we must recognize that the entire critical region will lie in one tail of the z probability distribution.

The simplest method for finding the critical value for a one-tailed test using the z distribution table is to locate column C (area beyond z) in Table 8.1 and move down the column to the selected alpha level, which in our example is .0505. As shown in Table 8.1, the z-score (Column A) that corresponds with the .05 alpha level (Column C) is the critical value that defines the beginning of the critical region. In our example, the critical value of z at the .05 alpha level equals 1.64. Remember, this value defines the lower boundary of the critical region. In order for us to reject the null hypothesis, the calculated z statistic must equal or exceed the critical z value found in the z distribution table.

TABLE 8.1 Sample z Distribution

Column A	Column B	Column C
z-score	Area between mean and z	Area beyond z
1.60	.4452	.0548
1.61	.4463	.0537
1.62	.4474	.0526
1.63	.4484	.0516
1.64	.4495	.0505
1.65	.4505	.0495
1.66	.4515	.0485
1.67	.4525	.0475
1.68	.4535	.0465

Step 6: Interpret findings.

The final step in our analysis is to interpret our findings. Our interpretation is based on making a decision about the null hypothesis. Since the value of the test statistic (calculated z = 3.74) is larger than the critical value (critical z = 1.64), we know that our test

FIGURE 8.5 Comparison of calculated *z* statistic with critical *z* value for a one-tailed test

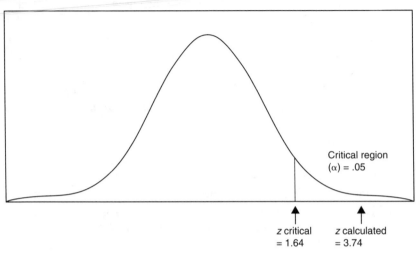

Critical region
(α) = .05

z critical   *z* calculated
= 1.64   = 3.74

statistic falls within the critical region, which indicates a statistically significant difference between the two means. Therefore, we can conclude that the 1998 recruits who
participated in the prep course scored significantly higher on the entrance exam when
compared to the population of recruits from previous years who did not take the prep
course. Thus, our research hypothesis is supported. We illustrate this interpretation in
Figure 8.5.

It is important to remember that with a directional hypothesis, the test statistic must
exceed the critical value in the hypothesized direction. As illustrated in Figure 8.5, the
critical value is 1.64. If the calculated *z* statistic equaled –3.74, we would not have
rejected the null hypothesis, because the difference between the sample mean and population mean would not be in the hypothesized direction. A negative *z* statistic would
indicate a lower average score for the sample compared to the population, which is
opposite of our research hypothesis.

What if we wanted to conduct a two-tailed test using a nondirectional hypothesis?
Using our example of scores on the police officer entrance exam, let's assume that the
sample of 1998 recruits scored worse than the population, resulting in a negative *z* statistic of –1.70. Because our hypothesis is nondirectional—that is, the sample mean
may be higher or lower than the population mean—our alpha level of .05 must be
divided into both tails of the *z* probability distribution. This results in two critical
regions comprised of the upper and lower 2.5% of the *z* probability distribution. To
determine the critical value that marks the lower boundary of the critical regions, we
once again must go to Column C in the *z* distribution table and find the *z* value that
corresponds with 2.5% of the area beyond *z*. As shown in Table A in Appendix A, the
critical *z* value that defines the lower boundary of the upper 2.5% of the distribution is

FIGURE 8.6 Comparison of calculated z statistic with critical z value for a two-tailed test

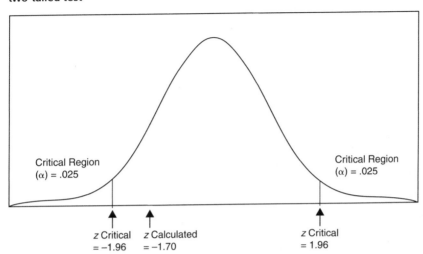

1.96. Because the z probability distribution is symmetrical, the value that marks the lower boundary of the lower 2.5% of the distribution is –1.96.

Because our calculated z statistic is negative, we know that we will be in the lower half of the distribution. As illustrated in Figure 8.6, comparing our calculated z (–1.70) with the critical z (–1.96) shows that our z statistic falls outside of the critical region. Thus, we are unable to reject the null hypothesis and must conclude that the difference between the means is the result of sampling error.

Now that you have a good understanding of the one sample z test, we recommend that you complete the TryIT! exercise in Box 8.2. Be sure to complete each step of the exercise and check your answers with those at the end of the chapter.

TryIT!   BOX **8.2**

The warden at a local juvenile residential facility recently began a program of family counseling for newly admitted juveniles. The warden would like to know if the program has an effect on institutional behavior. The average number of misconduct reports (MRs) for the population of juveniles during their initial six months of confinement equals 2.71. A random sample of seven program participants was selected for observation, and the number of misconduct reports for each subject is reported in the following table.

Subject No.	MRs (X)
1	0
2	2

Subject No.	MRs (X)
3	0
4	1
5	3
6	0
7	4

Step 1: State the research and null hypotheses.

Step 2: Compute the mean and standard deviation for the sample.

Step 3: Calculate the standard error of the mean.

Step 4: Calculate the *z* statistic.

Step 5: Compare the calculated *z* statistic with the critical *z* value.

Step 6: Interpret findings.

8.3 z Test for Proportions

In the previous section, we used the one-sample *z* test for testing a hypothesis about a known population mean and a sample mean. The comparison of means requires that our data be measured at the interval or ratio level. Criminal justice research often involves situations in which our data is measured at the nominal or ordinal level. In these instances, we are unable to calculate means and standard deviations as descriptive statistics for our data. Thus, the *z* test for means is not applicable.

The most commonly used descriptive statistics reported for nominal- and ordinal-level data are proportions and percentages. Testing a hypothesis using proportions requires us to use a *z* test designed to test whether two population proportions are equal. The **z test for proportions** is *a statistical technique used for comparing two population proportions.* You will recall that one of the main characteristics of the *z* probability distribution is that a certain proportion of cases falls within specified increments under the normal curve. Thus, we can calculate a *z*-score for a proportion to determine the proportion of cases falling above and below the calculated *z*-score. For example, a *z*-score of +2.00 has .02 (2%) of the cases falling above it and .98 (98%) of the cases falling below it. We can then use this information to test a null hypothesis concerning the probabilities associated with a proportion.

There are two types of hypotheses we can test using the *z* test for proportions. First, we can test a hypothesis similar to that used with the one-sample *z* test. That is, we can

z test for propor-tions

test whether a sample proportion is equal to a known population proportion. The second hypothesis we can test is whether two population proportions are equal. For the purposes of this text, we present an example using only the second type of hypothesis.

In order to test a hypothesis about two population proportions, we once again need to calculate a z statistic. The formula for the z test for proportions is given as:

$$z = \frac{p_1 - p_2}{sp_1 - p_2}$$

p_1 and p_2 = sample proportions for groups 1 and 2

$sp_1 - p_2$ = standard error of the difference in proportions

According to our formula, we need only to subtract the proportion of group 2 from the proportion of group 1 and divide by the standard error of the difference in proportions. Once we have calculated our z statistic, we simply compare that value to the critical value in the z distribution table and make a decision about the null hypothesis.

Let's assume that a researcher was interested in knowing college students' attitudes toward Megan's Law—a law in which convicted sex offenders must register with the police. Of particular interest is whether criminal justice majors and noncriminal justice majors have similar levels of support for the law. Thus, the researcher draws a random sample of 387 students from a state college and asks them to complete a short survey. The results are presented in Figure 8.7. From the results, we can see that 187 of the 220 criminal justice majors surveyed support Megan's Law, compared to 119 of the 167 noncriminal justice majors. We are now ready to proceed with a step-by-step illustration for testing our hypothesis.

FIGURE 8.7 Number of criminal justice and non–criminal justice majors in support of Megan's Law

	Criminal Justice Major	Non–Criminal Justice Major	Totals
Support Megan's Law			
Yes	187	119	306
No	33	48	81
Totals	220	167	387

Step 1: State the research and null hypotheses.

   H_1: The proportion of criminal justice majors who support Megan's Law is different from the proportion of noncriminal justice majors who support Megan's Law.

   $H_1: \pi_1 \neq \pi_2$

H_0: There is no difference between the proportion of criminal justice majors and the proportion of noncriminal justice majors who support Megan's Law.

$$H_0: \pi_1 = \pi_2$$

We use the Greek letter π (pi) to symbolize the population proportion, while p is the symbol for the sample proportion.

Step 2: Calculate the proportion of criminal justice majors (p_1) and the proportion of noncriminal justice majors (p_2) who support Megan's Law. You will recall that our formula for calculating a proportion is:

$$\text{proportion} \, (p) = \frac{\text{frequency} \, (f)}{\text{total} \, (n)}$$

The proportion of criminal justice majors who support Megan's Law equals .85 (187/220), while the proportion of noncriminal justice majors who support Megan's Law is .71 (119/167).

Step 3: Calculate the pooled sample proportion (P^*). The pooled sample proportion is calculated using the following formula:

$$P^* = \frac{n_1 p_1 + n_2 p_2}{n_1 + n_2}$$

The pooled sample proportion is a combination of the proportion of each group multiplied by its sample size divided by the total sample size. We simply place the appropriate values into the formula and solve for P^* as follows:

$$P^* = \frac{(220)(.85) + (167)(.71)}{220 + 167}$$

$$P^* = \frac{187 + 118.57}{387}$$

$$P^* = .79$$

Step 4: Calculate the standard error of the difference in proportions ($sp_1 - p_2$). The following formula is used to calculate the standard error of the difference in proportions:

$$sp_1 - p_2 = \sqrt{\left[P^* \left(1 - P^* \right) \left(n_1 + n_2 \right) \right] / \left(n_1 n_2 \right)}$$

Substituting our data into the formula, we obtain the following:

$$sp_1 - p_2 = \sqrt{[.79(1-.79)(220+167)]/(220*167)}$$

$$= \sqrt{[.79(.21)(387)]/36,740}$$

$$= \sqrt{[(.17)(387)]/36,740}$$

$$= \sqrt{65.79/36,740}$$

$$= \sqrt{.002}$$

$$= .04$$

Step 5: Calculate the z statistic. The z statistic is determined using the following formula:

$$z = \frac{p_1 - p_2}{sp_1 - p_2}$$

We simply subtract the proportion for group 2 from the proportion of group 1 and divide by the standard error of the difference in proportions. Substituting our data into the formula, we determine the z statistic as follows:

$$z = \frac{.85 - .71}{.04} = 3.50$$

Step 6: Compare the calculated z statistic with the critical z value.

We are now ready to compare the calculated z with the critical z value found in the z distribution table (Table A in Appendix A). Because our hypothesis is nondirectional, we must divide our alpha level by two, to ensure that an equal proportion of the critical region occurs in both tails of the z distribution. An alpha level of .05 results in a critical region of .025 in both the upper and lower tails of the distribution. Consulting the z distribution table, we locate column C (area beyond z) and proceed down the column until we have reached the selected alpha level of .025. The z-score that corresponds with an alpha level of .025 is 1.96. Remember, 1.96 is the critical value that defines the beginning of the critical region for the upper tail of the z distribution. What about the critical value that defines the critical region for the lower tail of the distribution? Because the z distribution is symmetrical, the lower half of the distribution is an exact duplicate of the upper half. Thus, if 1.96 defines the upper critical region, then −1.96 must define the lower critical region. In comparing the test statistic with the critical value, we find that z calculated (3.50) is larger than z critical (1.96). We illustrate this comparison in Figure 8.8.

FIGURE 8.8 *z* test for proportions for support of Megan's Law by major

Step 7: Interpret findings.

Now that we have determined that the *z* statistic exceeds the critical *z* value, we must interpret the meaning of this finding. Our interpretation is based on making a decision about the null hypothesis. Because the calculated *z* statistic falls within the critical region, our decision is to reject the null hypothesis of no difference between the two proportions and accept the research hypothesis that the two population proportions are different. More precisely, our findings show that, among the student population, a higher proportion of criminal justice majors supports Megan's Law (.85) than do non-criminal justice majors (.71).

You are now ready to give the *z* test for proportions a try. Complete TryIT! Box 8.3 before moving on to calculating *z* tests using Excel.

TryIT!

BOX 8.3

In a study of judicial attitudes toward sentencing guidelines, researchers hypothesized that a higher proportion of female judges than of male judges would support the guidelines. The data is presented below.

	Male Judges	Female Judges	Totals
Support Guidelines			
Yes	20	29	49
No	30	21	51
Totals	50	50	100

Step 1: State the research and null hypotheses.

Step 2: Calculate the proportion of male and female judges who support the sentencing guidelines.

Step 3: Calculate the pooled sample proportion.

Step 4: Calculate the standard error of the difference in proportions.

Step 5: Calculate the z statistic.

Step 6: Compare the calculated z statistic with the critical z value.

Step 7: Interpret findings.

8.4 Using Excel to Compute z Tests

We would now like to turn your attention to using Excel for calculating both one-sample z tests and z tests for proportions. Two research problems are presented that are accompanied by step-by-step illustrations for performing a z test.

One-Sample z Test

The parole board has decided to implement an orientation program for inmates soon to be released on parole. The program is designed to decrease the number of parole violations among parolees. The researcher has found that the average number of parole violations among the population of parolees over the past two years is 2.25. The researcher draws a random sample of 50 parolees who have gone through the new orientation program and finds that the average number of parole violations for the sample is equal to 2.06, with a standard deviation of 1.28. The researcher hypothesizes that the sample of parolees who have gone through the orientation program will have a lower number of parole violations than the population of parolees who have not gone through the program. The data is presented in Table 8.2 on page 210.

Step 1: State the research and null hypotheses. These are given in notational form in cell a2.

Step 2: Calculate the mean and standard deviation for the sample of parolees using the procedures outlined in Chapters 4 and 5 for frequency distributions.

Step 3: Calculate the standard error of the mean using the following formula:

$$s_{\bar{x}} = \frac{s}{\sqrt{n-1}}$$

Place the cursor in cell b14 and write: =b13/(sqrt(c10–1)).

b13 is the cell location for the standard deviation of the sample.
sqrt is the symbol for square root.
c10 is the cell location for the sample size.

Step 4: Calculate the z statistic using the following formula:

$$z = \frac{\bar{X} - \mu}{s_{\bar{x}}}$$

Place the cursor in cell b15 and write: =(b12–b11)/b14.

b12 is the cell location for the sample mean.
b11 is the cell location for the population mean.
b14 is the cell location for the standard error of the mean.

TABLE 8.2 One-Sample z Test

	A	B	C	D	E
1	TABLE 8.2 One-Sample z Test				
2	$H_1: \bar{X} < \mu$ $H_0: \bar{X} \geq \mu$				
3		Violations (X)	Frequency (f)	fx	$f(X - \bar{X})^2$
4		5	3	15	25.93
5		4	2	8	7.53
6		3	7	21	6.19
7		2	23	46	0.08
8		1	13	13	14.61
9		0	2	0	8.49
10	Sum		50	103	62.82
11	Population mean (μ)	2.25			
12	Sample mean ($\bar{X}$)	2.06			
13	Standard deviation (s)	1.28			
14	$s_{\bar{x}}$	0.18			
15	z statistic	−1.04			
16	Critical z	−1.64			

Step 5: Compare the calculated z statistic to the critical z value. Determine the critical z value using the z distribution table (Table A) located in Appendix A for a one-tailed test at the .05 alpha level. The critical z value is equal to 1.64—or, in our case, is −1.64, because we hypothesized that the sample mean would be lower than the population mean. The direction of the difference for our z statistic is correct ($z = -1.04$); however, the value of the calculated z statistic does not equal or exceed the critical z value of −1.64.

Step 6: Interpret findings. Because the calculated z (−1.04) does not fall within the critical region, we are unable to reject the null hypothesis, and must therefore conclude that there is no difference in the average number of violations between the sample of program participants and the population of nonparticipants. Thus, the difference between the two means is attributed to sampling error and not the effects of the program.

z Test for Proportions

A researcher believes that victim testimony at parole hearings has an effect on the parole board's decision to grant parole. She draws a random sample of 160 parole hearings with 80 having victim testimony and 80 without victim testimony. The data is presented in Table 8.3.

Step 1: State the research and null hypotheses. These are given in notational form in cell a2. Notice that the research hypothesis is nondirectional. That is, we are comparing the proportion of cases involving victim testimony in which the defendant was granted parole with the proportion of cases without victim testimony that were granted parole. The null hypothesis suggests that there is no difference between the two population proportions ($\pi_1 = \pi_2$).

Step 2: Calculate the proportions for both groups by dividing the frequency of each attribute by the sample size. For group 1 (victim testimony) place the cursor in cell d3 and write: =c3/c5. Click on the lower right-hand corner of cell d3 and drag the cursor down through cell d5. This will create the rest of the proportion column for group 1.

c3 is the cell location for the frequency of the victim testimony sample granted parole.
c5 is the cell location for the total frequency for victim testimony.
$ holds the column and row constant.

For group 2, place the cursor in cell f3 and write: =e3/e5. To create the rest of the proportion column for group 2, click on the lower right-hand corner of cell f3 and drag the cursor to cell f5.

e3 is the cell location for the frequency of the no victim testimony sample granted parole.

e5 is the cell location for the total frequency for no victim testimony.
$ holds the column and row constant.

Step 3: Calculate the pooled sample proportion ($P*$) using the following formula:

$$P* = \frac{n_1 p_1 + n_2 p_2}{n_1 + n_2}$$

Place the cursor in cell b6 and write the following formula: =((c5*d3)+(e5*f3))/ (c5+e5)

d3 and f3 are the cell locations for the proportions p_1 (victim testimony-granted parole) and p_2 (no victim testimony-granted parole).
c5 and e5 are the cell locations for the sample sizes n_1 (victim testimony) and n_2 (no victim testimony).
*, +, and /, are the symbols for multiplication, addition, and division respectively.

Step 4: Calculate the standard error of the difference in proportions ($sp_1 - p_2$) using the following formula:

$$sp_1 - p_2 = \sqrt{\left[P*\left(1 - P*\right)\left(n_1 + n_2\right)\right] / \left(n_1 n_2\right)}$$

Place the cursor in cell b7 and write: =sqrt((b6*(1-b6)*g5)/(c5*e5))

b6 is the cell location for the pooled sample proportion.
g5 is the cell location for the total sample size ($n_1 + n_2$).
c5 and e5 are the cell locations for the sample size of group 1 (victim testimony) and group 2 (no victim testimony).
sqrt is the symbol for square root.

Step 5: Calculate the z statistic. The formula is given as:

$$z = \frac{p_1 - p_2}{sp_1 - p_2}$$

Place the cursor in cell b8 and write: =(d3–f3)/b7

d3 is the cell location for the proportion for p1 (victim testimony-granted parole).
f3 is the cell location for the proportion for p2 (no victim testimony-granted parole).
b7 is the cell location for the standard error of the difference in proportions.

Step 6: Compare the calculated z statistic with the critical z value found in Table A (Appendix A). Because we have a nondirectional hypothesis, the critical regions must be located in both tails of the distribution to account for both types of directional differences ($\pi_1 > \pi_2$ or $\pi_1 < \pi_2$). Once again, this is accomplished by dividing our alpha level in half so that one-half of the critical region is in the upper tail of the

TABLE 8.3 z Test for Proportions

	A	B	C	D	E	F	G
1	TABLE 8.3 z Test for Proportions						
2	$H_1: \pi_1 \neq \pi_2$ $H_0: \pi_1 = \pi_2$		Victim Testimony (f_1)	Proportion (p_1)	No Victim Testimony (f_2)	Proportion (p_2)	Totals
3		Granted parole	54	0.68	64	0.80	118
4		Denied parole	26	0.33	16	0.20	42
5	Totals		80	1.00	80	1.00	160
6	*P**	0.74					
7	*sp*$_1$ - *p*$_2$	0.07					
8	z statistic	-1.80					
9	critical z	-1.96					

distribution and the other half is located in the lower tail of the distribution. With our standard alpha level of .05, each tail of the distribution is defined as .025 of the area beyond z (column C in the z distribution table). The critical z value that corresponds with .025 of the area beyond z is 1.96 and −1.96.

Step 7: Interpret findings. Because our calculated z statistic (−1.80) is not equal to or greater than the critical z value (−1.96), we are unable to reject the null hypothesis of no difference. We conclude that the proportion of offenders granted parole does not differ with regard to the presence of victim testimony at the parole hearing. More specifically, those who have victim testimony at the hearing are equally as likely to be granted parole as are those without victim testimony. The differences in the sample proportions are attributed to sampling error.

8.5 Assumptions of z Tests

Both the one-sample z test and the z test for proportions assume that the sample is drawn from a normally distributed population. This seems to be a reasonable assumption, given that the one-sample z test compares a sample mean with a known population mean. For large samples (n > 30), we can safely assume that the sample is normally distributed, which enables us to use the normal curve (z distribution) to make a decision concerning the null hypothesis. The z test for proportions, however, does not use means but, rather, proportions. Is it possible to assume that the sample for a proportion is normally distributed? Recall our discussion in Chapter 7 concerning the central limit theorem. This theorem informs us that, for sufficiently large samples, the sampling distribution of a statistic will be normally distributed regardless of the shape of the population distribution. Therefore, it is necessary that we have a large enough sample in order to satisfy this assumption. Once again, a sample size of 30 or more is usually sufficient to assume normality.

What if our sample is not large enough to assume normality? With small samples ($n < 30$), we simply use the t distribution in place of the z distribution. We used this procedure when constructing confidence intervals for small samples as discussed in Chapter 7. The t distribution raises the critical value that we need to exceed in order to reject the null hypothesis. For example, when using a two-tailed test at the .05 significance level, the critical value from the z distribution table is 1.96, regardless of the sample size. This is okay if the normality assumption is satisfied ($n > 30$). Let's assume, however, that our sample size was 20. Because we cannot assume normality, we are unable to use the z distribution but, rather, must use the one-sample t test in place of z. The critical value of t for a two-tailed test at the .05 significance level is 2.09.

If the normality assumption for the z test for proportions is violated—as is the case with a small sample—then we must use alternative statistical procedures, known as nonparametric statistics. These statistical procedures are commonly referred to as distribution free statistics, because they make no assumptions about the shape of the sampling distribution of the statistic. The appropriate statistical test for a nominal level variable is Chi-square and for an ordinal level variable is Spearman's rho. We discuss both of these statistical procedures in Chapter 9.

A second assumption that must be satisfied for the one-sample z test is that the dependent variable is measured at either the interval or ratio level. This is a requirement for the calculation of means. The z test for proportions assumes that the dependent variable is measured at the nominal or ordinal level; thus, we are unable to calculate a mean, and must rely on the proportions for each of the attributes.

8.6 Summary

This chapter presented the logic of hypothesis testing and how statistical tests are used to make decisions concerning the null hypothesis of no difference. A discussion of research and null hypotheses was presented as well as a discussion of directional and nondirectional hypotheses. The importance of the significance level and its effect on errors in decision making regarding the null hypothesis was also addressed. Decreasing the significance level guards against Type I error but increases the risk of making a Type II error, whereas increasing the significance level guards against Type II error but increases the risk of Type I error.

We presented two statistical tests in this chapter, known as the one-sample z test and the z test for proportions. The one-sample z test is used to test a hypothesis about a single population mean. This is accomplished by comparing differences between a sample mean and a known population mean. Specifically, researchers ask whether the sample mean is different than the population mean as the result of some intervention, program, or known differences between the sample and the population. This technique is commonly used for evaluating the effectiveness of a program in which an experimental design could not be used. In order to use this statistical procedure, we must assume that the dependent variable is measured at the interval or ratio level and that the sample mean is normally distributed.

The z test for proportions is used to test hypotheses concerning two population proportions. Researchers typically want to know whether two population proportions are equal, based on the analysis of sample proportions. Using this statistical test assumes that the dependent variable is measured at the nominal or ordinal level and that the sampling distribution of the proportion is normally distributed.

This chapter also provided step-by-step calculations for both the one-sample z test and z test for proportions. Furthermore, each of the statistical techniques were conducted using Excel. It is important to note that both of these techniques require sufficiently large sample sizes in order to satisfy the normality assumption.

Key Terms

research hypothesis	critical value
null hypothesis	statistically significant
nondirectional hypothesis	one-tailed test
directional hypothesis	two-tailed test
Type I error	one-sample z test
Type II error	z test for proportions
significance level (alpha)	

TryIT! Answers

Box 8.1

H_1: Probation officers are less satisfied or equally as satisfied with their careers compared to parole officers. (Directional Hypothesis)

H_2: The frequency of drug use between high school dropouts and high school graduates is equal. (Nondirectional Hypothesis)

H_3: The rate of institutional misconduct does not differ between Latino and Asian inmates. (Nondirectional Hypothesis)

H_4: Male police officers have lower or equal rates of burnout than female police officers. (Directional Hypothesis)

H_5: Private attorneys have a lower or equal average number of acquittals than do public defenders. (Directional Hypothesis)

H_6: The number of misdemeanor offenses committed by rural and urban adolescents is equal. (Nondirectional Hypothesis)

H_7: The level of fear of crime for females is less than or equal to the level of fear for males. (Directional Hypothesis)

H_8: The rate of absenteeism is not different between correctional officers and police officers. (Nondirectional Hypothesis)

Box 8.2

Step 1: State the research and null hypotheses.

H_1: Misconduct differs between program participants and nonparticipants.

H_0: Misconduct does not differ between program participants and nonparticipants.

$$H_1 : \bar{X} \neq \mu$$
$$H_0 : \bar{X} = \mu$$

Step 2: Compute the mean and standard deviation for the sample.

Subject No.	MRs (X)	$(X - \bar{X})^2$
1	0	2.04
2	2	0.33
3	0	2.04
4	1	0.18
5	3	2.47
6	0	2.04
7	4	6.61
Sum	10	15.71
Mean ($\bar{X}$)	1.43	
Standard deviation (s)	1.62	

Step 3: Calculate the standard error of the mean.

$$s_{\bar{x}} = \frac{1.62}{\sqrt{7-1}} = .66$$

Step 4: Calculate the z statistic.

$$z = \frac{1.43 - 2.71}{.66} = -1.94$$

Step 5: Compare the calculated z statistic with the critical z value.

We advanced a nondirectional hypothesis in which we hypothesized that the sample mean was different from the population mean. The critical value using a two-tailed test at the .05 significance level is equal to -1.96. Because our calculated z statistic of -1.94 does not exceed the critical value of -1.96, we are unable to reject the null hypothesis.

Step 6: Interpret findings.

There is no statistically significant difference between program participants and nonparticipants with regard to institutional misconduct. The difference between the sample mean and the population mean is the result of sampling error, and not an actual difference between the sample and the population.

Box 8.3

Step 1: State the research and null hypotheses.

> H_1: The proportion of female judges (π_1) who support sentencing guidelines is higher than the proportion of male judges (π_2) who support the guidelines.

> H_0: The proportion of female judges (π_1) who support sentencing guidelines is less than or equal to the proportion of male judges (π_2) who support the guidelines.

$H_1: \pi_1 > \pi_2$
$H_0: \pi_1 \leq \pi_2$

Step 2: Calculate the proportion of male and female judges who support the guidelines.

$$P_{1(males)} = \frac{20}{50} = .40$$
$$P_{2(females)} = \frac{29}{50} = .58$$

Step 3: Calculate the pooled sample proportion.

$$P* = \frac{(50)(.40)+(50)(.58)}{50+50} = .49$$

Step 4: Calculate the standard error of the difference in proportions.

$$SP_1 - P_2 = \sqrt{[.49(1-.49)(50+50)]/(50)(50)}$$
$$= \sqrt{[.49(.51)(100)]/2500}$$
$$= \sqrt{[(.25)(100)]/2500}$$
$$= \sqrt{25/2500}$$
$$= \sqrt{.01}$$
$$= .10$$

Step 5: Calculate the z statistic.

$$z = \frac{.40-.58}{.10} = -1.80$$

Step 6: Compare the calculated z statistic with the critical z value.

Because we hypothesized a directional difference between female and male judges, the critical region will be located in one tail of the z distribution table. Using a one-tailed test with a .05 significance level, we find that the critical z value is equal to 1.64. Because our calculated z statistic of 1.80 is larger than 1.64, we reject the null hypothesis of no difference. That is, −1.80 is larger than −1.64, and is in the hypothesized direction.

Step 7: Interpret findings.

Female judges are significantly more likely to support sentencing guidelines than are male judges. Because the difference between the two sample proportions was statistically significant, we concluded that, within the population of judges, a higher proportion of female judges than of male judges supports sentencing guidelines.

8.7 Problems

1. A researcher hypothesizes that juveniles will have a greater number of police contacts than will adults. Identify the type of hypothesis and whether a one-tailed or two-tailed test is warranted.

2. A statement of no difference is known as what type of hypothesis?

3. If a researcher fails to reject the null hypothesis when the null hypothesis is false, the researcher committed what type of error?

4. What proportion of the critical region is located in the upper tail of the probability distribution for a two-tailed test at the .05 alpha level?

5. A researcher hypothesizes a difference in disciplinary infractions between a sample of inmates who participated in an anger management program and the population of inmates who did not participate in the program. Write the research and null hypotheses in both text and notational form.

6. Which statistical technique is most appropriate for testing the hypothesis in question 5?

7. Conduct a statistical test for the hypothesis in question 6 using the following data and an alpha level of .05 (disciplinary infractions is the dependent variable):

$\mu = 5.40$
$\bar{X} = 5.10$
$s = 1.60$
$n = 120$

Identify the following: (a) calculated z statistic, (b) critical z value, and (c) decision about the null.

8. Using a .05 alpha level and a one-tailed test, identify whether the following calculated z statistics are statistically significant.

	z statistic
a.	1.98
b.	−2.15
c.	.98
d.	−3.12
e.	1.61

9. To say that a relationship is statistically significant, the calculated test statistic must _____ or _____ the critical value.

10. Using a .05 alpha level and a two-tailed test, make a decision regarding the null hypothesis for each of the following calculated z statistics.

	z statistic
a.	−2.34
b.	1.90
c.	3.21
d.	.45
e.	−2.05

11. A researcher believes that correctional officers are more likely than police officers to favor the death penalty. Write the research and null hypotheses in both text and notational form.

12. Which statistical technique is most appropriate for testing the hypothesis in question 11?

13. Conduct a statistical test for the hypothesis in question 12, using the following data and an alpha level of .05 (support of the death penalty is the dependent variable):

	Correctional Officers	Police Officers
Support of Death Penalty		
Favor	40	40
Oppose	25	38

Identify the following: (a) calculated z statistic, (b) critical z value, and (c) decision about the null.

14. Identify the critical z value for the following:

	Tailed Test	Alpha Level
a.	1	.05
b.	1	.01
c.	1	.10
d.	2	.10
e.	2	.01
f.	2	.05

15. What decision would you make concerning the null hypothesis for each of the following? Assume that the calculated z statistic is in the hypothesized direction.

	Calculated z statistic	Critical z value
a.	−1.78	1.64
b.	1.56	1.64
c.	1.96	1.96
d.	2.09	2.58

16. A researcher wants to know if high-income earners are more likely to support three strikes legislation than low-income earners. What would be the appropriate statistical test to answer this question?

17. A researcher hypothesizes that juveniles who participated in a behavior modification program will have a lower average number of school citations for behavioral problems than the population of juveniles from which the sample was drawn. The following data is given for the sample of 40 juveniles who participated in the program. The population mean (μ) is equal to 2.20. Enter the data into Excel and conduct a one-sample z test. Make a decision about the null hypothesis and interpret your findings.

Citations (X)	Frequency (f)
5	7
2	8
1	5
0	20

18. A researcher hypothesizes a difference between employed and unemployed persons in regards to being a victim of a crime. Enter the following data into Excel and conduct a z test for proportions to test the researcher's hypothesis. Be sure to make a decision about the null hypothesis and interpret your findings.

	Employed	*Unemployed*
Victim of Crime		
Yes	45	28
No	170	55

Statistical Analysis for Nominal and Ordinal Variables: Chi-Square and Spearman's Rho

ExploreIT!

You are a law student who has spent quite some time studying the sentencing process. You have observed that individuals who indicate remorse seem to be handed the minimum sentence more often than those who show no remorse. You design a study for your senior law project to address this issue. The study consists of variables measured at the nominal level. The independent variable is "remorse," measured in terms of Yes—the offender showed remorse—or No—the offender failed to show remorse. The dependent variable is "sentence length," measured in terms of Minimum—the convicted felon was given the minimum sentence—or Other—the offender received a sentence other than the minimum sentence. Is there support for your hypothesis that offenders showing remorse are more likely to be handed the minimum sentence than offenders who fail to show remorse? In this case, your hypothesis can be tested with a nonparametric procedure called chi-square.

We begin this chapter with a brief review of our discussion in Chapter 1, concerning two types of inferential statistics—parametric and nonparametric. Parametric statistics require us to make some explicit assumptions about the level of measurement of the variable and its distributional shape. Specifically, the variable must be measured at the interval or ratio level and must be normally distributed. What about situations in which these assumptions are violated, where either the variable is measured categorically or the distribution is skewed? Fortunately, there are statistical procedures designed to handle such situations. These statistical tests collectively are known as nonparametric statistics. **Nonparametric statistics** *are tests that do not make assumptions concerning the distribution of the variables in the population.* Thus, nonparametric statistics commonly are used to test hypotheses involving nominal- and ordinal-level variables. Two of the most common types of nonparametric tests used in criminal justice research include chi-square and Spearman's rho.

nonpara-
metric
statistics

In this chapter, the one-sample and two-sample chi-square are introduced. Next, we turn to two common tests used for measuring the strength of the relationship for nominal-level variables. The two measures are known as phi and Cramer's *V*. Before presenting Excel examples of the techniques presented in this chapter, we look at one final test called Spearman's rank-order correlation coefficient or Spearman's rho. This is an appropriate measure of the correlation or association between two variables when the variables are measured at the ordinal level and/or the assumption of normality is violated.

9.1 Chi-Square: Introduction

chi-square **Chi-square** *is a nonparametric statistical test used for assessing how well the distribution of observed frequencies of a categorical variable fits the distribution of expected frequencies.* Below are several hypotheses in which chi-square is an appropriate statistical test.

Hypothesis 1: Female defendants are more likely than male defendants to plead guilty.

Hypothesis 2: White officers are more likely to be charged with racial discrimination than non-White officers.

Hypothesis 3: The relative frequency of criminal justice students satisfied with their selection of a criminal justice major differs among seniors, juniors, sophomores, and freshmen.

Hypothesis 4: Sociology students will not choose criminal justice, family studies, and minority studies equally as their major area of concentration.

In the above examples, all the variables are categorical. In Hypothesis 1, there are two categorical variables, each with two attributes. The variable defendants' "sex" consists of the attributes Male and Female; the variable defendants' "plea" consists of the attributes Guilty and Not Guilty. Likewise, Hypothesis 2 contains two categorical variables, each with two attributes. What are the variables? What are the attributes? You are correct if you identified the variables "race" and "charged with racial discrimination" as the two variables. The attributes for the variable "race" are White and Non-White, and the attributes for the variable "charged with racial discrimination" are Yes and No. Similarly, there are two variables in Hypothesis 3. One variable is "students' satisfaction" with selection of major, and it consists of two attributes —Yes and No. The other variable is "academic class standing," and it consists of four attributes—Seniors, Juniors, Sophomores, and Freshmen.

Hypothesis 4 is a bit different from the other three hypotheses in that it consists of only one variable—"major area of concentration." This variable has three attributes—Criminal Justice, Family Studies, and Minority Studies. With all the hypotheses, the appropriate statistical analysis is the chi-square. Because the first three hypotheses consist of two categorical variables, the two sample chi-square test is appropriate. In contrast, the one-sample chi-square test is used in situations in which there is only one categorical variable as illustrated in Hypothesis 4. We will now examine the one-sample **one-sample** chi-square. Formally, a **one-sample chi-square** is *a statistical test used to examine how* **chi-square** *observations within a single sample distribute across a set of categories.*

9.2 One-Sample Chi-Square

Procedures for Calculating the One-Sample Chi-Square

We demonstrate the procedures for a one-sample chi-square by further examining Hypothesis 4. As with all statistical procedures, the first step requires stating the research and null hypotheses.

Step 1: State the research and null hypotheses.

In this example, the research hypothesis states that sociology students will not choose criminal justice, family studies, and minority studies equally as their major area of concentration. The null hypothesis is the logical opposite of the research hypothesis; that is, students will choose the three areas of concentration equally. More formally, the hypotheses are as follows:

H_1: Sociology students do not choose criminal justice, family studies, and minority studies equally as their academic major.

$$H_1: f_1 \neq f_2 \neq f_3$$

H_0: Sociology students do chose criminal justice, family studies, and minority studies equally as their academic major.

$$H_0: f_1 = f_2 = f_3$$

Our notational symbols indicate that the frequency (f) of each of the three groups is not equal for the research hypothesis, and the frequency for the three groups is equal for the null hypothesis. Suppose a researcher randomly selects 75 sociology students, and determines their major areas of concentration as: 30 (40%) criminal justice, 20 (27%) family studies, and 25 (33%) minority studies. By observing the data, it seems that students prefer some areas of concentration over others. The question is whether the discrepancy represents real differences in preference among the population of sociology students or whether such discrepancy is due purely to sampling error. To address this question, the researcher will compare the observed frequencies to the expected frequencies (also called theoretical frequencies). The expected frequencies are those that are expected if the null hypothesis is true; that is, the observations are equally distributed among the categories (usually called cells). In our example, it is expected—under the null hypothesis—that students will choose among the three areas of concentration equally. The chi-square statistic involves comparing the distribution of observed frequencies to the distribution of expected frequencies. The greater the discrepancy, the greater the value of the chi-square statistic (symbolized as X^2). In turn, a large X^2 value is likely to result in rejecting the null hypothesis rendering support for the research hypothesis.

Step 2: Determine the observed frequencies (f_o) and expected frequencies (f_e).

Although the observed frequencies are known, researchers must calculate the expected frequencies. In one sample case, this procedure is relatively easy. The calculations simply involve dividing the number of observations by the number of cells, as illustrated in the following formula:

$$f_e = \frac{n}{k}$$

n = total sample size
k = number of categories (cells)

In our example, 75 divided by 3 is 25. That is, the null hypothesis predicts that 25 students will select each of the three areas of concentration.

Step 3: For each cell, separately, obtain the squared difference between the observed and expected frequency and divide by the expected frequency. Sum the values across all cells.

Step 3 is the most difficult. It involves looking at the difference between the observed and expected frequency for each of the three cells. The difference is then squared and divided by the expected frequency. Summing the cell values produces a chi-square statistic. In other words, the chi-square statistic is obtained by subtracting the expected from the observed frequency, squaring that value, and dividing by the expected frequency.

This process is repeated for each of the cells. By summing the values for all of the cells, a chi-square statistic is calculated. The formula is as follows:

$$\chi^2 = \Sigma \frac{\left(f_o - f_e\right)^2}{f_e}$$

By applying the formula to our example, the following chi-square statistic is calculated:

$$\chi^2 = \frac{\left(30 - 25\right)^2}{25} + \frac{\left(20 - 25\right)^2}{25} + \frac{\left(25 - 25\right)^2}{25}$$

$$= \frac{25}{25} + \frac{25}{25} + \frac{0}{25}$$

$$= 1 + 1 + 0$$

$$= 2$$

Step 4: Compare the calculated chi-square statistic to the critical chi-square value found in the chi-square distribution table (Table E) located in Appendix A.

You will recall from earlier chapters that this step involves making a decision about the null hypothesis. We make this decision by comparing the calculated X^2 statistic with the critical X^2 value. In order to locate the critical value of X^2, two pieces of information are needed: (a) the degrees of freedom, which is determined by the number of cells (categories) minus one $(k-1)$ (in our example, the degrees of freedom is 2 $(3-1=2)$; and (b) the alpha level (α), or level of significance (p). Consistent with other statistical procedures discussed in this text, the conventional levels are .01 and .05. In our example, we select an alpha level of .05. With this information in hand, we can determine the critical chi-square value located in the chi-square distribution table. As shown in Table 9.1, the critical value of X^2 $(df = 2, \alpha = .05)$ equals 5.99. Because the calculated chi-square statistic of 2 is less than the critical value of 5.99, we fail to reject the null hypothesis. Thus, the sample observations do not support our research hypothesis.

TABLE 9.1 Sample Chi-Square Distribution Table

	Significance Level (α)			
df	0.1	0.05	0.01	0.001
1	2.71	3.84	6.64	10.83
2	4.61	5.99	9.21	13.82
3	6.25	7.82	11.35	16.27
4	7.78	9.49	13.28	18.48
5	9.24	11.07	15.09	20.52

Step 5: Interpret findings.

Our data failed to support the research hypothesis. We must conclude that the observed differences in students' selections of concentrations are simply the result of sampling error and not actual differences among the population of sociology students. As you can see, the calculations for a one-sample chi-square statistic are relatively straightforward and involve very few steps.

You are now ready to give a one-sample chi-square a try! Complete TryIT! Box 9.1 before moving on to section 9.3.

TryIT!   BOX **9.1**

The director of corrections is interested in knowing whether officers prefer a particular shift. Suppose 150 correctional officers indicated their shift preference, and the following observations were obtained: 85 officers prefer the day shift (7:00 A.M.–3:00 P.M.), 40 officers prefer the evening shift (3:00 P.M.–11:00 P.M.), and 25 officers prefer the night shift (11:00 P.M.–7:00 A.M.). Given this information, compute the chi-square statistic to test the director's hypothesis that officers prefer working particular shifts.

Step 1: State the research and null hypotheses.

Step 2: Determine the observed and expected frequencies.

Step 3: For each cell, separately, obtain the squared difference between the observed and expected frequencies and divide by the expected frequency. Sum values across all cells.

Step 4: Compare the calculated chi-square statistic with the critical chi-square value, using an alpha level of .05.

Step 5: Interpret findings.

9.3 Two-Sample Chi-Square

The one-sample chi-square test is used to examine how observations within a single sample will distribute across a set of categories. If you are interested in studying the frequency of defendants pleading guilty and not guilty, the one-sample chi-square is appropriate. In this case, you have one sample of defendants and two categories—guilty and not guilty. Let's extend this example. Suppose you think that male and female defendants differ in the relative frequency of guilty and not guilty pleas. In this study, you still have two categories (guilty and not guilty). Your hypothesis, however, now consists of comparing two samples of defendants (male and female) in terms of the distribution of guilty and not guilty pleas. More specifically, you are hypothesizing that the "offender's sex" (X) has an effect on the "type of plea" (Y). In this case, the two-sample chi-square statistic is appropriate. Formally, a **two-sample chi-square** is *a statistical test used to examine how observations with two samples distribute across a set of categories.*

two-sample chi-square

As you will see shortly, the logic and procedures for the two sample chi-square are very similar to the one sample chi-square discussed in the previous section. The two-sample chi-square statistic involves comparing the distribution of observed frequencies with the distribution of expected frequencies. A comparison is then made between the calculated chi-square statistic and the critical chi-square value found in the chi-square distribution table. If the calculated statistic equals or exceeds the critical value, then the researcher is able to reject the null hypothesis of no difference between the two samples in favor of the research hypothesis. That is, the researcher can say that the difference between the two samples (male and female defendants)—in terms of the relative frequency of guilty and not guilty pleas—is due to an actual difference among the population of defendants and not the result of sampling error. The logic and procedures of the two-sample chi-square test are presented in the following section.

Procedures for Calculating the Two-Sample Chi-Square

Let's say that you are interested in testing the relative frequency of guilty and not guilty pleas among male and female defendants. The first step is to state the hypotheses.

Step 1: State the research and null hypotheses.

H_1: Male and female defendants differ in the relative frequency of guilty and not guilty pleas.

$$H_1 : f_{group1} \neq f_{group2}$$

H_0: Male and female defendants do not differ in the relative frequency of guilty and not guilty pleas.

$$H_0 : f_{group1} = f_{group2}$$

Step 2: Record observed frequencies (f_o) in terms of a contingency table and calculate the row sum (RS), column sum (CS), and the grand sum (GS).

Suppose you test your hypothesis by observing the pleas of 25 male and 25 female defendants. At this point, you will record your observations in a contingency table. In this example, you will construct a 2×2 contingency table. The size of the contingency table depends on the number of attributes for each of our variables. Because our example consists of an independent and dependent variable, each with two attributes— "sex" (Male, Female) and "type of plea" (Guilty, Not Guilty)—a 2×2 contingency table is constructed. If our example, however, consisted of an independent variable with

TABLE 9.2 Contingency Table—Type of Plea by Sex

Type of Plea (Y)	Defendant's Sex (X)		Row Sums (RS)
	Male	Female	
Guilty			
observed frequencies (f_o)	15	5	20
expected frequencies (f_e)			
Column Percentages			
Not Guilty			
observed frequencies (f_o)	10	20	30
expected frequencies (f_e)			
Column Percentages			
$X^2 =$			
			Grand Sum (GS)
Column Sums (CS)	25	25	50

two attributes (Male, Female) and a dependent variable with three attributes (Guilty, Not Guilty, No Contest), then a 2×3 contingency table would be required.

Table 9.2 reports our observations in a 2×2 contingency table. As you can see, 15 guilty and 10 not guilty pleas are recorded for male defendants, while 5 guilty and 20 not guilty pleas are recorded for female defendants. At this point, we would like to stress an important point regarding setting up the contingency table. In our discussion of cross-tabulation tables in Chapter 2, we recommended that you always place the independent variable (X) in the columns and the dependent variable (Y) in the rows. Furthermore, we discussed the importance of calculating the percentages for the independent variable within each attribute of the dependent variable to determine the effect of X on Y. The same is true for contingency table analysis (also known as cross-tabulation analysis). If we consistently set our tables up with the independent variable in the columns and the dependent variable in the rows, then we will always calculate the column percentages to aid in our interpretation of the results.

At this step of the process, record the observed frequencies, row and column sums, and the grand sum of the observed frequencies. The row sums are calculated simply by adding the observed frequencies for each attribute of the dependent variable. The column sums require us to add the observed frequencies for each attribute of the independent variable. The grand sum can be calculated by adding either the row sums or the column sums. Be careful, however, to use one or the other, and not both. We have also included space in the contingency table for the expected frequencies, the X^2 statistic, and the column percentages. These values will appear in the contingency table as we complete each step of the analysis.

Step 3: Calculate the expected frequencies (f_e).

Although relatively straightforward, the calculations for the expected frequencies for a two-sample chi-square require a bit more work than the calculations for the one-sample chi-square. With the one-sample chi-square, expected frequencies were calculated by dividing the number of observations by the number of categories or cells. With the two-sample chi-square, the expected frequencies must be calculated for each of the cells containing the observed frequencies (f_o). Put another way, for each observed frequency, we must calculate a corresponding expected frequency (f_e). The number of expected frequencies must equal the number of observed frequencies. In our example, we have a 2×2 table that has four observed frequencies; therefore, we must have four expected frequencies to correspond with each observed frequency. In a 4×4 table, there would be 16 observed frequencies, necessitating the calculation of 16 expected frequencies.

To calculate expected frequencies (f_e), you must multiply the appropriate row sum (RS) by the appropriate column sum (CS), and divide by the grand sum (GS) of the observations. Thus, we use the following formula to calculate expected frequencies:

$$f_e = \frac{(CS)(RS)}{GS}$$

CS = Column Sum
RS = Row Sum
GS = Grand Sum

For instance, the expected frequencies for male defendants pleading guilty is calculated by multiplying 25 (CS) by 20 (RS) and then dividing by 50 (GS), yielding an expected frequency of 10. The expected frequency for male defendants pleading not guilty is calculated by multiplying 25 (CS) by 30 (RS) and then dividing by 50 (GS), yielding an expected frequency of 15. What are the expected frequencies for guilty and not guilty pleas of female defendants? The calculations are the same and are illustrated below:

Expected Frequencies (f_e)

Males / Guilty:	$(25 \times 20)/50 = 10$
Males / Not Guilty:	$(25 \times 30)/50 = 15$
Females / Guilty:	$(25 \times 20)/50 = 10$
Females / Not Guilty:	$(25 \times 30)/50 = 15$

TABLE 9.3 Contingency Table—Type of Plea by Sex

Type of Plea (Y)	Defendant's Sex (X)		Row Sums (RS)
	Male	Female	
Guilty			
observed frequencies (f_o)	15	5	20
expected frequencies (f_e)	10	10	
Column Percentages			
Not Guilty			
observed frequencies (f_o)	10	20	30
expected frequencies (f_e)	15	15	
Column Percentages			
$X^2 =$			
			Grand Sum (GS)
Column Sums (CS)	25	25	50

It should be noted that the expected frequencies for the male and female defendants were identical as the size of the two samples were equal. This will not always be the case. You also will notice that the expected frequencies for guilty and not guilty are quite different, because of the discrepancy between the number of observed guilty pleas (20) compared to the number of observed not guilty pleas (30). Once the expected frequencies have been calculated, we can place them into the contingency table, Table 9.3.

Step 4: For each cell, separately, obtain the sum of the squared difference between the observed and expected frequencies and then divide by the expected frequency. Sum values across all cells.

Although this step might seem complex, it is the same procedure used to calculate the one-sample chi-square. This step involves calculating the difference between the observed and expected frequencies for each cell. The difference is squared and divided by the expected frequency. Summing the values across the cells produces the chi-square statistic. The formula is the same as that used for the one-sample chi-square.

$$\chi^2 = \Sigma \frac{\left(f_o - f_e\right)^2}{f_e}$$

By applying the formula to our example, the chi-square statistic is calculated as follows:

$$\chi^2 = \underbrace{\frac{(15-10)^2}{10}}_{\text{males/guilty}} + \underbrace{\frac{(10-15)^2}{15}}_{\text{males/not guilty}} + \underbrace{\frac{(5-10)^2}{10}}_{\text{females/guilty}} + \underbrace{\frac{(20-15)^2}{15}}_{\text{females/not guilty}}$$

$$= \frac{25}{10} + \frac{25}{15} + \frac{25}{10} + \frac{25}{15}$$

$$= 2.50 + 1.67 + 2.50 + 1.67$$

$$= 8.34$$

Step 5: Calculate the degrees of freedom.

The degrees of freedom are calculated using the following formula:

$$df = (R-1)(C-1)$$
R = total number of rows
C = total number of columns

We simply multiply the total number of rows minus one $(R-1)$ by the total number of columns minus one $(C-1)$. In our example, the degrees of freedom is $(2-1)(2-1) = 1$.

Step 6: Compare the calculated chi-square statistic with the critical chi-square value found in Table E in Appendix A.

We are now ready to compare the calculated chi-square statistic to the critical chi-square value. As always, we also must select an alpha level. We select the conventional alpha level of .05. As can be seen from the chi-square distribution table (Table E in Appendix A), the critical value is equal to 3.84. Because the calculated chi-square statistic of 8.34 is greater than the critical value of 3.84, we are able to reject the null hypothesis and accept the research hypothesis.

Step 7: Interpret findings.

Our data supports the research hypothesis. We are able to conclude that the populations of male and female defendants do differ in the relative frequency of guilty and not guilty pleas. In order to determine *how* guilty pleas differ by sex, it is necessary for us to calculate the percentages for the independent variable. If we consistently place the independent variable in the columns, then we need only to remember to calculate the column percentages. To calculate the column percentages for males, we divide the observed frequency of each attribute of our dependent variable by the column sum. Of the 25 males, 15 plead guilty [(15/25) × 100], resulting in a column percentage of

60%. Repeat this process for males who plead not guilty and for females who plead guilty and not guilty.

Thus, we now know that a higher percentage of males in our sample plead guilty (60%), compared to females (20%). Because our chi-square statistic revealed a significant difference in the frequency of guilty pleas between males and females, we conclude that this difference is attributed to an actual difference in the population parameters (i.e., frequency of males and females pleading guilty) and not the result of sampling error. Even though the calculation of the chi-square statistic is based on the frequencies, it is necessary to calculate the column percentages to determine how the independent variable influences the dependent variable. The completed contingency table is shown in Table 9.4.

TABLE 9.4 Contingency Table—Type of Plea by Sex

Type of Plea (Y)	Defendant's Sex (X)		Row Sums (RS)
	Male	Female	
Guilty			
observed frequencies (f_o)	15	5	20
expected frequencies (f_e)	10	10	
Column Percentages	60%	20%	
Not Guilty			
observed frequencies (f_o)	10	20	30
expected frequencies (f_e)	15	15	
Column Percentages	40%	80%	
$X^2 = 8.34$			
			Grand Sum (GS)
Column Sums (CS)	25	25	50

As you can see, the calculations for a two-sample chi-square statistic are simply an extension of the one-sample case. The key differences are the procedures used to calculate the expected frequencies, the formula for determining the degrees of freedom, and the necessity for calculating percentages for the independent variable.

Try calculating a two-sample chi-square by completing TryIT! Box 9.2.

TryIT!

BOX **9.2**

As chair of the criminal justice department, you want to know whether your students are satisfied with their selection of a criminal justice major. You distribute a survey to a random sample of 100 students (25 at each of the four academic ranks). Using an alpha level of .01, test the chair's hypothesis. Here are your results.

Satisfaction	Academic Rank			
	Freshmen	*Sophomore*	*Junior*	*Senior*
Satisfied	8	15	18	23
Dissatisfied	17	10	7	2

Step 1: State the research and null hypotheses.

Step 2: Record your observations in a contingency table. Notice that this problem requires a 2 × 4 contingency table. You need to compute the row and column sums as well as the grand sum for the observed frequencies.

Step 3: Calculate the expected frequencies.

Step 4: For each cell, obtain the squared difference between the observed and expected frequencies and then divide by the expected frequency. Sum values across all cells.

Step 5: Calculate the degrees of freedom.

Step 6: Compare the calculated X^2 statistic with the critical X^2 value.

Step 7: Interpret findings.

9.4 Measures of Association: Phi Coefficient and Cramer's *V*

After a significant chi-square is detected, the researcher knows that there is a significant relationship between the two variables. The strength of the relationship and the amount of variance in the dependent variable explained by the independent variable are unknown. These two pieces of information can be quite easily obtained. The phi and Cramer's *V* statistics are two measures of association that may be appropriate following a significant chi-square. We look at each of these two measures of association in turn.

Phi Coefficient (Φ)

phi

Phi—*a measure of association appropriate for a 2 × 2 contingency table—is a statistic used to examine the strength of the relationship between two nominal-level variables, each with two attributes.* In an earlier example, we examined the relative frequency of male and female defendants pleading guilty and not guilty. This is an example of a 2 × 2 contingency in which the phi statistic is appropriate.

phi coefficient   The **phi coefficient** *indicates the strength of the relationship.* The larger the value of the coefficient, the stronger the relationship between the two variables. The phi coefficient ranges from 0 (no relationship between the two variables) to 1 (perfect relationship between the two variables). The phi coefficient is calculated by dividing the calculated chi-square statistic by the total sample size and taking the square root of that value. The formula for phi is as follows:

$$\text{phi}(\phi) = \sqrt{\frac{\chi^2}{n}}$$

In examining the relationship between defendant's sex and type of plea, a calculated chi-square of 8.34 was obtained, based on a sample size of 50. With this information, we calculate phi as follows:

$$\text{phi}(\phi) = \sqrt{\frac{8.34}{50}}$$

$$= \sqrt{.17}$$

$$= .41$$

To interpret the strength or magnitude of phi, we present in Figure 9.1 a guideline for interpreting the magnitude of phi. A phi of .41 indicates a moderate relationship between defendant's sex and type of plea.

The squared phi coefficient tells us the amount of variance explained in the dependent variable by the independent variable. In our example, a squared phi of .41 equals .17. This means that 17% of the variance in type of plea is explained or accounted for by defendant's sex. Overall, what can we say? We can conclude that there is a significant and moderate relationship between our two variables, with defendant's sex accounting for 17% of the variance in type of plea.

Cramer's V

In many instances, the chi-square statistic is based on a contingency table larger than a 2×2. In such cases, the phi coefficient is an inappropriate measure of association. For contingency tables larger than 2×2, Cramer's V is recommended as the appropriate measure of association. Like phi, Cramer's V is used for nominal-level variables, and is calculated following a significant chi-square statistic. The value of V ranges in magnitude from 0 (no relationship between the two variables) to 1 (a perfect relationship between the two variables), and its squared value is a measure of the amount of variance in the dependent variable explained by the independent variable. Unlike phi, however, **Cramer's V**   Cramer's V takes into account the size of the contingency table. In short, **Cramer's V—** *a measure of association appropriate for contingency tables larger than 2×2—is a statistic to examine the strength of the relationship between two nominal level variables.*

FIGURE 9.1 Guidelines for interpreting the strength of phi, Cramer's *V*, and rho

Coefficient	Interpretation
.00	none
.10	slight/weak
.20	low/definite
.40	moderate
.60	substantial
.80	high/strong
.90	very high/extremely strong
1.00	perfect

Cramer's *V* is calculated by dividing the calculated chi-square statistic (X^2) by the product of the sample size (n) and the *smaller* of the number of rows or columns minus one (k – 1), and then taking the square root of that value. The formula for Cramer's *V* is:

$$V = \sqrt{\frac{\chi^2}{n(k-1)}}$$

χ^2 = chi-square statistic
n = total sample size (Grand Sum)
k = smaller of the number of rows or number of columns

To illustrate, suppose that 25 males and 25 females indicated preferences for one of three entry-level job positions. This example produces a 2 × 3 contingency table. Suppose the results yielded a chi-square value of 12.31. Based on this information, Cramer's *V* is calculated as follows:

$$V = \sqrt{\frac{12.31}{50(2-1)}}$$

$$= \sqrt{\frac{12.31}{50}}$$

$$= \sqrt{.25}$$

$$= .50$$

[handwritten annotation:]

ans 5

$V = \sqrt{\dfrac{17.8^2}{568(3-1)}} =$

$= \sqrt{\dfrac{316.84}{1136}}$

$= \sqrt{.53}$

$= .53$

A Cramer's *V* statistic of .50 indicates a moderate association between gender and job preference. Like the phi coefficient, a squared Cramer's *V* indicates the amount of variance in the dependent variable explained by the independent variable. In our example, a squared Cramer's *V* of .50 equals .25, which means that 25% of the variance in preference for job position is explained by gender.

As you can see, chi-square is an appropriate statistical technique for data that does not meet the assumptions required for parametric statistical tests. Hence, chi-square is a nonparametric test that is part of a group of distribution free statistical techniques. It is important to note, however, that chi-square cannot be used indiscriminately. The following assumptions apply to its use: (a) the independent and dependent variables are measured at the nominal level, although chi-square can be used for data measured at higher levels; (b) probability sampling is used to select subjects; and (c) adjustments are made for small cell sizes. There should be no fewer than ten expected frequencies for any one cell. For situations involving fewer than ten expected frequencies, a correction procedure must be employed. The two common methods used for adjusting for small cell sizes are Yates's correction for continuity or collapsing the data into fewer cells.*

9.5 Spearman's Rank-Order Correlation Coefficient

Spearman's rank-order correlation coefficient (Spearman's rho)

Like the chi-square statistic, Spearman's rho (r_s) is another very useful nonparametric test. **Spearman's rho** is *a measure of the correlation or association among ordinal (rank) variables.* Thus, rho has more in common with Pearson's correlation coefficient—discussed in Chapter 12—than the chi-square. Because it is classified as a nonparametric test, however, we present it in this chapter. Spearman's rho is an appropriate statistical technique to use when one or both variables are ordinal and/or when the normality assumption required of parametric tests is violated, as is commonly the case with small samples ($n < 30$).

Spearman's rho is a type of correlation coefficient. A correlation coefficient is a numerical summary of the direction and strength of a relationship between two variables. In terms of direction, the coefficient can be positive or negative. A positive correlation means that the two variables covary in the same direction. For example, a positive correlation is expected between officer's rank for length of service and rank on exam score. In other words, a high rank for service length is associated with a high rank on the exam. Likewise, a low rank for service length is associated with a low rank on the exam. A negative correlation means that the two variables covary in the opposite direction. That is, high ranks on one variable are associated with low ranks on another variable. In terms of strength, a correlation coefficient ranges from .00 (no association between the two variables) to 1.00 (a perfect association between the two variables). The strength of a correlation coefficient can be interpreted using the guidelines presented in Figure 9.1.

---

*Miller and Whitehead (1996) provide a thorough explanation for both Yates's correction for continuity and collapsing data into fewer cells. The authors illustrate both correction processes with computational formulas and step-by-step instructions using practical criminal justice examples.

Spearman's rho is appropriate to examine the following hypotheses.

Hypothesis 1: There is a relationship between number of years serving as a police officer and one's ranking on the lieutenant's exam.

Hypothesis 2: Senior class standing is positively related to the number of job offers prior to graduation.

Hypothesis 3: Perception of community crime is related to violence rating of favorite television crime drama.

Procedures for Calculating Spearman's Rho

Let's consider one of these three hypotheses by outlining the steps involved in calculating Spearman's rho. Suppose a researcher is interested in whether greater length of service is related to better performance on the lieutenant's exam. As always, our first step is to state the hypotheses.

Step 1: State the research and null hypotheses.

H_1: An increased length of service as a police officer is related to higher ranking on the lieutenant's exam.

$r_s > 0$

H_0: There is a negative or no relationship between length of service as a police officer and ranking on the exam.

$r_s \leq 0$

Step 2: Rank both the X and Y variables.

The second step requires rank-ordering both the independent (X) and dependent (Y) variables. Suppose the researcher rank orders ten officers in terms of "length of service" (X) and "exam performance" (Y). The observations are presented in Table 9.5.

By observing the data presented in Table 9.5, we see that although Officer Mike ranked first in terms of length of service, he ranked third in performance on the exam; Diane ranked second in both terms of service and performance on the exam; and Officer Tom ranked last in both length of service and exam performance. After both the X and Y variables are ranked, we are ready to move to step 3.

But wait! In many instances, we are unable to rank respondents without encountering ties in the rankings. For example, we may have two officers that entered the police force at the same time; thus, both officers may log six years of service. If so, we must determine rank order by adding the tied ranks and dividing by the number of ties. Let's consider the following illustration, using the data presented in Table 9.6. Suppose that Officers Mike, Diane, and Sue all log ten years with the police, and are thus tied for the first three positions. Officers Patrick and Jeff also are tied, with six years of service. To determine the average rank order of Officers Mike, Diane, and Sue, you must add the first three positions (add tied ranks) and divide by three (number of ties). The average rank is calculated as follows:

$$\frac{1+2+3}{3} = 2$$

Thus, you would assign the three officers a rank of 2. You will notice that Officer Lou is next in terms of length of service. As there is not a tie, Officer Lou is assigned the fourth

TABLE 9.5 Rank-Order of Length of Service and Exam Score

Officer	Length of Service Rank-Order (X)	Lieutenant's Exam Rank-Order (Y)
Mike	1	3
Diane	2	2
Sue	3	1
Lou	4	5
Jim	5	4
Patrick	6	6
Jeff	7	9
Mark	8	7
Michelle	9	8
Tom	10	10

TABLE 9.6 Resolving Tied Ranks

Officer	Length of Service Actual Years (X)	Length of Service Rank-Ordering (X)
Mike	10	2
Diane	10	2
Sue	10	2
Lou	8	4
Jim	7	5
Patrick	6	6.5
Jeff	6	6.5
Mark	3	8
Michelle	2	9
Tom	1	10

position. Likewise, Officer Jim is assigned the fifth position. For the sixth and seventh positions, Officers Patrick and Jeff are tied. What would their relative position be? Once again, you need to add the position of the tied ranks (6 + 7) and divide by the number of ties (2). In this case, Officers Patrick and Jeff are assigned an average rank of 6.5. Officers Mark, Michelle, and Tom would be ranked as 8, 9, and 10, respectively, as shown in Table 9.6. All ties, whether occurring on the independent or dependent variable, should be resolved in this manner.

Step 3: Obtain the difference between X and Y ranks, square the difference, and sum the values.

Continuing with our example reported in Table 9.5, we must first find the difference between each of the X and Y ranks. To do this, we simply subtract the Y rank from the X rank. Next, we square the difference and then sum the squared difference scores. We illustrate this step in Table 9.7.

Step 4: Calculate the Spearman's rho (r_s) statistic.

At this point, you have all the information necessary to compute Spearman's rho. The formula is as follows:

$$r_s = 1 - \frac{6\left[\Sigma(X-Y)^2\right]}{n(n^2-1)}$$

TABLE 9.7 Rank-Order of Exam Score and Length of Service

Officer	Length of Service Rank-Order (X)	Lieutenant's Exam Rank-Order (Y)	(X – Y)	(X – Y)²
Mike	1	3	−2	4
Diane	2	2	0	0
Sue	3	1	2	4
Lou	4	5	−1	1
Jim	5	4	1	1
Patrick	6	6	0	0
Jeff	7	9	−2	4
Mark	8	7	1	1
Michelle	9	8	1	1
Tom	10	10	0	0
				$\Sigma(X-Y)^2 = 16$

Considering our example, Spearman's rho is calculated as follows:

$$r_s = 1 - \frac{6(16)}{10(100-1)}$$

$$= 1 - \frac{96}{999}$$

$$= 1 - .10$$

$$= .90$$

Step 5: Compare the calculated Spearman's rho correlation statistic (r_s) with the critical rho value found in Table G in Appendix A.

To determine whether the rho coefficient is significant, you need to compare the calculated rho statistic with the critical rho value found in the rho distribution table (Table G in Appendix A). For a one-tailed test (directional hypothesis), an alpha of .05 and n of 10, the critical value of rho is .56. Given that our calculated rho statistic exceeds the critical rho value, we are able to reject the null hypothesis and accept the research hypothesis.

Step 6: Interpret findings.

You need to interpret both the magnitude and sign of the correlation. In our example, we concluded that officers who ranked high in length of service achieved a higher rank on the lieutenant's exam. More precisely, there is a very strong positive relationship between an officer's length of service and his or her ranking on the lieutenant's exam.

Now take a minute and give Spearman's rho a try, by completing TryIT! Box 9.3.

TryIT!   BOX **9.3**

You hypothesize that senior class standing is positively related to the number of job offers prior to graduation. Calculate Spearman's rho to test your hypothesis. Your data is as follows:

Subject	Class Standing Rank-Order (X)	Job Offers Number	Job Offers Rank-Order (Y)
Samuel	1	5	
Isaac	2	3	
Hannah	3	5	
Michaela	4	3	
Elizabeth	5	2	
Sarah	6	1	

Step 1: State the research and null hypotheses.

Step 2: Rank X and Y variables. Notice the X variable (class standing) is already ranked. You will need to rank order the Y variable (job offers prior to graduation).

Step 3: Obtain the difference between X and Y ranks, square the difference, and sum the values.

Step 4: Calculate Spearman's rho.

Step 5: Compare the calculated rho statistic with the critical rho value.

Step 6: Interpret findings.

9.6 Using Excel to Compute Chi-Square and Spearman's Rho

We are now ready to incorporate Excel into the statistical calculations for nominal- and ordinal-level data. We present two research situations and proceed with step-by-step instructions for calculating a two-sample chi-square statistic and a Spearman's rho statistic.

Two-Sample Chi-Square

A researcher is interested in knowing if where one lives in the city has an effect on one's perceptions of crime. She conducts a survey with a random sample of 535 respondents from a small eastern city. Her data includes "residential location" (X) consisting of the following three categories: Central Business District, Middle City, and Suburbs; and "perception of crime" (Y), meaning the perception that crime has: Increased, Decreased, or Stayed About the Same. The data for this problem is presented in Table 9.8.

Step 1: State the research and null hypotheses. These are given in notational form in cell a2.

Step 2: Record observations in terms of a contingency table and calculate the row and column sums as well as the grand sum. The observed frequencies are already entered into the cells. To calculate the row sum for those who said crime Increased, place the cursor in cell e6, and click on the autosum button on the Excel menu.

$$\boxed{\Sigma}$$

Repeat this step for the other two attributes of "Perception of crime"—cell e11 for Decreased and cell e16 for Stayed the Same. To calculate the column sum for those living in the Central Business District, place the cursor in cell b20 and write: =sum(b6,b11,b16), then hit enter. This will create the column sum for those three cell values. Repeat this step for the remaining attributes of "Residential Location." We do not want to use the autosum function for the column sums, because the summed value will incorporate those cells that have the expected frequencies. This will create what is called a circular reference, which will not allow us to write our formulas to calculate the expected frequencies. To calculate the grand sum, place the cursor in cell e20 and autosum either the row sums or the column sums.

Step 3: Calculate the expected frequencies using the following formula:

$$f_e = \frac{(CS)(RS)}{GS}$$

CS = Column Sum
RS = Row Sum
GS = Grand Sum

Place the cursor in cell b7 and write: =(b20*e6)/e20. This will create the expected frequency for those living in the Central Business area who said crime Increased.

b20 is the cell location of the column sum for Central Business.
e6 is the cell location of the row sum for Increased.
e20 is the cell location for *n* (grand sum).
$ holds the cell constant.

To create the rest of the expected frequencies for the Increased attribute, simply click on the lower right-hand corner of cell b7 and drag the cursor over to cell d7.

For those who said crime Decreased, place the cursor in cell b12 and write: =(b20*e11)/e20. Then click and drag the cursor over to cell d12 to create the rest of the row. For Stayed the Same, place the cursor in cell b17 and write: =(b20*e16)/e20. Once again, click and drag the cursor over to cell d17 to create the expected frequencies for Middle City and Suburban residents.

Step 4: Obtain the squared difference between the observed and expected frequencies. Then sum the values across all cells. Place the cursor in cell b8 and write: =((b6–b7)^2)/b7. This will create the squared difference between the observed and expected frequency for those living in the Central Business area who said crime Increased.

b6 is the cell location for the observed frequency.
b7 is the cell location for the expected frequency.
^2 is the symbol for square.
/ is the symbol for division.

Click on the lower right-hand corner of cell b8 and drag the cursor over to cell d8 to create the rest of the row. Repeat this procedure for the remaining attributes of "Perception of Crime." For Decreased, place the cursor in cell b13 and write: =((b11–b12)^2)/b12. For Stayed the Same, place the cursor in cell b18 and write: =((b16–b17)^2)/b17. To calculate the chi-square statistic, use the following formula:

$$\chi^2 = \Sigma \frac{\left(f_o - f_e\right)^2}{f_e}$$

Thus, chi-square is calculated by summing all of the $(f_o - f_e)^2/f_e$ values. Place the cursor in cell b21 and write: =sum(b8:d8, b13:d13, b18:d18).

Step 5: Calculate the degrees of freedom. Because we have a 3×3 contingency table (3 rows and 3 columns) we place the cursor in cell b22 and write: =(3–1)*(3–1).

Step 6: Compare the calculated chi-square statistic with the critical chi-square value. We can use Excel's statistical function to determine the critical chi-square value.

6a. place the cursor in cell b23 and click on the paste function box.

6b. Click on the function category called **Statistical**.
6c. Click on the function name called **CHIINV**.
6d. A box will appear like the one below and will ask for the probability and degrees of freedom. Enter .05 in the Probability box (this is our alpha level) and 4 in the Deg_freedom box and click ok.

Probability	.05
Deg_freedom	4

The resulting value is the critical value of chi-square at the .05 significance level with four degrees of freedom. Comparing the calculated chi-square statistic of 31.04 to the critical value of 9.49 leads us to reject the null hypothesis and accept the research hypothesis that residential location affects respondents' perception of crime.

Step 7: Interpret findings. Interpretation of the findings requires us to express the independent variable as a percentage. To calculate the column percentage for those living in

TABLE 9.8 Two-Sample Chi-Square

	A	B	C	D	E
1	**TABLE 9.8 Two-Sample Chi-Square**				
2	$H_1: f_{group1} \neq f_{group2} \neq f_{group3}$ $H_0: f_{group1} = f_{group2} = f_{group3}$	Residential Location (X)			**Row Sums**
3		**Central Business**	**Middle City**	**Suburban**	
4	Perception of crime (Y)				
5	**Increased**				
6	Observed frequencies (f_o)	60	57	70	187
7	Expected frequencies (f_e)	36.00	63.61	87.38	
8	$(f_o - f_e)^2/f_e$	**16.00**	**0.69**	**3.46**	
9	Column percentage	58.25%	31.32%	28.00%	
10	**Decreased**				
11	Observed frequencies (f_o)	10	30	45	85
12	Expected frequencies (f_e)	16.36	28.92	39.72	
13	$(f_o - f_e)^2/f_e$	**2.48**	**0.04**	**0.70**	
14	Column percentage	9.71%	16.48%	18.00%	
15	**Stayed the same**				
16	Observed frequencies (f_o)	33	95	135	263
17	Expected frequencies (f_e)	50.63	89.47	122.90	
18	$(f_o - f_e)^2/f_e$	**6.14**	**0.34**	**1.19**	
19	Column percentage	32.04%	52.20%	54.00%	
20	**Column sums**	103	182	250	535
21	**Calculated X^2 statistic**	**31.04**			
22	**Degrees of freedom (df)**	**4.00**			
23	**Critical X^2 value**	**9.49**			
24	**Cramer's V**	**0.17**			

the Central Business area who said crime Increased, place the cursor in cell b9 and write: =(b6/b20)*100. Click on cell b9 and drag the cursor over to cell d9 to create the rest of the column percentages for Middle City and Suburban residents who said crime Increased. Repeat this procedure for the other attributes of "Perception of Crime" (Decreased and Stayed the Same). We are now able to determine how Residential Location affects perception of crime, by comparing the column percentages within each attribute of the dependent variable. More specifically, we see that a higher percentage of Central Business residents said crime Increased (58.25%) compared to both Middle City (31.32%) and Suburban residents (28%). Even though the chi-square statistic is calculated based on the frequencies, we must express the independent variable as a percentage in order to determine where the differences exist.

Step 8: Calculate a measure of association. Because we have a 3 × 3 table we must use Cramer's V to determine the strength of the association between "residential location" and "perception of crime." Our formula for Cramer's V is given as:

$$V = \sqrt{\frac{\chi^2}{n(k-1)}}$$

Place the cursor in cell b24 and write: =sqrt((b21/(e20*(3–1)))).

sqrt is the word for square root.
b21 is the cell location of the X^2 statistic.
e20 is the cell location for the sample size (grand sum).

The resulting value of .17 shows a weak correlation between "residential location" (X) and "perception of crime" (Y).

Spearman's Rho

A researcher wants to know if there is a relationship between "television viewing" (X) and "perceptions of television violence" (Y). She selects a random sample of 12 subjects and gives each subject a questionnaire that asks them to indicate the number of hours spent watching television per month and their ratings of the amount of violence on television (using a ten-point scale, with 10 a "very high amount" and 1 a "very low amount" of violence). Given that the sample size is small, Spearman's rho is an appropriate choice of techniques. The data is presented in Table 9.9. For clarification purposes we present the raw and rank-ordered data in Table 9.9.

Step 1: State the research and null hypotheses. These are given in notational form in cell a2. Notice that this is a nondirectional hypothesis indicating that r_s can be either positive or negative.

Step 2: Rank the X and Y variables. This must be done manually by entering the correct rank in columns D and E. Excel does have a rank function; however, it does not take into account tied scores. Therefore, we do not recommend using the rank function.

Step 3: Obtain the difference between the X and Y ranks, square the difference, and sum the values. Place the cursor in cell f4 and write: =(d4–e4)^2. This will subtract the Y rank from the X rank and square the difference for subject 1.

d4 is the cell location for the X rank.
e4 is the cell location for the Y rank.
^2 is the symbol for squaring the value.

To create the rest of the $(X- Y)^2$ column, click on the lower right-hand corner of cell f4 and drag the cursor down to cell f15.

Sum the column using the autosum function on the Excel menu.

Step 4: Calculate Spearman's rho statistic using the following formula:

$$r_s = 1 - \frac{6\left[\Sigma\left(X-Y\right)^2\right]}{n\left(n^2-1\right)}$$

Place the cursor in cell b18 and write: = 1 – ((6*f16)/(b17*((b17)^2)–1)).

f16 is the cell location for $\Sigma(X- Y)^2$.
b17 is the cell location for the sample size (n).
^2 is the symbol for squaring the value.
–, *, / are the symbols for subtraction, multiplication, and division respectively.

Step 5: Compare the calculated r_s statistic with the critical value of r_s. There is no function in Excel that will assist us in getting the critical value for r_s. Therefore, we must look at the Spearman's rho distribution table (Table G) in Appendix A, to determine the critical value. With an alpha level of .05 and n equal to 12, the critical value of r_s is equal to .59. We can simply type this value into cell b19. Because our calculated r_s statistic is less than the critical r_s, we are unable to reject the null hypothesis.

Step 6: Interpret findings. We conclude that there is no statistically significant relationship between "television viewing" (X) and "perceptions of television violence" (Y). Any observed differences are attributed to sampling error and not the result of actual differences among the population parameters.

TABLE 9.9 Spearman's Rho

	A	B	C	D	E	F
1	TABLE 9.9 Spearman's Rho					
2	H_1: $r_s \neq 0$ H_0: $r_s = 0$					
3	Subject	Hours of Television	Ratings of Violence Scale	Hours of Television Rank-Ordered (X)	Ratings of Violence Rank-Ordered (Y)	$(X-Y)^2$
4	1	220	10	1	1.5	0.25
5	2	140	1	2	11.5	90.25
6	3	120	2	3.5	9	30.25
7	4	120	5	3.5	6.5	9
8	5	100	5	5	6.5	2.25
9	6	80	6	6.5	5	2.25
10	7	80	2	6.5	9	6.25
11	8	40	2	8.5	9	0.25
12	9	40	1	8.5	11.5	9
13	10	30	8	10	3.5	42.25
14	11	20	8	11	3.5	56.25
15	12	10	10	12	1.5	110.25
16	Sum					358.50
17	Sample (n)	12				
18	Calculated r_s statistic	−0.25				
19	Critical r_s value	0.59				

9.7 Summary

Nonparametric tests are appropriate whenever assumptions of parametric tests are violated. This chapter presented two common nonparametric tests appropriate with nominal- or ordinal-level dependent variables known as chi-square and Spearman rank-order correlation coefficient (Spearman's rho). The chi-square examines how well the pattern of observed frequencies fits the distribution of expected frequencies. The greater the discrepancy between the observed and the expected, the greater the likelihood of a significant chi-square. If a significant chi-square is detected, the phi coefficient or Cramer's *V* is used to assess the strength of the relationship between the two nominal-level variables.

Spearman's rho is a correlation coefficient among ranked-ordered variables. Spearman's rho is used when one or both variables are ordinal and/or when the normality assumption is violated. Spearman's rho ranges in value from 0 (no relationship between the variables) to 1 (perfect relationship between the variables), and can be positive or negative. Thus, the strength and the sign of the relationship must be interpreted. The significance of rho is assessed by comparing the calculated statistic to the critical value.

Step-by-step hand and computer calculations were presented for the one- and two-sample chi-square, measures of association known as phi and Cramer's *V*, and Spearman's rho. It is important to keep in mind that these techniques are appropriate alternatives to the more powerful parametric tests; thus, these techniques are to be used sparingly when parametric tests are deemed inappropriate.

Key Terms

nonparametric statistics	phi
chi-square	phi coefficient
one-sample chi-square	Cramer's *V*
two-sample chi-square	Spearman's rank-order correlation coefficient (Spearman's rho)

Try IT! Answers

Box 9.1

Step 1: State the research and null hypotheses.

H_1: Correctional officers do not choose equally first, second, or third shift as their preferred shift.

$$H_1: f_1 \neq f_2 \neq f_3$$

H_0: Correctional officers equally choose first, second, or third shift as their preferred shift.

$$H_0: f_1 = f_2 = f_3$$

Step 2: Determine the observed and expected frequencies.

Observed Frequencies (f_o)	Expected Frequencies (f_o)
Day Shift = 85	Day Shift = 50
Evening Shift = 40	Evening Shift = 50
Night Shift = 25	Night Shift = 50

Step 3: Obtain the squared difference between each observed frequency and expected frequency divided by the expected frequency. Sum the values across the cells.

$$\chi^2 = \frac{(85-50)^2}{50} + \frac{(40-50)^2}{50} + \frac{(25-50)^2}{50}$$

$$= \frac{1225}{50} + \frac{100}{50} + \frac{625}{50}$$

$$= 24.50 + 2 + 12.50$$

$$= 39$$

Step 4: Compare the calculated chi-square statistic with the critical chi-square value found in the chi-square distribution table (Table E in Appendix A).

With two degrees of freedom at the .05 alpha level, we find that the critical value is equal to 5.99. Because our calculated chi-square statistic of 39 is larger than the critical value of 5.99, we are able to reject the null hypothesis and accept the research hypothesis.

Step 5: Interpret findings.

We conclude that the population of correctional officers differ in their shift preference. The majority of officers prefer the day shift with the night shift being the least preferred.

Box 9.2

Step 1: State the research and null hypotheses.

H_1: The relative frequency of satisfied and dissatisfied students differs by academic rank.

$$H_1: f_{group1} \neq f_{group2} \neq f_{group3} \neq f_{group4}$$

H_0: The relative frequency of satisfied and dissatisfied students does not differ by academic rank.

$$H_0: f_{group1} = f_{group2} = f_{group3} = f_{group4}$$

Step 2: Record the observations in a contingency table.

Satisfaction	Academic Rank				Row Sums (RS)
	Freshman	Sophomore	Junior	Senior	
Satisfied					
observed frequencies (f_o)	8	15	18	23	64
expected frequencies (f_e)					
Dissatisfied					
observed frequencies (f_o)	17	10	7	2	36
expected frequencies (f_e)					Grand Sum
Column Sums (CS)	25	25	25	25	(GS) 100

Step 3: Calculate the expected frequencies. Once these values have been calculated, place them in the appropriate location in the contingency table.

Expected Frequencies (f_e)

Freshman/Satisfied:	$(25 \times 64) / 100 = 16$
Sophomore/Satisfied:	$(25 \times 64) / 100 = 16$
Junior/Satisfied:	$(25 \times 64) / 100 = 16$
Senior/Satisfied:	$(25 \times 64) / 100 = 16$
Freshman/Dissatisfied:	$(25 \times 36) / 100 = 9$
Sophomore/Dissatisfied:	$(25 \times 36) / 100 = 9$
Junior/Dissatisfied:	$(25 \times 36) / 100 = 9$
Senior/Dissatisfied:	$(25 \times 36) / 100 = 9$

Satisfaction	Academic Rank				Row Sums (RS)
	Freshman	Sophomore	Junior	Senior	
Satisfied					
observed frequencies (f_o)	8	15	18	23	64
expected frequencies (f_e)	16	16	16	16	
Dissatisfied					
observed frequencies (f_o)	17	10	7	2	36
expected frequencies (f_e)	9	9	9	9	Grand Sum
Column Sums (CS)	25	25	25	25	(GS) 100

Step 4: Calculate the sum of the squared differences between the observed and expected frequencies and then divide by the expected frequency. Sum the values across all cells.

$$\chi^2 = \frac{(8-16)^2}{16} + \frac{(15-16)^2}{16} + \frac{(18-16)^2}{16} + \frac{(23-16)^2}{16}$$
$$+ \frac{(17-9)^2}{9} + \frac{(10-9)^2}{9} + \frac{(7-9)^2}{9} + \frac{(2-9)^2}{9}$$
$$= \frac{64}{16} + \frac{1}{16} + \frac{4}{16} + \frac{49}{16} + \frac{64}{9} + \frac{1}{9} + \frac{4}{9} + \frac{49}{9}$$
$$= 4 + .06 + .25 + 3.06 + 7.11 + .11 + .44 + 5.44$$
$$= 20.47$$

Step 5: Calculate the degrees of freedom.

With two rows and four columns, the degrees of freedom $(2-1) \times (4-1)$ is equal to 3.

Step 6: Compare the calculated chi-square statistic with the critical chi-square value found in the chi-square distribution table (Table E in Appendix A). Using the standard .01 alpha level, we find that the critical value equals 11.34. Because our calculated chi-square statistic of 20.47 is greater than the critical value, we reject the null hypothesis.

Step 7: Interpret findings.

We conclude that satisfaction with the criminal justice major differs by academic rank among the population of college students. The observed differences in satisfaction among the sample of students is attributed to actual differences in the population. More specifically, juniors and seniors are more satisfied with the major (72% and 92% respectively) than are freshmen and sophomores (32% and 60% respectively).

Box 9.3

Step 1: State the research and null hypotheses.

H_1: There is a positive relationship between class standing and number of job offers.

$r_s > 0$

H_0: There is a negative or no relationship between class standing and number of job offers.

$r_s \leq 0$

Step 2: Rank-order the independent *(X)* and dependent *(Y)* variables

Subject	Class Standing Rank-Order (X)	Job Offers Number (Y)	Job Offers Rank-Order (Y)
Samuel	1	5	1.5
Isaac	2	3	3.5
Hannah	3	5	1.5
Michaela	4	3	3.5
Elizabeth	5	2	5
Sarah	6	1	6

Step 3: Obtain the difference between *X* and *Y* ranks, square the difference, and sum the values

Officer	Class Standing Rank-Order (X)	Job Offers Rank-Order (Y)	(X – Y)	(X – Y)²
Samuel	1	1.5	−0.5	0.25
Isaac	2	3.5	−1.5	2.25
Hannah	3	1.5	1.5	2.25
Michaela	4	3.5	0.5	0.25
Elizabeth	5	5	0	0
Sarah	6	6	0	0
				$\Sigma(X - Y)^2 = 5$

Step 4: Calculate Spearman's rho.

$$r_{\text{Spearman's rho}} = 1 - \frac{6(5)}{6(36 - 1)}$$

$$= 1 - \frac{30}{210}$$

$$= 1 - .14$$

$$= .86$$

Step 5: Compare the calculated rho statistic with the critical rho value.

Because our hypothesis is directional, we are conducting a one-tailed test at the .05 alpha level with an *n* of 6. We find that the critical value is equal to .83. The calculated rho statistic of .86 exceeds the critical value; thus, we reject the null hypothesis and accept the research hypothesis.

Step 6: Interpret findings.

We conclude that there is a strong positive relationship between class standing and the number of job offers received.

9.8 Problems

1. Determine the critical X^2 value for each of the following:

	Degrees of freedom	Alpha level
a.	1	.01
b.	5	.05
c.	3	.01
d.	3	.05
e.	10	.01
f.	2	.01

2. Make a decision regarding the null hypothesis for each of the following:

	Calculated X^2 statistic	Degrees of freedom	Alpha level
a.	4.25	1	.05
b.	5.34	1	.01
c.	13.45	4	.01
d.	15.28	8	.05
e.	34.91	18	.01
f.	8.21	3	.05

3. A researcher has found a significant chi-square statistic for a 3 × 4 contingency table. What measure of association should the researcher use? Cramer's V

4. Chi-square and Spearman's rho belong to what class of statistical techniques?

5. Spearman's rho is commonly used for _____ data, while chi-square is most often used for _____ level data.

6. A researcher finds that 67% of females favor gun control, compared to 54% of males, with a calculated X^2 statistic of 2.85, with 1 degree of freedom at the .05 alpha level. How would you interpret the difference between males and females?

7. Determine the critical value of r_s for each of the following:

	N	Alpha level	Tails
a.	5	.01	1
b.	7	.05	1
c.	12	.01	2
d.	8	.01	2
e.	20	.05	1

8. A researcher calculates a Spearman's rho coefficient of .45 with n equal to 20. Using a two-tailed test at the .05 alpha level, what decision should be made regarding the null hypothesis?

9. A researcher conducts a survey with college students and obtains their opinions on the campus drinking policy. Using the data below, write (a) a testable hypothesis, (b) calculate a chi-square statistic to test your hypothesis, (c) calculate column percentages, and (d) interpret your findings.

	Student	
Campus Drinking Policy	*Undergraduate*	*Graduate*
Support	150	75
Oppose	245	38

10. Researchers obtained rankings for the amount of alcohol consumption (X) and level of crime (Y) for eight college campuses. Using the data below, write (a) a testable hypothesis, (b) calculate a Spearman's rank-order correlation coefficient (Spearman's rho) to test your hypothesis, and (c) interpret your findings using a two-tailed test and .05 alpha level.

Campus	*Alcohol Consumption—Rank Order*	*Level of Crime—Rank Order*
A	1	2
B	2	1
C	3	4
D	4	5
E	5	3
F	6	8
G	7	6
H	8	7

11. Calculate the degrees of freedom for the following contingency tables:

a. 2×3
b. 4×6
c. 2×8
d. 6×6
e. 3×5

12. Make a decision regarding the null hypothesis for each of the following Spearman's rho coefficients:

	Calculated r_s	*N*	*Alpha level*	*Tails*
a.	.45	20	.05	1
b.	.32	6	.01	1
c.	.78	12	.01	2
	Calculated r_s	*N*	*Alpha level*	*Tails*
d.	.93	8	.01	2
e.	.85	14	.05	1
f.	.65	12	.05	2

13. A researcher calculates a Spearman's rho of .67 with N equal to 8. Using an alpha level of .05 and a two-tailed test, (a) what decision does the researcher make regarding the null hypothesis, and (b) how does the researcher interpret the differences in the rankings?

14. A researcher has hypothesized that lower staff /inmate ratios are positively correlated with less violence in correctional institutions. Below is a list of 12 correctional institutions ranked from best (1) to worst (12) in terms of the amount of violence and the staff/inmate ratio. Enter the data into Excel, rank the staff/inmate ratio, and calculate a Spearman's rank-order correlation coefficient to test the researcher's directional hypothesis using an alpha level of .05. Be sure to interpret your findings.

Institution	Violence (X)	Staff/Inmate Ratio
A	1	1:15
B	2	1:15
C	3	1:25
D	4	1:20
E	5	1:18
F	6	1:33
G	7	1:25
H	8	1:28
I	9	1:30
J	10	1:45
K	11	1:45
L	12	1:30

15. A researcher conducts a study on automobile values and alarms. The results of the study are given below. Enter the data into Excel and calculate a chi-square statistic, phi coefficient, and column percentages. Be sure to interpret your findings.

	Value of Automobile	
Own Auto Alarm	$15,000 or less	over $15,000
Yes	135	64
No	193	65

Statistical Analysis for Comparing Two Population Means: *t* Tests

ExploreIT!

The mayor of a medium-sized city has hired you as a research consultant to determine what the citizens think of the neighborhood crime watch program. The mayor wants you to recommend whether the city should continue funding this program or whether it should be eliminated from the budget. You decide to conduct a survey and immediately begin designing a simple questionnaire asking citizens their perceptions of the effectiveness of the program using a 7-point rating scale. You think that senior citizens might differ from others in terms of their assessment of the program; hence, the questionnaire also asks respondents to indicate their age. The respondents are then grouped as younger (under age 55) or older (55 and over) citizens. How can you determine whether the older citizens view the program differently than the younger ones? In this case, the appropriate statistical test is the *t* test.

If we asked you to generate a list of hypotheses of potential interest to criminal justice practitioners, many of the hypotheses would undoubtedly involve comparing different groups of people in terms of a specific variable. Your research hypotheses may look something like the following:

Research Hypothesis 1: Women police officers make more arrests than do male officers.

Research Hypothesis 2: Light and heavy TV viewers differ in their perception of law enforcement officers.

Research Hypothesis 3: Younger inmates differ from older ones in terms of the number of disciplinary infractions.

Research Hypothesis 4: Recidivism rates are higher among individuals of low rather than high socioeconomic status (SES).

In all of these examples, you are proposing that a difference exists between two different groups of individuals—female versus male officers, heavy versus light viewers, young versus old inmates, and individuals of high versus low SES. You are also proposing that these groups differ in a very specific way—number of arrests, perceptions of law enforcement officers, number of disciplinary infractions, and recidivism rates. The question that arises, "How do we know whether these groups differ as hypothesized?," cannot be answered without conducting a statistical test called a *t* test.

This chapter discusses the *t* test as a statistical technique for hypotheses testing two population means. The *t* test is a parametric inferential statistic that allows us to make inferences about the population parameters through the analysis of sample statistics. Specifically, we want to determine whether observed differences between two sample means are the result of actual differences among the population means or the result of sampling error. We discuss two specific types of *t* tests—independent and dependent samples—as well as the assumptions for using the *t* test. This chapter also demonstrates several methods for calculating *t* tests using Excel.

10.1 Independent-Samples t Test

independent-samples t test

An **independent-samples *t* test** is *a statistical technique used to assess the mean difference between two different groups drawn from the same sample*. This technique is commonly used when comparing two different groups on a single dependent measure. Let's say that we want to compare light and heavy TV consumers in terms of their perceptions of law enforcement officers. It is important to note that the independent variable is categorical; that is, the level of measurement of the independent variable is nominal or ordinal. Additionally, the *t* test can be used only if the independent variable consists of two levels or categories. In our example, we have two categories—light versus heavy TV viewers. Thus, we proceed to test our hypothesis by selecting our sample of light and heavy TV consumers on the basis of individuals' self-reports of their viewing habits. For our study, we have elected to classify individuals who report watching four or more hours per day as heavy viewers, and those who report watching less than four hours per day as light viewers.

Although the independent variable must be categorical, the dependent variable must be numerically measured at the interval or ratio level. Perceptions of law enforcement officers, for example, could be measured on a 7-point rating scale, with higher values reflecting more favorable perceptions. If we had our respondents indicate their perceptions of officers, we could calculate a mean for the sample of light viewers and a mean for the sample of heavy viewers. Thus, we are seeing whether mean ratings differ between group 1 (light viewers) and group 2 (heavy viewers). Our research and null hypotheses are:

H_1: Light and heavy TV viewers differ in their perception of law enforcement officers.
H_0: There is no difference between light and heavy TV viewers in terms of their perceptions of law enforcement officers.

As discussed in Chapter 8, statistical techniques are based on testing the null hypothesis, with the goal of rejecting the null so we can infer support for our research hypothesis. With this in mind, we are now ready to look at our observations. The data for this example is reported in Table 10.1. The numerical values represent the scores for each subject on our dependent variable—"perceptions of law enforcement officers."

TABLE 10.1 Perceptions of Law Enforcement Officers by Television Viewers

	Group 1	*Group 2*
	Light TV Viewers	*Heavy TV Viewers*
	7	4
	6	3
	7	4
	5	4
	5	2
	5	6
	7	5
Sample size (*n*)	7	7
Sum	42	28
Mean ($\bar{X}$)	6	4

Furthermore, these values range from 1 to 7, with higher values reflecting more favorable perceptions of law enforcement officers.

After calculating the mean for each sample, we observe that the ratings of law enforcement officers among light viewers is 6 and the mean rating among heavy viewers is 4. The question becomes: "Is the mean difference (6 – 4) of 2 a statistically significant difference between the two groups in the population or is the difference due to sampling error?" What if the mean difference was 1.50? What about 1.10? How large a difference is necessary to reject the null hypothesis of no difference and accept the research hypothesis that the two populations differ in terms of their perceptions of officers?

One additional piece of the equation must be calculated before answering this question: We must first calculate the standard error of the difference. The logic behind calculating a *t* statistic involves comparing not only the mean difference but looking at the difference in relation to the standard error of the difference between the means. The **standard error of the difference between means** is a *measure of the variability (e.g., standard deviation) of the sampling distribution of differences between two sample means*. The standard error of the difference between means is based on a probability distribution of an infinite number of differences between two sample means. That is, if we drew an infinite number of samples and measured the differences between the means for two groups, those mean differences would form a sampling distribution, and the standard error of the difference between means would be the standard deviation of that sampling distribution.

standard error of the difference between means

The general formula for the *t* statistic is:

$$t = \frac{\overline{X}_1 - \overline{X}_2}{s_{\overline{x}_1 - \overline{x}_2}}$$

$\overline{X}_1$ and $\overline{X}_2$ = Sample means for groups 1 and 2

$s_{\overline{x}_1 - \overline{x}_2}$ = Standard error of the difference between means

The numerator involves calculating the mean difference between the two groups by subtracting the mean of group 2 from the mean of group 1. The denominator, the standard error of the difference between means, is calculated differently depending on factors such as whether the variance of the samples are approximately the same (pooled versus separate estimates of the variance), the two samples are related (dependent versus independent), and the sample size. Regardless of the specific formula for calculating the standard error of the difference, the main ingredient is the sum of the squared deviation scores; that is, we are looking at how much each individual score deviates from the mean of its distribution. This process is not new to you; you looked at how much variability exists in a distribution when calculating measures of dispersion known as variance and standard deviation in Chapter 5.

How do we know the value of the standard error of the difference between means? Although the true standard error is rarely known, we are able to estimate error based on our samples. The formula for the standard error estimates how different the means of the two samples can be due to sampling error alone. Suppose we had a mean difference between the two groups of 10 and a standard error of 2. If we plug the information into the general formula, we would obtain a t statistic of 5 (10 divided by 2). By contrast, let's say that the mean difference between our two groups is still 10; however, now our standard error is equal to 10. If we plug this information into the general formula, we would obtain a t statistic of 1 (10 divided by 10). This example illustrates that increasing error leads to smaller t values. And, as we will see shortly, the smaller our calculated t value, the less chance we have of rejecting the null hypothesis and accepting the research hypothesis. We conclude that any difference between the two sample means is the result of sampling error and not actual differences between the population means.

The following formula is used to estimate the standard error of the difference between the means:

$$ s_{\bar{x}_1 - \bar{x}_2} = \sqrt{ \left(\frac{n_1 s_1^2 + n_2 s_2^2}{n_1 + n_2 - 2} \right) \left(\frac{n_1 + n_2}{n_1 n_2} \right) } $$

n_1 and n_2 = Sample size for groups 1 and 2

s_1^2 and s_2^2 = Variance for groups 1 and 2

As true error is usually unknown, this formula is used for estimating error based on the observations from our samples. The standard error of the difference serves as the denominator for calculating a t statistic for independent samples. We are now ready to resume our example and calculate the t statistic.

Procedures for Independent-Samples t Test

Step 1: State the research and null hypotheses.

H_1: Light and heavy TV viewers differ in their perceptions of law enforcement officers.

$H_1 : \mu_1 \neq \mu_2$

H_0: Light and heavy TV viewers do not differ in terms of their perceptions of law enforcement officers.

$H_0 : \mu_1 = \mu_2$

It is important to remember that your goal is to reject the null hypothesis and accept the research hypothesis.

Step 2: Calculate the mean $(\bar{X})$ and variance (s^2) for each group.

	Group 1 Light TV Viewers	$(X - \bar{X})^2$	Group 2 Heavy TV Viewers	$(X - \bar{X})^2$
	7	1	4	0
	6	0	3	1
	7	1	4	0
	5	1	4	0
	5	1	2	4
	5	1	6	4
	7	1	5	1
Sum (Σ)	42	6	28	10
Sample Size (n)	$n_1 = 7$		$n_2 = 7$	
$\bar{X} = \Sigma X/n$	$\bar{X}_1 = 42/7 = 6$		$\bar{X}_2 = 28/7 = 4$	
$s^2 = \Sigma(X - \bar{X})^2/ n-1$	$s_1^2 = 6/(7-1) = 1$		$s_2^2 = 10/(7-1) = 1.67$	

Step 3: Calculate the standard error of the difference.

$$s_{\bar{x}_1 - \bar{x}_2} = \sqrt{\left(\frac{n_1 s_1^2 + n_2 s_2^2}{n_1 + n_2 - 2}\right)\left(\frac{n_1 + n_2}{n_1 n_2}\right)}$$

$$s_{\bar{x}_1 - \bar{x}_2} = \sqrt{\left(\frac{(7)(1) + (7)(1.67)}{7 + 7 - 2}\right)\left(\frac{7 + 7}{(7)(7)}\right)}$$

$$s_{\bar{x}_1 - \bar{x}_2} = \sqrt{\left(\frac{18.69}{12}\right)\left(\frac{14}{49}\right)}$$

$$s_{\bar{x}_1 - \bar{x}_2} = \sqrt{(1.56)(.29)}$$

$$s_{\bar{x}_1 - \bar{x}_2} = \sqrt{.45}$$

$$s_{\bar{x}_1 - \bar{x}_2} = .67$$

Step 4: Calculate the t statistic.

$$t = \frac{\bar{X}_1 - \bar{X}_2}{s_{\bar{x}_1 - \bar{x}_2}}$$

$$t = \frac{6 - 4}{.67}$$

$$t = 2.99$$

Step 5: Calculate the degrees of freedom.

The formula for calculating the degrees of freedom for an independent-samples t test is $n_1 + n_2 - 2$. In our example, the degrees of freedom is 12. That is, $7 + 7 - 2 = 12$.

Step 6: Compare the calculated t statistic with the critical t value from Table B in Appendix A. It is important to recall that two pieces of information are needed to locate the correct critical value:

1. **Are you conducting a one-tailed or a two-tailed test?**
2. **What is your degrees of freedom?**

In our example, we advanced a nondirectional hypothesis with 12 degrees of freedom. Looking at the t distribution table (Table B in Appendix A) for a two-tailed test, we first find the column with an alpha level of .05 and then proceed to the row with 12 degrees of freedom. The critical value in this case is 2.18. It is important to remember that the critical value is the minimum value your calculated t statistic must achieve in order to reject the null hypothesis and accept the research hypothesis.

If the calculated t statistic—regardless of whether the direction is positive or negative—is equal to or larger than the critical t value (tabled value), you reject the null hypothesis and the research hypothesis is accepted. If the calculated t statistic is smaller than the critical value, however, then you are likely to be disappointed, as you are unable to reject the null hypothesis of no difference between the two group means.

In our example, the calculated t statistic is 2.99 and the critical t value is 2.18. Because the calculated t statistic is larger than the critical t value, we are able to reject the null hypothesis and accept the research hypothesis.

Step 7: Interpret findings.

In our experience, students often neglect this step. It is important, however, to interpret your findings. In our example, it is accurate to conclude that the researcher must reject the null and accept the research hypothesis. Yet, it is more desirable to continue and state that the researcher is able to argue that there is a statistically significant difference between the population of light and heavy TV viewers regarding their perceptions of law enforcement officers. In fact, she can argue that light TV viewers have more favorable perceptions of law enforcement officers than do heavy TV viewers.

Let us suppose that the researcher advanced a directional rather than a nondirectional hypothesis. That is, she proposed that light viewers report *more favorable perceptions* of law enforcement officers than do heavy viewers. The calculated t statistic would still be 2.99. The piece of information that changes is the critical value. As found in Table B in Appendix A, the critical t value for a one-tailed test with 12 degrees of freedom and an alpha of .05 is 1.78. The fact that the calculated t statistic (2.99) is larger than the critical t value of 1.78 enables us to reject the null hypothesis and accept the research hypothesis. Once again, we can say that light TV viewers report significantly more favorable perceptions of law enforcement officers than do heavy viewers.

It is important to notice that the critical value is smaller with a one-tailed than with a two-tailed test; this will always be the case. The implication is that we are able to reject the null hypothesis with a smaller calculated *t* statistic for a one-tailed than for a two-tailed test. This is because of the size of the rejection region of our distribution. If we have selected a .05 alpha level and we are performing a one-tailed test, then the entire .05 rejection region is located in one tail of the *t* distribution. If we perform a two-tailed test, however, the .05 rejection region must be split into the two tails, such that each tail accounts for .025 of the *t* distribution. This process, in turn, increases the critical value that we must equal or exceed in order to reject the null hypothesis.

To illustrate, let's assume that our calculated *t* statistic is 2.10. If we were conducting a one-tailed test with 12 degrees of freedom, we would reject the null hypothesis as our calculated *t* statistic of 2.10 is larger than the critical *t* value of 1.78. As shown in Figure 10.1, our calculated *t* statistic falls in the rejection region beyond the critical *t* value of 1.78. By contrast, if we had selected a two-tailed test with 12 degrees of freedom, we would be unable to reject the null hypothesis, as the calculated *t* statistic of 2.10 is smaller than the needed critical *t* value of 2.18. Thus, our *t* statistic fails to reach the critical region, and we must conclude that the difference between the two means is because of sampling error and not differences among the population parameters. We illustrate this in Figure 10.2. This process demonstrates that a directional hypothesis (one-tailed test) will always have more power to detect a difference than a nondirectional hypothesis (two-tailed test), assuming that everything else is equal.

FIGURE 10.1 Critical region of *t* distribution for a one-tailed test with 12 degrees of freedom

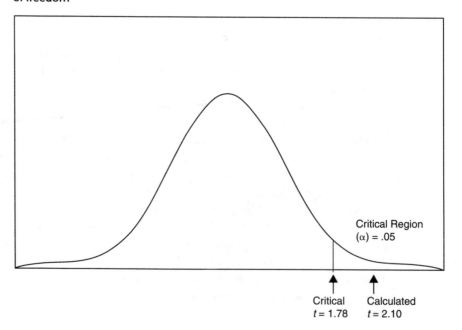

Critical Region
$(\alpha) = .05$

Critical
$t = 1.78$

Calculated
$t = 2.10$

FIGURE 10.2 Critical regions of *t* distribution for a two-tailed test with 12 degrees of freedom

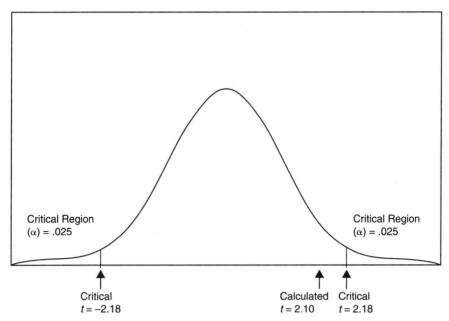

Critical Region
(α) = .025

Critical Region
(α) = .025

Critical
t = –2.18

Calculated
t = 2.10

Critical
t = 2.18

If a directional hypothesis is more powerful, the question that arises is: "Is it always advantageous to conduct a one-tailed test?" The answer is no. The key is in the direction of the difference. It is important to notice what would happen if light viewers reported a mean of 4 and heavy viewers reported a mean of 6; that is, light viewers actually reported less favorable impressions than heavy viewers. In this case, the calculated *t* statistic would be *negative* rather than positive. The numerator, the mean difference between the two groups (4 – 6), would be –2, leading to a calculated *t* statistic of –2.99. The critical values for rejecting the null remain the same; the critical *t* value for a two-tailed test is 2.18 and the value for a one-tailed test is 1.78. In both cases, the critical *t* value is smaller than the absolute value of the calculated *t* statistic, and so it seems that we are able to reject the null and accept the research hypothesis. Such a conclusion, however, would be correct only for a nondirectional hypothesis. The directional hypothesis requires you to examine the *direction* of the difference between the two groups. The researcher argued that light viewers would have more favorable impressions than heavy viewers. The results showed just the opposite. That is, light viewers reported less favorable impressions. Thus, the researcher is unable to reject the null hypothesis. She can state that there was no support to suggest that light viewers have more favorable impressions of law enforcement officers than do heavy viewers.

Students often ask, "Well, isn't it accurate to say that there is a statistically significant difference between the two groups but in the *opposite direction* than predicted?" The answer is no. The researcher elected to test a directional hypothesis; that is, she was willing to state "how" the two groups differ. She was wrong. The critical value is based on probability theory; the critical value for a one-tailed test is smaller than for a two-tailed test, as the researcher is willing to stipulate a direction and stick to that decision. This point is often difficult to digest, especially given that researchers often violate this principle.

You are now ready to calculate an independent-samples t test. Take a few moments to complete TryIT! Box 10.1, before moving on to the next section.

TryIT!   BOX **10.1**

Let's say that a researcher is interested in knowing whether male and female police officers differ in terms of number of arrests. A random sample of eight male and eight female officers was obtained from a local police department. The number of arrests each officer made during the past 30 days is reported as follows:

Male Officers	Female Officers
4	3
6	4
6	4
5	4
5	2
4	2
6	3
4	2

Step 1: State the research and null hypotheses.

Step 2: Calculate the mean and variance for each group.

Step 3: Calculate the standard error of the difference between means.

Step 4: Calculate the t statistic.

Step 5: Calculate the degrees of freedom.

Step 6: Compare the calculated t statistic with the critical t value.

Step 7: Interpret findings.

10.2 Dependent- or Matched-Samples t Test

Our discussion of the *t* test has focused on the difference between two means drawn from independent samples. That is, the probability of selection for one sample has no effect on the probability of selection for the other sample. In several instances, however, the researcher deliberately seeks dependent samples. This often occurs with pre–post experimental designs, in which only one sample is drawn, then measures of the depend-

depen-
dent- or
matched-
samples
***t* test**

ent variable are taken at two different points in time. Thus, a **dependent- or matched-samples *t* test** is *a statistical technique used to test the difference scores for a single sample of respondents*. To illustrate, a researcher may be interested in the effects of a particular institutional program on inmate conduct. The researcher would select a sample of inmates and record the number of disciplinary infractions eight weeks prior to implementing the program and, again, eight weeks after the completion of the program. In this case, there is only one sample, and the subjects are observed repeatedly on the dependent variable. This type of data is often referred to as repeated measures.

Often dependent samples occur as a result of researchers deliberately selecting samples in which participants in the two groups are comparable on a number of important characteristics. This type of dependent sample often occurs with experiments consisting of a treatment and a control group. In this type of a sample, a participant in the treatment group is matched with a person in the control group. For instance, a researcher interested in the effects of a particular institutional program on inmate conduct may want to match inmates on a number of variables such as age, gender, and type of offense when selecting participants for the treatment and the control groups. Thus, the researcher will be more confident that any observed differences between the two groups is due to the effects of the treatment, in this case the institutional program, rather than inmate characteristics. With both dependent and matched samples, the assumption of independent samples is violated; that is, we can no longer say that the probability of being selected for one sample has no effect on the probability of being selected for another sample. Our procedure in calculating a *t* statistic with dependent or matched samples, therefore, must deal with this deliberate violation of the assumption of independence.

The main procedure for handling this violation is to treat dependent and matched samples as one rather than two groups. In other words, the experiment is thought of as having one sample or group, with "paired" or "matched" observations. Hence, rather than calculating the mean difference between the two groups, we look at the mean difference between each pair of observations. Our focus is on the *difference* between the two observations, often referred to as the difference score. As our key observation is the difference score, sample size, commonly referred to as *n,* is determined differently with independent and dependent samples. With independent samples, *n* refers to the total number of subjects or scores in both groups combined. With dependent samples, *n* is the total number of "pairs" or "matched" observations. Keeping these few differences in mind, calculating the dependent- or matched-samples *t* statistic is not unlike calculating the independent t statistic. We now outline the procedures for calculating a dependent-samples t test.

Procedures for Dependent- or Matched-Samples t Statistic

Pre-Post Design

Suppose you are interested in assessing the effectiveness of a domestic violence counseling program designed to decrease the number of domestic abuse incidents among convicted abusers. The case files of ten offenders are randomly selected from the population of convicted abusers. The number of abuse incidents (verbal or physical) reported six months before the implementation of the counseling program and six months following the completion of the program are reported in Table 10.2.

Step 1: State the research hypothesis and null hypothesis.

H_1: The number of abuse incidents will significantly decrease after implementation of the domestic violence counseling program.

$$H_1 : \mu_1 > \mu_2$$

H_0: The number of abuse incidents is equal to or greater after the implementation of the domestic violence counseling program than before the program.

$$H_0 : \mu_1 \leq \mu_2$$

TABLE 10.2 Number of Abuse Incidents Before and After Implementation of the Domestic Violence Counseling Program

File Number	Before (X_1)	After (X_2)
Offender 1	4	2
Offender 2	3	1
Offender 3	1	1
Offender 4	0	0
Offender 5	1	2
Offender 6	3	1
Offender 7	4	3
Offender 8	0	0
Offender 9	4	2
Offender 10	4	2

Notice that we have a directional hypothesis in which we have hypothesized that the program will decrease incidents of domestic abuse. Directional hypotheses are very common with this type of design as researchers usually expect a program to have an expected effect on participants.

Step 2: Calculate the means for before-program scores $(\bar{X}_1)$ and after-program scores $(\bar{X}_2)$.

Step 3: For each pair of observations, calculate the difference (D) between before-program scores and after-program scores. Then, square the difference scores (D^2) and sum.

  The calculation of difference scores (D) is accomplished by subtracting the second score from the first score $(\bar{X}_1 - \bar{X}_2)$ for each subject in the sample. Once the difference scores have been calculated, we simply square each of those scores to complete the D^2 column. Steps 2 and 3 are illustrated in Table 10.3.

Step 4: Calculate the standard deviation of the *difference* between X_1 and X_2. The formula is given as:

$$s_D = \sqrt{\frac{\Sigma D^2}{n} - \left(\bar{X}_1 - \bar{X}_2\right)^2}$$

TABLE 10.3 Difference Scores, Squared Difference Scores, Means, and Sums

File Number	Before (X_1)	After (X_2)	Difference (D)	Difference squared (D^2)
Offender 1	4	2	+2	4
Offender 2	3	1	+2	4
Offender 3	1	1	0	0
Offender 4	0	0	0	0
Offender 5	1	2	−1	1
Offender 6	3	1	+2	4
Offender 7	4	3	+1	1
Offender 8	0	0	0	0
Offender 9	4	2	+2	4
Offender 10	4	2	+2	4
Sample (n)	10			
Sum (Σ)	24	14		22
Mean ($\Sigma X/n$)	$\bar{X}_1 = 2.40$	$\bar{X}_2 = 1.40$		

Substituting our data into the above formula, we obtain the standard deviation of the difference as follows:

$$s_D = \sqrt{\frac{22}{10} - (2.40 - 1.40)^2}$$

$$= \sqrt{2.2 - 1}$$

$$= \sqrt{1.2}$$

$$= 1.10$$

Step 5: Calculate the standard error of the mean difference. The formula requires us to divide the standard deviation of the difference by the square root of the sample size minus one.

$$s_{\overline{D}} = \frac{s_D}{\sqrt{n-1}}$$

Entering our data into the formula, we calculate the standard error as follows:

$$s_{\overline{D}} = \frac{1.10}{\sqrt{10-1}}$$

$$= \frac{1.10}{3}$$

$$= .37$$

Step 6: Calculate the t statistic. According to the formula, we simply subtract the mean of group 2 from the mean of group 1 and divide by the standard error of the mean difference.

$$t = \frac{\overline{X}_1 - \overline{X}_2}{s_{\overline{D}}}$$

Placing our data into the formula, we compute the t statistic in the following manner:

$$t = \frac{2.40 - 1.40}{.37}$$

$$= \frac{1}{.37}$$

$$= 2.70$$

Step 7: Calculate the degrees of freedom. The formula for calculating the degrees of freedom for a dependent sample t test is $n - 1$. In our example, the degrees of freedom is 9. That is, $10 - 1 = 9$.

Step 8: Compare the calculated t statistic with the critical t value from Table B in Appendix A. The critical value is determined using a one-tailed test with nine degrees of freedom. We use a one-tailed test because our research hypothesis was directional; that is, we stated that the number of domestic violence incidents would be significantly lower after the program compared to the number before the program. We stated "how" the dependent variable (i.e., incidents of domestic violence) would change as a result of the program. Thus, the critical t value is 1.83. Because the calculated t statistic of 2.70 is larger than the critical t value (1.83), we are able to reject the null hypothesis and accept the research hypothesis.

Step 9: Interpret findings.

The significance of the t statistic enables the researcher to argue that the domestic violence counseling program was effective in reducing incidents of domestic abuse. We know that the incidents of abuse decreased, because the after-program mean is less than the before-program mean. Thus, the program is effective at reducing domestic violence incidents among the population of convicted abusers.

Now that you understand the differences between an independent and dependent samples t test, take a moment to complete TryIT! Box 10.2.

TryIT! BOX 10.2

As a criminal justice (CJ) instructor, you are interested in whether a popular program, "How to Study and Get Better Grades," will improve students' overall academic performance. You randomly select eight criminal justice students from the population of CJ students. The grade point averages (GPAs) of the eight students for Fall 2001 are recorded (X_1). The students participate in the program prior to the beginning of the Spring 2002 term. The GPAs of the students for the Spring semester (2002) are recorded (X_2).

Student Number	Before-Program GPAs (X_1)	After-Program GPAs (X_2)
CJ Student 1	3.0	3.5
CJ Student 2	3.0	3.2
CJ Student 3	2.5	2.5
CJ Student 4	2.5	3.0
CJ Student 5	4.0	3.7
CJ Student 6	2.0	3.0
CJ Student 7	2.0	3.3
CJ Student 8	3.3	4.0

Step 1: State the research and null hypotheses.

Step 2: Calculate the mean GPA for X_1 (before-program) and X_2 (after-program).

Step 3: For each pair of observations, calculate the difference between before-program GPA and after-program GPA. Then, square the difference scores and sum.

Step 4: Calculate the standard deviation of the difference between X_1 and X_2.

Step 5: Calculate the standard error of the mean difference.

Step 6: Calculate the t statistic.

Step 7: Calculate the degrees of freedom. The formula is $n - 1$.

Step 8: Compare the calculated t statistic with the critical t value from Table B in Appendix A.

Step 9: Interpret findings.

10.3   Assumptions of the t Test

The amount of confidence we are able to place in our findings is determined, at least in part, by the care the researcher took in designing the study and meeting the assumptions of the t test. The four assumptions of an independent t test are:

- The researcher selects two random samples.
- The two samples are drawn from normally distributed populations.
- The dependent variable is measured at the interval or ratio level; recall that the independent variable is categorical consisting of only two categories.
- The variances of the two samples are homogeneous.

In evaluating or conducting a research study reporting a t statistic, it is important to be sure that the two samples are randomly selected. Did the researcher draw two random samples from the same population? Are you confident that the probability of being selected for one group had no effect on the probability of being selected for the other group? If only one random sample is drawn, as in the case of dependent and matched-samples, then a dependent rather than an independent t statistic should be considered.

A second assumption of the t statistic is that the two samples must be drawn from normally distributed populations. If you draw large enough samples—let's say 30 or more for each group—you can assume that this assumption has been met. We often use small sample sizes in this text for the sake of illustration and ease of computation; however, the t statistic requires obtaining sufficiently large samples. If a researcher is unable to obtain large samples, a specific t statistic formula designed for small sample sizes should be considered.

A third assumption of the *t* statistic is that the dependent variable must be measured at the interval or ratio level. If this assumption is violated, you should consider using non-parametric alternatives to the *t* statistic as discussed in the previous chapter (Chapter 9).

The final assumption that a researcher must address is that the variances of the two groups must be homogeneous; that is, the two variances must approximate the same value. This assumption is often the most difficult to evaluate. To meet this assumption, the researcher should draw large samples (i.e., 30 or more) of equal sample size. Second, the researcher should calculate the variances for each of the two samples and determine whether the variances are indeed "fairly similar." Although what constitutes "fairly similar" is a decision left to the researcher, one suggested guideline is that the difference between the standard deviations (square root of the variances) of the two groups must be less than 1 to say that the variances of the two groups are equal (Miller and Whitehead, 1996, p. 258).

It is important that the assumptions of the *t* test are met; any extreme violations render the value of the *t* statistic meaningless. It is also important to stress, however, that the *t* statistic is meaningless unless the researcher paid close attention to the details of the research process. If the study is haphazardly conducted (e.g., careless selection of subjects, inconsistent presentation of the treatment, inaccurate recording of the observations), then we will have little confidence in our findings regardless of the value of our *t* statistic. It is our experience that *t* statistics are more often rendered meaningless, because of careless research practices than violations of the assumptions.

10.4 Using Excel to Compute t Tests

Now that you are able to perform the *t* test calculations by hand, we turn our attention to Excel. As always, we begin with the assumption that the data has already been entered into the spreadsheet, and then proceed with step-by-step instructions for calculating a *t* test involving a hypothetical research scenario.

Independent-Samples t Test

A researcher believes that, in sentencing, there are some fundamental differences between juveniles and adults. To answer her research question, she begins by drawing a random sample of juveniles and adults who have been sentenced to probation for a specific number of months following the conviction of a DUI (Driving Under the Influence) offense. Specifically, she hypothesizes that the offender's age status (X) has an effect on length of sentence (Y). This is a nondirectional hypothesis, because she is not hypothesizing "how" the groups are different by suggesting that one group receives longer sentences than the other group; she only argues that the two groups are different in terms of sentence length. The data for this example is presented in Table 10.4.

Step 1: State the research null hypotheses. We provide this in notational form in cell a2.

Step 2: Calculate the mean and variance for both juveniles and adults using the paste function box as learned in Chapters 4 and 5.

Step 3: Calculate the standard error of the difference between means using the following formula:

$$s_{\bar{x}_1 - \bar{x}_2} = \sqrt{\left(\frac{n_1 s_1^2 + n_2 s_2^2}{n_1 + n_2 - 2} \right) \left(\frac{n_1 + n_2}{n_1 n_2} \right)}$$

Place the cursor in cell b18 and write:
=sqrt(((((b15*b17)+(c15*c17))/(b15+c15-2))*((b15+c15)/(b15*c15)))).

b15 and c15 are cell locations for the sample size of juveniles and adults, respectively. b17 and c17 are cell locations for the variances for juveniles and adults, respectively. sqrt is the symbol for square root.

Step 4: Calculate the *t* statistic using the following formula:

$$t = \frac{\bar{X}_1 - \bar{X}_2}{s_{\bar{x}_1 - \bar{x}_2}}$$

Place the cursor in cell b19 and writing: =(b16-c16)/b18.

b16 is the cell location for the mean sentence length for juveniles. c16 is the cell location for the mean sentence length for adults. b18 is the cell location for the standard error of the difference.

Step 5: Calculate the degrees of freedom. Place the cursor in cell b20 and write: =b15+c15-2.

b15 and c15 are cell locations for the sample sizes for juveniles and adults, respectively.

Step 6: Compare the calculated *t* statistic with the critical *t* value. When we performed these calculations by hand, we found the critical *t* value in the *t* distribution table located in Appendix A (Table B). We make this comparison to determine whether our *t* statistic is statistically significant. With Excel, we can compute the significance level of our *t* statistic by performing a *t* test with the paste function box, thus eliminating the need to look at the *t* distribution table.

a. Place the cursor in cell b21 and click on the paste function box to calculate the significance level of our *t* statistic:

$$\boxed{fx}$$

TABLE 10.4 Independent-Samples *t* Test

	A	B	C
1	**TABLE 10.4 Independent-Samples *t* Test**		
2	H_1: $\mu_1 \neq \mu_2$ H_0: $\mu_1 = \mu_2$	Juveniles Sentence (X_1)	Adults Sentence (X_2)
3		8	7
4		12	7
5		6	6
6		7	12
7		6	13
8		14	16
9		8	14
10		8	12
11		3	7
12		3	9
13		6	9
14		9	13
15	**Sample size (*n*)**	12	12
16	**Mean ($\bar{X}$)**	7.50	10.42
17	**Variance (s^2)**	10.27	10.99
18	**Standard error of difference ($s_{\bar{x}_1 - \bar{x}_2}$)**	1.39	
19	***t* statistic**	-2.10	
20	***df***	22	
21	**Significance level**	0.04	

b. Click on the function category called **statistical.**

c. Click on the name category called **TTEST.**

d. Click **ok** and a box will appear that will ask for the following information: array 1, array 2, tails, and type. Array 1 and 2 are the data values for our two groups, tails is whether we are performing a one-tailed or two-tailed test, and type is the specific type of t test we are performing (independent or dependent samples). Thus, our box should look like the following:

array 1	b3:b14
array 2	c3:c14
tails	2
type	2

array 1: All juveniles in the sample located in cells b3 through b14.
array 2: All adults in the sample located in cells c3 through c14.
tails: 2 specifies a two-tailed test.
type: 2 specifies an independent-samples *t* test assuming equal variances.

Once the correct values have been typed into the box, click **ok** and the resulting value will be the significance level for the calculated *t* statistic.

Step 7: Interpret the findings. Our analysis concludes that the *t* statistic of –2.10 is significant at the .04 level, thus indicating that the difference in average probation sentences for DUI offenses among juveniles and adults is due to an actual difference among the population parameters and not the result of sampling error. In simpler terms, adults receive significantly longer probation sentences than juveniles for DUI offenses. It is important to remember that to conclude that our *t* statistic is statistically significant the significance level must be .05 or less. Because a significance level of .04 is less than .05, we can conclude that adults receive longer sentences than juveniles.

Although our *t* statistic is negative, we simply ignore the sign when comparing the calculated *t* to the critical *t*. The sign indicates the direction of the relationship. Specifically, the average sentence for adults is 10.42 months, which is longer than the juvenile average of 7.50 months. Because we are subtracting the larger mean from the smaller mean, we will get a negative *t* statistic. Our comparison, however, focuses on the absolute value of the calculated *t* statistic compared to the critical *t* value in determining whether the difference is statistically significant.

Dependent-Samples t Test

Let's now look at an example in which we would want to perform a dependent-samples *t* test. Suppose a researcher is interested in studying the effects of DARE (Drug Abuse Resistance Education) among a group of adolescents. The researcher believes that DARE (X) has an effect on drug use (Y), and he has drawn a random sample of 12 9th graders from among the population of 9th graders who have admitted using drugs within the past year and have participated in the DARE program. His specific hypothesis is that drug use will be significantly lower after the program compared to drug use before the program. This is a directional hypothesis because the researcher is specifying "how" the two means should differ—the postprogram mean should be lower than the preprogram mean. Table 10.5 provides the data for this example with X_1 being the number of times each student used drugs one year prior to the start of the program and X_2 representing the number of times each student used drugs during the year following the completion of the program. The researcher's goal is to compare the average amount of drug use before the program with the average amount of use after the program to determine if DARE has an effect on drug use.

Step 1: State the research and null hypotheses. These are given in notational form in cell a2.

Step 2: Calculate the mean for $\bar{X}_1$—preprogram drug use—and $\bar{X}_2$—postprogram drug use—using the paste function box.

Step 3: Create a difference score squared column (D^2) by subtracting each after-program score from its corresponding preprogram score and squaring it. Place the cursor in cell d3, and write: =(b3-c3)^2.

b3 is the cell location for preprogram drug use for the first student.
c3 is the cell location for the postprogram drug use for the first student.
^2 is the symbol used to square the value in the parentheses.

Click on the lower right-hand corner of cell d3 and drag the cursor down to cell d14. This will automatically create the rest of the D^2 column.

Place the cursor in cell d15, click on the autosum button on the Excel menu, and hit the return key. This will automatically sum the D^2 column.

Step 4: Calculate the standard deviation of the difference (s_D) between X_1 and X_2 using the following formula:

$$s_D = \sqrt{\frac{\Sigma D^2}{n} - \left(\bar{X}_1 - \bar{X}_2\right)^2}$$

Place the cursor in cell b17 and write: =sqrt((d15/b15)–((b16–c16)^2)).

d15 is the cell location for the sum of D^2.
b15 is the cell location for the sample size.
b16 and c16 are the cell locations for the means for X_1 and X_2, respectively.
^2 is the symbol for squaring a value.
sqrt is the symbol for square root.

Step 5: Use the following formula to calculate the standard error of the difference ($s_{\overline{D}}$):

$$s_{\overline{D}} = \frac{s_D}{\sqrt{n-1}}$$

Place the cursor in cell b18 and write: =b17/(sqrt(b15-1)).

b17 is the cell location for the standard deviation of the difference.
b15 is the cell location for the sample size.
sqrt is the symbol for square root.

Step 6: Calculate the t statistic. The formula is given as:

$$t = \frac{\overline{X}_1 - \overline{X}_2}{s_{\overline{D}}}$$

Place the cursor in cell b19 and write: =(b16-c16)/b18.

b16 and c16 are the cell locations for the means for X_1 and X_2, respectively.
b18 is the cell location for the standard error of the difference.

Step 7: Calculate the degrees of freedom by placing the cursor in cell b20 and writing: =b15-1.

Step 8: Determine the significance level of t. Once again we can use the paste function box to determine this value. The steps are exactly the same as those used for the independent-samples t test; however, the values in the box are slightly different, and should read as follows:

array 1	b3:b14
array 2	c3:c14
tails	1
type	1

array 1: The preprogram scores for each student are located in cells b3 through b14.
array 2: The postprogram scores for each student are located in cells c3 through c14.
tails: 1 Specifies a one-tailed test.
type: 1 Specifies a dependent-samples t test.

After the values have been entered into the box, click **ok,** and the resulting value will indicate the exact significance level of the t statistic.

Step 9: Interpret the findings. As shown in Table 10.5, the calculated t statistic of 1.95 is statistically significant at the .04 level. Therefore, we are able to reject the null hypothesis of no difference and conclude that DARE significantly reduces drug use

TABLE 10.5 Dependent-Samples *t* Test

	A	B	C	D
1	**TABLE 10.5 Dependent-Samples *t* Test**			
2	$H_1: \mu_1 > \mu_2$ $H_0: \mu_1 \leq \mu_2$	Before DARE X_1	After DARE X_2	D^2
3	Student 1	5	3	4
4	Student 2	3	3	0
5	Student 3	3	0	9
6	Student 4	1	2	1
7	Student 5	1	2	1
8	Student 6	7	3	16
9	Student 7	6	2	16
10	Student 8	5	4	1
11	Student 9	3	4	1
12	Student 10	2	0	4
13	Student 11	1	2	1
14	Student 12	1	0	1
15	**Sample size (*n*)**	12	Sum	55
16	**Mean ($\bar{X}$)**	3.17	2.08	
17	**Standard deviation of difference (s_D)**	1.85		
18	**Standard error of difference ($s_{\bar{D}}$)**	0.56		
19	***t* statistic**	1.95		
20	***df***	11		
21	**Significance**	0.04		

among the population of 9th graders who have previously used drugs. Our research hypothesis, therefore, is supported.

Although we have already discussed the implications for conducting a one-tailed or two-tailed test, it is worth revisiting. In this example, our researcher hypothesized a directional difference, because he believed that DARE would have a positive effect on drug use; that is, drug use would decrease among individuals who participated in the program. According to the *t* distribution table in Appendix A (Table B), the critical value for a one-tailed test with 11 degrees of freedom at the .05 level of significance is 1.80. Because the calculated *t* statistic (1.95) exceeds the critical *t* value, our researcher was able to reject the null hypothesis.

Suppose the researcher hypothesized that DARE has an effect on drug use but is unsure whether it will increase or decrease use. This is a nondirectional hypothesis, which requires us to perform a two-tailed test. The critical value for a two-tailed test with 11 degrees of freedom at the .05 level of significance is 2.20. Because the calculated *t* statistic of 1.95 is less than the critical value, the researcher is unable to reject the null hypothesis.

In most instances involving a program such as DARE, researchers are able to formulate a directional hypothesis because the program is designed to accomplish a specific goal. DARE is designed to reduce and/or prevent drug use among adolescents. Once again, the advantage of a directional hypothesis is that the critical *t* value is smaller, as the critical region is located entirely in one tail of the *t* distribution.

As mentioned in Chapter 1, there is—in many instances—more than one way to perform statistical analyses using Excel. Although we recommend performing the *t* test using the formula method demonstrated, one must be aware that the resulting *t* statistic will be accurate only if the formulas have been written correctly. How do we know if the formulas are correct? We could calculate the *t* statistics by hand to double-check the work done in Excel; however, such work seems to defeat the purpose of using Excel. Therefore, we recommend using Excel's other functions as a check on your formula calculations.

We would now like to demonstrate the calculation of a dependent-samples *t* test using the data analysis tool in Excel. We use the same data presented in Table 10.5.

Step 1: Select the **tools** option on the Excel menu bar.
Step 2: Select **data analysis** under the tools option.
Step 3: In the analysis tool box, select **t test: Paired Two-Sample for Means.**
Step 4: Enter b2:b14 for the Variable *1* Range (X_1) and c2:c14 for the Variable *2* Range (X_2). Click on the labels box so the X_1 and X_2 labels will appear in the output table.
Step 5: Click **ok** and an output table like that shown in Table 10.6 will be produced.

A comparison of Tables 10.5 and 10.6 demonstrates identical results with regard to the means, sample sizes, degrees of freedom, calculated *t* statistic, and significance level, using the two different techniques for computing a dependent-samples *t* test. The Data Analysis Tool provides some additional information, including the critical values and significance levels for both one-tailed and two-tailed tests. We can see that the critical value for a one-tailed test is 1.80 (cell b9) and the significance value of our *t* statistic— labeled $P(T \le = t)$—is .04 (cell b8). The steps for computing an independent-samples *t* test are exactly the same, with the exception of step 3, in which case we would select **t test: Two-Sample Assuming Equal Variance.** We recommend use of the Data Analysis Tool—not as a substitute for the formula method but, rather, as a procedural check on your work to ensure that your calculations are correct.

TABLE 10.6 Dependent *t* Test Using Data Analysis Tool

	A	B	C
1	TABLE 10.6 Dependent *t* Test Using Data Analysis Tool		
2		*Before DARE* X_1	*After DARE* X_2
3	Mean	3.17	2.08
4	Variance	4.52	2.08
5	Observations	12	12
6	*df*	11	
7	*t* stat	1.95	
8	$P(T \leq t)$ one-tail	0.04	
9	*t* critical one-tail	1.80	
10	$P(T \leq t)$ two-tail	0.08	
11	*t* critical two-tail	2.20	

10.5 Summary

This chapter presented the *t* test to analyze hypotheses proposing a difference between two groups on a specific dependent measure. Some examples of hypotheses in which using the *t* test would be appropriate include: "Celebrities are more knowledgable on stalking laws than are noncelebrities." "Drug use is higher among urban than rural youths." The independent variable must consist of two groups or categories (e.g., celebrities vs. noncelebrities, urban vs. rural youths). The two groups are measured on a specific dependent measure (e.g., knowledge of stalking laws, amount of drug use). The dependent variable must be measured at the interval or ratio level (e.g., number of correct responses on a stalking law test, number of different types of illegal drugs used during a specific time period).

We presented the *t* test for both independent and dependent samples. The *t* test for independent samples is appropriate when the two samples are selected in such a way that the likelihood of selection for one sample has no effect on the likelihood of selection for the other sample. The *t* test for dependent or matched samples is appropriate when the two samples are selected in such a way that the likelihood of selection for one sample directly affects the likelihood of selection for the other sample. This often occurs in pre-post experimental designs, in which only one sample is drawn and measures of the dependent variable are taken at two different points in time. A researcher may also deliberately seek dependent samples on matching subjects in terms of important characteristics prior to placing them in the treatment and control group. In this case, a subject in the treatment group is matched with one in the control group to heighten confidence that any observed differences can be attributed to the treatment rather than to subject characteristics.

Step-by-step hand and computer calculations of the *t* test for both independent and dependent/matched samples were presented. The *t* test for independent samples compares the means of two different samples on a single dependent measure. One of the main assumptions of the independent *t* test—that the researcher draws two random samples—is deliberately violated with the dependent- and matched-samples *t* test. To handle this violation, the researcher focuses on the pair of observations and looks at the difference or change scores from a single sample.

This chapter also discussed the assumptions of the *t* test. The four assumptions are (1) that the researcher selects two random samples, (2) that the samples are drawn from normally distributed populations, (3) that the dependent variable is measured at the interval or ratio level, and (4) that the variances of the two samples are homogeneous. If these assumptions are met and if the study was carefully designed and executed, then the researcher can meaningfully interpret the *t* statistics.

Key Terms

independent-samples *t* test

standard error of the difference between means

dependent- or matched-samples *t* test

TryIT! Answers

Box 10.1

Step 1: State the research and null hypotheses.

H_1: Male and female officers differ in terms of number of arrests.

$H_1: \mu_{1males} \neq \mu_{2females}$

H_0: Male and female officers do not differ in terms of number of arrests.

$H_0: \mu_{1males} = \mu_{2females}$

Step 2: Calculate the mean and variance for each group.

Male officers: mean = 5, variance = .86
Female officers: mean = 3, variance = .86

Step 3: Calculate the standard error of the mean difference.

$$S_{\bar{x}_1-\bar{x}_2} = .49$$

Step 4: Calculate the *t* statistic.

$$t = 4.08$$

Step 5: Calculate the degrees of freedom.

$$8 + 8 - 2 = 14$$

Step 6: Compare the calculated *t* statistic with the critical *t* value in Table B (Appendix A). We advanced a two-tailed hypothesis with 14 degrees of freedom. The critical value is 2.15. As the calculated *t* statistic of 4.08 is greater than the critical *t* value of 2.15, we reject the null hypothesis and accept the research hypothesis.

Step 7: Interpret findings.
There is a statistically significant difference between the population of male and female officers in terms of number of arrests. Male officers make significantly more arrests than do female officers.

Box 10.2

Step 1: State the research and null hypotheses.

H_1: Criminal justice students' after-program GPA will be higher than their before-program GPA.

$$H_1: \mu_{1\text{Before GPA}} < \mu_{2\text{After GPA}}$$

H_0: Criminal justice students' after-program GPA will be equal to or less than their before-program GPA.

$$H_0: \mu_{1\text{Before GPA}} \geq \mu_{2\text{After GPA}}$$

Step 2: Calculate the mean GPA before and after the program.

Before-program (X_1): mean = 2.79
After-program (X_2): mean = 3.28

Step 3: For each pair of observations, calculate the difference between before-program GPA (X_1) and after-program GPA (X_2). Then square the difference scores and sum.

Sum of the difference scores squared = 3.81

Step 4: Calculate the standard deviation of the difference between X_1 and X_2.

Standard deviation of the difference = .49

Step 5: Calculate the standard error of the mean difference.

Standard error of the mean difference $= .18$

Step 6: Calculate the t statistic.

$t = -2.72$

Step 7: Calculate degrees of freedom.

$8 - 1 = 7.$

Step 8: Compare the calculated t statistic with the critical t value from Table B (Appendix A). We advanced a one-tailed hypothesis with seven degrees of freedom. The critical value is 1.89. The calculated t statistic of -2.78 is greater in absolute value than the critical t value of 1.89; thus, we reject the null hypothesis only on confirming that the difference is in the hypothesized direction. We expected a negative t statistic, because we hypothesized that after-program GPA (X_2) would be larger than before-program GPA (X_1). The research hypothesis is confirmed.

Step 9: Interpret findings.

The findings show that the program "How to Study and Get Better Grades" is effective at improving the academic performance for the population of criminal justice students.

10.6 Problems

1. This chapter began with the mayor of a mid-sized city hiring you to determine what the citizens think about the neighborhood crime watch program. You think that older citizens might differ from younger ones in their assessment of the program. Eight older and eight younger citizens were selected randomly to participate in the study. On a 7-point scale, the volunteers marked their perceptions of the effectiveness of the neighborhood crime watch program. With higher scores reflecting more favorable evaluations, the observations are recorded as follows:

Younger Citizens	Older Citizens
5	3
5	4
7	5
7	7
7	4
6	4
5	3
6	2

Determine the following: (a) calculated t statistic, (b) degrees of freedom, (c) critical t value, and (d) the decision about the null hypothesis.

2. A one-tailed test is used for a _____ hypothesis, while a two-tailed test is used for a _____ hypothesis.

3. To use a *t* test, the dependent variable must be measured at what level?

4. Determine the critical *t* value for the following conditions:

	Tailed Test	*Alpha Level*	*Degrees of Freedom*
a.	2	.05	22
b.	1	.01	18
c.	1	.05	40
d.	2	.01	10
e.	2	.05	75
f.	1	.10	15

5. A researcher hypothesizes that criminal justice majors will score higher on a statistics exam than will psychology majors. Identify (a) the appropriate *t* test and (b) whether a one-tailed or two-tailed test is warranted.

6. Calculate the degrees of freedom for the following research conditions:

	Type of t *Test*	*Sample Size*
a.	Dependent	45
b.	Independent	Group 1 = 15, Group 2 = 21
c.	Independent	Group 1 = 8, Group 2 = 12
d.	Dependent	29
e.	Dependent	100
f.	Independent	Group 1 = 27, Group 2 = 31

7. Define the following:

   a. Independent samples *t* test
   b. Dependent samples *t* test

8. Make a decision concerning the null hypothesis for each of the following research conditions:

	Calculated t *Statistic*	*Critical* t *Value*
a.	−1.97	−1.85
b.	1.56	2.13
c.	2.34	2.34
d.	2.89	3.01
e.	−1.14	−1.16

9. As a member of the police board, you have been assigned the task of evaluating the effectiveness of an arrest policy for domestic disturbances. The program has been implemented in a number of cities and was expected to increase the number of reported cases. The number of reported cases of domestic disturbances before and after implementation of the arrest policy for seven randomly selected cities are reported below.

Before Implementation	After Implementation
10	15
15	20
15	20
5	15
10	15
10	5
0	5

Determine the following: (a) calculated t statistic, (b) degrees of freedom, (c) critical t value (alpha = .05), and the (d) decision about the null hypothesis.

10. A researcher believes that differences exist between single-parent children and two-parent children with regard to the number of school days skipped during the fall semester. Write a directional hypothesis in both text and notational form, and identify the type of t test most appropriate for testing your hypothesis.

11. In a study of 50 high school seniors (25 from a public school and 25 from a private school) and their attitudes toward community sanctions for convicted offenders, researchers conducted an independent-samples t test that revealed a calculated t statistic equal to 1.85. Using an alpha level of .05 and a two-tailed test, determine the (a) degrees of freedom, (b) critical t value, and (c) decision about the null hypothesis. 2.02 > 1.85 ∴ accept Ho.

12. A researcher hypothesizes that incarcerated drug offenders have fewer misconduct violations in prison than nondrug offenders. After drawing a random sample of 24 offenders (12 drug and 12 nondrug offenders), the researcher measures each subject on the number of violations received during the first six months of incarceration. Enter the following data into Excel and calculate an independent samples t test to test the researcher's hypothesis. Be sure to include the research and null hypotheses, mean and variance for both groups, standard error of the difference, t statistic, degrees of freedom, significance level, and decision about the null hypothesis.

Drug Offenders (X_1)	Nondrug Offenders (X_2)
1	3
1	0
3	1
3	1
2	0
3	2
4	2
2	0
3	1
1	3
2	0
2	1

13. The chief of police believes that directed patrols in high crime areas will reduce the number of calls from those areas. You have been hired as a researcher to test this assumption. Data was collected over a five-week period from eight different high crime areas. The number of calls was counted for each area over a two-week period prior to the implementation of directed patrols. Directed patrols were conducted for one week. Data was then collected over a two-week period after the directed patrols had ended. The data follows. Enter this data into Excel and calculate a dependent-samples *t* test. Be sure to include the research and null hypotheses, before and after means, standard deviation of the difference, standard error of the difference, *t* statistic, degrees of freedom, significance level, and decision about the null hypothesis.

Area	No. Calls Before (X_1)	No. Calls After (X_2)
1	125	83
2	150	175
3	93	94
4	100	90
5	110	81
6	75	65
7	80	90
8	120	100

Statistical Analysis for Comparing Three or More Population Means: Analysis of Variance

ExploreIT!

The Office of Juvenile Justice and Delinquency Prevention has awarded you a federal grant to study school violence across America. The agency is particularly interested in knowing if the amount of violence differs by the type of school. You have decided to analyze violence among four different types of schools: public, private-Christian, private-non-Christian, and charter schools. After selecting a probability sample of 100 schools (25 of each type), you count the number of violent acts that were reported to school administrators within each school during the 2000–2001 school year. How do you know if the frequency of violence varies by type of school? You will use analysis of variance to compare the mean number of violent acts across the four types of schools.

In the preceding chapter we examined a statistical test, referred to as the t test, for the difference between two means. We compared two groups on a single dependent variable. For instance, we looked at whether younger and older citizens differ in their perceptions of the neighborhood crime watch program. The independent variable consisted of two groups—younger versus older citizens. The dependent variable was measured at the interval level—perceptions of the crime watch program on a 7-point rating scale.

We now turn to the situation in which there is one independent variable with more than two groups. Let's say we wish to compare three age groups of citizens—adolescents, middle-aged people, and seniors—in terms of their perceptions of the crime watch program. Our independent variable is "age," which consists of three different groups—Adolescents, Middle-aged, and Seniors—and our dependent variable is "perceptions of the crime watch program," which is measured on a 7-point rating scale. Our research hypothesis would suggest that the mean levels of perception of the crime watch program are different among the three groups of respondents. Alternatively, the null hypothesis would indicate that the three group means are equal. In this case, with one independent variable having three or more groups and one dependent variable measured at the interval or ratio level, the appropriate statistical analysis is called a one-way or single-factor analysis of variance (ANOVA).

Let's extend this example and decide to consider both "age" (Adolescents, Middle-aged, and Seniors) and "race" (Black, White) of citizens in drawing conclusions about the perceptions of the crime watch program. In this situation, we have two independent variables, "age" and "race," and one dependent variable, "perceptions of the program." If your project focuses on the impact of two independent variables on a single continuous dependent measure, the appropriate analysis is the two-way or two-factor **analysis of variance**. Thus, **analysis of variance** (ANOVA) is *defined as a class of statistical techniques designed to test if different groups, or various combinations of groups, differ in terms of a continuous dependent measure.*

analysis of variance (ANOVA)

In many ways, ANOVA is an extension of the t statistic; hence, we begin with a discussion of a comparison between the two types of analyses. This chapter will also discuss three different types of ANOVA techniques commonly used in criminal justice research to test various hypotheses concerning population means involving three or more groups. This chapter concludes with illustrations on calculating the different types of ANOVAs using Excel.

11.1 Comparison of t Statistic and ANOVA

The t statistic and ANOVA are similar in several ways. First, the nature of the independent and dependent variables is the same. The independent variable is categorical and the dependent variable is continuous. Second, the goal of both types of analyses is to see whether the differences between the groups represent actual differences in the population rather than sampling error. Third, the analyses are based on the same set of assumptions. The samples are randomly selected, the dependent variable is measured at the interval or ratio level, and the variances of the samples are homogeneous.

The two analyses differ in terms of the number of comparisons that can be made. As you know, the *t* statistic compares the means of two groups. In contrast, a single-factor ANOVA compares the means of more than two groups on a specific dependent variable. In addition, the researcher can look at differences between combinations of groups; for example, the researcher is able to compare the mean of one group to the means of two groups combined. The number of independent variables also can distinguish the types of analyses. Whereas there is always only one independent variable with a *t* statistic and a single-factor ANOVA, a two-factor or multiple-factor ANOVA consists of two or more independent variables.

In performing a *t* test, the researcher needs to be concerned with only one type of variability; in contrast, ANOVA considers two types of variability. Both the *t* test and ANOVA are concerned with within-group variability, which pertains to how much each individual observation deviates from the mean of its own distribution. The *t* statistic examines the mean difference between two groups in relation to the variability or error that exists within each group. The same principle characterizes ANOVA. Analysis of variance examines the mean differences between groups taking into account how much variability or error exists within each group. Our goal is to have as little within-group variability as possible. Let's examine this principle.

Suppose we took a random sample of eight inmates from each of three classification groups: minimum, medium, and maximum. If we recorded the number of disciplinary infractions of each inmate in each of the three groups, we hope to observe little within-group variability. In other words, we hope that the number of infractions does not vary widely for individuals within each group. In this example, we hope that most of the minimum-classified inmates had about the same number of disciplinary infractions, most of the medium-classified inmates had about the same number of infractions, and so on. If so, the sample mean would be a good estimate for representing the group of observations. Figure 11.1a shows little variability, as measured by the standard deviation, among the observations in each group; by contrast, Figure 11.1b illustrates much greater within-group variability as the range of scores for each group increases. For example, in Figure 11.1a, the number of disciplinary infractions for maximum-custody inmates ranges from a low of 1 to a high of 4, resulting in a small standard deviation of 1.09. In Figure 11.1b, the standard deviation is much larger (4.54), because the amount of variation among the scores ranges from a low of 0 to a high of 12.

For both the *t* test and ANOVA, the researcher is concerned with minimizing within-group variability. With ANOVA, the researcher also must be concerned with a second type of variability known as between-group variability. Between-group variability pertains to the amount of variability among the sample means of the different groups. The greater the difference between the sample means of each group—assuming little within-group variation—the more confidence we have that any observed differ-

FIGURE 11.1a Illustration of little variability among scores within each group

	Minimum	Medium	Maximum
	2	2	4
	1	0	3
	0	0	4
	1	2	2
	0	3	3
	0	2	4
	2	0	4
	1	0	4
	0	1	1
Mean ($\bar{X}$)	0.78	1.11	3.22
Standard deviation (s)	0.83	1.17	1.09

FIGURE 11.1b Illustration of much variability among scores within each group

	Minimum	Medium	Maximum
	5	7	12
	1	3	1
	0	2	3
	2	2	9
	1	1	8
	0	0	1
	0	0	1
	5	5	0
	7	0	0
Mean ($\bar{X}$)	2.33	2.22	3.89
Standard deviation (s)	2.65	2.44	4.54

ences are because of actual differences between the population parameters and not sampling error. Thus, our goal is to maximize between-group variability.

Suppose that the sample means representing the number of disciplinary infractions of the three groups of inmates were identical; for instance, each group had a sample mean of 2.40. If so, there would be no between-group variability. By contrast, the more the sample means of the three groups of inmates differ, the greater the between-group variability.

ANOVA is a method for testing hypotheses involving three or more sample means. The calculations of an ANOVA yield a statistical value called F. The F statistic is represented as the amount of variance between-group divided by the amount of variance within-group.

$$F = \frac{\text{Between-Group Variance}}{\text{Within-Group Variance}}$$

As with the t value, the F statistic is compared to a probability distribution to determine whether the value is large enough to reject the null hypothesis and accept the research hypothesis. The more between-group variance exceeds within-group variance, the greater the value of F. This explains why the goal is to maximize between-group variability and minimize within-group variability.

Because ANOVA is concerned with two types of variation, it has two types of degrees of freedom associated with it. ANOVA has both between-group degrees of freedom and within-group degrees of freedom. In order to look up the critical value in the F probability distribution, you must know the degrees of freedom for both between-group and within-group variance. Between-group degrees of freedom is determined by the number of groups minus 1, represented as $k - 1$. Within-group degrees of freedom is determined by the total number of subjects (e.g., sample size) minus the number of groups, represented as $n - k$.

We have tried to show that ANOVA is an extension of the t test. Both methods consist of at least one categorical independent variable and a continuous dependent variable. The assumptions of the tests are similar. Furthermore, the two procedures allow us to determine if the observed sample differences are the result of actual differences among the population parameters or the result of sampling error. ANOVA is an extension of the t test that allows for more comparisons often involving more than one independent variable. Whereas the t test is concerned only with within-group variance, ANOVA also must consider between-group variance. As such, the t is able to consider only within-group degrees of freedom, while ANOVA must consider both between-group and within-group degrees of freedom. For both analyses, the research hypothesis is tested by comparing the yielded value, t or F, to a probability distribution.

Assumptions of ANOVA

The assumptions of ANOVA parallel those of a t test. The four basic assumptions of ANOVA are:

- The scores are drawn randomly from normally distributed populations.
- The scores are independent of each other.

- The dependent variable is measured at the interval or ratio level; recall that the independent variable is categorical.
- The variances are homogeneous.

The first assumption is the assumption of normality. The observations must be drawn from normally distributed populations. That is, the shape of the distribution for the dependent variable within each group should approximate the normal or bell-shaped curve. We can evaluate the extent to which this assumption is met by looking at the distribution of scores. If the sample sizes of each group are equal, the sample sizes are greater than 15, and the shape of the distribution approximates normality, then— for practical consideration—the assumption is considered to be met. If one or more of these conditions are violated, then it may be necessary to entertain other alternatives such as data transformation—a procedure discussed in advanced texts (see Kirk, 1982). Although the researcher should test for normality and proceed with caution using ANOVA in extreme violations, in general, the *F* distribution is not greatly affected by violations of this assumption.

A second assumption of ANOVA is independence of scores. That is, the scores, for both between-group and within-group are not in anyway related or dependent on each other. If the researcher designs the study carefully, this assumption should never be violated. For experimental designs, this assumption is met as along as two conditions prevail—the researcher randomly assigns individuals to treatment groups, and the researcher tests each individual independently. For survey designs, independence of scores is achieved by means of probability sampling.

A third assumption of ANOVA is that the dependent variable must be measured at the interval or ratio level. We must be able to calculate a mean for the dependent variable at each level or category of the independent variable.

The final assumption that a researcher must address is that the variances of the groups must be homogeneous; that is, the variances must approximate the same value. This assumption is often the most difficult to evaluate. Research involving equal samples of 30 or more subjects in each group is one method for meeting this assumption. This is not to say that you have violated this assumption if you have fewer than 30 subjects or unequal sample sizes in each group. Thus, it is highly recommended that researchers calculate the variances for each of the groups to determine whether the variances are indeed "fairly similar." Once again, we recommend following the guidelines as discussed in Chapter 10 to determine whether the variances are similar. As you recall, we can assume that the variances are similar if the differences between the standard deviations for each group are less than 1 (Miller and Whitehead, 1996, p. 258). Keeping in mind that ANOVA is really an extension of the *t* test, we are ready to turn our attention to a closer examination of a single-factor ANOVA.

11.2 Single-Factor ANOVA

single-factor ANOVA   A **single-factor ANOVA** is *a statistical test for comparing the sample means of three or more groups in terms of a continuous dependent measure*. A single-factor ANOVA would be appropriate to test the following research hypotheses:

Hypothesis 1: Children at four grade levels (1st, 4th, 8th, and 12th) differ in terms of their perceptions of violence in crime dramas.

Hypothesis 2: Sentence length is a function of judges' political affiliation—Republican, Democrat, and Independent.

Hypothesis 3: The level of satisfaction with the new campus crime prevention strategy differs among various members of the campus community—Undergraduates, Graduates, Faculty, and Staff.

In the above hypotheses, there is one categorical independent variable (grade level, political affiliation, members of the campus community). Moreover, each independent variable consists of three or more groups or levels (grade levels: 1st, 4th, 8th, and 12th; political affiliation: Republican, Democrat, and Independent; members of campus community: Undergraduates, Graduates, Faculty, and Staff). The researcher claims that these groups differ in terms of a specific continuous dependent variable—perceptions of violence in crime dramas, sentence length, and satisfaction with the crime prevention strategy. Which hypothesis is of most interest to you?

Procedures for Calculating a Single-Factor ANOVA

Let's say that you are most interested in studying children's perceptions of violence in crime dramas. As researchers, we think that there will be some differences in the level of "perceptions of violence"(Y) among children at different "grade levels"(X).

Step 1: State the research and null hypotheses.

H_1: Children at four grade levels (1st, 4th, 8th, and 12th) differ in terms of their perceptions of violence in crime dramas.

$$H_1: \mu_1 \neq \mu_2 \neq \mu_3 \neq \mu_4$$

H_0: Children at four grade levels (1st, 4th, 8th, and 12th) do not differ in terms of their perceptions of violence in crime dramas.

$$H_0: \mu_1 = \mu_2 = \mu_3 = \mu_4$$

Your goal is to reject the null hypothesis that the children at the four grade levels do not differ in terms of their perceptions of violence in crime dramas. If you are able to reject the null hypothesis of no difference among sample means, you are able to accept the research hypothesis and conclude that the children's perceptions of violence in crime dramas varied depending on grade level. It is important to note that ANOVA will only tell us that there is significant variation among the means at the four grade levels. In other words, a significant *F* statistic means that somewhere among the four means there is at least one significant difference. ANOVA will *not* tell us which means are significantly different from each other. You *cannot* say things like "The 4th graders perceived more violence in the crime dramas than did the 1st graders." In order to know which pair of means (e.g., 1st vs. 12th grade) or combinations of means (e.g., 1st and 4th vs. 8th and 12th grade) differ, you must conduct further analyses called *post hoc* or *follow-up* tests. An explanation of how to perform post hoc tests and a discussion of some important considerations in performing these tests are presented later in this chapter.

Let's say that you proceed to test your hypothesis that perceptions of violence in crime dramas differ by grade level. You randomly select five children at each of the four grade levels to participate in your study. You administer a questionnaire to obtain the children's perceptions of violence in TV crime dramas. Of particular interest to you is the children's perceptions of the level of violence in such dramas. The scores range from 1 to 10, with higher values reflecting greater perceptions of violence. Table 11.1 reports the observations.

By observing Table 11.1, we might be tempted to conclude that the sample means differ among the four grade levels. Yet, as you know by now, we cannot draw such conclusions without first considering sources of variation. How do we measure variation? This concept was discussed in calculating the variance and standard deviation in Chapter 5. Furthermore, the *t* test involves calculating variation by looking at how each score **sum of** deviates from the mean of its own distribution. A similar procedure is used to look at **squares** variability in ANOVA. In ANOVA, variation is referred to as **sums of squares**, defined

TABLE 11.1 Perceptions of Violence in Crime Dramas by Grade Level

	Grade Level			
	1st	*4th*	*8th*	*12th*
	8	6	5	1
	9	6	4	2
	8	2	4	3
	7	4	3	3
	8	7	4	1
Sum	40	25	20	10
Mean	8	5	4	2

as *the sums of the squared deviation scores*. We used squared deviation scores when calculating the variance and standard deviation. Sums of squares is the descriptive term that represents the sum of the squared deviation scores. There are three sources of variation in ANOVA: There are sums of squares between-group, sums of squares within-group, and total sums of squares. We will look at each of these sources of variation in our calculations of ANOVA.

Step 2: Calculate the group means, grand mean, and the sums of squares between-group ($SS_{Between}$).

sums of squares between-group

Sums of squares between-group ($SS_{Between}$) refers to *how much the means of each group deviate from the grand mean*. The grand mean is the mean of all of the scores combined, whereas the group means are the means for the scores within each of the groups. Thus, we use the following formulas to calculate the group means and the grand mean:

$$\bar{X}_{Group} = \frac{\Sigma X_{iGroup}}{n_{Group}}$$

$$\bar{X}_{Grand} = \frac{\Sigma X_i}{n_{Total}}$$

According to the preceding formulas, the group means are calculated by dividing the sum of the individual scores within each group (ΣX_{iGroup}) by the sample size of the group (n_{Group}). The grand mean is calculated by dividing the sum of **all** of the individual scores (ΣX_i) by the total sample size (n_{Total}). Table 11.2 illustrates the calculations of the group means and the grand mean.

Once we have calculated the means, we can proceed with the calculation of sums of squares between-group. We use the following formula to calculate $SS_{Between}$:

$$SS_{Between} = \Sigma \left[n_{Group} \left(\bar{X}_{Group} - \bar{X}_{Grand} \right)^2 \right]$$

$\bar{X}_{Group}$ = Group mean of the individual
scores within each group
$\bar{X}_{Grand}$ = Grand mean of all the
individual scores
n_{Group} = Sample size of each group

The formula requires us to subtract the grand mean ($\bar{X}_{grand}$) from each group mean ($\bar{X}_{group}$) separately, then square that value. We then multiply the squared deviation by the number of observations in each group. Continuing with our example, the process for calculating $SS_{Between}$ is summarized in Table 11.2.

TABLE 11.2 Calculating the Sums of Squares Between-Group

	Grade Level			
	1st	*4th*	*8th*	*12th*
	8	6	5	1
	9	6	4	2
	8	2	4	3
	7	4	3	3
	8	7	4	1
Sums (Σ)	40	25	20	10
$\bar{X}_{Group} = \Sigma X_{iGroup}/n_{Group}$	8	5	4	2
$\bar{X}_{Grand} = \Sigma X_i/n_{total} = 4.75$				
$\bar{X}_{Group} - \bar{X}_{Grand}$	3.25	.25	−.75	−2.75
$(\bar{X}_{Group} - \bar{X}_{Grand})^2 =$	10.56	.06	.56	7.56
$n\,(\bar{X}_{Group} - \bar{X}_{Grand})^2 =$	52.81	.31	2.81	37.81
$\Sigma[n(\bar{X}_{Group} - \bar{X}_{Grand})^2] = 93.74$				

Step 3: Calculate the sums of squares within-group (SS_{Within}).

sums of squares within-group

We have just taken into account how much between-group variability exists. Our hope is that there is a lot of variability between the means of the four groups. We now look at the variability among observations in the same group; that is, we will examine within-group variability, referred to as the sums of squares within-group. **Sums of squares within-group** (SS_{Within}) is *how much each individual score deviates from the mean of its own group*. Thus, SS_{Within} reflects the sums of the squared deviations of the individual observations from the mean of its own group. It should be relatively easy to calculate as the procedures are nearly the same as for calculating the within-group variability using the *t* test. The formula is as follows:

$$SS_{Within} = \Sigma\left[\Sigma\left(X_{iGroup} - \bar{X}_{Group}\right)^2\right]$$

X_{iGroup} = Individual scores within each group

$\bar{X}_{Group}$ = Group mean of the individual
scores within each group

The formula requires us to subtract the group mean from each of the individual scores within that group. Next, for each group separately, square the deviations and sum the squared deviation scores. Finally, sum the sum of the squared deviations for each of the groups. It is important to recognize that we must compute a sum twice. The first sum is the sum of the squared deviation scores within each group. The second sum is the sum of the summed squared deviation scores across each of the groups. We illustrate the calculation of SS_{Within} in Table 11.3.

TABLE 11.3 Calculating the Sums of Squares Within-Group

Group 1: 1st Grade (X_1)

Violence Rating	Group Mean	Deviation	Squared Deviation
8	8	0	0
9	8	1	1
8	8	0	0
7	8	−1	1
8	8	0	0

Sum of the Squared Deviations = 2

Group 2: 4th Grade (X_2)

Violence Rating	Group Mean	Deviation	Squared Deviation
6	5	1	1
6	5	1	1
2	5	−3	9
4	5	−1	1
7	5	2	4

Sum of the Squared Deviations = 16

Group 2: 8th Grade (X_3)

Violence Rating	Group Mean	Deviation	Squared Deviation
5	4	1	1
4	4	0	0
4	4	0	0
3	4	−1	1
4	4	0	0

Sum of the Squared Deviations = 2

Group 2: 12th Grade (X_4)

Violence Rating	Group Mean	Deviation	Squared Deviation
1	2	−1	1
2	2	0	0
3	2	1	1
3	2	1	1
1	2	−1	1

Sum of the Squared Deviations = 4

$$SS_{Within} = 2 + 16 + 2 + 4 = 24$$

Step 4: Calculate the sums of squares total (SS_{Total}).

So far, we have examined two main sources of variability: sums of squares between-group and sums of squares within-group. Combining these two sources, we have the total amount of variability referred to as sums of squares total, SS_{Total}. **Sums of squares total** (SS_{Total}) is *the total amount of variability in analysis of variance.* To calculate, we could simply add the two sources of variability as shown in the following formula:

sums of squares total

$$SS_{Total} = SS_{Between} + SS_{Within}$$

Continuing our example, we could simply plug in the appropriate values to the above formula as follows: $SS_{Total} = 93.74 + 24 = 117.74$. We recommend that you use the procedure to check your work. More formally, however, SS_{Total} is the sum of the squared deviations of each individual score minus the grand mean. The formula is as follows:

$$SS_{Total} = \Sigma\left(X_i - \overline{X}_{Grand}\right)^2$$
$$X_i = \text{Individual scores}$$
$$\overline{X}_{Grand} = \text{Grand mean of all the}$$
$$\text{individual scores}$$

Using this formula, we simply subtract the grand mean from each individual score, then square the deviation score, and, finally, sum all of the squared deviation scores. In our example, the process for computing the sum of squares total is presented in Table 11.4.

TABLE 11.4 Calculating the Sums of Squares Total

Violence Rating (X)	Grand Mean	Deviation	Squared Deviation
8	4.75	3.25	10.56
9	4.75	4.25	18.06
8	4.75	3.25	10.56
7	4.75	2.25	5.06
8	4.75	3.25	10.56
6	4.75	1.25	1.56
6	4.75	1.25	1.56
2	4.75	−2.75	7.56
4	4.75	−0.75	0.56
7	4.75	2.25	5.06
5	4.75	0.25	0.06
4	4.75	−0.75	0.56
4	4.75	−0.75	0.56

(Continued)

TABLE 11.4 *continued*

Violence Rating (X)	Grand Mean	Deviation	Squared Deviation
3	4.75	−1.75	3.06
4	4.75	−0.75	0.56
1	4.75	−3.75	14.06
2	4.75	−2.75	7.56
3	4.75	−1.75	3.06
3	4.75	−1.75	3.06
1	4.75	−3.75	14.06
		$SS_{Total} = 117.74$	

In summary, our total amount of squared deviations is 117.74 and is partitioned as $SS_{Between}$ of 93.74 and SS_{Within} of 24. Our goal is to have larger between-group variability and small within-group variability. By observing our findings thus far, it appears that our goal is met. One more factor has to be taken into account, however—sample size.

Step 5: Calculate $MS_{Between}$ and MS_{Within}.

You know that sample size is an important component in assessing variability among scores, and that degrees of freedom is a function of sample size. The measure known as mean square—*MS*—is calculated by dividing the sums of squares by its corresponding degrees of freedom. As we need to look at between-group variability, we can obtain $MS_{Between}$ by dividing $SS_{Between}$ by $df_{Between}$. $df_{Between}$ is the number of groups minus 1, represented as $k − 1$. In our example, $SS_{Between}$ is 93.74 and $df_{Between}$ is 3; thus, $MS_{Between}$ is 31.25.

We also need to look at within-group variability. We can obtain MS_{Within} by dividing SS_{Within} by df_{Within}. Recall that df_{Within} is the number of scores minus the number of groups, represented as $n − k$. In our example, SS_{Within} is 24 and df_{Within} is 16; thus, MS_{Within} is 1.50. We would like to point out that df_{Total} is the number of total scores minus 1, represented as $n − 1$. In our example, df_{Total} is 19. If we add $df_{Between}$ and df_{Within}, 3 + 16 = 19, we obtain df_{Total}. We recommend that df_{Total} is calculated with both methods as a way to check your work.

Step 6: Calculate the *F* statistic.

At last we are ready to calculate the *F* statistic. The *F* statistic is determined using the following formula:

$$F = \frac{MS_{Between}}{MS_{Within}}$$

Placing the appropriate values into the formula, we solve for F:

$$F = \frac{31.25}{1.50} = 20.83$$

Thus, in our example, $MS_{Between}$ (31.25) divided by MS_{Within} (1.50), yields an F statistic of 20.83.

Step 7: Compare the calculated F statistic to the critical F value found in Table D in Appendix A. Is 20.83 a large enough value to reject the null hypothesis and accept the research hypothesis? In order to answer this question, we must compare the calculated F statistic to the critical F value reported in the F distribution table. The F distribution table is a bit more complex to read than the t distribution table, and may take a little practice to master. With the F table, you need to know the $df_{Between}$ (reported in the columns of the F distribution), df_{Within} (reported in the rows of the F distribution), and the desired alpha level ($p \le .05$ is the generally acceptable level). In our example, we know that our $df_{Between}$ is 3 and df_{Within} is 16, and that an alpha of .05 is selected. To find the critical value, we simply find the column that contains three degrees of freedom, and proceed down to the row that contains 16 degrees of freedom. As shown in Table 11.5, the critical value is 3.24, which is located at the intersection of the column with 3 df and the row with 16 df. Comparing our calculated F statistic of 20.83 to the critical F value of 3.24, we reject the null hypothesis of no difference between the means and accept the research hypothesis.

Step 8: Interpret findings.

The results of our analysis indicate a statistically significant relationship between perceptions of crime drama violence and grade level. More specifically, we can say that the ratings of violence among the population of 1st, 4th, 8th, and 12th graders significantly differ. The differences among the sample means are the result of actual differences between the population parameters and not the result of sampling error.

TABLE 11.5 Sample F Distribution Table $\alpha = .05$

df_{Within}	$df_{Between}$		
	3	4	5
10	3.71	3.48	3.33
11	3.59	3.57	3.20
12	3.49	3.26	3.11
13	3.41	3.18	3.03
14	3.34	3.11	2.96
15	3.29	3.06	2.90
16	**3.24**	3.01	2.85
17	3.20	2.97	2.81
18	3.16	2.93	2.77
19	3.13	2.90	2.74

Remember that $p \leq .05$ is generally considered the minimum significance level for rejecting the null hypothesis. In our example, the calculated F statistic exceeds the critical F value of 5.29 at $p \leq .01$. Thus, the probability is very small that the differences in the sample means for the four grade levels are due to sampling error. More formally, the probability that we have made a Type I error (i.e., rejected the null hypothesis when the null hypothesis is true) is less than .01.

Step 9: Construct an ANOVA summary table.

As the different steps involved in ANOVA are performed, the findings should be summarized in an ANOVA table. The table provides a way to organize the results of the calculations. The first column in an ANOVA summary table states the sources of variation, the second column reports the sums of squares, the third column reports the degrees of freedom, the fourth column reports the mean squares, and the fifth reports the F statistic. Finally, the researcher indicates significance of the F statistic by using an asterisk (*). The number of asterisks depends on the significance level (α) of the F statistic. The general rule usually applies: * = .05(α), ** = .01(α), and *** = .001(α). In this text, we determine significance levels at .05 and .01 levels, only because the F distribution table reported in Appendix A contains critical values for these two levels. The ANOVA summary table for our hypothetical example is presented in Table 11.6.

In Table 11.7, we review the key formulas involved in calculating the F statistic. We hope you find this table useful. You are now ready to compute a single-factor ANOVA. Complete TryIT! Box 11.1 before moving on to the next section.

TABLE 11.6 ANOVA Summary Table: Children's Perceptions of Violence in Crime Dramas

Sources of Variation	Sums of Squares	Degrees of Freedom	Mean Square	F
Between-Group	93.74	3	31.25	20.83**
Within-Group	24	16	1.50	
Total	117.74	19		

**$p \leq .01$

TABLE 11.7 Summary of ANOVA Formulas

Sources of Variation	Sums of Squares (SS)	Degrees of Freedom (df)	Mean Square (MS)	F
Between-Group	$\Sigma n_{Group}(\bar{X}_{iGroup} - \bar{X}_{Grand})^2$	$k - 1$	$SS_{Between}/df_{Between}$	$MS_{Between}/MS_{Within}$
Within-Group	$\Sigma[\Sigma(X_i - \bar{X}_{Group})^2]$	$n - k$	SS_{Within}/df_{Within}	
Total	$\Sigma(X_i - \bar{X}_{Grand})^2$	$n - 1$		

TryIT! BOX **11.1**

Wisconsin's Department of Social Services (WDSS) implemented a campaign to educate residents about WDSS. Residents of the lower, middle, and upper social class were asked their level of support for WDSS. The residents' perceptions were measured using a 7-point rating scale, with higher values reflecting higher levels of support for WDSS.

| | Social Class | |
Lower	Middle	Upper
4	2	2
5	1	2
6	1	3
5	2	4
5	4	4

Step 1: State the research and null hypotheses.

Step 2: Calculate the group means, grand mean, and sums of square between-group ($SS_{Between}$).

Step 3: Calculate the sums of squares within-group (SS_{Within}).

Step 4: Calculate the sums of squares total (SS_{Total}).

Step 5: Calculate $MS_{Between}$ and MS_{Within}.

Step 6: Calculate the *F* statistic.

Step 7: Compare the calculated *F* statistic with the critical *F* value from Table D in Appendix A.

Step 8: Interpret findings.

Step 9: Construct an ANOVA summary table.

11.3 Post Hoc Comparisons

ANOVA is an overall test for comparing three or more sample means. By rejecting the null hypothesis, we are simply saying that there is significant variation among the sample means. The results do *not* tell us what means statistically differ from each other. To identify which means are significantly different from which other means, one must

post hoc (posteriori) perform additional analyses. **Post hoc (posteriori)** *or follow-up comparisons are a set of statistical procedures used for determining significant differences among sample means.* As the name implies, post hoc tests are conducted *only after* an ANOVA yields a significant *F* statistic.

To illustrate the need for post hoc comparisons, let's consider the results of our hypothetical study. By observing the means at the four grade levels, 1st graders ($\bar{X}_{First}$ = 8) appear to perceive more violence in crime dramas than do children at the three higher grades ($\bar{X}_{Fourth}$= 5; $\bar{X}_{Eighth}$ = 4; and $\bar{X}_{Twelfth}$ = 2). The questions become: "Are first graders significantly different from fourth graders in terms of their perceptions of violence in crime dramas?," "Is there a statistically significant difference between fourth and eighth graders?," and so on. It might be tempting to say that 1st and 4th graders differ, but not 4th and 8th graders, by comparing the mean difference of 3 to the mean difference of 1. What about the mean difference of 2 between 8th and 12th graders? Is that significantly different? How great must a mean difference be for one to argue that the observed differences are due to actual differences among the population parameters and not to sampling error? Post hoc comparisons allow us to pinpoint the means that differ significantly from one another.

With one main exception, post hoc comparisons are much like the t test for independent samples. The exception is that post hoc tests control for the number of comparisons to be made. Why is this so important? It is essential to remember that the critical values of the t distribution are based on conducting *one* comparison between two sample means. The probability of Type I error (rejecting the null hypothesis of no difference between group means when the null hypothesis is true) increases as a function of the number of tests. Making a greater number of comparisons is likely to lead to the incorrect conclusion that the differences between the two means represent true differences in the population, when such differences are actually the result of sampling error. The number of possible pairwise comparisons increases substantially as the number of groups increases. The number of possible pairwise comparisons can be determined by $k (k - 1)/2$, with k = the number of groups. With four groups, six pairwise comparisons are possible, $4(4 - 1)/2 = 6$. With eight groups, 28 pairwise comparisons are possible, $8 (8 - 1)/2 = 28$. Thus, the probability of Type I error increases greatly, from four to eight groups. The point is that researchers *must,* and post hoc tests *do,* control for Type I error.

Procedures for Calculating Tukey's HSD Test

There are a number of excellent methods for making comparisons after a significant F statistic has been found. Some of the more common procedures include Tukey's Honestly Significant Difference (HSD) test, Duncan's multiple range test, the Scheffe method, and the Newman–Keuls test. The selection of a particular method depends on a number of factors, such as the number and types of comparisons to be made, groups of equal or unequal sample size, and so on. We present Tukey's HSD test; this method is recommended over other procedures for making pairwise comparisons with samples **Tukey's** of equal size (Kirk, 1982). In general, **Tukey's HSD** *involves comparing the difference* **HSD** *between any two means to a critical difference score using a sampling distribution* *called the studentized range statistic* q. If the mean difference exceeds the critical difference score, the means are statistically different. The steps are as follows:

Step 1: Find the studentized range value (q) from Table F in Appendix A.

To determine q, three pieces of information are required: df_{Within}, number of groups (k), and desired alpha (α) level of .05 or .01. We refer again to our investigation of differences in perceptions of violence in crime dramas among children at four grade levels. In our example, Table F in Appendix A reports that the studentized range value q, with df_{Within} = 16, k = 4, and α = .05, is 4.05. When α = .01, our q value is 5.19.

Step 2: Calculate the critical difference score.

The critical difference score is the value that the mean difference of any two groups must exceed in order to conclude that the means are statistically different. The critical difference score for Tukey's HSD (CD_{HSD}) is calculated using the following formula:

$$CD_{HSD} = q\sqrt{\frac{MS_{Within}}{n_k}}$$

To locate MS_{Within}, refer to the ANOVA Summary Table (Table 11.6). The symbol n_k is the number of subjects in each group. This is based on the assumption that each group has the same number of subjects. Thus, the critical difference score at the .05 alpha level is calculated as:

$$CD_{HSD} = 4.05\sqrt{\frac{1.50}{5}} = 2.22$$

To calculate the critical difference score at the .01 level of significance, we simply change the value of q from 4.05 (.05α) to 5.19 (.01α), and recalculate using the formula:

$$CD_{HSD} = 5.19\sqrt{\frac{1.50}{5}} = 2.84$$

Step 3: Construct a matrix of differences among sample means.

A matrix is constructed of the absolute values of the differences among the four sample means. For presentational purposes, the means often are ordered from largest to smallest, although it is not necessary to do this. Table 11.8 illustrates a matrix of mean differences among sample means with our data from the study on children's perceptions of violence in crime dramas.

TABLE 11.8 Matrix of Differences among Sample Means

	$\bar{X}_{First} = 8$	$\bar{X}_{Fourth} = 5$	$\bar{X}_{Eighth} = 4$	$\bar{X}_{Twelfth} = 2$
$\bar{X}_{First}$ = 8	—	3**	4**	6**
$\bar{X}_{Fourth}$ = 5		—	1	3**
$\bar{X}_{Eighth}$ = 4			—	2
$\bar{X}_{Twelfth}$ = 2				—

* Statistically significant at $p \leq .05$.
** Statistically significant at $p \leq .01$.

Step 4: Compare the CD_{HSD} value to the differences among means presented in the matrix. Any pairwise comparison that exceeds the CD_{HSD} is considered significant. Referring to our example, any mean difference exceeding 2.22 is significant at $p \leq .05$, and any difference exceeding 2.84 is significant at $p \leq .01$. The pairs of means that are statistically different from each other are noted with asterisks in Table 11.8.

Step 5: Interpret findings.
Although it is often unnecessary to interpret all of the results shown in the table, key findings should be brought to the reader's attention. Thus, for example, one might conclude that 1st graders are significantly more likely to perceive violence in crime dramas than are children at the three higher grade levels. Although a difference between 4th and 8th graders was not detected, children at these two grade level perceived more violence in the dramas than did children in the 12th grade. Overall, the study found that children at lower grade levels perceive more violence in crime dramas than do those at higher grade levels.

Try calculating Tukey's HSD by completing TryIT! Box 11.2.

TryIT!   BOX **11.2**

The following summarizes the findings of an investigation of stress among police officers. The researcher argues that change in blood pressure before and after an officer's shift is an effective physiological measure of stress, with higher readings associated with greater stress. The average change in blood pressure readings at four different ranks are reported below.

Patrol	Sergeant	Lieutenant	Captain
$\bar{X} = 15.1$	$\bar{X} = 10.3$	$\bar{X} = 11.5$	$\bar{X} = 16.5$
$n = 11$	$n = 11$	$n = 11$	$n = 11$

$MS_{Within} = 8.50$
$df_{Within} = 40$
Number of groups $(k) = 4$

Step 1: Find the studentized range value (q) for α .05 and α .01 in Table F of Appendix A.

Step 2: Determine the critical difference score using Tukey's HSD for both the .05 and .01 alpha levels.

Step 3: Construct a matrix of mean differences among ranks and indicate which pairs of means are statistically different.

Step 4: Interpret key findings.

11.4 Repeated-Measures ANOVA

The single-factor ANOVA is a statistical technique for comparing sample means of three or more *independent* groups. What procedure is used for comparing sample means of three or more *dependent* groups? As you know from our *t* test discussion, dependent samples cannot be treated in the same manner as independent samples. The most common research design with a dependent sample involves the same individuals measured repeatedly on a specific variable. The same inmates, for example, may be asked their perceptions of the criminal justice system at three different time periods. The appropriate statistical technique for this type of a design, described as a repeated-measures or within-subjects design, is a repeated-measures ANOVA. A **repeated-measures ANOVA** is *a statistical technique used for comparing the means of three or more dependent groups.*

repeated-measures ANOVA

Let's assume that a researcher believes that the level of stress among parole officers differs depending on length of time on the job. He randomly selects a sample of parole officers for his study and administers a 20-point stress questionnaire after one, three, and five years on the job. We begin our analysis by stating our hypotheses.

Step 1: State the research and null hypotheses.

  H_1: The level of stress among parole officers is different at one, three, and five years on the job.

  $$H_1 : \mu_1 \neq \mu_2 \neq \mu_3$$

  H_0: The level of stress among parole officers is not different at one, three, and five years on the job.

  $$H_0 : \mu_1 = \mu_2 = \mu_3$$

Step 2: For step 2, we perform some intermediate calculations on our data that will allow us to determine the different sums of squares needed to calculate the F statistic. Table 11.9 illustrates the calculations involved in this step.

a: Calculate the mean of the X scores for each group ($\bar{X}_{Group}$).
b: Sum all of the X scores for each subject (SXi).
c: Square each of the X scores for each subject (X_i^2).
d: Sum all of the columns.

TABLE 11.9 Calculating the Means and Sums for a Repeated-Measures ANOVA

Subject	1 year X_1	3 years X_2	5 years X_3	ΣX_i	1 year X_1^2	3 years X_2^2	5 years X_3^2
1	5	8	18	31	25	64	324
2	4	6	8	18	16	36	64
3	4	7	8	19	16	49	64
4	7	6	6	19	49	36	36
5	3	8	5	16	9	64	25
6	1	4	12	17	1	16	144
7	1	5	13	19	1	25	169
8	4	5	11	20	16	25	121
Means ($\bar{X}$)	3.63	6.13	10.13				
Sums (Σ)	29	49	81	159	133	315	947

Step 3: Calculate the sums of squares total (SS_{Total}), using the following formula:

$$SS_{Total} = \Sigma\left(X^2\right) - \left[\left(X_{Total}\right)^2 / nk\right]$$

X_{Total} = Sum of the ΣX_i scores
n = Sample size
k = Number of measures

In our example, we add the summed values of the three X squared values $\Sigma(X^2)$. Next, we square the summed value of all the ΣX_i scores and divide by the sample size times the number of measures [$(X_{Total})^2 / nk$]. Thus, we calculate SS_{Total} as:

$$\Sigma\left(X^2\right) - \left[\left(X_{Total}\right)^2 / nk\right] = (133 + 315 + 947) - \left[(159)^2 / (8)(3)\right]$$
$$= 1395 - \left[25,281 / 24\right]$$
$$= 1395 - 1053.38$$
$$= 341.62$$

Step 4: Calculate the sums of squares between-group ($SS_{Between}$), using the following formula:

$$SS_{Between} = \left[\Sigma(\Sigma X)^2 / n \right] - \left[(X_{Total})^2 / nk \right]$$

X_{Total} = Sum of the ΣX_i scores

n = Sample size

k = Number of measures

Once again, $SS_{Between}$ represents the amount of variability between the different groups. Thus, we calculate $SS_{Between}$ by squaring the sum of each group of X scores, dividing by the sample size, and then summing across the three groups $[\Sigma(\Sigma X)^2 / n]$. Next, we square the summed value of all the ΣX_i scores and divide by the sample size times the number of measures $[(\Sigma X_{Total})^2 / nk]$. Thus, $SS_{Between}$ is calculated as follows:

$$\left[\Sigma(\Sigma X)^2 / n \right] - \left[(X_{Total})^2 / nk \right] = \left[(29^2 / 8) + (49^2 / 8) + (81^2 / 8) \right] - \left[(159)^2 / (8)(3) \right]$$
$$= \left[105.13 + 300.13 + 820.13 \right] - \left[25,281 / 24 \right]$$
$$= 1225.39 - 1053.38$$
$$= 172.01$$

Step 5: Calculate the sums of squares within-subjects, using the following formula (use as a measure of the amount of variability within each subject's scores across the different measurement points).

$$SS_{Within} = \left[\Sigma(\Sigma X_i)^2 / k \right] - \left[(X_{Total})^2 / nk \right]$$

ΣX_i = Sum of the total X scores for each subject

X_{Total} = Sum of the ΣX_i scores

This formula first requires us to square the ΣX_i scores for each subject, divide by the number of scores for each subject, and then sum $[\Sigma(\Sigma X_i)^2 / k]$. Once again, we square the summed value of all the ΣX_i scores and divide by the sample size times the number of measures $[(X_{Total})^2 / nk]$. Thus, SS_{Within} is calculated as:

$$\left[\Sigma(\Sigma X_i)^2 / k \right] - \left[(X_{Total})^2 / nk \right] = \left[(31^2 / 3) + (18^2 / 3) + (19^2 / 3) + (19^2 / 3) + (16^2 / 3) + (17^2 / 3) \right.$$
$$\left. + (19^2 / 3) + (20^2 / 3) \right] - [25,281 / 24]$$
$$= [320.33 + 108 + 120.33 + 120.33 + 85.33 + 96.33 + 120.33$$
$$+ 133.33] - [25,281 / 24]$$
$$= 1104.31 - 1053.38$$
$$= 50.93$$

Step 6: Calculate the sums of squares error (SS_{Error}), using the following formula:

$$SS_{Error} = SS_{Total} - SS_{Between} - SS_{Within}$$

We simply subtract the three values that have been calculated already. The resulting value is the amount of variation that is unexplained by the other three sources of variation. SS_{Error} is calculated as:

$$SS_{Error} = SS_{Total} - SS_{Between} - SS_{Within}$$
$$= 341.62 - 172.01 - 50.93$$

Step 7: Calculate the degrees of freedom for all four sources of variation—
$$df_{Total} = nk - 1, df_{Between} = k - 1, df_{Within} = n - 1, \text{ and } df_{Error} = nk - n - k + 1.$$

$$df_{Total} = (8)(3) - 1 = 24 - 1 = 23$$
$$df_{Between} = 3 - 1 = 2$$
$$df_{Within} = 8 - 1 = 7$$
$$df_{Error} = (8)(3) - 8 - 3 + 1 = 24 - 8 - 3 + 1 = 14$$

Step 8: Calculate the mean square between group $MS_{Between}$ and the mean square error MS_{Error}, using the following formulas:

$$MS_{Between} = SS_{Between} / df_{Between} = 172.01 / 2 = 86.01$$
$$MS_{Error} = SS_{Error} / df_{Error} = 118.68 / 14 = 8.48$$

Step 9: Calculate the *F* statistic using the following formula:

$$F = \frac{MS_{Between}}{MS_{Error}}$$

Step 10: Compare the calculated *F* statistic with the critical *F* value in Table D in Appendix A.

With 2 and 14 degrees of freedom, we determine the critical value to be 3.74 at the .05 alpha level. Because our *F* statistic of 10.51 exceeds the critical value of 3.74, we reject the null hypothesis of no difference and accept the research hypothesis.

Step 11: Interpret findings.

We conclude that there is a statistically significant relationship between the level of stress and years on the job and that these differences are attributed to actual differences among the population parameters. Specifically, officers who have been on the job for five years had the highest average level of stress (10.13), while officers who had been on the job for the least amount of time—one year—had the lowest average (3.63). Additionally, the calculated *F* statistic is significant at the .01 alpha level (critical value = 6.51).

You can see that the calculations for a repeated-measures ANOVA are somewhat more complex than those for a single-factor ANOVA. With a little practice, however, you will be able to master the calculations. Try calculating a repeated-measures ANOVA by completing TryIT! Box 11.3.

TryIT!   BOX **11.3**

The warden at a state penitentiary developed a prison work program designed to decrease idleness and lower the rate of misconduct among incarcerated offenders. A sample of five offenders participated in the work program and were measured on the number of misconduct reports they accumulated at three different time intervals—before the program, six months after, and 12 months after completing the program.

Subject	Before	6 Months	12 Months	ΣX_i	Before^2	6 Months^2	12 Months^2
1	8	3	2	13	64	9	4
2	5	5	0	10	25	25	0
3	4	2	0	6	16	4	0
4	5	0	0	5	25	0	0
5	4	2	1	7	16	4	1

Step 1: State the research and null hypotheses.

Step 2: Calculate the means for the number of misconduct reports and the sums.

Step 3: Calculate the sums of squares total (SS_{Total}).

Step 4: Calculate the sums of squares between-group ($SS_{Between}$).

Step 5: Calculate the sums of squares within-subjects (SS_{Within}).

Step 6: Calculate the sums of squares error (SS_{Error}).

Step 7: Calculate the degrees of freedom for all four sources of variation.

Step 8: Calculate the $MS_{Between}$ and MS_{Error}.

Step 9: Calculate the F statistic.

Step 10: Compare the calculated F statistic with the critical F value in Table D in Appendix A.

Step 11: Interpret findings.

11.5 Two-Factor ANOVA

two-factor ANOVA

multiple-factor ANOVA

With both single-factor ANOVA and repeated-measures ANOVA, the research design consists of one independent variable. A **two-factor ANOVA** is *a statistical technique used for designs (often referred to as factorial designs), that have two independent variables (factors), each variable consisting of two or more groups or levels.* A **multiple-factor ANOVA** is *used for designs incorporating more than two independent variables,* *each variable with two or more groups.* Such factorial designs are described in terms of the number of independent variables and the number of groups or levels corresponding to each of the variables. If the design consists of two independent variables each with three levels, then the design is a 3 × 3 factorial design. If the research design consists of three independent variables, all with two levels, then the design is described as a 2 × 2 × 2 factorial design. A 3 × 2 × 3 factorial design has three independent variables—the first variable with three levels, the second variable with two levels, and the third variable with three levels. As seen, factorial designs can be quite complex; hence, the ANOVA procedures for handling these designs are also complex, rendering hand calculations of these procedures beyond the scope of this text. We provide an overview, however, of the two-factor ANOVA, along with an Excel computer application.

The complexity of the two-factor ANOVA—more so in a multiple-factor ANOVA—stems in part from the number of testable hypotheses. In a two-factor ANOVA, there are three hypotheses—one associated with the first independent variable, one associated with the second independent variable, and one associated with the interaction between the two independent variables. To clarify, let's extend our example of children's perceptions of violence in crime dramas and consider a 4 (grade) × 2 (sex) factorial design. As with the single-factor ANOVA, you test whether perceptions differ across the four grade levels. This is known as a **main effect**, which *means that the influence of one independent variable is examined apart from the influence of other variables in the design.* In this example, you test a main effect for grade.

main effect

By expanding the design, you are able to test two further hypotheses. First, you can test whether boys and girls differ in their perceptions—a main effect for sex. You also can test whether there is an *interaction* between the two independent variables—grade and sex. An **interaction effect** *means that the impact of one independent variable depends on the level of another independent variable.* For instance, you can test whether differences between boys' and girls' perceptions of violence portrayed in crime dramas vary depending on grade level.

interaction effect

For each of these three hypotheses—the two main effects and the interaction effect—an *F* statistic is calculated. The *F* statistic is similar to the single-factor ANOVA, in that it represents the amount of between-group variability divided by the amount of within-group variability. To declare an effect significant, the calculated *F* statistic must equal or exceed the critical *F* value found in the *F* distribution table.

11.6 Using Excel to Compute Analysis of Variance

Now that you have a good understanding of ANOVA and have had several opportunities to practice the calculations by hand, we turn our attention to the use of Excel. We present several research designs—single-factor, repeated-measures, and two-factor ANOVA—that will require us to compute an *F* statistic using Excel.

Single-Factor ANOVA

A criminologist is interested in studying criminal activity among juveniles. He believes that the amount of unreported criminal activity is different among those living in rural, urban, and suburban areas. The researcher carefully draws a probability sample of 15 juveniles from each area—urban, suburban, and rural—who previously have been arrested. Each juvenile is given a self-report criminal history survey that asks respondents to identify the number of nonviolent crimes in which they have been involved during the past 12 months that were not reported to the police. The data for this problem is presented in Table 11.10.

Step 1: State the research and null hypotheses. These are given in notational form in cell a2.

Step 2: Calculate the group means and the grand mean using the paste function box. Remember, the grand mean is the average of all of the group scores ($n = 45$), while the group means are the averages for the scores within each of the three groups ($n = 15$). Use the group means and grand mean to calculate $SS_{Between}$ using the following formula:

$$SS_{Between} = \Sigma\left[n_{Group}\left(\overline{X}_{Group} - \overline{X}_{Grand}\right)^2\right]$$

Place the cursor in cell b22 and write the following formula: =(b18*((b20-b21)^2) +(c18*((c20-b21)^2)+(d18*((d20-b21)^2)))).

b18, c18, and d18 are the cell locations for the sample size for each of the three groups.
b20, c20, and d20 are the cell locations for the group means for each group.
b21 is the cell location for the grand mean that is subtracted from each group mean.
^2 is the symbol used for squaring a value.
+ is the symbol for addition.

The resulting value for $SS_{Between}$ is 98.31.

Step 3: Calculate SS_{Within} using the following formula:

$$SS_{Within} = \Sigma\left[\Sigma\left(\overline{X}_{iGroup} - \overline{X}_{Group}\right)^2\right]$$

We first need to create a squared deviation score column for each group before we can sum the values. Columns E, F, and G represent the squared deviation score columns for each of the three groups. We created these columns before, when we calculated the variance and standard deviation for a frequency distribution (see Chapter 5). We only need to write a formula for the first score in each column. Thus, in cell e3 we write: =(b3-b20)^2; in cell f3 we write: =(c3-c20)^2; and

TABLE 11.10 Single-Factor ANOVA

	A	B	C	D	E	F	G
1	TABLE 11.10 Single-Factor ANOVA						
2	$H_1: \mu_1 \neq \mu_2 \neq \mu_3$ $H_0: \mu_1 = \mu_2 = \mu_3$	Urban (X_1)	Suburban (X_2)	Rural (X_3)	Urban $(X_{iGroup} - \bar{X}_{Group1})^2$	Suburban $(X_{iGroup} - \bar{X}_{Group2})^2$	Rural $(X_{iGroup} - \bar{X}_{Group3})^2$
3		8	2	0	10.67	0.75	6.76
4		2	0	4	7.47	1.28	1.96
5		0	0	5	22.40	1.28	5.76
6		1	3	4	13.94	3.48	1.96
7		6	2	4	1.60	0.75	1.96
8		5	1	0	0.07	0.02	6.76
9		7	1	0	5.14	0.02	6.76
10		4	0	1	0.54	1.28	2.56
11		5	0	2	0.07	1.28	0.36
12		0	4	0	22.40	8.22	6.76
13		6	2	0	1.60	0.75	6.76
14		8	1	3	10.67	0.02	0.16
15		7	0	6	5.14	1.28	11.56
16		7	0	5	5.14	1.28	5.76
17		5	1	5	0.07	0.02	5.76
18	Sample size (n)	15	15	15			
19	Sum (Σ)				106.93	21.73	71.60
20	Means $(\bar{X}_{group})$	4.73	1.13	2.60			
21	Mean $(\bar{X}_{grand})$	2.82					
22	$SS_{Between}$	98.31			Matrix of Sample Mean Differences		
23	SS_{Within}	200.27				$\bar{X}_{1Urban}$	$\bar{X}_{2Suburban}$	$\bar{X}_{3Rural}$
24	SS_{Total}	298.58		$\bar{X}_{1Urban}$	-	3.60**	2.13*
25	$df_{Between}$	2		$\bar{X}_{2Suburban}$		-	1.47
26	df_{Within}	42		$\bar{X}_{3Rural}$			-
27	$MS_{Between}$	49.16		* Statistically significant at $p \leq .05$.			
28	MS_{Within}	4.77		** Statistically significant at $p \leq .01$.			
29	F Statistic	10.31					
30	Significance	0.0002					
31	$CD_{HSD\ (.05\alpha)}$	1.94					
32	$CD_{HSD\ (.01\alpha)}$	2.46					

=(d3-d20)^2 in cell g3. We use the dollar signs to hold a particular cell constant, which in this case is the group mean for each column. This allows us to click on the first row and drag to the last row for each of the columns, which automatically creates the rest of the column. Once the three columns have been created, simply click on the autosum button [Σ] on the menu to sum the squared deviation scores for each group. These values are located in cells e19, f19, and g19. To calculate SS_{Within}, we simply sum the three columns by placing the cursor in cell b23 and writing: =e19+f19+g19. The value for SS_{Within} equals 200.27.

Step 4: Calculate SS_{Total} ($SS_{\text{Between}} + SS_{\text{Within}}$), by placing the cursor in cell b24 and writing: =b22+b23.

b22 is the cell location for SS_{Between}.
b23 is the cell location for SS_{Within}.

SS_{Total} equals 298.58.

Step 5: Calculate MS_{Between} and MS_{Within}. In order to calculate the mean squares, we must first determine the degrees of freedom—$df_{\text{Between}} = k - 1$; therefore, place the cursor in cell b25 and write: =3–1. For df_{Within} ($n - k$), place the cursor in cell b26 and write: (b18+c18+d18)–3. To calculate MS_{Between} ($SS_{\text{Between}}/df_{\text{Between}}$) place the cursor in cell b27 and write: =b22/b25. For MS_{Within} ($SS_{\text{Within}}/df_{\text{Within}}$), place the cursor in cell b28 and write:=b23/b26.

b22 is the cell location for SS_{Between}.
b25 is the cell location for df_{Between}.
b23 is the cell location for SS_{Within}.
b26 is the cell location for df_{Within}.

Step 6: Calculate the *F* statistic ($MS_{\text{Between}}/MS_{\text{Within}}$) by placing the cursor in cell b29 and writing: =b27/b28.

b27 is the cell location for MS_{Between}.
b28 is the cell location for MS_{Within}.

The calculated *F* statistic is equal to 10.31.

Step 7: Compare the calculated *F* statistic with the critical *F* value. We can determine the significance level of the calculated *F* statistic by using the paste function box in Excel.

a: Place the cursor in cell b30 and click on the paste function box:

$$\boxed{fx}$$

b: Click on the function category called **statistical**.
c: Click on the name category called **FDIST**.

d: Click **ok** and a box will appear that will ask for the following: x, deg_freedom1, and deg_freedom2. The box should look like the following:

x	b29
deg_freedom1	b25
deg_freedom2	b26

x contains the calculated *F* statistic (cell b29).
deg_freedom1 contains $df_{Between}$ (cell b25).
deg_freedom2 contains df_{Within} (cell b26).

Once the values have been typed into the appropriate cells, click **ok**, and the resulting value will be the exact significance level for the calculated *F* statistic. Because the significance level is less than .05, we are able to reject the null hypothesis and accept the research hypothesis.

Step 8: Interpret findings. We conclude that there is a statistically significant difference in the number of crimes committed by juveniles living in urban, suburban, and rural areas. The difference in the mean number of crimes committed among the sample of juveniles is the result of actual differences between the population parameters and not sampling error. Unfortunately, we do not know which means are significantly different. As stated earlier, any time our analysis results in a significant *F* statistic, we must perform post hoc comparisons to determine which means are significantly different from each other.

Tukey's HSD

We used the following formula earlier to calculate the critical difference score:

$$CD_{HSD} = q\sqrt{\frac{MS_{Within}}{n_k}}$$

It is common to calculate the Tukey test using both the .05 and .01 alpha levels and report the results accordingly. To do so, we must first find the value of *q* at both alpha levels from Table F in Appendix A. The value of *q* equals 3.44 (.05α) and 4.37 (.01α). MS_{Within} equals 4.77 and is located in cell b28, while n_k is the sample size for each group (*n* = 15), which is located in cells b18, c18, and d18. Because the sample is the same for each group, we only need to use one of the cells in our formula. Thus, to obtain CD_{HSD} at the .05 alpha level, place the cursor in cell b31 and write: =3.44*(sqrt(b28/b18)) and at the .01 alpha level place the cursor in cell b32 and write: =4.37*(sqrt(b28/b18)). The resulting values of 1.94 and 2.46 are the minimum differences that must be achieved for any two means to be significantly different at the .05 and .01 alpha levels, respectively.

We then construct our matrix of mean differences by making three pairwise comparisons as shown in the matrix of sample mean differences in Table 11.10. You want to be sure that you always subtract the smaller mean from the larger one; otherwise you will end up with negative numbers. Our interest is in the absolute value of the mean differences. Remember, we need only to conduct the Tukey test if we obtain a significant F statistic from the ANOVA.

No doubt that you have realized that ANOVA requires many steps, and it is quite easy to make a mistake whether performing the calculations by hand or with Excel. You will recall that step 9 on page 302 of our hand calculations required us to construct an ANOVA Summary Table. We can use Excel's data analysis tool to produce the ANOVA Summary Table, which will allow us to compare our formula statistics with those generated by the computer. Although it is relatively easy to compute the statistics using the data analysis tool, we suggest that this tool be used as a method for producing the ANOVA Summary Table and for checking the accuracy of your calculations, and not as a replacement for writing your own formulas.

Step 1: Select the **tools** option on the Excel menu bar.
Step 2: Select **data analysis** under the tools option.
Step 3: In the analysis tool box select **Anova: Single Factor.**
Step 4: Enter b2:d17 for the input range. Click on the labels box so that the group labels will appear in the output table.
Step 5: Click **ok,** and an ANOVA Summary Table will be produced like that shown in Table 11.11. We can now check the results from our calculations in Table 11.10 with those obtained using the data analysis tool in Table 11.11. Pay particular attention to the sources of variation and the F statistic when making comparisons. The data analysis tool also provides the exact significance level of the F statistic (P–value = .0002) located in cell f12 as well as the critical value of F at the .05 level (3.22) located in cell g12.

Repeated-Measures ANOVA

Assume that the Massachusetts Department of Juvenile Justice and Delinquency Prevention Office enacted a gang intervention program in 1996 designed to decrease gang activity among known gang members. The department would like to do a three-year follow-up study to determine if the program had its intended effect. The researchers have selected Boston as the test site, and have drawn a probability sample of 15 subjects from the Boston area who went through the program in 1996. The dependent variable "gang activity" is measured as the number of police contacts by the Boston gang unit. The data for this example is presented in Table 11.12.

Step 1: State the research and null hypotheses. These are presented in notational form in cell a2.
Step 2: Calculate the means (cells b20 through e20) and the sums (cells b21 through e21) for the four different measurement times using the paste function box and the autosum [Σ] button on the menu. Calculate the sums of the four scores for each

TABLE 11.11 Single-Factor ANOVA Summary Table

	A	B	C	D	E	F	G
1	TABLE 11.11 Single-Factor ANOVA Summary Table						
2							
3	SUMMARY						
4	*Groups*	*Count*	*Sum*	*Average*	*Variance*		
5	Urban (X_1)	15	71	4.73	7.64		
6	Suburban (X_2)	15	17	1.13	1.55		
7	Rural (X_3)	15	39	2.60	5.11		
8							
9							
10	ANOVA						
11	*Source of Variation*	*SS*	*df*	*MS*	*F*	*P-value*	*F crit*
12	Between-Groups	98.31	2	49.16	10.31	0.0002	3.22
13	Within-Groups	200.27	42	4.77			
14							
15	Total	298.58	44				

subject (ΣX_i). These values are located in column F. Square each score (X_i^2) for each subject. These values are located in columns G through J. Sum the remaining columns (F through J) using the autosum [Σ] button.

Step 3: Calculate SS_{Total} using the following formula:

$$SS_{Total} = \Sigma\left(X^2\right) - \left[\left(X_{Total}\right)^2 / nk\right]$$

Place the cursor in cell b22 and write: =(sum(g21:j21)-(f21^2)/(b19*4))

g21 through j21 are the cell locations for the sums of the *X* squared scores $\Sigma(X^2)$.
f21 is the cell location for X_{Total}.
b19 is the cell location for the sample size (*n*).
The number 4 is the number of *X* scores for each subject.

The resulting value for SS_{Total} equals 556.93.

Step 4: To calculate SS_{Between}, we use the following formula:

$$SS_{\text{Between}} = \left[\Sigma\left(\Sigma X\right)^2 / n \right] - \left[\left(X_{\text{Total}}\right)^2 / nk \right]$$

Place the cursor in cell b23 and write the following: =((b21^2)/b19)+((c21^2)/b19) +((d21^2)/b19+((e21^2)/b19))-(f21^2)/(b19*4)

b21 through e21 are the cell locations for the sums of the X scores (ΣX). These values are squared and then divided by n (15) and then summed, which is given as [$\Sigma(\Sigma X)^2 / n$].

The second half of the formula [$(X_{\text{Total}})^2 / nk$] is the same as that shown in step 3. The resulting value for SS_{Between} is 290.27.

Step 5: Use the following formula to calculate SS_{Within}:

$$SS_{\text{Within}} = \left[\Sigma\left(\Sigma X_i\right)^2 / k \right] - \left[\left(X_{\text{Total}}\right)^2 / nk \right]$$

The first part of the formula requires us to sum the four scores for each subject, square them, and divide by the number of scores for each subject. We already have created a column of summed scores for each subject labeled ΣX_i (column F). Therefore, we recommend creating another column labeled $(\Sigma X_i)^2 / k$. To create this column, simply place the cursor in cell k4 and write: =(f4^2)/4. To complete the column click on the lower right-hand corner of cell k4 and drag the cursor down to the last row of scores (cell k18). To finish calculating SS_{Within}, place the cursor in cell b24 and write: =k21-(f21^2)/(b19*4).

k21 is the cell location for the sum of [$\Sigma(\Sigma X_i)^2 / k$].

The second half of the formula [$(X_{\text{Total}})^2 / nk$] is the same as that shown in steps 3 and 4. The resulting value for SS_{Within} is 153.43.

Step 6: Calculate SS_{Error}, with the following formula:

$$SS_{\text{Error}} = SS_{\text{Total}} - SS_{\text{Between}} - SS_{\text{Within}}$$

Place the cursor in cell b25 and write: =b22-b23-b24. The resulting value equals 113.23.

Step 7: Calculate the degrees of freedom for df_{Total} ($nk - 1$), df_{Between} ($k - 1$), df_{Within} ($n - 1$), and df_{Error} ($nk - n - k + 1$). Thus, we compute the following:

For df_{Total}, place cursor in cell b26 and write: =(b19*4)-1.
For df_{Between}, place cursor in cell b27 and write: =4-1.

TABLE 11.12 Repeated-Measures ANOVA

	A	B	C	D	E	F	G	H	I	J	K
1	**TABLE 11.12 Repeated-Measures ANOVA**										
2	$H_1: \mu_1 \neq \mu_2 \neq \mu_3 \neq \mu_4$ $H_0: \mu_1 = \mu_2 = \mu_3 = \mu_4$										
3	Subject #	Before X_1	1 yr. X_2	2 yrs. X_3	3 yrs. X_4	$\sum X_i$	Before X_1^2	1 yr. X_2^2	2 yrs. X_3^2	3 yrs. X_4^2	$(\sum X_i)^2/k$
4	1	12	7	8	12	39	144	49	64	144	380.25
5	2	8	5	2	1	16	64	25	4	1	64
6	3	7	4	1	2	14	49	16	1	4	49
7	4	5	4	2	2	13	25	16	4	4	42.25
8	5	7	1	5	4	17	49	1	25	16	72.25
9	6	7	3	0	1	11	49	9	0	1	30.25
10	7	6	4	2	3	15	36	16	4	9	56.25
11	8	8	6	3	0	17	64	36	9	0	72.25
12	9	12	5	1	1	19	144	25	1	1	90.25
13	10	8	4	3	2	17	64	16	9	4	72.25
14	11	8	5	2	1	16	64	25	4	1	64
15	12	6	4	1	0	11	36	16	1	0	30.25
16	13	7	3	3	1	14	49	9	9	1	49
17	14	7	7	1	1	16	49	49	1	1	64
18	15	6	5	0	2	13	36	25	0	4	42.25
19	**Sample size (*n*)**	15									
20	**Mean ($\bar{X}$)**	7.60	4.47	2.27	2.20						
21	**Sum ($\sum$)**	114	67	34	33	248	922	333	136	191	1178.5
22	SS_{Total}	556.93									
23	$SS_{Between}$	290.27									
24	SS_{Within}	153.43									
25	SS_{Error}	113.23									
26	df_{Total}	59									
27	$df_{Between}$	3									
28	df_{Within}	14									
29	df_{Error}	42									
30	$MS_{Between}$	96.76									
31	MS_{Error}	2.70									
32	**F statistic**	35.89									
33	**Significance**	1.2E-11	or_p <.001								

For df_{Within}, place cursor in cell b28 and write: =b19-1.

For df_{Error}, place cursor in cell b29 and write: =(b19*4)-b19-4+1.

Step 8: Calculate $MS_{Between}$ and MS_{Error} by dividing the sums of squares by the corresponding degrees of freedom. For $MS_{Between}$ $(SS_{Between} / df_{Between})$, place the cursor in cell b30 and write: =b23/b27, and for MS_{Error} $(SS_{Error} / df_{Error})$, place the cursor in cell b31 and write: =b25/b29.

Step 9: Calculate the F statistic by dividing $MS_{Between}$ by MS_{Error}. Place the cursor in cell b32 and write: =b30/b31. The results of our analysis yield a calculated F statistic of 35.89.

Step 10: Compare the calculated F statistic with the critical F value. Once again, use the paste function to calculate the significance level for the calculated F statistic. The procedure is the same as before:

x is the calculated F statistic.

deg_freedom1 is $df_{Between}$.

deg_freedom2 is df_{Error}.

The resulting significance value of 1.2E–11 (cell b33) simply means that we move the decimal point 11 places to the left of the 1. Put another way, our calculated F statistic is highly significant, enabling us to reject the null hypothesis and accept the research hypothesis.

Step 11: Interpret findings. We conclude that the program significantly reduced the number of police contacts for the population of gang members who participated in the program. The most striking decline in police contacts appears to occur at one and two years after completion of the program.

Two-Factor ANOVA

In Section 11.5, we introduced the concept of a two-factor ANOVA, in which we examine the effect of two independent variables simultaneously on a dependent variable. We also indicated that the calculations for such a design are rather lengthy and complex when performed by hand and suggested that you perform this type of analysis using the data analysis tool in Excel.

Suppose a researcher is interested in knowing whether the number of parole violations varies by "type of offender" and/or "community service." The number of parole violations is our dependent variable and "type of offender" is one independent variable consisting of two attributes—Violent and Nonviolent. The other independent variable is "community service," consisting of two attributes—Service and Nonservice. This design is known formally as a 2×2 factorial design, because each of our two independent variables has two attributes or levels. The data for this example is presented in Table 11.13.

There are a total of 48 subjects in this study who were on parole. The numbers in cells b3 through b14 represent the number of parole violations for violent offenders

TABLE 11.13 Two-Factor ANOVA

	A	B	C
1	**TABLE 11.13 Two-Factor ANOVA**		
2		Service	Nonservice
3	Violent	3	2
4		2	5
5		6	3
6		4	2
7		3	4
8		4	4
9		5	4
10		6	4
11		1	4
12		5	3
13		1	5
14		2	5
15	Nonviolent	0	4
16		2	0
17		0	4
18		1	3
19		2	4
20		0	2
21		0	5
22		1	3
23		0	4
24		2	0
25		1	3
26		2	5

who received community service; c3 through c14 represent the number of violations for violent offenders who did not receive community service. In cells b15 through b26, we find the number of violations for nonviolent offenders who received community service. Finally, cells c15 through c26 represent the number of violations for nonviolent offenders who did not receive community service. As stated earlier, this type of analysis allows us to test three different hypotheses: a main effect for "type of offender"(violent versus nonviolent), a main effect for "community service"(service versus nonservice), and an interaction effect between "type of offender" and "community service"(violent/service—violent/nonservice versus nonviolent/service—nonviolent/nonservice). The following procedures are used to conduct a two-factor ANOVA:

Step 1: Select the **tools** option on the Excel menu bar.

Step 2: Select **data analysis** under the tools option.

Step 3: In the analysis tool box, select **Anova: Two Factor with Replication**.

Step 4: Enter a2:c26 for the **input range**. You want to be sure to get the labels into the input range as well (e.g., violent, service, etc.), so that the means will be appropriately identified.

Step 5: Enter 12 into the **rows per sample** box. This indicates that there are 12 subjects in each condition.

Step 6: Click **ok** and an output table like that shown in Table 11.14 will be produced.

The summary section of Table 11.14 (cells b5 through c20) provides descriptive statistics of the number of parole violations (dependent variable) for each group. For example, cells b11 through b14 provide the count (sample size), sum, mean, and variance for the number of parole violations for nonviolent offenders who received community service. The totals for violent and nonviolent offenders are located under Total in column D (cell d3), while the totals for service and nonservice are located in columns B and C under Total (cell a16).

We have modified the ANOVA portion of Table 11.14 by adding labels in parentheses to assist in the interpretation of the results. Row 25, which is labeled Sample, reports the results for the main effect for "offender type." This main effect comparison looks at the means between violent (3.63 in cell d7) and nonviolent (2.00 in cell d13) offenders, and determines whether they are significantly different. We can see that the calculated F statistic of 16.01 (cell e25) exceeds the critical F value of 4.06 (cell g25). We also simply can look at the P-value located in column F and see that the probability level associated with our calculated F statistic is equal to .000 (cell f25), which informs us that the difference between the two means is statistically significant.

We now move to row 26, labeled Columns, to determine the main effect for the second independent variable—"community service" on parole violations. Once again, the calculated F statistic of 8.85 (cell e26) has a probability value equal to .005 (cell f26), which indicates that the difference in the mean number of violations for service inmates (2.21 in cell b19) is significantly less than the average for nonservice inmates

TABLE 11.14 Two-Factor ANOVA

	A	B	C	D	E	F	G
1	TABLE 11.14 Two-Factor ANOVA						
2							
3	Summary	Service	Nonservice	Total			
4	*violent*						
5	Count	12	12	24			
6	Sum	42	45	87			
7	Average	3.50	3.75	3.63			
8	Variance	3.18	1.11	2.07			
9							
10	*nonviolent*						
11	Count	12	12	24			
12	Sum	11	37	48			
13	Average	0.92	3.08	2.00			
14	Variance	0.81	2.81	2.96			
15							
16	*total*						
17	Count	24	24				
18	Sum	53	82				
19	Average	2.21	3.42				
20	Variance	3.65	1.99				
21							
22							
23	ANOVA						
24	*Source of variation*	*SS*	*df*	*MS*	*F*	*P*-value	*F* crit
25	Sample (offender type)	31.69	1	31.69	16.01	0.000	4.06
26	Columns (community service)	17.52	1	17.52	8.85	0.005	4.06
27	Interaction	11.02	1	11.02	5.57	0.023	4.06
28	Within (error)	87.08	44	1.98			
29							
30	Total	147.31	47				

(3.42 in cell c19). Thus far, we have determined that the average number of parole violations is influenced by "type of offender" and "community service." That is, violent offenders have more violations than nonviolent offenders, and offenders with no community service have a higher number of violations than offenders with community service. We now want to know whether there is an interaction effect between offender type and community service. That is, does the impact of community service on parole violations vary by type of offender?

The analysis of the interaction effect is located in row 27. The calculated F statistic is equal to 5.57 (cell f27), and has an associated probability of .023 (cell e27). Because the probability level is less than .05, we determine that the interaction effect is statistically significant. We interpret this finding by saying that the effect of community service on parole violations depends on the type of offender. By observing the means, we determine that community service had little to no impact on the average number of parole violations among violent offenders. The mean for violent offenders with service is 3.50 (cell b7), compared to 3.75 (cell c7) for violent offenders without service. Among nonviolent offenders, however, community service had a significant effect on the number of parole violations. Nonviolent offenders with service had an average of .92 violations (cell b13), compared to 3.08 violations (cell c13) for nonviolent offenders without service.

We illustrate the significant interaction effect for the above analysis in Figure 11.2. Among nonviolent offenders, the difference between the mean number of violations for service and nonservice offenders is greater (3.08 − .92 = 2.16) than is the difference among violent offenders who received community service and those who did not (3.75 − 3.50 = .25). This illustrates a significant interaction effect between our two independent variables.

FIGURE 11.2 Significant interaction effect between type of offender and community service

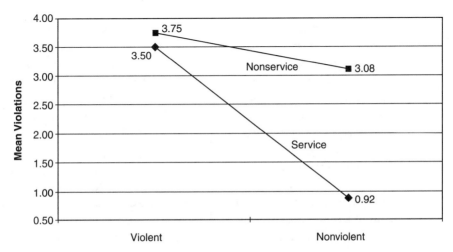

FIGURE 11.3 Nonsignificant interaction effect between type of offender and community service

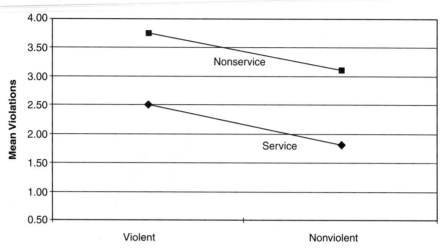

Had the analysis revealed a nonsignificant interaction between "offender type" and "community service," we would find that the differences between violent and non-violent offenders within each attribute of service would be parallel, as illustrated in Figure 11.3. Although the average number of violations among offenders who received community service is significantly less than offenders with nonservice, the difference is the same for both violent and nonviolent offenders. That is, among violent offenders, the difference between service and nonservice is the same as that for nonviolent offenders.

11.7 Summary

We began this chapter by demonstrating that ANOVA is an extension of the *t* statistic. Whereas the *t* statistic compares two groups on a single continuous dependent variable, ANOVA is the statistical technique for comparing more than two groups on a specific dependent variable. The calculations of ANOVA yield a value called *F*, represented as the amount of between-group variance divided by within-group variance. This calculated *F* statistic is compared to an *F* probability distribution to determine whether the value is large enough to reject the null hypothesis of no difference among groups and accept the research hypothesis.

There were three types of ANOVA presented in this chapter—single-factor, repeated-measures, and two-factor. A single-factor ANOVA, often referred to as a one-way ANOVA, is a technique for comparing the sample means of three or more groups in terms of a continuous dependent variable. It is called single-factor, as it involves only one categorical independent variable consisting of more than two groups or levels. It is important to remember that, in general, ANOVA is used for comparing sample means of *independent* groups. If a researcher compares sample means of more than two *dependent* groups, then a repeated-measures ANOVA is the appropriate technique. The most common research design resulting in a dependent sample is when the same individual is measured repeatedly on a specific variable. Finally, a two-factor ANOVA is used for research designs, often referred to as factorial designs, having two independent variables (factors) with each variable consisting of two or more groups or levels. As the complexity of the technique increases from a single-factor to a two-factor ANOVA, the number of testable hypotheses also increases. In a two-factor ANOVA, there are three hypotheses—a main effect associated with the first independent variable, a main effect associated with the second independent variable, and an interaction effect associated with the interaction between the two independent variables. The chapter concluded with a presentation of the procedures for performing each of the three types of ANOVA using Excel.

Key Terms

analysis of variance (ANOVA)	Tukey's HSD
single-factor ANOVA	repeated-measures ANOVA
sums of squares	two-factor ANOVA
sums of squares between-group	multiple-factor ANOVA
sums of squares within-group	main effect
sums of squares total	interaction effect
post hoc (posteriori)	

TryIT! Answers

Box 11.1

Step 1: State the research and null hypotheses.

H_1: Support of the Wisconsin Department of Social Services varies by social class.

$$H_1: \mu_1 \neq \mu_2 \neq \mu_3$$

H_0: Support of the Wisconsin Department of Social Services does not vary by social class.

$$H_0: \mu_1 = \mu_2 = \mu_3$$

Step 2: $\bar{X}_{Lower} = 5$, $\bar{X}_{Middle} = 2$, $\bar{X}_{Upper} = 3$, $\bar{X}_{Grand} = 3.33$, $SS_{Between} = 23.35$

Step 3: $SS_{Within} = 12$

Step 4: $SS_{Total} = 35.35$

Step 5: $MS_{Between} = 23.25/2 = 11.63$

$MS_{Within} = 12/12 = 1$

Step 6: $F = 11.63/1 = 11.63$

Step 7: Calculated $F = 11.63$; Tabled critical value [$df_{Between} = 2$, $df_{Within} = 12$, $p \le .05$] $= 3.89$

Step 8: As the calculated F of 11.63 is larger than the critical value of 3.89, the null hypothesis is rejected. The research hypothesis—that support of the Wisconsin Department of Social Services does vary by social class—is accepted. Lower-, middle-, and upper-class residents differ in their support of the WDSS.

Step 9: ANOVA Summary Table

Sources of Variation	Sums of Squares	Degrees of Freedom	Mean Square	F
Between-group	23.35	2	11.63	11.63
Within-group	12	12		1
Total	35.35	14		

Box 11.2

Step 1: At $\alpha = .05$, $q = 3.79$; at $\alpha = .01$, $q = 4.70$

Step 2: At $\alpha = .05$, $CD_{(HSD)} = 3.34$; at $\alpha = .01$, $CD_{(HSD)} = 4.14$

Step 3: *Absolute Values of Differences Among Sample Means*

	Patrol ($\bar{X} = 15.1$)	Sergeant ($\bar{X} = 10.3$)	Lieutenant ($\bar{X} = 11.5$)	Chief ($\bar{X} = 16.5$)
Patrol ($\bar{X} = 15.1$)	—	4.80**	3.60*	1.40
Sergeant ($\bar{X} = 10.3$)		—	1.20	6.20**
Lieutenant ($\bar{X} = 11.5$)			—	5.00**
Chief ($\bar{X} = 16.5$)				—

* = statistically significant at $p \le .05$.
** = statistically significant at $p \le .01$.

Step 4: The results show no differences in stress between sergeants and lieutenants and between chiefs and patrol officers. Both chiefs and patrol officers, however, experience more stress than do sergeants and lieutenants.

Box 11.3

Step 1: State the research and null hypotheses.

H_1: The rate of misconduct is different before, 6 months after, and 12 months after the work program.

$$H_1{:}\mu_1 \neq \mu_2 \neq \mu_3$$

H_0: The rate of misconduct is not different before, 6 months after, and 12 months after the work program.

$$H_0{:}\mu_1 = \mu_2 = \mu_3$$

Step 2:

	Means ($\bar{X}$)	Sums (Σ)
Before	5.20	26
6 Months	2.40	12
12 Months	.60	3
ΣX_i		41
Before^2		146
6 Months^2		42
12 Months^2		5

Step 3: $SS_{Total} = 80.93$

Step 4: $SS_{Between} = 53.73$

Step 5: $SS_{Within} = 14.25$

Step 6: $SS_{Error} = 12.95$

Step 7: $df_{Total} = 14$

$df_{Between} = 2$

$df_{Within} = 4$

$df_{Error} = 8$

Step 8: $MS_{Between} = 26.87$

$MS_{Error} = 1.62$

Step 9: $F = 16.59$

Step 10: Reject the null hypothesis, as the calculated F statistic (16.59) exceeds the critical F value of 4.46.

Step 11: The rate of misconduct among the population of offenders who participated in the program was different before, 6 months after, and 12 months after the work program.

11.8 Problems

1. Using Table D in Appendix A, determine the critical F value for each of the following:

	Alpha level	$df_{Between}$	df_{Within}
a.	.05	4	15
b.	.05	2	25
c.	.01	2	30
d.	.01	6	10
e.	.05	10	12
f.	.01	4	60

2. The F statistic is calculated by dividing the _____ by the _____.

3. A researcher conducts a study of attitudes toward sentencing guidelines using a 20-point rating scale, with higher values representing more favorable attitudes. The sample consists of 25 police officers, 25 parole officers, and 25 correctional officers. Identify the following:

   a. The ANOVA test that is most appropriate to use
   b. $df_{Between}$
   c. df_{Within}
   d. Critical F value (alpha level of .01)
   e. Critical F value (alpha level of .05)

4. Define the following:

   a. Single-Factor ANOVA
   b. Repeated-Measures ANOVA
   c. Two-Factor ANOVA

5. Determine the studentized range value (q) for each of the following:

	df_{Within}	Number of groups (k)	Alpha level
a.	16	4	.05
b.	22	6	.01
c.	14	3	.01
d.	32	10	.05
e.	10	5	.01

6. What is the primary difference between the t test and ANOVA?

7. Make a decision about the null hypothesis for each of the following:

	Calculated F statistic	Critical F value
a.	4.50	6.78
b.	3.45	2.85
c.	2.79	2.79
d.	1.45	1.54

8. In a study of drunk driving incidences (Y) with a sample of convicted DUI offenders, researchers believe that the amount of the fine for the past prior offense (X)—categorized as small, medium, and large—is related to future incidences. Write the research and null hypotheses for the study.

9. In the study presented in Question No. 8, researchers found that the average number of incidences for those with small fines $(n = 10)$ was 3.4, medium fines $(n = 10)$ was 2.8, and large fines $(n = 10)$ was 2.2, and the calculated F statistic equaled 2.44. Determine (a) the critical F value, and (b) the appropriate decision about the null hypothesis. $df_w = 30 - 3 = 27$ $df_{b/w} = 3 - 1 = 2$

10. Researchers believe that individuals' participation in criminal activity will decrease at three age levels: age 16, age 18, and age 21. A sample of eight juveniles were followed for five years to determine their involvement in crime at three different ages (ages 16, 18, and 21). Using the data below, conduct a repeated-measures ANOVA and report the following: (a) $MS_{Between}$, (b) MS_{Error}, (c) calculated F statistic, (d) critical F value, and (e) decision about the null hypothesis.

Subject	Age 16	Age 18	Age 21
1	4	5	3
2	3	3	1
3	3	1	0
4	2	1	1
5	5	2	0
6	4	4	1
7	2	2	3
8	5	2	0

11. Calculate the F statistic for each of the following:

	$SS_{Between}$	SS_{Within}	$df_{Between}$	df_{Within}
a.	158.04	48.14	4	12
b.	220.45	86.24	8	16
c.	120.34	34.00	5	17
d.	350.87	110.42	10	21

12. What is the purpose of conducting post hoc comparisons?

13. What are the four assumptions of ANOVA?

14. What is the appropriate decision regarding the null hypothesis $(\alpha = .05)$ for each of the following:

	Calculated F statistic	P-value
a.	3.45	.06
b.	2.89	.03
c.	1.87	.10
d.	.45	.95
e.	2.34	.05
f.	1.54	.04

15. A researcher undertakes a study of physical force incidences among a sample of correctional officers. Specifically, the researcher is interested in knowing if officer use of force differs by the height of the officer. The researcher has selected a random sample of 30 officers (ten officers representing each of the three height categories). The values under each category represent the number of times an officer used physical force (Y) within the past 12 months. Enter the data below into Excel and conduct a single-factor ANOVA. Be sure to include the research and null hypotheses, the group means, grand mean, the sums of squares, degrees of freedom, mean squares, F statistic, significance level, and decision about the null hypothesis.

5'0"–5'10" (X_1)	5'11"–6'4" (X_2)	Over 6'4" (X_3)
0	0	2
3	0	3
1	1	1
1	2	0
0	0	0
2	0	3
2	1	3
0	1	1
2	2	1
0	0	1

16. A researcher wants to study the effects of solitary confinement on aggression. She selects a random sample of 12 inmates housed in solitary confinement. She has decided to measure aggression by counting the number of aggressive acts displayed by each inmate during his/her one hour of yard time per day. She will conduct her observations at 5, 10, 15, and 20 days after the inmate entered solitary confinement. The data is presented below, and represents the total number of aggressive acts displayed by each offender over the five-day time intervals. Enter the data into Excel and conduct a repeated-measures ANOVA. Be sure to include the research and null hypotheses, the group means, sums of squares, degrees of freedom, mean squares, F statistic, significance level, and decision about the null hypothesis.

Subject	5 days	10 days	15 days	20 days
1	1	3	3	2
2	3	2	3	2
3	1	1	0	1
4	0	0	2	3
5	1	0	0	2
6	0	2	1	1
7	2	2	1	3
8	3	1	0	1
9	0	0	1	2
10	1	0	2	4
11	1	1	0	1
12	0	0	1	0

Statistical Analysis for Assessing Relationships: Correlation

ExploreIT!

The mayor of a large eastern city believes that increasing the education level of police officers will produce better officers, ones less likely to receive citizen complaints. The mayor wants to implement a police incentive program that offers additional monies to police officers based on their level of education. Specifically, for each additional year of formal education past high school, officers would receive an additional 5% of their salary. In order to fund the program, however, the city council has hired you as an independent research consultant to assess the relationship between education level and officer complaints. How will you determine if education level is associated with citizen complaints? After selecting a random sample of police officers from the population of officers within the city, you will use correlation analysis to test the following hypothesis: As education level increases, the number of citizen complaints decreases.

Chapters 10 and 11 presented statistical analyses for testing hypotheses asserting a difference between categories of nominal independent variables. Examples of such hypotheses are as follows:

Hypothesis 1: Victims are more supportive of the three strike law than are nonvictims.
Hypothesis 2: Voters are more supportive of the three strike law for violent than nonviolent offenders.

To address these hypotheses, we described tests for examining differences in the categories of a nominal independent variable on a single-interval/ratio-level dependent variable. We now turn from testing differences among categories to assessing relationships among variables measured at the interval or ratio level. We no longer ask the question, "Is there a difference between groups?" Rather, we now ask the question, "Is there a relationship between variables?" Is there a relationship between age and drug use? Is there a relationship between employment length and job satisfaction?

This chapter presents correlational techniques. Correlational analysis is used for testing hypotheses that state two variables are related or associated in some manner. As you recall, we discussed a nonparametric correlation statistic in Chapter 9 known as Spearman's rho. This test is appropriate for variables measured at the ordinal level. In this chapter, we discuss a parametric statistical test known as Pearson's product moment correlation. This statistic is more commonly used in criminal justice research and is appropriate for variables measured at the interval or ratio level. We first turn our attention to correlation analysis by examining the nature of a correlation. We present how to interpret a correlation coefficient and illustrate the procedures for calculating and assessing the significance of a correlation. Partial correlations are also discussed. The chapter concludes with a demonstration using Excel to calculate correlation coefficients.

12.1 Nature of Correlation

correlation   **Correlation analysis** is *a statistical test to determine the extent to which two variables*
analysis   *are related.* What does it mean to say that variables are related? Suppose you observe that juvenile delinquency and school performance tend to go together. That is, the more a person is involved in delinquent activities, the lower his/her school performance. In this case, you have observed a relationship between two variables. In other words, how one variable behaves (school performance) varies depending on another variable (delinquent activities). In such instances, we say that the two variables are related or tend to covary. Or, put another way, we say that there is an association between the variables. More formally, we say that delinquency involvement and school performance are correlated.

It should be noted that researchers are often cautious in making a distinction between which variable is independent and which one is dependent, especially when both variables are measured simultaneously and hypothesized to covary. Why? It is often possible to reverse which variable is the cause (independent) and which variable is the effect (dependent variable). To illustrate, consider the relationship between length of employment and the level of criminal activity. You might see unemployment as a cause leading to increased criminal activity. By contrast, it could be argued that higher levels of criminal activity make it more difficult to maintain employment. If so, criminal activity rather than length of employment is the causal variable. Although we need to be very careful in identifying what variable is the cause, correlation analysis allows us to examine whether the two variables are related. In short, correlation analysis focuses on the relationship between variables, and does not easily lend itself to arguing for causation.

We are now ready to advance several hypotheses appropriate for correlational analysis.

Hypothesis 1: Severity of inmate misconduct and segregation time are related.

Hypothesis 2: There is a relationship between drug use and frequency of criminal activity.

Hypothesis 3: A positive relationship exists between news consumption and knowledge of stalking laws.

Hypothesis 4: There is a negative relationship between age and sentence length.

In each of the hypotheses, the two variables are argued to covary. It is also reasonably easy to visualize the variables as measured at the interval or ratio level. You will note that Hypotheses 1 and 2 simply argue that two variables are related. Thus, these are nondirectional hypotheses. Hypotheses 3 and 4, however, are directional hypotheses. That is, they are more specific, and state "how" the two variables are related. What does it mean to say that there is a *positive* relationship between variables? What does a *negative* relationship mean? To answer these questions, we must look at how correlation coefficients are interpreted.

12.2 Interpreting Correlation Coefficients

correlation coefficient A **correlation coefficient** is *a numerical summary of the direction and strength of the relationship between variables*. A correlation coefficient is often symbolized as r_{xy}, representing the correlation (r) between two variables—an independent (X) and dependent (Y) variable. By direction of the relationship, we mean that the relationship between the variables is either positive or negative. A **positive correlation coefficient** *indicates* **positive correlation coefficient** *that the variables covary in the same direction.* As one variable increases, the other variable also increases. In other words, high values of one variable (news consumption) are associated with high values of another variable (knowledge of stalking laws). Thus, another—and perhaps preferable—way of saying Hypothesis 3 is the following:

Hypothesis 3: As TV news watching increases, one's knowledge of stalking laws also increases.

FIGURE 12.1 Positive relationship between TV news viewing and knowledge of stalking laws

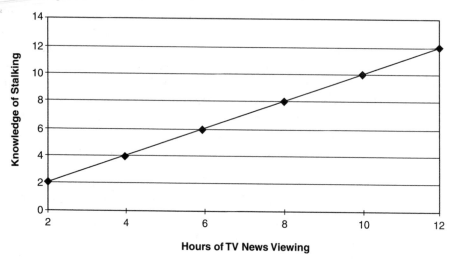

The reverse is also true. That is, as news consumption decreases, one's knowledge of stalking laws also decreases. Figure 12.1 illustrates a positive relationship between TV news viewing and knowledge of stalking laws. Each respondent's scores on both variables are represented by a single dot on the graph. The dot furthest on the left of the graph, for example, represents one individual's response of watching two hours of "TV news"(X) and obtaining a score of two on a "knowledge of stalking laws"(Y) test. The next dot represents another individual's responses. This individual indicated watching four hours of TV news and obtained a score of four on the knowledge test. The pattern continues, with higher values of TV news consumption tending to go with higher scores on the knowledge test. In this case, a positive correlation between the two variables results. A plus sign (+) is used to indicate a positive correlation.

negative correlation coefficient   A **negative correlation coefficient** *indicates that the two variables covary in the opposite direction.* As one variable increases, the other variable will decrease. That is, high values of one variable (age) is associated with low values of another variable (sentence length). Thus, another way of saying Hypothesis 4 is the following:

Hypothesis 4: As age increases, sentence length decreases.

The reverse is also true. In other words, as age decreases, sentence length increases. Figure 12.2 presents a negative relationship between age and sentence length. Once again, take a look at the dot furthest on your left. In this graph, you will notice that a 20-year-old respondent was handed a sentence length of 20 months. The next dot shows that a 30-year-old respondent was handed a sentence length of 16 months. As this pattern continues, with higher values of age tending to go with shorter sentence lengths, a neg-

FIGURE 12.2 Negative relationship between age and sentence length

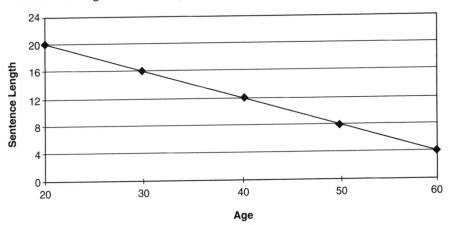

ative correlation between the two variables results. A negative sign (–) is used to indicate a negative correlation between the variables.

An examination of Figures 12.1 and 12.2 illustrates another feature of correlation analysis. If the two variables are related, then the dots on the graph will form a straight line, also known as a linear relationship. If the two variables are unrelated, the dots will be scattered. The more the dots cluster around an imaginary straight line, the stronger the relationship between the two variables. Thus, the strength of a correlation coefficient is illustrated in terms of the extent to which the dots form a straight line.

By strength of the relationship, we mean how much or the extent to which the two variables are linearly related. The strength of the relationship is referred to as the magnitude of the relationship. The magnitude of a correlation coefficient ranges from 0 to 1, with 0 meaning the two variables are unrelated, and 1 meaning that there is a perfect relationship between the two variables. A close look at the graphs in Figures 12.1 and 12.2 shows a perfect positive and a perfect negative relationship, respectively. Very rarely do researchers find that two variables are either perfectly related or completely unrelated. It is almost always the case that a correlation coefficient will fall somewhere in between 0 and 1. Figures 12.3 and 12.4 are illustrative of various correlation values. Figure 12.3 shows that increasing values of X correspond with increasing values of Y, which results in a positive correlation of .56. Although none of the values fall directly on the line, the values do cluster relatively close to the line. Figure 12.4 illustrates a negative correlation, in which increasing values of X correspond with decreasing values of Y. The values in Figure 12.4 do not cluster as closely around the line as the values in Figure 12.3. The result of this increased deviation is a weaker correlation coefficient (–.39).

Interpreting a correlation coefficient requires considering *both* the direction and the strength of the relationship. Thus, a correlation coefficient of +.45 is interpreted as a

FIGURE 12.3 A positive correlation between *X* and *Y* (correlation = .56)

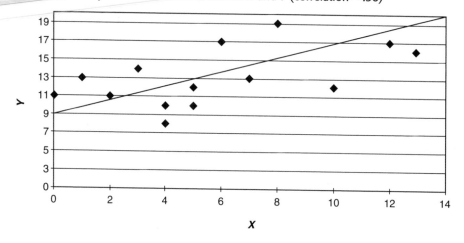

FIGURE 12.4 A negative correlation between *X* and *Y* (correlation = −.39)

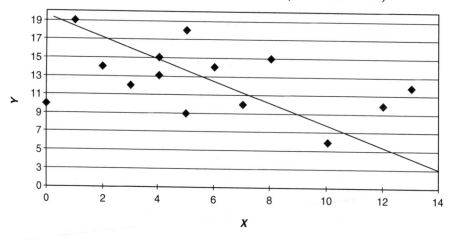

moderate positive relationship, whereas a correlation coefficient of −.45 is interpreted as a moderate negative relationship. In both cases, the strength of the relationship between the two variables is identical; the coefficients differ only in direction. You will notice that the *sign* (+ or −) and the *strength* (ranging from 0 to 1) are interpreted independently. That is, the sign says *nothing* about the strength of the relationship. It has been our experience that students often incorrectly think that a correlation coefficient of, let's say, −.34 indicates a weaker relationship than a correlation coefficient of +.20. Such is *not* the case. A correlation of −.34 indicates a stronger relationship than does a correlation of +.20. It is worth repeating that the sign of the correlation coefficient says *nothing* about the strength of the relationship, and that both the sign and strength of the relationship must be interpreted separately. To assist you in interpreting the strength of correlation coefficients, we offer the following guidelines in Figure 12.5. It

FIGURE 12.5 Guidelines for interpreting the strength of correlation coefficients

.00	none
.10	slight/weak
.20	low/definite
.40	moderate
.60	substantial
.80	high/strong
.90	very high/extremely strong
1.00	perfect

should be noted that these are merely guidelines, and should not be taken as strict rules of interpretation.

You are now ready to give interpreting a correlation coefficient a try. Complete TryIT! Box 12.1 before moving on to Section 12.3.

TryIT!   **BOX 12.1**

First, interpret the following six correlation coefficients. Next, order the correlations in terms of the strength of the relationship, from the weakest to the strongest.

$r_{XY} = +.50$

$r_{XY} = -.19$

$r_{XY} = -.93$

$r_{XY} = +.04$

$r_{XY} = +.25$

$r_{XY} = +.79$

12.3 Pearson's Correlation Coefficient (r)

Pearson's product–moment correlation coefficient
One of the most popular correlation procedures, named after its originator, Karl Pearson, is referred to as Pearson's correlation coefficient, Pearson's product–moment correlation coefficient, or simply Pearson's *r*. **Pearson's product–moment correlation coefficient** *is a statistical test to assess the relationship between two interval-ratio-level variables.* The following assumptions must be met to correctly use Pearson's *r:*

- The X and Y variables are measured at the interval or ratio level.
- Both the X and Y variables are normally distributed in the population.
- The relationship between X and Y is linear—it takes the form of a straight line.
- A probability sample was drawn from the population.

The logic and procedures of Pearson's r are based on examining the deviations of the individual X and Y values from their respective means. The summed product of the deviations represents how much the two distributions actually have in common. The square root of the summed product of the squared deviations for each of the distributions represents how much the two distributions could have in common. Thus, Pearson's r is a ratio of how much the distributions actually have in common to how much the two distributions could have in common. The formula for Pearson's r is:

$$r_{XY} = \frac{\Sigma d_x d_y}{\sqrt{\left(\Sigma d_x^2\right)\left(\Sigma d_y^2\right)}}$$

$$d_x = \left(X - \bar{X}\right)$$

$$d_y = \left(Y - \bar{Y}\right)$$

$$d_x^2 = \left(X - \bar{X}\right)^2$$

$$d_y^2 = \left(Y - \bar{Y}\right)^2$$

The numerator represents how much the two deviations have in common. The denominator represents the maximum amount of deviation the two distributions could have in common. A perfect correlation ($r_{XY} = 1.00$) informs us that the two variables share all possible variance. No correlation ($r_{XY} = .00$) means that the two variables share none of the possible variance. Hence, the stronger the relationship between the two variables, the greater the amount of shared variance in relation to total variance.

Procedures for Calculating Pearson's Product–Moment Correlation Coefficient

Let's assume that a researcher is interested in examining the relationship between "TV news consumption" and "knowledge of stalking laws." She measures TV news consumption (X) as the number of hours of TV news watched during a one-week period—a ratio-level variable. Knowledge of stalking laws (Y) is measured on a ten-item knowledge quiz—another ratio-level variable. Scores on the knowledge test could range from 0 (no questions answered correctly) to 10 (all questions answered correctly). The researcher obtains a random sample of ten individuals. She administers a questionnaire requiring the individuals to take the ten-question knowledge test and to indicate the number of hours of TV news they watched last week. Thus, she can see whether high TV news consumption tends to go with high scores on the knowledge test. Likewise, low TV news consumption should go with low scores on the knowledge test. As always, the first step is to state the research and its corresponding null hypothesis.

Step 1: State the research and null hypotheses.

In our example, the research and null hypotheses are:

H_1: TV news consumption is positively correlated with knowledge of stalking laws.

$$\rho_{XY} > 0$$

H_0: TV news consumption is not positively correlated with knowledge of stalking laws.

$$\rho_{XY} \leq 0$$

Up to this point, we have used r as the symbol for Pearson's correlation coefficient. This is correct; however, our concern is knowing whether there is a relationship between the population parameters. Therefore, we use rho (ρ) as the symbol for the population correlation coefficient. Statistical inference enables us to use our sample statistic (r) to make a decision regarding the population parameter (p).

We have hypothesized a directional relationship between TV news consumption and knowledge of stalking laws. That is, our research hypothesis is stipulating that the population correlation coefficient rho (ρ) will be larger than zero (positive), recalling that a correlation coefficient of .00 indicates no relationship between the variables. Statistical techniques are based on testing the null hypothesis with the goal of rejecting the null, so as to logically infer support for the research hypothesis. Thus, the null hypothesis indicates either no relationship between TV news consumption and knowledge of stalking laws, "or" the relationship between TV news consumption and knowledge of stalking laws is less than zero (negative). Because we have a directional hypothesis, we will be conducting a one-tailed test of our correlation coefficient.

How would the null hypothesis be stated if the research hypothesis indicated a negative relationship between variables? In this case, the null hypothesis is that there is either no relationship or a positive relationship between the two variables. Symbolically, the research and its corresponding null hypothesis would be:

$$H_1: \rho_{XY} < 0$$
$$H_0: \rho_{XY} \geq 0$$

If the research hypothesis does not specify the direction of the relationship (+ or −) and simply states that the two variables are related, then the hypothesis is nondirectional. In this case, the research hypothesis states that the population correlation coefficient between the two variables does not equal zero. The corresponding null hypothesis would be that the relationship between the two variables does equal zero. That is, TV news consumption and knowledge of stalking laws are not related. A nondirectional hypothesis requires the use of a two-tailed test in assessing the significance of Pearson's r. Symbolically, the research and null hypotheses for a two-tailed test are:

$$H_1: \rho_{XY} \neq 0$$
$$H_0: \rho_{XY} = 0$$

With this in mind, we are now ready to look at our observations. Take a close look at the data presented in Table 12.1. Is the researcher likely to find support for her hypothesis that there is a positive relationship between "TV news consumption" and "knowledge of stalking laws"? Do high scores on news consumption tend to go with high scores on the knowledge test? What about low scores? Do low scores tend to go together? By observing the data, we are able to answer yes to these questions. Thus, it appears that the two variables are positively related, as the researcher predicted. Are the two variables related enough to argue that there is a statistically significant positive relationship between the two variables in the population? As you know by now, answering this question involves testing our hypothesis using an appropriate statistical test on our sample observations with the goal of making inferences to the population. Let's proceed with our test by looking at the procedures outlined in the next several steps.

Step 2: Calculate the means and the sums for the X and Y variables.

Step 3: Calculate the deviations of X (d_x) and Y (d_y) scores from the mean of their own distributions.

This step involves subtracting the mean of the $\bar{X}$ scores from each of the individual scores of the X distribution. Similarly, the mean of the $\bar{Y}$ scores must be subtracted from each of the individual scores of the Y distribution. In Table 12.1, the mean of the $\bar{X}$ distribution is reported as 6.50. Thus, 6.50 is subtracted from each of the individual scores of the X distribution. For example, $10 - 6.50$, $3 - 6.5$, $5 - 6.5$, and so on. The mean of the $\bar{Y}$ distribution is 5. Thus, 5 is subtracted from each of the individual scores of the Y distribution. For example, $9 - 5$, $1 - 5$, $3 - 5$, and so on. The deviations of the X and Y scores from the mean of their own distribution are reported in Table 12.2 under columns 3 and 4, respectively.

Step 4: Calculate the sum of the products of the deviations of X and Y symbolized as $\Sigma(d_x d_y)$.

The sum of the products of the deviations of X and Y represents the total amount of deviation the two distributions have in common. This is represented in the numerator of the Pearson's r formula. Step 3 is easy to calculate. You simply multiply the deviations of X (d_x) and the deviations of Y (d_y). In other words, multiply the values located in columns 3 and 4. Be very careful to keep track of the sign. To illustrate with the data reported in Table 12.2, this step requires multiplying 3.50 and 4, -3.50 and -4, and -1.50 and -2, and so on. Once these values have been calculated for each X and Y score, we simply sum the column. The calculations are reported in Table 12.2 in column 5.

TABLE 12.1 Correlation Analysis of TV News Consumption and Knowledge of Stalking Laws

	TV News Consumption (X)	Knowledge of Stalking Laws (Y)
	10	9
	3	1
	5	3
	9	8
	10	8
	3	3
	2	1
	4	3
	9	7
	10	7
Sample size (n)	10	10
Sum (Σ)	65	50
Mean	$\bar{X} = 6.50$	$\bar{Y} = 5$

TABLE 12.2 Pearson's *r*: Assessing the Relationship between TV News Consumption (*X*) and Knowledge of Stalking Laws (*Y*)

Individual Scores		Deviations		Product	Squared Deviations	
X	Y	d_x	d_y	$d_x d_y$	d_x^2	d_y^2
10	9	3.50	4	14	12.25	16
3	1	−3.50	−4	14	12.25	16
5	3	−1.50	−2	3	2.25	4
9	8	2.50	3	7.5	6.25	9
10	8	3.50	3	10.5	12.25	9
3	3	−3.50	−2	7	12.25	4
2	1	−4.50	−4	18	20.25	16
4	3	−2.50	−2	5	6.25	4
9	7	2.50	2	5	6.25	4
10	7	3.50	2	7	12.25	4
$\Sigma x = 65$	$\Sigma y = 50$			$\Sigma d_x d_y = 90$	$\Sigma d_x^2 = 102.50$	$\Sigma d_y^2 = 86$
$\bar{X} = 6.50$	$\bar{Y} = 5$					

Step 5: Calculate the sum of the squared deviations of X, $\Sigma(d_x^2)$ and Y, $\Sigma(d_y^2)$.

The product of the summed squared deviations is the maximum amount of the squared deviations that the two distributions could have in common. This is represented in the denominator of the Pearson's r formula. For the X and Y distributions, separately, step 4 requires you to square each of the deviations and sum those values. For the X distribution, you will calculate 3.50^2, -3.50^2, and -1.50^2 and so on. These values are then summed. For the Y distribution, you will calculate 4^2, -4^2, -2^2 and so on. These values are also summed. The calculations are reported in Table 12.2 in columns 6 and 7, respectively. After you have completed these calculations, you have all the values needed for plugging the information into the formula for Pearson's r.

Step 6: Calculate Pearson's r.

$$r_{XY} = \frac{\Sigma d_X d_Y}{\sqrt{\left(\Sigma d_X^2\right)\left(\Sigma d_Y^2\right)}}$$

$$= \frac{90}{\sqrt{(102.50)(86)}}$$

$$= \frac{90}{\sqrt{8815}}$$

$$= \frac{90}{93.89}$$

$$= .96$$

At this point, the calculated statistic does not yet tell us whether we are able to reject the null hypothesis and accept the research hypothesis. Significance testing requires us to determine whether the correlation statistic (Pearson's r) of .96 represents a true relationship between the two variables in the population or whether the correlation coefficient is the result of sampling error.

Step 7: Calculate the degrees of freedom.

The formula for calculating the degrees of freedom for Pearson's r is n − 2, where n is the number of XY pairs. In our example, the degrees of freedom is 8. That is, 10 − 2 = 8.

Step 8: Compare the calculated r statistic with the critical r value from Table C in Appendix A.

Once we have completed our calculations, we need to compare the calculated r statistic with the critical r value found in the r probability distribution table, Table C in Appendix A. Using a one-tailed test (directional hypothesis) with eight degrees of freedom and an alpha level of .05, we determine the critical value of r to be .55 (see

TABLE 12.3 Sample *r* Distribution Table

Two-Tailed Test Significance Level (α)			One-Tailed Test Significance Level (α)		
df	.05	.01	df	.05	.01
1	1.00	1.00	1	.99	1.00
2	.95	.99	2	.90	.98
3	.88	.96	3	.81	.93
4	.81	.92	4	.73	.88
5	.75	.87	5	.67	.83
6	.71	.83	6	.63	.79
7	.67	.80	7	.58	.75
8	.63	.76	8	.55	.72

Table 12.3). Because our calculated *r* statistic (correlation coefficient) of +.96 is larger than the critical *r* value of .55 *and the relationship is in the direction predicted,* we are able to reject the null hypothesis and accept the research hypothesis.

Step 9: Interpret findings.

The significance of Pearson's *r* enables the researcher to say that there is a statistically significant correlation between TV news consumption and knowledge of stalking laws. Because the correlation coefficient was +.96, we know there is a *very strong positive* relationship between these two variables. It is important to remember that both the direction and strength of the relationship must be considered in interpreting a correlation coefficient. The direction is determined by the sign, positive (+) or negative (–), and the strength can be evaluated in light of the guidelines suggested in Figure 12.5. It is worth remembering that the values of a correlation coefficient, including Pearson's *r*, range from .00 (no relationship) to 1 (perfect relationship). If, when calculating Pearson's *r*, you obtain a value outside of this range—let's say –2.56—you know that a calculation error has been made and you need to check the accuracy of your computations.

Now that you have a good understanding of the calculations for Pearson's *r*, take a few minutes to practice calculating Pearson's correlation coefficient by completing TryIT! Box 12.2.

TryIT!   BOX **12.2**

A researcher is interested in knowing whether there is a relationship between legislators' views on the effectiveness of antidrug programs and their support for the needle exchange initiative. He randomly selects six legislators and obtains scores, on ten-point rating scales, measuring belief of the "effectiveness of antidrug programs"(X) and level of "support for the needle exchange program"(Y). Higher scores reflect more favorable ratings of effectiveness and support. The data is given below:

Subject Number	Effectiveness of Antidrug Programs (X)	Support for Needle Exchange Program (Y)
Legislator 1	6	8
Legislator 2	4	2
Legislator 3	7	9
Legislator 4	3	5
Legislator 5	4	4
Legislator 6	6	8

Step 1: State the research and null hypotheses.

Step 2: Calculate the means and sums of X and Y.

Step 3: Calculate the deviations of X and Y scores from the mean of their own distributions.

Step 4: Calculate the sum of the products of the deviations of X and Y.

Step 5: Calculate the sum of the squared deviations of X and Y. Construct a table containing the answers for steps 2, 3, 4, and 5.

Step 6: Calculate Pearson's r.

Step 7: Calculate the degrees of freedom. The formula is $n - 2$.

Step 8: Compare the calculated r with the critical r value from Table C in Appendix A.

Step 9: Interpret findings.

12.4 Using Scatterplots in Correlation Analysis

By now you are aware that correlation analysis is an extremely useful statistical technique for assessing the relationship between an independent and dependent variable. Often, however, decisions concerning the significance or importance of a correlation coefficient based only on the value of r may be misleading or misinterpreted. For example, suppose a researcher was interested in assessing the relationship between the "number of offenders on parole"(X) and the "crime rate"(Y) for six equally populated counties within a particular state. The data is presented below.

County	No. of Parolees (X)	Crime Rate (Y)
A	103	689.23
B	114	695.43
C	115	708.11
D	125	1235.44 *outlier*
E	158	800.76
F	160	821.65

We can see, by observing our data, that higher values of X tend to correspond with higher values of Y. That is, as the number of parolees increases, so does the crime rate. Assume that our researcher proposed a nondirectional hypothesis and proceeded to calculate a correlation coefficient. Using the data above, Pearson's r is equal to .18. The critical value of Pearson's r for a two-tailed test at the .05 alpha level with 4 degrees of freedom is equal to .81. Because our calculated r of .18 is less than the critical r value of .81, we would fail to reject the null hypothesis.

Although this interpretation is correct based on the data above, there is a problem with one of the data values. Notice that the crime rate (Y) for county D is significantly higher than the crime rates for the other five counties. This value represents an extreme

outlier case commonly referred to as an outlier. An **outlier** is *an extreme or atypical case that distorts the data distribution.* We discussed measures of central tendency and dispersion in Chapters 4 and 5, and discovered that high or low values will affect the mean and standard deviation in such a way that the data distributions will be either positively or negatively skewed. Because one of the major assumptions of correlation analysis is that the variables are normally distributed in the population, correlation coefficients are adversely affected when the data distribution is skewed by an outlier or group of outliers.

Scatterplots provide a simple method for detecting outliers. We first introduced you to scatterplots in Section 12.1, where we illustrated several different scatterplots show-

scatterplot ing both positive and negative correlation values. A **scatterplot** is *a graph that plots the values of the independent and dependent variables simultaneously for each subject.* Using the data above, we would generate a scatterplot like that shown in Figure 12.6. It is easy to visualize the relationship between the independent and dependent variables. Another assumption of correlation analysis is that the relationship between X and Y is linear. Observation of the scatterplot shows that this assumption holds true for five of the six counties, with one county (county D) being identified as an outlier—its data point occurs on Y, way above the other data points.

There are several methods for dealing with outliers, with most beyond the scope of this text. One common method is to drop the case from the analysis. In our example, we would simply eliminate county D from the analysis and recalculate Pearson's r using the other five counties. Our calculated r statistic, excluding county D, now equals .99. Compared to the critical r value of .88 (two-tailed test, .05 alpha level, 3 df), we are now able to reject the null hypothesis and accept the research hypothesis that there is in

FIGURE 12.6 Scatterplot of parolees and crime rate

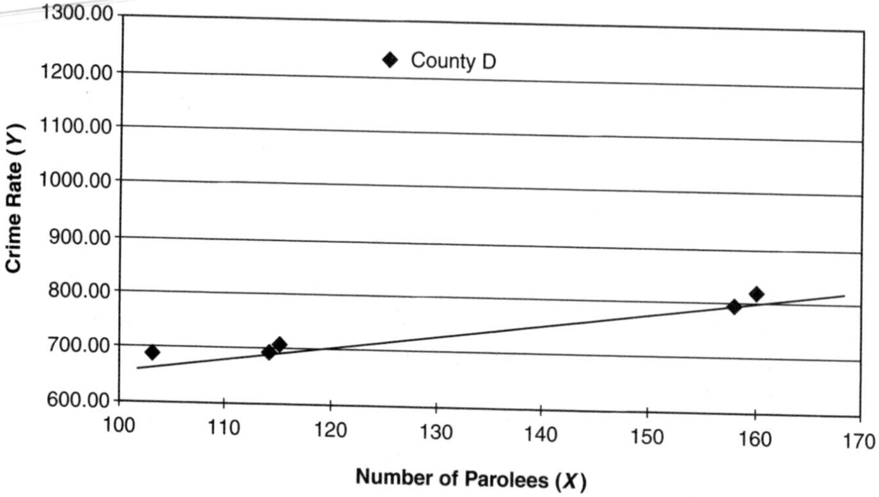

fact a statistically significant relationship between the number of offenders on parole and the crime rate.

It is important to note that outliers can occur on either the dependent or independent variable. In our example, we presented a case in which an outlier occurred on the dependent variable, which ultimately affected the results of the correlation coefficient. That is, with the outlier included in the analysis, the calculated *r* was not statistically significant. On removal of the outlier, however, the results were drastically different, as we were able to conclude that *X* and *Y* were significantly related in the population.

For illustration purposes, Figure 12.7 presents a scatterplot involving a larger sample (30 cities), in which we have some outliers on both our independent (percentage unemployed) and dependent variables (robbery rate). The majority of cities vary between 1% and 14% for unemployment, with cities 3 and 4 identified as outliers on the independent variable only (28% and 29% unemployment, respectively). For the dependent variable, the majority of cities have a robbery rate between 8.5 and 16.4, with city 1 being identified as an outlier on the dependent variable only with a robbery rate of 32.8. City 2 is considered an outlier on both the independent (percent unemployed = 30%) and dependent variables (robbery rate = 32.8).

It is relatively easy to detect outliers by visually inspecting a scatterplot. Based on our observations of the graph, we know that corrective action is warranted to decrease the adverse effects these outliers will have on the correlation coefficient. Failure to deal with outliers will result in a biased correlation coefficient as the assumptions of normality and linearity will be violated. Although we have suggested eliminating outliers from the analysis, it is important to note that this is only one method of correction that is typi-

FIGURE 12.7 Scatterplot of unemployment and robbery

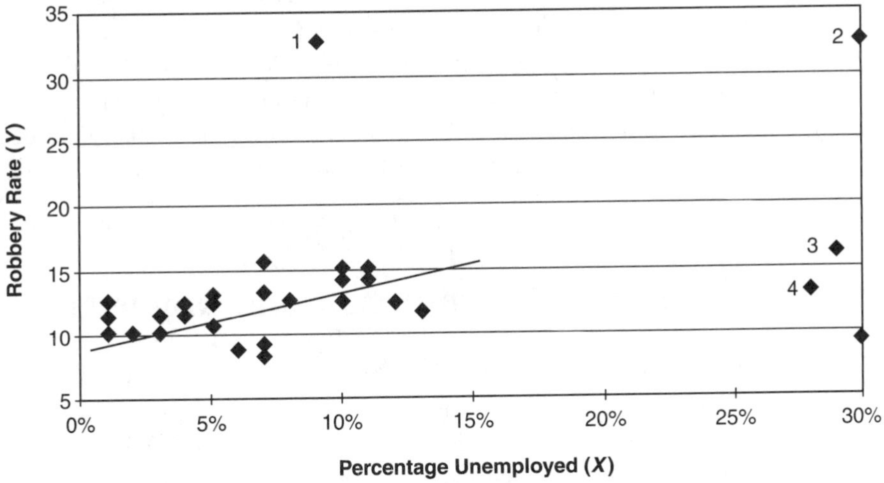

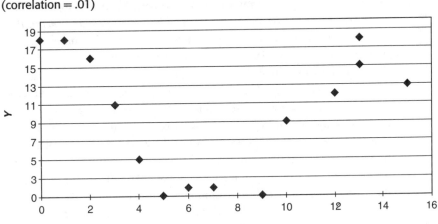

cally used. Other methods of correction may be more suitable, depending on the values of the outliers and other theoretical considerations.

One final point concerning scatterplots: One of the assumptions of Pearson's r is that the relationship between the independent and dependent variable is linear. It is imperative that we validate this assumption prior to calculating a correlation coefficient. Assume that we constructed a scatterplot like that shown in Figure 12.8 for a set of data. Is the linearity assumption violated? Our visual inspection of the graph would indicate yes—the assumption is violated. Specifically, there does not appear to be any

FIGURE 12.8 Scatterplot illustrating a U-shaped relationship between X and Y (correlation = .01)

positive or negative pattern between the *X* and *Y* values. In fact, in this particular graph, the pattern is U-shaped, which indicates a negative correlation at lower values of *X*, no correlation at the middle values of *X*, and a positive correlation at larger values of *X*. Because the pattern is inconsistent across all values of *X*, the calculation of Pearson's *r* is unwarranted—the value would be rendered meaningless. Visual inspection of a scatterplot is necessary prior to the calculation of a correlation coefficient to detect not only outliers within the data but also to determine if the linearity assumption has been met.

12.5 Coefficients of Determination and Nondetermination

A correlation coefficient indicates the direction and strength of the relationship between two variables. It does not say anything about the percentage or proportion of variability in one variable that is explained by the other variable. In order to understand the amount of change in the dependent variable (*Y*) explained by the independent variable (*X*), a coefficient of determination must be calculated. It is also important to keep in mind that a correlation coefficient is not expressed as a percentage or a proportion; thus, we cannot say, for instance, that a correlation coefficient of .60 indicates twice the relationship as a coefficient of .30. Making such comparisons involves computing coefficients of determination. The **coefficient of determination**, or r^2, is *the percentage of variance in the Y variable explained or accounted for by the X variable.* The coefficient of determination (r^2) is simply the square of the correlation coefficient (*r*). For example, a researcher obtains an *r* of .60. Expressed as a coefficient of determination, we would say that 36% of the variability in the dependent variable (*Y*) can be explained by its association with the independent variable (*X*). Coefficients of determination are comparable; thus, it is appropriate to say that an r^2 of .60 explains twice the variability as an r^2 of .30.

coefficient of determination

Another useful piece of information is the **coefficient of nondetermination** defined as *the percentage of variance in the Y variable unexplained or unaccounted for by the X variable.* The coefficient of nondetermination is simply the complement of r^2, or $1 - r^2$. An r^2 of .30, for example, yields a coefficient of nondetermination of .70 ($1 - .30 = .70$), indicating that 70% of the variance in *Y* is not explained by its association with *X*.

coefficient of nondetermination

It is wise to consider r^2 and $1 - r^2$ in interpreting correlation coefficients, especially with coefficients of low magnitude, as low values of *r* result in a negligible amount of common variance. An *r* of .30, for instance, may signify a significant relationship, yet only 9% (coefficient of determination) of the variance in *Y* is explained by its association with *X*, leaving 91% unexplained (coefficient of nondetermination). In contrast, the decrease is not as sharp at higher values of *r*. An *r* of .90, for instance, indicates that the two variables share 81% of common variance, leaving only 19% unexplained.

Take a moment to complete TryIT! Box 12.3 before moving to partial correlation coefficients.

TryIT!

BOX **12.3**

For the following correlation coefficients, determine the coefficient of determination (r^2) and coefficient of nondetermination ($1-r^2$). What does a coefficient of determination of .25 mean? What does a coefficient of nondetermination of .75 mean?

Correlation Coefficient	Coefficient of Determination	Coefficient of Nondetermination
.05	0.00 (.05×0.05)	1−0.25=0.75
.25		
.50		
.75		
.95		

12.6 Partial Correlation Coefficient

The degree of confidence in the results of a correlation analysis depends, to a great extent, on the ability to rule out possible confounding variables that may account for the relationship between the independent and dependent variables. A researcher might report, for example, a strong negative association between "age"(X) and "sentence length"(Y). She reports that older individuals are more likely to be awarded shorter sentence lengths. Before making such claims, she must carefully consider what other relevant variables might account for the relationship between age and sentence length. One possible variable is "education"(Z). Individuals with higher education tend to be older and receive more favorable sentences; thus, education might account for the detected relationship between "age" and "sentence length." A **partial correlation coefficient** is *a statistic used to analyze the correlation between two variables, while controlling for the influence of one or more other variables.*

partial correlation coefficient

Symbolically, a partial correlation coefficient is written as $r_{XY \cdot Z}$, and it is read as the partial correlation coefficient between two variables (X and Y), while statistically ruling out the influence of another variable (Z). In our example, a partial correlation allows us to examine the relationship between age and sentence length while ruling out the effects of education.

Procedures for Calculating a Partial Correlation Coefficient

Step 1: Determine the correlation coefficients.

To calculate a partial correlation, we must first calculate correlation coefficients (Pearson's r). In our example, we need the correlations between age and sentence length (r_{XY}), age and education level (r_{XZ}) and sentence length and education (r_{YZ}). Let us suppose that the following correlation coefficients were calculated:

$$r_{XY} = -.85$$
$$r_{XZ} = +.50$$
$$r_{YZ} = -.30$$

Step 2: Calculate the partial correlation coefficient ($r_{XY \cdot Z}$).
The partial correlation coefficient is computed using the following formula:

$$r_{XY \cdot Z} = \frac{r_{XY} - (r_{XZ})(r_{YZ})}{\sqrt{1 - (r_{XZ})^2} \sqrt{1 - (r_{YZ})^2}}$$

Although the formula looks intimidating, the process is straightforward. In the numerator, we simply multiply the correlation of XZ (r_{XZ}) with the correlation of YZ (r_{YZ}), which is then subtracted from the correlation of XY (r_{XY}). The denominator requires us to multiply the square root of the coefficient of nondetermination for XZ, which is given as: $1 - (r_{XZ})^2$, by the square root of the coefficient of nondetermination for YZ, shown as: $1 - (r_{YZ})^2$. Substituting our values into the formula, we calculate the partial correlation coefficient in the following manner:

$$r_{XY \cdot Z} = \frac{-.85 - (.50)(-.30)}{\sqrt{1 - (.50)^2} \sqrt{1 - (-.30)^2}}$$

$$= \frac{-.85 - -.15}{\sqrt{1 - .25} \sqrt{1 - .09}}$$

$$= \frac{-.70}{\sqrt{.75} \sqrt{.91}}$$

$$= \frac{-.70}{(.87)(.95)}$$

$$= \frac{-.70}{.83}$$

$$r_{XY \cdot Z} = -.84$$

Step 3: Interpret findings.
The partial correlation coefficient ($r_{XY \cdot Z} = -.84$) looks at the relationship between age and sentence length controlling for the effects of education. It is almost identical to the original correlation between age and sentence length ($r_{XY} = -.85$). It is apparent that the relationship between our independent variable "age" and dependent variable

"sentence length" is independent from its joint relationship with "education." The researcher is safely able to rule out education as a rival explanation for the association detected between age and sentence length.

What conclusion would you draw if the results showed a drop in the partial correlation coefficient compared to the original coefficient? Suppose $r_{XY \cdot Z}$ was $-.38$, compared to the original coefficient, $r_{XY} = -.85$. By considering education, the correlation between age and sentence length is weaker than earlier suspected. In this case, education cannot be ignored in drawing conclusions about the relationship between age and sentence length.

What conclusion would you draw if the results showed a sharp increase in the partial correlation coefficient compared to the original coefficient? Suppose $r_{XY \cdot Z}$ was $-.98$, compared to the original coefficient, $r_{XY} = -.85$. In this case, education suppresses the detected association between age and sentence length; thus, the relationship between age and sentence length is actually stronger than originally detected. Once again, education cannot be ignored in making conclusions about the relationship between age and sentence length.

Partial correlation is useful for controlling possible rival explanations that may account for the detected relationship between an independent and dependent variable. Its usefulness, however, is limited to your skill in isolating possible alternative variables *and* your insight to include the variables in the research design. Failure to include education in your questionnaire, for example, makes it impossible to statistically control for this variable using partial correlation analysis.

Try calculating a partial correlation coefficient by completing TryIT! Box 12.4.

TryIT!   BOX 12.4

As a juvenile probation officer, you are interested in the relationship between income and involvement in juvenile delinquency, controlling for the effects of drug use. Compute and interpret the partial correlation coefficient of interest.

Step 1: Determine the correlation coefficients.

The following are the correlation coefficients among the variables "income" (X), "involvement in juvenile delinquency" (Y), and "drug use" (Z).

$r_{XY} = -.60$

$r_{XZ} = +.25$

$r_{YZ} = -.20$

Step 2: Calculate the partial correlation coefficient ($r_{XY \cdot Z}$).

Step 3: Interpret findings.

12.7 Using Excel for Correlation Analysis

Now that you are able to calculate correlation coefficients by hand, we now want to incorporate computer technology into our statistical applications. We provide step-by-step instructions using Excel to calculate both Pearson's *r* and a partial correlation coefficient.

Pearson's r

At the beginning of this chapter, we introduced you to the mayor of a large eastern city, who believes that increasing the education level of police officers will produce better officers less likely to receive citizen complaints. Let's assume we have decided to study this issue and select a probability sample of 15 police officers from this particular city. The two variables of interest are "education level"(*X*), measured as the number of years of formal schooling each officer has had, and "citizen complaints"(*Y*), measured as the number of complaints filed against each officer. The data for this problem is presented in Table 12.4.

Step 1: State the research and null hypotheses. These are given in notational form in cell a2.

Notice that we have proposed a directional hypothesis in keeping with the mayor's assumption that increased levels of education will lead to fewer citizen complaints. More specifically, we are assuming that the correlation coefficient between education level and citizen complaints will be negative.

Step 2: Calculate the means and sums for both education level and complaints using the paste function box and the autosum button on the menu.

Step 3: Calculate the deviations of the $X\,(d_x)$ and $Y\,(d_y)$ scores from the mean of their own distribution, using the following formulas:

$$d_x = \left(X - \overline{X}\right)$$
$$d_y = \left(Y - \overline{Y}\right)$$

To calculate the deviations for education level, place the cursor in cell d4 and write: =b4-b19.

b4 is the cell location for the education level of Officer 1.
b19 is the mean education level.
$ holds the column (b) and row (19) constant.

Click the lower right-hand corner of cell d4 and drag the cursor down to cell d18. This will automatically create the rest of the d_x column.

$$\boxed{\text{-1.13}}\ \blacksquare \longleftarrow$$

To calculate the deviations for complaints, place the cursor in cell e4 and write: =c4-c19.

c4 is the cell location for the number of complaints for Officer 1.
c19 is the cell location for the mean number of complaints.
$ holds the column (c) and row (19) constant.

To create the rest of the d_y column, click the lower right-hand corner of cell e4 and drag the cursor down to cell e18.

Step 4: Calculate the sum of the product of the deviations of X and Y, $\Sigma(d_x d_y)$.
Place the cursor in cell f4 and write: =d4*e4

d4 is the cell location for deviation of X for Officer 1.
e4 is the cell location for the deviation of Y for Officer 1.

To create the rest of the product column, click the lower right-hand corner of cell f4 and drag the cursor down to cell f18.

To create the sum of the product column, place the cursor in cell f20 and click the autosum button on the menu.

Step 5: Calculate the sum of the squared deviations of X, $\Sigma(d_x^2)$ and Y, $\Sigma(d_y^2)$.
To create the squared deviations for education, place the cursor in cell g4 and write: =d4^2.

d4 is the cell location for the deviation of X for Officer 1.
^2 is the symbol used to square a value.

Click the lower right-hand corner of cell g4 and drag the cursor down to cell g18 to create the rest of the d_x^2 column.

To create the squared deviations for complaints, place the cursor in cell h4 and write: =e4^2.

e4 is the cell location for deviation of Y for Officer 1.
^2 is the symbol used to square a value.

Click the lower right-hand corner of cell h4 and drag the cursor down to cell h18 to create the rest of the d_y^2 column.

TABLE 12.4 Pearson's *r* Correlation Coefficient

	A	B	C	D	E	F	G	H
1	TABLE 12.4 Pearson's *r* Correlation Coefficient							
2	H_1: $p_{XY} < 0$ H_0: $p_{XY} \geq 0$			Deviations		Product	Squared Deviations	
3	Officer	Education (X)	Complaints (Y)	d_x	d_y	$d_x d_y$	d_x^2	d_x^2
4	1	12	0	-1.13	-1.13	1.28	1.28	1.28
5	2	14	1	0.87	-0.13	-0.12	0.75	0.02
6	3	16	2	2.87	0.87	2.48	8.22	0.75
7	4	11	1	-2.13	-0.13	0.28	4.55	0.02
8	5	12	1	-1.13	-0.13	0.15	1.28	0.02
9	6	12	1	-1.13	-0.13	0.15	1.28	0.02
10	7	14	3	0.87	1.87	1.62	0.75	3.48
11	8	18	2	4.87	0.87	4.22	23.68	0.75
12	9	10	1	-3.13	-0.13	0.42	9.82	0.02
13	10	10	0	-3.13	-1.13	3.55	9.82	1.28
14	11	12	2	-1.13	0.87	-0.98	1.28	0.75
15	12	12	0	-1.13	-1.13	1.28	1.28	1.28
16	13	14	0	0.87	-1.13	-0.98	0.75	1.28
17	14	14	2	0.87	0.87	0.75	0.75	0.75
18	15	16	1	2.87	-0.13	-0.38	8.22	0.02
19	Mean ($\bar{X}$) ($\bar{Y}$)	13.13	1.13					
20	Sum					13.73	73.73	11.73
21	r_{xy}	0.47						
22	*df*	13						
23	Critical *r*	0.44						

Use the autosum button to create the sum of the squared deviation scores for both d_x^2 (cell g20) and d_y^2 (cell h20).

Step 6: Calculate Pearson's r (r_{xy}), using the following formula:

$$r_{xy} = \frac{\Sigma d_x d_y}{\sqrt{\left(\Sigma d_x^2\right)\left(\Sigma d_y^2\right)}}$$

Place the cursor in cell b21 and write: =f20/(sqrt(g20*h20)).

f20 is the numerator $\Sigma(d_x d_y)$.
g20 and h20 are the $\Sigma(d_x^2)$ and $\Sigma(d_y^2)$, respectively.
sqrt is the symbol for square root.
/ is the symbol for division.

Step 7: Calculate the degrees of freedom ($n-2$). Place the cursor in cell b22 and write: =a18-2.

a18 is the cell location for the sample size (n).

Step 8: Compare the calculated r statistic with the critical r value from Table C in Appendix A.
   The critical value of r for a one-tailed test, an alpha level of .05, and 13 degrees of freedom is determined to be .44. The calculated r statistic of .47 is larger than the critical value of .44; however, the direction is the opposite of that which was hypothesized. We hypothesized that the relationship would be negative, with higher levels of education associated with lower numbers of complaints. Because the relationship is positive, we are unable to reject the null hypothesis.

Step 9: Interpret findings.
   Our findings require us to say that there is no statistically significant relationship between education level and number of citizen complaints among the population of police officers. Any association that we found is primarily the result of sampling error and not due to an actual relationship within the population.

Excel offers several different methods for calculating Pearson's r. The first method of calculation is the formula approach, which we demonstrated with the data in Table 12.4. An alternative method for calculating Pearson's r is to make use of the paste function box. Using the same research scenario as above, the data is presented in Table 12.5 and the following steps are performed:

Step 1: Place the cursor in cell b19 and click the paste function box (also known as function wizard):

$$\boxed{fx}$$

358   *Chapter 12*

Step 2: Click the function category called **statistical**.

Step 3: Click the name category called **PEARSON** (you can also use **CORREL** in the name category).

Step 4: Click **next** and a box will appear that will ask for the values for array1 (independent values) and array2 (dependent values). For array1, type in the range of cells within which the *X* values lie (b4:b18), or highlight the range by selecting cell b4 and dragging the cursor down to cell b18. For array2, type in the range of cells within

TABLE 12.5 Pearson's *r*—Paste Function

	A	B	C
1	TABLE 12.5 Pearson's *r*—Paste Function		
2	$H_1: p_{XY} < 0$ $H_0: p_{XY} \geq 0$		
3	Officer	Education (*X*)	Complaints (*Y*)
4	1	12	0
5	2	14	1
6	3	16	2
7	4	11	1
8	5	12	1
9	6	12	1
10	7	14	3
11	8	18	2
12	9	10	1
13	10	10	0
14	11	12	2
15	12	12	0
16	13	14	0
17	14	14	2
18	15	16	1
19	r_{XY}	0.47	
20	*df*	13	
21	Critical *r*	0.44	

which the *Y* values lie (c4:c18), or highlight the range by selecting cell c4 and dragging the cursor down to cell c18. Then click **finish**.

array 1	b4:b18
array 2	c4:c18

As shown in Table 12.5, use of the paste function allows us to eliminate the calculations found in columns D through H, as illustrated in Table 12.4. Furthermore, it is not necessary to calculate the means or the sums for either variable when using the paste function box. Whereas the paste function approach allows us to combine steps 3, 4, and 5 into one step, it is necessary to perform steps 1, 6, 7, and 8 as previously mentioned using the formula method.

Criminal justice research often involves situations in which a researcher may want to calculate correlation coefficients among several variables. Although we can perform these calculations using both the formula and paste function methods, this is more time-consuming. Thus, when several variables are involved, it is more efficient to make use of the data analysis tool as a method for calculating the correlations. This is the third method of calculating Pearson's *r* using Excel. You should be familiar with this tool, as we introduced you to this function in earlier chapters on *t* tests and ANOVA. Using the data in Table 12.6, we see that we have four independent variables and two dependent variables. Assume that our researcher wants to test the relationship between each independent variable and each dependent variable. This will require the calculation of eight correlation coefficients (X_1 through X_4 with Y_1 and Y_2). We would also need to have eight research and null hypotheses concerning each of the correlation coefficients. We provide only one hypothesis for years of service and awards. This is given in cell a2.

Using the data analysis tool, we perform the following steps:

Step 1: Select the **tools** option on the Excel menu bar.
Step 2: Select **data analysis** under the tools option.
Step 3: In the analysis tool box, select **correlation**.
Step 4: Enter b3:g18 for the input range. It is important to note that the range includes the labels for the *X* and *Y* variables; thus, the **Labels in First Row** box must be checked.
Step 5: Click **ok** and a correlation matrix table will be produced like that shown in Table 12.7.

As shown in Table 12.7, the data analysis tool calculates correlation coefficients among all of the variables. That is, Pearson's *r* is not only calculated between each *X* and *Y* variable, it is also calculated between each of the *X* variables and *Y* variables. Although the data analysis tool is a more efficient method for calculating Pearson's *r* for several variables simultaneously, we must perform steps 1, 6, 7, and 8. We cannot make

TABLE 12.6 Pearson's *r* Correlation Coefficient—Data Analysis Tool

	A	B	C	D	E	F	G
1	TABLE 12.6 Pearson's *r* Correlation Coefficient—Data Analysis Tool						
2	$H_1: p_{X2Y2} > 0$ $H_0: p_{X2Y2} \leq 0$						
3	Officer	Education (X_1)	Service (X_2)	Training (X_3)	Exam (X_4)	Complaints (Y_1)	Awards (Y_2)
4	1	12	5	80	75	0	0
5	2	14	2	120	77	1	1
6	3	16	8	100	88	2	1
7	4	11	1	60	80	1	0
8	5	12	1	60	70	1	0
9	6	12	4	80	75	1	1
10	7	14	1	80	77	3	0
11	8	18	1	150	95	2	5
12	9	10	10	60	70	1	1
13	10	10	4	80	76	0	0
14	11	12	2	60	80	2	2
15	12	12	2	60	88	0	0
16	13	14	1	80	90	0	3
17	14	14	1	80	70	2	1
18	15	16	12	200	98	1	3

TABLE 12.7 Correlation Matrix

	Education (X_1)	Service (X_2)	Training (X_3)	Exam (X_4)	Complaints (Y_1)	Awards (Y_2)
Education (X_1)	1.00					
Service (X_2)	0.04	1.00				
Training (X_3)	0.75	0.44	1.00			
Exam (X_4)	0.68	0.21	0.68	1.00		
Complaints (Y_1)	0.47	−0.12	0.14	−0.03	1.00	
Awards (Y_2)	0.72	0.19	0.73	0.72	0.17	1.00

use of the correlation matrix unless we have specified our hypotheses, determined the degrees of freedom, and compared the calculated r with the critical r found in Table C in Appendix A. For example, let's assume that we hypothesized a negative relationship between training and complaints but a positive relationship between training and awards. Because both hypotheses are directional, we will be using a one-tailed test. With 13 degrees of freedom and an alpha level of .05, we determine the r critical value to be .44. Looking at the correlation matrix, we find the column that has the variable "training" (X_3) and proceed down to the row that has the variable "complaints" (Y_1). Therefore, the calculated Pearson's r is equal to .14. Because the calculated r is less than the critical r, we fail to reject the null hypothesis of no relationship between training and complaints. To test the next hypothesis, we simply move down the matrix to the next row that contains the variable "awards" (Y_2), where we find the value of Pearson's r is equal to .73. Because the calculated r is larger than the critical r "and" it is in the hypothesized direction, we are able to reject the null hypothesis and conclude that there is a statistically significant relationship between training and awards among the population of police officers. More specifically, the more training an officer has, the more awards he/she is likely to receive.

Although the paste function and data analysis tools provide quick easy methods for calculating Pearson's r, we highly recommend that you use the formula method as the primary mode of operation for computing statistics with Excel. Both of these latter functions can be used as procedural checks on the accuracy of your calculations. We also recommend using the data analysis tool when a large number of variables are involved.

Partial Correlation Coefficient

Here is one example for the calculations of a partial correlation coefficient using Excel. Suppose our researcher believes (using the correlation matrix in Table 12.8) that the relationship between "training" (X_3) and "awards" (Y_2) may be confounded by the "length of service" (X_2). To rule out any possibility of confounding effects, the researcher would like to calculate a partial correlation coefficient between training and awards, while controlling for service. We have labeled the partial correlation coefficient in cell a10 to indicate the specified relationship.

Step 1: Determine the correlation coefficients. This was done using the data analysis tool.

Step 2: Calculate the partial correlation coefficient $(r_{XY \cdot Z})$ using the following formula:

$$r_{XY \cdot Z} = \frac{r_{XY} - (r_{XZ})(r_{YZ})}{\sqrt{1 - (r_{XZ})^2} \sqrt{1 - (r_{YZ})^2}}$$

Place the cursor in cell b10 and write: =(d8-(c5*c8))/((sqrt(1-(c5^2))*(sqrt(1-(c8^2)))))).

TABLE 12.8 Correlation Matrix and Partial Correlation Coefficient

	A	B	C	D	E	F	G
1	**TABLE 12.8 Correlation Matrix and Partial Correlation Coefficient**						
2		Education (X_1)	Service (X_2)	Training (X_3)	Exam (X_4)	Complaints (Y_1)	Awards (Y_2)
3	Education (X_1)	1.00					
4	Service (X_2)	0.04	1.00				
5	Training (X_3)	0.75	0.44	1.00			
6	Exam (X_4)	0.68	0.21	0.68	1.00		
7	Complaints (Y_1)	0.47	-0.12	0.14	-0.03	1.00	
8	Awards (Y_2)	0.72	0.19	0.73	0.72	0.17	1.00
9							
10	$r_{X_3 Y_2 - Z_2}$	0.74					

d8 is the cell location for the correlation coefficient between Training and Awards.
c5 is the cell location for the correlation coefficient between Training and Service.
c8 is the cell location for the correlation coefficient between Service and Awards.
sqrt is the symbol for square root and ^2 is the symbol for squaring a value.
-, *, / are the symbols for subtraction, multiplication, and division, respectively.

Step 3: Interpret findings. With a partial correlation coefficient of .74, we determine that the relationship between "training"(X_3) and "awards"(Y_2) remains statistically significant when controlling for "years of service"(X_2).

12.8 Summary

In this chapter, we explored correlational techniques appropriate for assessing the extent to which two interval-ratio-level variables are related. We presented some common ways to assess the relationship between variables. One way to assess relationships is in terms of direction, either positive or negative. A positive relationship means that the two variables covary in the same direction; that is, an increase in one variable is associated with an increase in the other variable. A negative relationship means that the variables covary in opposite directions; that is, an increase in one variable is marked by a decrease in the other variable. A second way to assess relationships is in terms of strength, with values ranging from .00 to 1. A correlation coefficient of .00 represents no relationship between the two variables; a coefficient of 1 represents a perfect relationship between the two variables. Most relationships fall somewhere between these two extremes. It is important to keep in mind that the direction and strength of a correlation coefficient must be interpreted separately.

A third way to assess relationships is to examine the amount of variance that can be explained in one of the variables (Y) by its association with the other variable (X). This is known as the coefficient of determination, or r^2. Similarly, the researcher can look at how much variance in one variable (Y) is left unexplained by its association with another variable (X). This is known as the coefficient of nondetermination, or $1 - r^2$. Finally, the researcher can investigate the relationship between two variables while ruling out the effects of another variable. This is known as partial correlation.

We provided step-by-step calculations for both Pearson's product-moment correlation coefficient and partial correlation coefficient. Each of these two techniques was demonstrated using Excel.

Key Terms

correlation analysis

correlation coefficient

positive correlation coefficient

negative correlation coefficient

Pearson's product–moment correlation coefficient

outlier

scatterplot

coefficient of determination

coefficient of nondetermination

partial correlation coefficient

TryIT! Answers

Box 12.1

Interpretation of correlation coefficients:

$r_{xy} = +.50$ Moderate positive relationship

$r_{xy} = -.19$ Slight negative relationship

$r_{xy} = -.93$ Very strong negative relationship

$r_{xy} = +.04$ Slight positive relationship

$r_{xy} = +.25$ Low positive relationship

$r_{xy} = +.79$ Substantial positive relationship

Order the correlations in terms of strength (weakest to strongest):

$r_{xy} = +.04, r_{xy} = -.19, r_{xy} = +.25, r_{xy} = +.50, r_{xy} = +.79, r_{xy} = -.93$

Box 12.2

Step 1: State the research and null hypotheses.

H_1: The legislators' perceptions of the effectiveness of antidrug programs and their level of support for the needle exchange program are related.

$\rho_{xy} \neq 0$

H_0: The legislators' perceptions of the effectiveness of antidrug programs and their level of support for the needle exchange program are not related.

$\rho_{xy} = 0$

Step 2: Calculate the means and sums of X and Y.

Step 3: Calculate the deviations of X and Y scores from the mean of their own distributions.

Step 4: Calculate the sum of the products of the deviations of X and Y.

Step 5: Calculate the summed squared deviations of the two distributions.

[Construct a table containing the answers for steps 2–5.]

Table Box 12.2: Pearson's *r*: Assessing the relationship between perceptions of effectiveness of antidrug programs and support for the needle exchange program

Individual Scores		Deviations		Product	Squared Deviations	
X	Y	d_x	d_y	$d_x d_y$	d_x^2	d_y^2
6	8	+1	+2	+2	+1	+4
4	2	−1	−4	+4	+1	+16
7	9	+2	+3	+6	+4	+9
3	5	−2	−1	+2	+4	+1
4	4	−1	−2	+2	+1	+4
6	8	+1	+2	+2	+1	+4
$\Sigma X = 30$	$\Sigma Y = 36$			$\Sigma d_x d_y = 18$	$\Sigma d_x^2 = 12$	$\Sigma d_y^2 = 38$
$\bar{X} = 5$	$\bar{Y} = 6$					

Step 6: Calculate Pearson's *r*:

$$r_{xy} = \frac{18}{\sqrt{(12)(38)}}$$
$$= .84$$

Step 7: Calculate the degrees of freedom ($n - 2$).

$$6 - 2 = 4$$

Step 8: Compare the calculated *r* with the critical *r* from Table C in Appendix A.

We advanced a two-tailed hypothesis with 4 degrees of freedom. The critical *r* at alpha $= .05$ is .81. The calculated *r* of .84 is greater than the critical *r*. Thus, we reject the null hypothesis and accept the research hypothesis.

Step 9: Interpret findings.

The data supports a statistically significant relationship between legislators' perceptions of the effectiveness of antidrug programs and their support for the needle exchange program. Because the correlation coefficient is +.84, we know that there is a strong positive relationship between these two variables.

Box 12.3

Correlation Coefficient	Coefficient of Determination	Coefficient of Nondetermination
.05	.00	1.00
.25	.06	.94
.50	.25	.75
.75	.56	.44
.95	.90	.10

A coefficient of determination of .25 means that 25% of the variability in *Y* can be explained by its association with *X*. A coefficient of nondetermination of .75 means that 75% of the variance in *Y* is left unexplained by its association with *X*.

Box 12.4

Step 1: Determine the correlation coefficients. The following correlation coefficients were provided in the problem:

$$r_{XY} = -.60$$
$$r_{XZ} = +.25$$
$$r_{YZ} = -.20$$

Step 2: Calculate the partial correlation coefficient ($r_{XY \cdot Z}$).

$$r_{XY \cdot Z} = \frac{-.60 - (.25)(-.20)}{\sqrt{1-(.25)^2}\sqrt{1-(-.20)^2}}$$

$$= -.58$$

Step 3: Interpret findings. There is only a slight reduction in the size of the partial correlation ($r_{XY \cdot Z} = -.58$), compared to the original correlation ($r_{XY} = -.60$). Hence, we are able to conclude that the relationship between income and criminal activity is independent of its joint relationship with age. Age can safely be ruled out as an alternative explanation for the detected association between income and criminal activity.

12.9 Problems

1. A researcher believes that there is a positive association between alcohol use and domestic violence. That is, as alcohol use increases, the frequency of domestic violence also increases. She selects a random sample of ten offenders who were previously arrested for domestic violence, within the past year. She measures alcohol use (X) as the average number of drinks per month over the past year, and frequency of domestic violence (Y) as the number of police contacts for domestic violence incidences within the past year. The data is given as follows:

Alcohol Use (X)	Domestic Violence (Y)
3.5	4
8.4	2
6.0	1
12.2	5
1.7	1
2	2
1	1
9.8	6
5.2	3
0	1

Answer the following:

a. What type of research hypothesis is being proposed? Should you perform a one-tailed or two-tailed test? Explain.

b. Calculate Pearson's *r*. Interpret the direction and strength of the correlation coefficient.

c. Is the correlation coefficient significant at the .05 alpha level? What conclusions would you make about the relationship between alcohol usage and domestic violence?

2. In order to calculate a Pearson correlation coefficient, both variables must be measured at what level(s)?

3. For the following hypotheses indicate whether a one-tailed or two-tailed test is appropriate. If one-tailed, indicate if the researcher is proposing a positive or negative relationship between the two variables.

   a. As news coverage of terrorism increases, citizens are less likely to travel abroad.
   b. The degree of taxpayer support for NASA is related to the number of scheduled NASA flights.
   c. There is a relationship between level of unemployment and likelihood of investing in the stock market.
   d. As judges' years on the bench increase, trial length decreases.
   e. As years on the police force increase, officers are more likely to have negative attitudes toward police work.

4. Consider the five correlation coefficients presented below.

   $$r_{XY} = -.98 \qquad r_{XY} = -.02 \qquad r_{XY} = +.85 \qquad r_{XY} = +.40 \qquad r_{XY} = +.10$$

   a. Which coefficient represents the greatest magnitude (strength) between the two variables?
   b. Which coefficient represents the least magnitude (strength) between the two variables?
   c. For $r_{XY} = -.98$, what is the coefficient of determination? Coefficient of nondetermination?
   d. Which of the correlation coefficients are significant at alpha = .05, assuming that each coefficient tests a directional hypothesis from a sample size of ten.

5. A researcher is interested in the relationship between amount of "TV viewing" (X) and "fear of victimization" (Y). She would like to control for the effects of "age" (Z). Calculate a partial correlation of X and Y controlling for the effects of Z. What conclusions can the researcher draw? The following correlation coefficients are given.

   $$r_{XY} = -.55$$
   $$r_{XZ} = +.80$$
   $$r_{YZ} = -.44$$

6. A criminal justice researcher is testing the negativity effect, which holds that people are more likely to remember negative than positive information. If so, the researcher reasons that people should recall unfavorable newspaper accounts of the criminal justice system more readily than favorable ones. He provided a sample of eight adults with newspaper articles that had been pretested and rated for negativity. Each participant read one article. After reading the article followed by a ten-minute distraction task, participants were asked to recall as much of the article as possible. The researcher obtained the following results, with higher values reflecting greater negativity ratings and more information recalled, respectively.

Ratings of Negativity (X)	Number of Pieces of Information Recalled (Y)
6	10
7	12
4	4
7	9

Ratings of Negativity (X)	Number of Pieces of Information Recalled (Y)
2	4
5	2
6	10
3	5

a. Is the researcher advancing a positive or negative association between negativity and recall? Should he perform a one-tailed or two-tailed test? Explain.

b. Calculate a Pearson correlation coefficient. Interpret the direction and strength of the coefficient.

c. Is the coefficient significant at the .05 alpha level? What conclusions can the researcher draw?

7. Determine the critical r value for the following conditions:

	Tailed Test	Alpha Level	Degrees of Freedom
a.	1	.01	14
b.	1	.05	8
c.	2	.01	20
d.	2	.05	10
e.	1	.05	25

8. Make a decision regarding the null hypothesis for each of the following research conditions:

	Calculated r Statistic	Critical r Value
a.	−.86	.84
b.	−.67	.71
c.	.54	.45
d.	.98	.25
e.	−.65	.68

9. The magnitude of the correlation coefficient indicates the _____ of the relationship, while the sign indicates the _____ of the relationship.

10. Correlation analysis should always be accompanied by visual examination of _____ for the purpose of detecting outliers.

11. A researcher hypothesizes a negative relationship between parental income level and juvenile delinquency. Specifically, as the parents' income level increases, the number of delinquent acts decreases. The researcher has selected a probability sample of 15 7th graders and records yearly income level and delinquent acts committed within the past year. Enter the following data into Excel and calculate Pearson's r. Be sure to include the research and null hypotheses, means, sums, deviation and squared deviation scores, degrees of freedom, critical r value, and decision about the null hypothesis.

Income Level (X)	Delinquent Acts (Y)
$45,000	3
$56,000	2
$28,000	4
$25,000	2
$55,000	1
$45,000	1
$40,000	0
$37,500	3
$39,000	1
$67,000	0
$50,000	1
$28,000	1
$35,000	0
$30,000	3
$39,000	1

12. In a study of employment history and drug use among parolees, researchers hypothesize a positive relationship between number of jobs held and frequency of drug use. After selecting a random sample of 13 parolees, researchers counted the number of jobs each subject held over the past six months, and the number of times each subject used illegal drugs during the past six months. Enter the data below into Excel and calculate Pearson's r. Be sure to include the research and null hypotheses, means, sums, deviation and squared deviation scores, degrees of freedom, critical r value, and decision about the null hypothesis.

Number of Jobs (X)	Drug Use (Y)
2	3
1	2
5	4
3	2
0	0
5	3
1	1
3	4
5	2
3	4
5	4
2	0
1	0

13. Enter the following data into Excel and use the data analysis tool to calculate a correlation matrix among the four variables. Determine the degrees of freedom and the critical r value. Use a two-tailed test and identify which variables are statistically significant, using a single * for $p \leq$ .05 and a double ** for $p \leq .01$.

No. of Arrests (Y_1)	No. of Convictions (Y_2)	Education Level (X_1)	Income (X_2)
3	2	9	$25,000
2	0	8	$15,000
2	1	11	$30,000
1	0	12	$45,000
1	0	14	$40,000
3	3	10	$25,000
3	2	12	$15,000
1	0	12	$18,000
1	1	12	$22,000
5	3	9	$15,000
4	2	10	$18,000
5	3	9	$35,000

Statistical Analysis for Prediction: Regression

ExploreIT!

The state juvenile court of Massachusetts wants to know what factors influence technical violations among juvenile probationers. The court has hired you as an independent research consultant to determine which independent factors influence technical violations. Based on your knowledge of juvenile delinquency you believe the following factors may be predictive of technical violations among juvenile probationers: officer contacts, extracurricular activities, and parental nonsupervision. How will you determine if these factors accurately predict technical violations? You will need to select a random sample of juvenile probationers and conduct a regression analysis to test the following hypotheses: (a) there is a positive linear relationship between the number of officer contacts and the number of technical violations, (b) there is a negative linear relationship between the hours of extracurricular activities and the number of technical violations, and (c) there is a positive linear relationship between the hours of parental nonsupervision and the number of technical violations.

In Chapter 12, we discussed correlation analysis as a method for assessing the relationship or association between two or more variables. Although correlation analysis is useful for testing both directional and nondirectional hypotheses, it does not require us to distinguish between the independent and dependent variables. That is, correlation analysis can be used to test the relationship between two independent variables or it can be used to test the relationship among several dependent variables. We presented research situations in which the independent and dependent variables were identified. We believe that this facilitates a better understanding of the statistical technique. Furthermore, it is often the case that criminal justice researchers identify the independent and dependent variables before conducting statistical analysis.

We now move beyond the process of simply determining whether there is an association between variables to specifying how changes in the independent variable affect **regression** changes in the dependent variable. **Regression analysis** is *a statistical technique used* **analysis** *for predicting values of a dependent variable based on values of one or more independent variables*. To make these predictions, it is absolutely necessary to specify the independent variable and the dependent variable.

This chapter demonstrates the usefulness of regression analysis for prediction. We first discuss the regression equation and how it enables us to predict changes in the dependent variable based on differing values of the independent variable(s). Next, we explain the regression line (line of best fit) and show how the line is used to fit the data into a linear relationship. We follow this discussion with step-by-step procedures for estimating the slope and the intercept in the regression analysis, as well as testing the significance of the regression model. We conclude with procedures for performing regression analysis using Excel.

13.1 The Regression Equation

Before discussing the regression equation, it is important to recognize that regression analysis—like all other inferential statistics—must meet certain assumptions. The following requirements must be met in order to use regression analysis appropriately as a statistical tool:

- Both the independent and dependent variable must be measured at the interval or ratio level. It should be noted, however, that there are a variety of regression techniques, beyond the scope of this text, that allow for analysis of nominal- and ordinal-level variables.
- Each variable must be normally distributed in the population. Specifically, the variables should not be skewed either positively or negatively by the presence of extreme cases.
- A probability sample must be drawn from the population.

- The relationship between the independent and dependent variable must be linear—that is, it takes the form of a straight line. Once again, the visual inspection of a scatterplot is essential for determining whether this assumption is correct for a set of sample data. If this assumption is violated, there are alternative regression techniques that allow for the analysis of nonliner relationships. These techniques are beyond the scope of this text.

If these assumptions have been met, regression analysis is an appropriate statistical technique for prediction.

The basic premise underlying regression analysis is the specification of the relationship between the independent and dependent variable in the form of an equation. This equation defines the linear relationship between X and Y and is specified as follows:

$$Y = \alpha + \beta X + \varepsilon$$

Y = Value of the dependent variable
α = Population intercept
β = Population slope
X = Value of the independent variable
ε = Residual error

bivariate regression model This equation represents a **bivariate regression model**, *a statistical technique used to determine the predictive power of a single independent variable on a single dependent variable*. Formally, the dependent variable (Y) is a function of the population intercept (α), the population slope (β), and error ($\in$). As you recall, statistical inference uses sample statistics to estimate population parameters. Both α and β are unknown parameters that must be estimated from the sample data. Thus, the sample equation for a bivariate regression model takes the following form:

$$Y = a + bX + e$$

To represent the sample equation, the definition of the model stays the same, only the symbols change. Specifically, a represents the sample intercept, b the sample slope, and e residual error within the sample. Both a and b are sample statistics used to estimate the population parameters—α and β respectively.

We now turn to a discussion of the components of the regression equation. Y is the value of the dependent variable and is equal to the sum of the other components. The **intercept** first component, a, is known as the **intercept**, defined as *the point at which the regression line crosses the Y axis.* This represents the predicted value of Y when the value of X is equal to zero. Assume that our dependent variable (Y) is "missed school days" and our independent variable (X) is "drug use." Our goal is to predict the number of missed school days based on the amount of drug use. Suppose that a is equal to 4. The value of Y (number of missed school days) is equal to the intercept (a), which in this case is 4, when the value of X (drug use) equals zero. This represents the value of Y (constant), given for each subject in the sample without considering X.

slope

The second component of the regression equation is b, called the slope. The **slope** is *the amount of change in the value of the dependent variable per one unit change in the value of the independent variable.* For example, assume that the slope for drug use is equal to +2. This indicates that the value of Y (missed school days) increases by 2 as the value of X increases by 1. More specifically, the value of Y for a juvenile with zero drug use is equal to 4 (*a*), whereas the value of Y for a juvenile with 1 instance of drug use is equal to 6 (*a* + *b*).

There are several points regarding the slope worthy of mention. First, the slope often is referred to as the regression coefficient. Second, the regression coefficient can be either positive (+) or negative (–). A positive slope indicates an increase in the value of Y per one unit increase in the value of X, while a negative slope indicates a decrease in the value of Y per one unit increase in X. Third, we determine the predicted values of Y by multiplying different values of X by the value of the slope and then adding that value to the intercept. For instance, in our example, we assumed that the value of the slope was 2. To determine the predicted value of missed school days (Y) for an individual with 4 instances of drug use (X), we simply place these values into the regression equation and solve as follows:

$$\hat{Y} = 4 + (2)(4) = 12 \qquad a + bX$$

We can repeat this process several times over for varying values of drug use (X). We use the following symbols to differentiate between actual and predicted values of the dependent variable:

$$Y = \text{Actual values of dependent variable}$$

$$\hat{Y} \text{ (pronounced "Y hat")} = \text{Predicted values of dependent variable}$$

residual error

The final component in the regression equation is e, which is known as the error term or residual error. We define **residual error** as *the amount of variation in the dependent variable unexplained or unaccounted for by the regression model.* In other words, residual error is the difference between the predicted value of Y based on the regression equation and the actual value of Y. To explain further, let's assume that we had a sample of ten juveniles who had four instances of drug use each. Using our regression equation, we would predict that the number of missed school days for each of those ten students would be 12. It is unlikely, however, that each of the ten students would have missed 12 days exactly. Some of the students would have missed fewer than ten days, while others would have missed more than ten days. Thus, while our best prediction of missed school days is 12 (based on the function of the intercept and slope), there will be instances in which the predicted value of the dependent variable differs from the actual value of the dependent variable. This difference is referred to as residual error. A more thorough discussion of residual error is presented in section 13.4.

13.2 The Regression Line

The regression equation explained in Section 13.1 is the mathematical equation used for a straight line. In regression analysis, we assume that the relationship between X and Y is linear (straight line), and, therefore, we are able to use the regression equation to define what is commonly called the regression line or line of best fit. We define the **regression** **line** as *the best fitting line that accurately portrays the linear relationship between X and Y.* More simply, we attempt to fit a straight line to our data that allows us to predict values of the dependent variable using various values of the independent variable. Returning to our example of "drug use"(X) and "missed school days"(Y), let's assume that we sample five students and record their values on both X and Y. The data is given as follows:

Student	Drug Use (X)	Missed School Days (Y)
1	1	5
2	2	10
3	3	15
4	4	20
5	5	25

You will notice that each unit increase in X corresponds with a five-unit increase in Y. The intercept (a) for this data is 0, while the slope (b) is equal to 5. We present the data in a scatterplot in Figure 13.1 along with a regression line. Each point on the graph represents the intersection of the X and Y value for each subject. The regression line indicates a perfect linear relationship between X and Y. That is, we can predict the value of Y on the basis of our knowledge of the value of X. This is important, because regression analysis is an inferential statistical technique that is used to make inferences about the population based on observations obtained from a sample.

FIGURE 13.1 Perfect linear relationship between drug use and missed school days

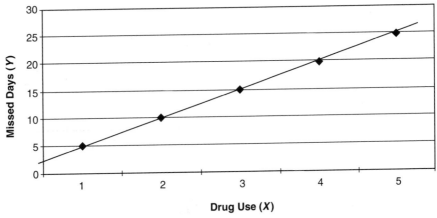

The regression line enables us to move beyond the limited scope of our sample and actually predict the number of missed school days for the population of students. We do this by substituting various values of X (drug use) into the regression equation to arrive at predicted values of $\hat{Y}$ (missed school days). For instance, what would be the predicted number of missed school days for a student who used drugs six times? Using the formula below, we plug in the values of the intercept (a), the slope (b), and the actual value of X (6), and then solve. Thus, we would predict that a student who used drugs six times would miss 30 days of school.

$$\hat{Y} = a + b(X)$$
$$\hat{Y} = 0 + 5(6) = 30$$

What would our prediction be for a student who had never used drugs? We simply change the X value from 6 to 0, and then solve the equation. The resulting value is 0, which is equal to the intercept. The predicted value for a dependent variable is equal to the intercept when the value of X equals 0.

$$\hat{Y} = 0 + 5(0) = 0$$

The data in Figure 13.1 represents a situation in criminal justice research that is very uncommon. Simply put, rarely do we find a perfect relationship between two variables. In the above example, each predicted value of missed school days would be equal to the actual value in the population. This, in turn, means there would be no residual error between predicted and actual values. Ideally, our goal is to have as minimal an amount of residual error as possible, which enhances our ability of predicting Y based on X. The majority of criminal justice research involving regression analysis includes residual error. A more realistic picture of the relationship between drug usage and missed school days is shown in Figure 13.2. Notice that the regression line defines a linear relationship

FIGURE 13.2 Regression line for drug use and missed school days

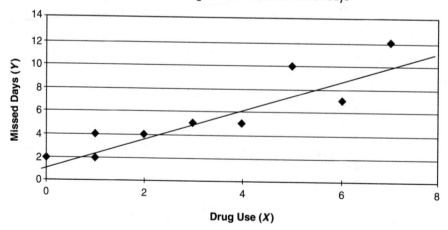

between X and Y; however, only one of the data points lies directly on the regression line. Most of the data points occur either above or below the line, indicating the presence of residual error. What does this mean? In practical terms, the regression line represents the line of best fit for the data. It is the linear relationship that most accurately represents the data values by minimizing the residual error. We want a regression line that cuts through the data points so that none of the Y values deviates from the line by very much. The line in Figure 13.2 appears to have this quality.

You are now ready to solve regression equations for various values of X, using information about the intercept and the slope. Take a minute to complete TryIT! Box 13.1 before moving on to section 13.3.

TryIT! Box **13.1**

Write and solve the regression equation $b = .25$ and $a = 1.30$, for each of the following X values.

X	$\hat{Y} = a + b(X)$	$\hat{Y}$
0		
2		
5		
13		
9		

13.3 Calculating the Slope (b) and the Intercept (a)

You are now able, after reading section 13.2, to solve the regression equation with known values of the intercept and the slope. In most research situations, these values are unknown and must be estimated using sample data. We now turn to the steps involved in calculating the values of the intercept and the slope based on sample observations.

Calculation of the intercept and the slope is straightforward and closely resembles the steps used for calculating a correlation coefficient. Because the formula for calculating the intercept is dependent on the value of the slope, we present the calculations for the slope first, followed by the intercept. Once we have determined the values of a and b, we can calculate predicted values of the dependent variable using the regression equation.

The formula for calculating the slope is given as:

$$b = \frac{\Sigma d_x d_y}{\Sigma d_x^{\,2}}$$
$$d_x = \left(X - \bar{X}\right)$$
$$d_y = \left(Y - \bar{Y}\right)$$
$$\Sigma d_x^{\,2} = \Sigma\left(X - \bar{X}\right)^2$$

A comparison of this formula with that of the correlation coefficient finds a marked similarity between the two. In fact, the numerator of both formulas is identical. The denominator, by contrast, changes for the slope, in that we are only concerned with the squared deviation scores of the independent variable. Thus, the formula requires us to divide the product of the deviation scores for both X and Y by the sum of the squared deviation scores for X. The result of this formula provides us with the best least squares estimate of the slope (Judd and McClelland, 1989).

Once we have calculated the slope, we use this information in our calculation of the intercept. The formula for the intercept is given as:

$$a = \bar{Y} - b\left(\bar{X}\right)$$

The intercept is determined by multiplying the slope by the mean of $\bar{X}$ and subtracting the resulting value from the mean of $\bar{Y}$. This value represents the best least squares estimate of the intercept. As stated earlier, the intercept is the point at which the regression line crosses the Y axis when the value of X equals zero.

Procedures for Regression Analysis

Let's turn our attention to a research situation involving regression analysis. Suppose we believe that there is a strong relationship between delinquency and parental supervision. More specifically, we find that the number of hours a child is left unsupervised correlates with the number of delinquent acts he/she will commit. Thus, our goal is to use "hours of nonsupervision"(X) as a predictor of "delinquent acts"(Y).

Our researcher randomly selects a sample of 12 juveniles aged 10 to 14 years old and administers a self-report questionnaire. The survey instrument asks each respondent to report (a) the number of hours spent at home without parental supervision during the past seven days, and (b) the number of delinquent acts committed in the past seven days. The data is presented in Table 13.1.

Step 1: State the research and null hypotheses.

Up to this point, we have always begun our analysis (step 1) with a statement of the research and null hypotheses. In regression analysis, our hypothesis is centered around the slope. Specifically, is the slope (i.e., regression coefficient) significantly different from zero? If it is, then we are able to predict the dependent variable based on our knowledge of the values of the independent variable. If the regression coefficient is not significantly different from zero, then knowing the value of X does not help us in predicting Y. Our best prediction of the dependent variable, then, refers back to the mean of $\bar{Y}$. In our example, we state the hypotheses as:

H_1: There is a linear relationship between parental supervision and delinquency.

$\beta \neq 0$

H_0: There is no linear relationship between parental supervision and delinquency.

$\beta = 0$

The research hypothesis simply states that the population slope (β) is significantly different than zero, which indicates a linear relationship between parental supervision and delinquency in the population. The sample slope, symbolized as b, is the basis for our analysis.

Step 2: Calculate the means and standard deviations for both the X and Y variables.

We perform this step in Table 13.1. Refer to Chapters 4 and 5 for the formulas used to calculate the mean and standard deviation.

TABLE 13.1 Regression Analysis of Parental Nonsupervision and Delinquency

Hours of Nonsupervision (X)	Delinquent Acts (Y)
50	5
10	1
20	2
20	2
45	4
40	5
20	1
15	3
25	2
40	5
40	4
20	3
$\bar{X} = 28.75$	$\bar{Y} = 3.08$
$s_X = 13.34$	$s_Y = 1.51$

Step 3: Calculate the deviations of X (d_x) and Y (d_y) scores from the mean of their own distributions.

This step involves subtracting the mean of the $\bar{X}$ scores from each of the individual X scores. For example, the mean of $\bar{X}$ (hours of nonsupervision) is reported as 28.75. This value is subtracted from each X score in the distribution as follows: $50 - 28.75$, $10 - 28.75$, $20 - 28.75$, and so on. Similarly, the mean of $\bar{Y}$ (delinquent acts) is equal to 3.08, which must then be subtracted from each of the individual Y values: $5 - 3.08$, $1 - 3.08$, $2 - 3.08$, and so on. This step is illustrated in Table 13.2, in columns 3 and 4, respectively.

Step 4: Calculate the sum of the products of the deviations of X and Y, $\Sigma(d_x d_y)$.

Performing this step requires us to multiply the deviations of X (d_x) by the deviations of Y (d_y). This step is illustrated in Table 13.2, column 5, where we multiply the values in column 3 (d_x) with the values in column 4 (d_y), and then sum the values in column 5.

Step 5: Calculate the sum of the squared deviations of X, $\Sigma(d_x^2)$.

To perform this step, we simply square the deviation scores of X found in column 3 and place the squared deviation scores in column 6. We then sum the squared deviation scores of X (d_x^2). This provides the denominator for the slope equation.

TABLE 13.2 Regression Analysis of Parental Nonsupervision and Delinquency

Individual Scores		Deviations		Product	Squared Deviations
X	Y	d_X	d_Y	$d_X d_Y$	d_X^2
50	5	21.25	1.92	40.73	451.56
10	1	−18.75	−2.08	39.06	351.56
20	2	−8.75	−1.08	9.48	76.56
20	2	−8.75	−1.08	9.48	76.56
45	4	16.25	.92	14.90	264.06
40	5	11.25	1.92	21.56	126.56
20	1	−8.75	−2.08	18.23	76.56
15	3	−13.75	−.08	1.15	189.06
25	2	−3.75	−1.08	4.06	14.06
40	5	11.25	1.92	21.56	126.56
40	4	11.25	.92	10.31	126.56
20	3	−8.75	−.08	.73	76.56
Sum (Σ)				191.25	1956.25

$\bar{X} = 28.75$ $\bar{Y} = 3.08$

$s_X = 13.34$ $s_Y = 1.51$

Step 6: Calculate the slope.

Our formula for the slope was given as:

$$b = \frac{\Sigma d_X d_Y}{\Sigma d_X^2}$$

Substituting the appropriate values into the formula, we solve for the slope as follows:

$$b = \frac{191.25}{1956.25} = .10$$

Step 7: Calculate the intercept.

The intercept is calculated by using the following formula:

$$a = \bar{Y} - b(\bar{X})$$

Substituting the appropriate values into the formula, we obtain the following intercept:

$$a = 3.08 - .10(28.75)$$
$$= 3.08 - 2.88$$
$$= .20$$

Step 8: Determine the significance of the slope.

In our previous statistical analysis, this step primarily involved comparing the calculated statistic with a critical value and then making a decision to either reject or fail to reject the null hypothesis. In regression analysis, however, there is no probability distribution for determining the critical value of the slope with which to compare the calculated value of b. Therefore, in order to determine whether the slope is significantly different from zero, we convert the regression coefficient (b) to a correlation coefficient, using the following formula:

$$r_{XY} = b\left(\frac{s_x}{s_y}\right)$$

Determining the correlation coefficient simply requires us to divide the standard deviation of the independent variable (s_x) by the standard deviation of the dependent variable (s_y), and then to multiply by the slope (b). Thus, r_{XY} is calculated as:

$$r_{XY} = .10\left(\frac{13.34}{1.51}\right)$$
$$= .10(8.83)$$
$$= .88$$

We now can use the correlation coefficient to make a determination about the null hypothesis using the same procedure outlined in Chapter 12. We simply compare the calculated r statistic with the critical r value found in Table C. Because the null hypothesis was nondirectional ($b = 0$), we find the critical value of r using a two-tailed test at the .05 alpha level with 10 degrees of freedom ($n - 2$), equal to .58. A comparison of the calculated r (.88) with the critical r (.58) causes us to reject the null hypothesis and conclude that the slope is significantly different from zero.

Step 9: Interpret the findings and plot the regression line.

To say that the slope is significantly different from zero is to say that there is a linear relationship between "hours of nonsupervision"(X) and "delinquent acts"(Y) among the population of juveniles from which the sample was drawn. We can refine this point further by saying that parental nonsupervision is a significant predictor of delinquency. More specifically, the number of delinquent acts increases by .10 for each additional hour a juvenile is left unsupervised. We can predict the number of delinquent acts for various hours of nonsupervision simply by placing differing values of X into the regression equation and solving. This, however, would be somewhat time-consuming. An easier approach is to plot a regression line on a scatterplot.

When the slope is statistically significant, it is recommended that we plot the regression line on a scatterplot in order to visualize the effect of the independent variable on the dependent variable. Plotting the regression line involves connecting two points on the scatterplot. The intercept (a) is commonly used as the left point connection. This point is .20, as illustrated in Figure 13.3. The right point connection is determined by selecting a value of X and solving the regression equation for the predicted value of $\hat{Y}$. We selected 60 hours for X and solved the following formula:

$$\hat{Y} = .20 + (.10)(60)$$
$$= .20 + 6$$
$$= 6.2$$

The right point connection is 6.2, which is the predicted value of delinquent acts for a juvenile with 60 hours of nonsupervision. The usefulness of plotting the regression line is to aid in understanding the impact of X on Y. We can see how much effect various numbers of hours of nonsupervision has on delinquent acts when we look at Figure 13.3. A visual inspection of the scatterplot shows us that a juvenile with ten hours of nonsupervision would have committed approximately 1.2 delinquent acts. Each additional ten hours of nonsupervision corresponds with one additional delinquent act.

There are two other things to observe in Figure 13.3. First, it is important to note that none of the actual data points fall directly on the regression line. Remember, the regression line represents the predicted values of delinquent acts, and not the actual values at various hours of nonsupervision. Second, the scatterplot shows that none of the data points stray very far from the regression line. This is an extremely important concept in regression analysis. It is more important that all of our data points fall

FIGURE 13.3 Regression line for hours of nonsupervision and delinquent acts

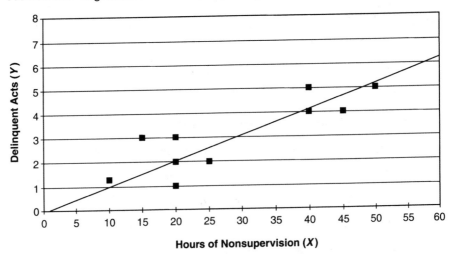

within close proximity to the regression line than it is for some of the points to fall directly on the line. We want to minimize the amount of residual error between the predicted values and actual values of the dependent variable. In regression analysis, we seek a regression line that minimizes the sum of the squared errors (SS_{Error}). The lower the value of SS_{Error}, the better the regression model (i.e., regression line) fits the data. That is, the accuracy of our predictions for the dependent variable increases as the residual error decreases. To understand this process, we now turn to a more detailed discussion of residual error.

Before moving on to Section 13.4, take a moment to practice calculating both the slope and the intercept by completing TryIT! Box 13.2.

TryIT!   BOX **13.2**

A researcher hypothesizes a negative linear relationship between "attorney experience"(X) and "sentence length"(Y). The researcher draws a probability sample of eight felons convicted of drug possession and measures attorney experience—number of months experienced as a criminal attorney—and sentence length—number of months sentenced to incarceration. Perform a regression analysis using the data below.

Subject	Attorney Experience (X)	Sentence Length (Y)
1	12	36
2	28	35
3	48	18

Subject	Attorney Experience (X)	Sentence Length (Y)
4	42	22
5	28	24
6	22	25
7	18	32
8	15	25

Step 1: State the research and null hypotheses.

Step 2: Calculate the means and standard deviations for X and Y.

Step 3: Calculate the deviations of X (d_x) and Y (d_y).

Step 4: Calculate the sum of the products of the deviations $\Sigma(d_x d_y)$.

Step 5: Calculate the sum of the squared deviations of X, $\Sigma(d_x^2)$.

Step 6: Calculate the slope.

Step 7: Calculate the intercept.

Step 8: Determine the significance of the slope.

Step 9: Interpret findings and plot the regression line if b is statistically significant.

13.4 Residual Error

As defined earlier, residual error is simply the difference between the predicted and actual values of the dependent variable. For instance, with the regression equation derived in Figure 13.3, we predicted that an offender with 25 hours of nonsupervision would have 2.70 delinquent acts. The actual number of delinquent acts for this individual was 2. The difference between the predicted value and the actual value is referred to as error. Error is calculated using the following formula:

$$e = Y - \hat{Y}$$

Thus, we can determine the amount of error in our predictions simply by subtracting the predicted value of $\hat{Y}$ for each subject from the actual value of Y. Remember, our goal is to have a regression line that minimizes the sum of the squared errors (SS_{Error}). We use SS_{Error} instead of e, because the sum of e is equal to zero, which does not provide information about the fit of the regression line to the data. Therefore, we use the following formula to calculate SS_{Error}:

$$SS_{Error} = \left(Y - \hat{Y}\right)^2$$

We use information about SS_{Error} to determine two important features of the regression model. First, we use this information to test the statistical significance of the regression model. Second, we use it to determine how much variability in the dependent variable is accounted for or explained by the independent variable(s).

The most common method for testing the statistical significance of a regression model is to use an *F* test, like that used in ANOVA. In regression analysis, the *F* test represents a measure of the difference between the predicted variance and the unpredicted variance. The *F* test is calculated using the following formula:

$$F = \frac{MS_{Regression}}{MS_{Error}}$$

The numerator ($MS_{Regression}$) represents the amount of variance in *Y* that is due to the regression equation. The denominator (MS_{Error}) is the unpredicted variance or the average deviation of the predicted values of $\hat{Y}$ from the actual values of *Y*. In order to calculate $MS_{Regression}$ and MS_{Error}, we first must decompose the sums of squares. You will recall from Chapter 11 that sums of squares represent the sum of the squared deviation scores. Specifically, we need to determine SS_{Error}, SS_{Total}, and $SS_{Regression}$. The following formulas are used to calculate the sums of squares associated with regression analysis:

$$SS_{Total} = \Sigma \left(Y - \bar{Y} \right)^2$$
$$SS_{Error} = \Sigma \left(Y - \hat{Y} \right)^2$$
$$SS_{Regression} = SS_{Total} - SS_{Error}$$

Calculating SS_{Total} requires us to subtract the mean of $\bar{Y}$ from each value of *Y* and then square the difference. To calculate SS_{Error}, we must first determine the predicted value of $\hat{Y}$ for each subject using the regression equation. Then we simply subtract the predicted value of $\hat{Y}$ from the actual value of *Y* and square the difference. Finally, we calculate $SS_{Regression}$ by subtracting SS_{Error} from SS_{Total}. We illustrate the process of calculating the sums of squares in Table 13.3 using our example of parental nonsupervision and delinquency.

Now that we have calculated the sums of squares, we are ready to calculate $MS_{Regression}$ and MS_{Error}. We determine the values of the mean squares by dividing the sums of squares by the corresponding degrees of freedom. The following formula is used to calculate $MS_{Regression}$:

$$MS_{Regression} = \frac{SS_{Regression}}{df_{Regression}}$$
$$df_{Regression} = PA - 1$$
$$= \frac{18.69}{1}$$
$$= 18.69$$

TABLE 13.3 Calculating SS_{Total}, SS_{Error}, and $SS_{Regression}$

Individual Scores		SS_{total}	Regression Equation	SS_{Error}
X	Y	$(Y - \bar{Y})^2$	$\hat{Y} = a + bX$	$(Y - \hat{Y})^2$
50	5	3.69	5.20	.04
10	1	4.33	1.20	.04
20	2	1.17	2.20	.04
20	2	1.17	2.20	.04
45	4	.85	4.70	.49
40	5	3.69	4.20	.64
20	1	4.33	2.20	1.44
15	3	.01	1.70	1.69
25	2	1.17	2.70	.49
40	5	3.69	4.20	.64
40	4	.85	4.20	.04
20	3	.01	2.20	.64
Sums (Σ)		24.92		6.23

Mean ($\bar{Y}$) 3.08

$SS_{Regression} = 24.92 - 6.23 = 18.69$

Determining the degrees of freedom requires us to subtract one from the number of parameters (*PA*) in the regression model. In our example, we have two parameters: the *a* (intercept) and the *b* (slope). Each independent variable counts as one parameter, as does the intercept. So, for example, if we had three independent variables, $df_{Regression}$ would be equal to 3 (*a*, b_1, b_2, b_3 = 4 – 1 = 3). To calculate MS_{Error}, the following formula is used:

$$MS_{Error} = \frac{SS_{Error}}{df_{Error}}$$

$$df_{Error} = n - PA$$

$$= \frac{6.23}{10}$$

$$= .62$$

The degrees of freedom error (df_{Error}) is determined by subtracting the number of parameters in the model from the sample size. Thus, since we have 12 subjects and two parameters (one intercept and one slope), df_{Error} is equal to 10 (12 – 2 = 10).

We are now ready to conduct an F test to determine if our regression model is statistically significant. In other words, does knowing the hours of nonsupervision significantly decrease the amount of error in predicting delinquent acts? Placing the appropriate values into the equation, we solve for F as follows:

$$F = \frac{18.69}{.62}$$

$$= 30.15$$

We now compare the calculated F statistic to the critical F value found in the F probability distribution table located in Table D (Appendix A). To determine the critical value using the F distribution table, $df_{\text{Regression}}$ is located in the columns labeled df_{Between}, and df_{Error} is located in the rows labeled df_{Within}. Using this information, we determine the critical value of F is equal to 4.96 (.05 alpha) and 10.04 (.01 alpha). Because the calculated F statistic of 30.15 is larger than both critical F values, we conclude that the regression model is statistically significant at the .01 alpha level. Specifically, taking into account hours of nonsupervision significantly improves our predictions of delinquent acts over and above a model that uses only the mean of Y.

Although we have just demonstrated how to test the significance of a bivariate regression model using ANOVA, one other question remains to be answered. How much of the variability in the dependent variable is accounted for by the independent **R-squared** variable? In regression analysis, we designate this value as **R-squared** (R^2), the coefficient of determination, defined as *the amount of variance in the dependent variable explained by the independent variable*. To calculate R^2, we simply divide $SS_{\text{Regression}}$ by SS_{Total}. Thus, the amount of variation in delinquent acts accounted for or explained by hours of nonsupervision is given as:

$$R^2 = \frac{SS_{\text{Regression}}}{SS_{\text{Total}}}$$

$$= \frac{18.69}{24.92}$$

$$= .75$$

Approximately 75% of the variance in delinquent acts is explained by hours of nonsupervision. Put another way, the prediction errors of delinquent acts decrease by 75% when we take into account hours of nonsupervision. In a bivariate regression model, R^2 can also be calculated by squaring the correlation coefficient (r^2).

Decomposing the sums of squares is the same process as used in ANOVA (Chapter 11). The primary difference between ANOVA and regression is that the independent variable in regression is numerical as opposed to categorical as in ANOVA. The use of the F test is the same for both types of analyses, and informs us as to whether the model is statistically significant.

You are now ready to calculate the sums of squares for a bivariate regression model. Complete TryIT! Box 13.3 before moving to Section 13.5.

TryIT!   BOX 13.3

Using the data below, calculate the sums of squares for SS_{Total}, SS_{Error}, and $SS_{Regression}$. Test the statistical significance of the model by conducting an F test. Also, determine the amount of variance in Y that is explained by X (R^2). The intercept and slope are given as follows: $a = 36.45$, $b = -.35$.

Individual Scores				
Attorney Experience (X)	Sentence Length (Y)	SS_{Total} $(Y - \bar{Y})^2$	Regression Equation $\hat{Y} = a + b\,(X)$	SS_{Error} $(Y - \hat{Y})^2$
12	36			
28	35			
48	18			
42	22			
28	24			
22	25			
18	32			
15	25			
Sums (Σ)				
Mean ($\bar{Y}$)				
$SS_{Regression}$				

13.5 Multiple Regression Analysis

multiple regression analysis **Multiple regression analysis** is *a statistical technique used to determine the predictive power of a set of independent variables on a single dependent variable*. It stands to reason that if we can improve our predictions of Y by knowing the values of a single independent variable, we might be able to further refine our predictions of Y (decrease residual error) by knowing the values of several independent variables. The equation for a multiple regression model takes the following form:

$$Y = \alpha + \beta_1 X_1 + \beta_2 X_2 + \beta_3 X_3 + \beta_k X_k + \varepsilon$$
$$k = \text{Number of independent variables}$$

Once again, this is the population equation. Our sample equation has the following notation:

$$\hat{Y} = a + b_1 X_1 + b_2 X_2 + b_3 X_3 + b_k X_k + e$$

In the multiple regression equation, we incorporated several independent variables into the regression model to improve our predictions of the dependent variable. The intercept (a) still represents the point at which the regression line crosses the Y-axis. It is the value of Y when all of the values of X equal zero. The subscript $_k$ simply represents the number of independent variables in the model. For example, if we had six independent variables in a multiple regression model, we would then have six slopes to correspond with each of the six X variables. The slopes (b) in a multiple regression model are commonly referred to as partial slopes. A **partial slope** is *the effect of an independent variable on a dependent variable while controlling for the effects of other independent variables in the model.* For example, the slope b_1 represents the amount of change in the value of Y per one unit change in the value of X_1, while holding the values of all other X variables constant. This important feature of the regression model allows us to determine the individual effect of each independent variable on the dependent variable. That is, multiple regression tests the statistical significance of each X variable independent of the effects of the other X variables. Let's look at an example to further clarify this point.

partial slope

Suppose we hypothesize that "delinquent acts"(Y) not only are influenced by "hours of nonsupervision"(X_1) but also by "hours worked"(X_2) and "number of nondelinquent friends" (X_3). Thus, we now have three independent variables that we believe influence the dependent variable. The incorporation of three independent variables into the regression analysis changes the regression equation from a bivariate regression model, in which we tested the predictive power of a single independent variable, to a multiple regression model, whereby we are testing the predictive power of several independent variables. Assume that we have calculated the multiple regression model and have obtained the following values for the intercept and partial slopes:

$$\hat{Y} = 1.56 + .25X_1 + .31X_2 + -.18X_3$$

In the above equation, we determine that the predicted value of $\hat{Y}$ without considering any of the X values is 1.56 (intercept), which also represents the average of Y. Our interpretation of the slope for the first independent variable X_1 (hours of nonsupervision) indicates that the number of delinquent acts increases by .25 for each additional hour of nonsupervision. The slope for X_2 shows that the number of delinquent acts increases by .31 for each additional hour worked. The interpretation of the final slope is that the number of delinquent acts decreases by .18 for each additional nondelinquent friend. Remember, the interpretation of each slope is based on the individual impact of each independent variable on the dependent variable, while holding the other independent variables constant.

Multiple regression analysis not only allows us to assess the effects of each X variable on the Y variable separately, but it also provides us with a measure of the total effect of all the independent variables on the dependent variable simultaneously. You will recall that this measure is referred to as R^2. Once again, R^2 represents the amount of variance or variability in the dependent variable (Y) that is explained or accounted for by the set of independent variables (Xs). Thus, we want to select independent variables that are correlated with the dependent variable in order to minimize residual error, which in turn increases the predictive power of the overall model. In selecting good predictor variables, however, we must be aware of the assumptions of the multiple regression model.

The initial assumptions of bivariate regression discussed in Section 13.1 also apply to multiple regression analysis. The following additional assumption is necessary, however, for the correct use of multiple regression: The independent variables should be uncorrelated with each other.

Our goal with regression analysis is to determine the amount of variability in Y accounted for by the set of X variables and to determine the effect of each X variable separately on the Y variable. When the independent variables in a regression model are highly correlated with each other, it is extremely difficult to determine the independent effects of each X variable on the Y variable. For example, assume that we have a regression model with three X variables that are correlated with each other and that all three variables have emerged as significant predictors of the dependent variable. The result of this correlation among the X variables confounds the interpretation of the partial slopes. That is, we are unable to determine how much of the effect is unique to each X variable—attributed only to that variable—and how much is the result of a shared effect between all three X variables. This problem is commonly referred to as **multicollinearity**, defined as the *correlation among a set of independent variables in a regression model that confounds the individual effects of the independent variables on the dependent variable.*

multicol- linearity

The primary method for determining whether multicollinearity exists is to calculate a correlation matrix among the set of independent variables and dependent variable. This enables us to assess the magnitude of the correlations among the independent variables as well as the correlations between the independent variables and dependent variable. Our goal is to develop a model that is predictive of the dependent variable. Therefore, we want to select a set of independent variables that correlate with the dependent variable and yet do not correlate with each other. The correlation matrix provides the necessary information with regard to selecting an appropriate model.

How strong a correlation between two variables suggests a problem with multicollinearity? Although there is some debate, the absolute values of correlation coefficients greater than .70 between independent variables are problematic for the regression model. The most appropriate action for this problem is to remove some of the correlated variables from the model. For example, if two X variables are highly correlated with each other as well as with the dependent variable, the removal of one of the independent variables from the model should correct the problem. Other correction procedures may be warranted; however, such techniques are beyond the scope of this text.

In criminal justice research, multiple regression is more common than bivariate regression. Because of the nature of the model with its multiple partial slopes, hand calculations are rather tedious and complex. Hence, we demonstrate the calculation of a multiple regression model using Excel's data analysis tool in section 13.6.

13.6 Using Excel for Regression Analysis

Now that you have a good understanding of regression analysis and are able to calculate a regression equation by hand, we turn our attention to using Excel. We present a research situation followed by step-by-step instructions for calculating the slope and the intercept. We also provide an example of bivariate regression analysis using the formula method and multiple regression analysis using the data analysis tool.

Bivariate Regression

We began this chapter with the Massachusetts juvenile court wanting to know if the number of probation officer contacts is predictive of the number of technical violations. To answer this question, assume we have drawn a random sample of 15 juveniles from across the state of Massachusetts, and measured the number of "officer contacts"(X) and the number of "technical violations"(Y) for each subject during the last six months. Our goal is to determine if the independent variable (officer contacts) can be used to predict the dependent variable (technical violations). More specifically, can we decrease the amount of error in our predictions of Y based on our knowledge of X? The data for this problem is presented in Table 13.4. We present step-by-step instructions for calculating the slope and the intercept. We also demonstrate the steps for determining the significance of the slope.

Step 1: State the research and null hypotheses. These are given in notational form in cell a2.

Step 2: Calculate the mean and standard deviation for both the X and Y variables. This can be done rather easily by using the paste function box on the menu bar.

Step 3: Calculate the deviations of $X(d_x)$ and $Y(d_y)$ scores from the mean of their own distributions. To calculate the deviation scores of X, place the cursor in cell d4 and write: =b4-b19.

b4 is the cell location for officer contacts for subject 1.
b19 is the cell location for the mean number of officer contacts.
$ holds the column and row constant (b19).

To create the rest of the d_x column, click the lower right-hand corner of cell d4 and drag the cursor down to cell d18.

-0.67

To create the deviation scores for Y, place the cursor in cell e4 and write: = c4-c19.

c4 is the cell location for technical violations for subject 1.
c19 is the cell location for the mean number of technical violations.
$ holds the column and row constant (c19).

Click the lower right-hand corner of cell e4 and drag the cursor down to cell e18 to create the rest of the d_y column.

-1.67

Step 4: Calculate the sum of the products of the deviations of X and Y, $\Sigma(d_x d_y)$. Place the cursor in cell f4 and write: =d4*e4.

d4 is the cell location for d_x for subject 1.
e4 is the cell location for d_y for subject 1.
* is the symbol for multiplication.

Click the lower right-hand corner of cell f4 and drag the cursor down to cell f18 to create the rest of the $d_x d_y$ column.

1.11

To sum the column, place the cursor in cell f21 and use the autosum button on the menu bar.

Step 5: Calculate the sum of the squared deviations of X, $\Sigma(d_x^2)$. Place the cursor in cell g4 and write: =d4^2.

d4 is the cell location of d_x for subject 1.
^2 is the symbol for squaring a value.

Click the lower right-hand corner of cell g4 and drag the cursor down to cell g18 to create the rest of the d_x^2 column.

.44

Sum the d_x^2 column by placing the cursor in cell g21 and using the autosum button on the menu bar.

TABLE 13.4 Bivariate Regression Analysis

	A	B	C	D	E	F	G
1	**TABLE 13.4 Bivariate Regression Analysis**						
2	$H_1: \beta \neq 0$ $H_0: \beta = 0$			Deviations		Product	Squared Deviations
3	Subject	Officer Contacts (X)	Technical Violations (Y)	d_X	d_Y	$d_X d_Y$	$d_X{}^2$
4	1	7	0	-0.67	-1.67	1.11	0.44
5	2	12	3	4.33	1.33	5.78	18.78
6	3	5	1	-2.67	-0.67	1.78	7.11
7	4	4	2	-3.67	0.33	-1.22	13.44
8	5	5	2	-2.67	0.33	-0.89	7.11
9	6	10	2	2.33	0.33	0.78	5.44
10	7	5	1	-2.67	-0.67	1.78	7.11
11	8	15	4	7.33	2.33	17.11	53.78
12	9	7	0	-0.67	-1.67	1.11	0.44
13	10	5	0	-2.67	-1.67	4.44	7.11
14	11	5	2	-2.67	0.33	-0.89	7.11
15	12	10	2	2.33	0.33	0.78	5.44
16	13	10	1	2.33	-0.67	-1.56	5.44
17	14	5	2	-2.67	0.33	-0.89	7.11
18	15	10	3	2.33	1.33	3.11	5.44
19	**Mean**	**7.67**	**1.67**				
20	**Standard deviation**	**3.29**	**1.18**				
21	**Sum**					32.33	151.33
22	**Slope (*b*)**	0.21					
23	**Intercept (*a*)**	0.03					
24	***r* statistic**	0.60					
25	***r* critical**	0.51					
26	**R^2**		0.36				

Step 6: Calculate the slope (b) using the following formula:

$$b = \frac{\Sigma d_x d_y}{\Sigma d_x^2}$$

Place the cursor in cell b22 and write: = f21/g21.

f21 is the cell location for $\Sigma(d_x d_y)$.
g21 is the cell location for $\Sigma(d_x^2)$.
/ is the symbol for division.

Step 7: Calculate the intercept (a) using the following formula:

$$a = \bar{Y} - b(\bar{X})$$

Place the cursor in cell b23 and write: =c19-(b22*b19).

c19 is the cell location for the mean of Y (Technical Violations).
b22 is the cell location for b (slope).
b19 is the cell location for the mean of X (Officer Contacts).
-, / are the symbols for subtraction and division, respectively.

Step 8: Determine the significance of the slope.

To do this, we simply convert the slope (b) to a correlation coefficient (r) and compare the calculated r statistic to the critical r value found in Table C in Appendix A. Place the cursor in cell b24 and write: =b22*(b20/c20).

b22 is the cell location for the slope.
b20 is the cell location for the standard deviation of X.
c20 is the cell location for the standard deviation of Y.
*, / are the symbols for multiplication and division, respectively.

Because the calculated r statistic of .60 is larger than the critical r value of .51, we reject the null hypothesis and conclude that the population slope (β) is significantly different from zero. More specifically, there is a linear relationship between officer contacts and technical violations. Thus, knowing the number of officer contacts enables us to predict the number of technical violations. We calculated R^2 (which equals r^2 in a bivariate regression model) by placing the cursor in cell b26 and writing: = b24^2.

b24 is the cell location for the correlation coefficient.
^2 is the symbol for squaring a value.

Once again, we interpret this finding as 36% of the variance in technical violations is accounted for or explained by officer contacts. Put another way, the residual error in predicting technical violations decreases by 36% when we take into account the number of officer contacts.

Multiple Regression

Let's return to our study of juvenile probationers. In the bivariate regression model, we found that officer contacts predict the number of technical violations. We now want to determine if we can improve our predictions of technical violations (decrease residual error) by incorporating other independent variables into the model—specifically, "extracurricular activity" and "parental nonsupervision." Assume that "extracurricular activity" is measured as the average number of hours spent on extracurricular activities per week, and "parental nonsupervision" is the average number of hours per week left unsupervised by parents.

As stated earlier, multiple regression analysis is more complex than bivariate regression; therefore, we will make use of Excel's data analysis tool to perform the necessary calculations. The data for this example is presented in Table 13.5. The following steps are performed to calculate a multiple regression model.

TABLE 13.5 Multiple Regression Analysis

	A	B	C	D	E
1	**TABLE 13.5 Multiple Regression Analysis**				
2	Subject	Officer Contacts (X_1)	Extracurricular Activity (X_2)	Parental Nonsupervision (X_3)	Technical Violations (Y)
3	1	7	10	0	0
4	2	12	0	20	3
5	3	5	5	10	1
6	4	4	2	20	2
7	5	5	0	12	2
8	6	10	0	5	2
9	7	5	3	0	1
10	8	15	1	25	4
11	9	7	12	4	0
12	10	5	15	2	0
13	11	5	5	2	2
14	12	10	3	2	1
15	13	10	3	2	1
16	14	5	1	10	2
17	15	10	0	10	3

Step 1: Select the **tools** option on the Excel menu bar.

Step 2: Select **data analysis** under the tools option.

Step 3: In the analysis tool box select **Regression** and click **ok**.

Step 4: Enter e2:e17 for the input Y range and enter b2:d17 for the input X range. Click the **labels** box so the labels for each of the variables will appear in the output table. Click **ok** and an output table like that shown in Table 13.6 will be produced.

Let's turn our attention to interpreting the various components of Table 13.6. The partial slopes (regression coefficients) for each of the independent variables are listed in the last section of the table. Observation of this section informs us that both "extracurricular activity" and "parental nonsupervision" are statistically significant, as noted by the t statistic and the corresponding P-value. Remember, when the P-value (alpha or significance level) is less than .05, we say the relationship is statistically significant. The

TABLE 13.6 Multiple Regression Analysis Output Table

SUMMARY OUTPUT

Regression Statistics

Multiple R	0.93
R-square	0.86
Adjusted R-square	0.82
Standard error	0.50
Observations	15

ANOVA

	df	SS	MS	F	Significance F
Regression	3	16.64	5.55	22.63	0.00
Residual	11	2.70	0.25		
Total	14	19.33			

	Coefficients	Standard Error	t Stat	P-value
Intercept	1.01	0.43	2.34	0.04
Officer contacts (X_1)	0.09	0.04	2.07	0.06
Extracurricular Activity (X_2)	−0.13	0.03	−3.89	0.00
Parental nonsupervision (X_3)	0.06	0.02	2.73	0.02

computer uses a *t* test to assess the significance of the slopes, whereas when we were using the bivariate regression model we used *r*. Both methods are appropriate for significance testing of the regression coefficients. When doing the calculations by hand or writing our own formulas using Excel, *r* is much easier to calculate.

In looking at the value of the slope (b_2) for "extracurricular activity" (−.13), we interpret this as a decrease of .13 in the number of technical violations for each unit increase in activity. For "parental nonsupervision," we find the slope (b_3) equal to .06. This indicates a positive relationship, which means that every unit increase in nonsupervision corresponds with a .06 increase in the number of technical violations.

Our regression equation for predicting technical violations now looks like the following:

$$\hat{Y} = a + .09X_1 + -.13X_2 + .06X_3$$

If we wanted to predict the number of technical violations for a juvenile who had ten contacts, ten hours of extracurricular activity, and ten hours of parental nonsupervision, we simply substitute these values into the regression equation and solve as follows:

$$\hat{Y} = a + .09(10) + -.13(10) + .06(10)$$
$$= 1.01 + .9 + -1.3 + .6$$
$$= 1.21$$

Thus, the predicted number of technical violations for a juvenile with these characteristics is approximately 1.

As stated earlier, we also can assess how well the set of independent variables account for the variability in the dependent variable. To determine this, we need to look at the section entitled "Summary Output." For the purposes of this text, we only concern **Multiple R** ourselves with the Multiple *R* and *R*-Square. The **Multiple R** is *the multiple correlation coefficient that assesses the correlation between the set of independent variables and the* **coefficient** *dependent variable*. The **coefficient of multiple determination, R squared**, is defined **of multiple** as *the amount of variance in the dependent variable that is explained or accounted for* **determi-** *by the set of independent variables*. The coefficient of multiple determination (R^2) is **nation (R^2)** equal to .86. Thus, 86% of the variability in "technical violations" (*Y*) is explained by the set of independent variables included in the model (e.g., "officer contacts," "extracurricular activity," and "parental nonsupervision"). In terms of residual error, the regression model reduces the residual error in predicting technical violations by 86% when taking into account the three independent variables. Put another way, only 14% of the variability is unaccounted for in our regression model. An R^2 of .86 in criminal justice research would be considered an exceptional explanatory model.

The regression output table also provides an ANOVA summary table within the regression analysis. This analysis informs us as to whether the regression model is statistically significant. You will recall that SS_{Total} represents the squared difference between the individual Y values and the mean of $\bar{Y}$, SS_{Residual} (SS_{Error}) represents the squared difference between the predicted and actual values of Y, and $SS_{\text{Regression}}$ is the difference between SS_{Total} and SS_{Residual}. Dividing $MS_{\text{Regression}}$ by MS_{Residual} results in an F statistic. The F statistic of 22.63 with its corresponding probability ($p \leq .00$) informs us that the regression model is statistically significant at the .00 alpha level. Thus, we can reduce the residual error in predicting technical violations by 86% (R^2) by basing our predictions on the regression model.

13.7 Summary

This chapter explained the conceptual issues and procedures for using regression analysis as a method of prediction. We discussed the elements of the regression equation, which include the intercept, slope, and residual error, and also how the equation forms a regression line. Plotting this line on a scatterplot allows us to visualize how the dependent variable changes as a function of the independent variable. Furthermore, we can use the regression equation to calculate predicted values of the dependent variable that take us beyond the scope of our sample data.

We demonstrated step-by-step procedures for calculating the intercept and the slope in a regression model and for determining the significance of the slope. We further illustrated the process of decomposing the sums of squares and how this allows us to test the significance of the regression model using ANOVA. Regression analysis is similar to correlation analysis in that it enables us to determine the amount of variance in the dependent variable (R^2) that is accounted for or explained by the independent variable(s). We explained how this value represents the reduction in residual error when making predictions about the dependent variable using the regression equation.

Finally, we provided some hypothetical research situations in which we could use Excel for performing regression analysis. We demonstrated the procedures both for a bivariate regression model and for a multiple regression model.

Key Terms

regression analysis	R-squared
bivariate regression model	multiple regression analysis
intercept	partial slope
slope	multicollinearity
residual error	Multiple R
regression line	coefficient of multiple determination (R^2)

TryIT! Answers

Box 13.1

X	$\hat{Y}=a+b(X)$	$\hat{Y}$
0	1.30 + .25(0) =	1.30
2	1.30 + .25(2) =	1.80
5	1.30 + .25(5) =	2.55
13	1.30 + .25(13) =	4.55
9	1.30 + .25(9) =	3.55

Box 13.2

Step 1: State the research and null hypotheses.

H_1: There is a negative linear relationship between attorney experience and sentence length.

H_1: $\beta < 0$

H_0: There is either a positive linear relationship or no linear relationship between attorney experience and sentence length.

H_0: $\beta \geq 0$

Step 2: Calculate the means and standard deviations for X and Y.

Step 3: Calculate the deviations of X (d_x) and Y (d_y).

Step 4: Calculate the sum of the products of the deviations $\Sigma(d_x d_y)$.

Step 5: Calculate the sum of the squared deviations of X $\Sigma(d_x^2)$.

[Construct a table containing the answers for steps 2–5.]

Table Box 13.2 Regression Analysis

Subject	Attorney Experience (X)	Sentence Length (Y)	d_x	y_d	$d_x d_y$	d_x^2
1	12	36	−14.63	8.88	−129.80	213.89
2	28	35	1.38	7.88	10.83	1.89
3	48	18	21.38	−9.13	−195.05	456.89
4	42	22	15.38	−5.13	−78.80	236.39

Subject	Attorney Experience (X)	Sentence Length (Y)	d_x	y_d	$d_x d_y$	d_x^2
5	28	24	1.38	−3.13	−4.30	1.89
6	22	25	−4.63	−2.13	9.83	21.39
7	18	32	−8.63	4.88	−42.05	74.39
8	15	25	−11.63	−2.13	24.70	135.14
Mean	**26.63**	**27.13**				
Standard deviation	**12.77**	**6.47**				
Sums					**−404.63**	**1141.88**

Step 6: Calculate the slope:

$$b = \frac{-404.63}{1141.88}$$

$$b = -.35$$

Step 7: Calculate the intercept:

$$a = 27.13 - -.35(26.63)$$
$$a = 27.13 - -9.32$$
$$a = 36.45$$

Step 8: Determine the significance of the slope:

$$r = -.35\left(\frac{12.77}{6.47}\right)$$

$$= -.35(1.97)$$

$$= -.69$$

Because the calculated r of −.70 is larger than the critical r of .62 (one-tailed test with 6 df at the .05 alpha level) and it is in the hypothesized direction, we reject the null hypothesis and conclude that the population slope is significantly less than zero.

Step 9: Interpret findings and plot the regression line if b is statistically significant. The sentence length for convicted burglars decreases by .35 for each additional month of attorney experience. We plot the regression line using the intercept as the left-point connection and a value of 60 months (attorney experience) as the right-point connection.

Scatterplot of Sentence Length and Attorney Experience

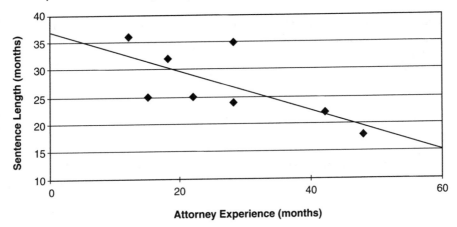

Box 13.3

Individual Scores

Attorney Experience (X)	Sentence Length (Y)	SS_{Total} $(Y - \bar{Y})^2$	Regression Equation $\hat{Y} = a + b\,(X)$	SS_{Error} $(Y - \hat{Y})^2$
12	36	78.77	32.25	14.06
28	35	62.02	26.65	69.72
48	18	83.27	19.65	2.72
42	22	26.27	21.75	0.06
28	24	9.77	26.65	7.02
22	25	4.52	28.75	14.06
18	32	23.77	30.15	3.42
15	25	4.52	31.2	38.44
Sums (Σ)		**292.88**		**149.52**

Mean ($\bar{Y}$)	27.13
$SS_{Regression}$	143.36
$df_{Regression}$	1
df_{Error}	6
$MS_{Regression}$	143.36
MS_{Error}	24.92
F statistic	5.75
F critical	5.59
R^2	0.49

13.8 Problems

1. Using the regression equation $a = 1.5$ and $b = .55$, determine the predicted values of $\hat{Y}$ for the following values of X:

   a. $X = 0$
   b. $X = 2$
   c. $X = 10$
   d. $X = 20$
   e. $X = 32$

2. Convert the following regression coefficients (b) into correlation coefficients:

	b	s_x	s_y
a.	.20	1.32	2.45
b.	.08	.56	.97
c.	.45	1.50	1.20
d	.70	.40	.90

3. Regression analysis involving one X variable and one Y variable is known as what type of regression?

4. Regression analysis involving multiple X variables and one Y variable is known as what type of regression?

5. The regression equation is a function of what three components?

6. A researcher believes that there is a negative linear relationship between the high school graduation rate and the crime rate. She selects a probability sample of 12 cities and measures the rate of high school graduations per 1,000 seniors during the 2000/2001 academic year, and the crime rate per 1,000 persons during the same time period. The data is presented below.

City	Graduation Rate (X)	Crime Rate (Y)
A	885.45	150.68
B	945.20	75.55
C	765.00	135.90
D	880.00	110.45
E	900.12	100.10
F	550.34	210.25
G	860.10	120.35
H	500.25	220.35
I	440.10	189.00
J	650.60	152.56
K	700.20	125.00
L	680.10	145.25

Complete the following:

   a. Write the research and null hypotheses concerning the population slope (β) in notational form.

   b. Calculate the slope and the intercept.

   c. Test the significance of the slope using a correlation coefficient.

   d. Make a decision about the null hypothesis and interpret your findings.

   e. Determine the amount of variability in the crime rate that is accounted for by the graduation rate.

7. Calculate the residual error for each of the following:

	Y	$\hat{Y}$	e
a.	5	6.20	
b.	2	2.80	
c.	3	2.20	
d.	7	9.20	
e.	11	12.80	
f.	1	1.40	
g.	15	16.20	

8. Using the data in question 7, calculate the mean of Y and determine each of the following:

   a. SS_{Total}, SS_{Error}, and $SS_{Regression}$

   b. $MS_{Regression}$ and MS_{Error}

   c. F statistic and R^2

9. Based on your analysis in question 8, what conclusions would you make concerning the regression model?

10. Define the following terms:

   a. slope

   b. intercept

   c. residual error

11. In a study of correctional officer stress, the director of institutional research believes that there is a linear relationship between "length of employment" (X) and "stress level" (Y). The director has elected to measure stress level using a 100-point stress exam, with higher values representing higher levels of stress. Length of employment is measured as the number of months employed within the department. The data is given below for a probability sample of ten correctional officers.

Officer	Months Employed	Stress Score
1	12	86
2	24	83
3	38	74
4	20	70
5	25	65
6	40	88
7	48	88
8	36	79
9	29	77
10	18	70

Complete the following:

    a. Write the research and null hypotheses concerning the population slope (β) in notational form.

    b. Calculate the slope and the intercept.

    c. Test significance of the slope using a correlation coefficient.

    d. Make a decision about the null hypothesis and interpret your findings.

    e. SS_{Total}, SS_{Error}, and $SS_{Regression}$

    f. $MS_{Regression}$ and MS_{Error}

    g. F statistic and R^2

    h. Determine the amount of variability in the stress score that is accounted for by the months employed.

12. A nonsignificant slope indicates that our predictions of Y are not an improvement over making predictions based on _____.

13. The regression line represents the _____ values of Y.

14. The best fitting line (i.e., regression line) is the line that minimizes _____.

15. Using an intercept (a) of 5.19 and a slope (b) of –.37, enter the following data into Excel and calculate the sums of squares—SS_{Total}, SS_{Error}, and $SS_{Regression}$—the mean squares—$MS_{Regression}$ and MS_{Error}—the F statistic, and R^2. Is the regression model statistically significant?

X	Y
1	7
2	8
1	8
2	5
4	5
6	2

X	Y
3	2
10	2
8	1
8	1
3	1
9	3
9	4
3	1
1	2

16. A criminal justice researcher hypothesizes a positive linear relationship between study time and exam performance. She measures the study time, the number of hours studied, of a sample of 15 police cadets. She then measures exam performance as the score on a police officer entrance exam. Enter the data below into Excel and perform a bivariate regression analysis. Be sure to report the research and null hypotheses, slope, intercept, calculated r statistic, critical r value, decision about the null hypothesis, and predicted values for 5, 10, 15, 20, and 25 hours of study.

Hours Studied (X)	Exam Score (Y)
2	74
12	72
10	83
15	83
8	80
8	92
3	78
5	70
5	82
12	90
15	98
10	89
10	88
8	88
4	78

17. A researcher believes that arrests can be predicted using the following independent variables: education level—years of formal education, unemployment—months unemployed during the last two years, and alcohol use—average number of drinks per month. Specifically, she hypothesizes a negative linear relationship between education and arrests, a positive linear relationship between unemployment and arrests, and a positive relationship between alcohol use and arrests. She has selected a probability sample of 12 arrested persons to test her hypotheses. Enter the

following data into Excel and calculate a multiple regression analysis using the data analysis tool. Determine which independent variables (e.g., slopes) are statistically significant, whether the overall model is significant, and the meaning of R^2.

No. Arrests (Y)	Education (X_1)	Unemployment (X_2)	Alcohol Use (X_3)
2	12	3	8
1	14	0	12
1	12	5	5
3	10	5	0
5	12	5	0
6	8	2	6
6	9	8	6
2	14	0	12
1	12	2	4
2	8	6	4
4	12	6	0
2	12	2	2

Probability Distribution Tables

TABLE A: z Distribution Table (Normal Curve)

z	A Area Between Mean and z	B Area Beyond z	z	A Area Between Mean and z	B Area Beyond z	z	A Area Between Mean and z	B Area Beyond z
0.00	.0000	.5000	0.41	.1591	.3409	0.82	.2939	.2061
0.01	.0040	.4960	0.42	.1628	.3372	0.83	.2967	.2033
0.02	.0080	.4920	0.43	.1664	.3336	0.84	.2995	.2005
0.03	.0120	.4880	0.44	.1700	.3300	0.85	.3023	.1977
0.04	.0160	.4840	0.45	.1736	.3264	0.86	.3051	.1949
0.05	.0199	.4801	0.46	.1772	.3228	0.87	.3078	.1922
0.06	.0239	.4761	0.47	.1808	.3192	0.88	.3106	.1894
0.07	.0279	.4721	0.48	.1844	.3156	0.89	.3133	.1867
0.08	.0319	.4681	0.49	.1879	.3121	0.90	.3159	.1841
0.09	.0359	.4641	0.50	.1915	.3085	0.91	.3186	.1814
0.10	.0398	.4602	0.51	.1950	.3050	0.92	.3212	.1788
0.11	.0438	.4562	0.52	.1985	.3015	0.93	.3238	.1762
0.12	.0478	.4522	0.53	.2019	.2981	0.94	.3264	.1736
0.13	.0517	.4483	0.54	.2054	.2946	0.95	.3289	.1711
0.14	.0557	.4443	0.55	.2088	.2912	0.96	.3315	.1685
0.15	.0596	.4404	0.56	.2123	.2877	0.97	.3340	.1660
0.16	.0636	.4364	0.57	.2157	.2843	0.98	.3365	.1635
0.17	.0675	.4325	0.58	.2190	.2810	0.99	.3389	.1611
0.18	.0714	.4286	0.59	.2224	.2776	1.00	.3413	.1587
0.19	.0753	.4247	0.60	.2257	.2743	1.01	.3438	.1562
0.20	.0793	.4207	0.61	.2291	.2709	1.02	.3461	.1539
0.21	.0832	.4168	0.62	.2324	.2676	1.03	.3485	.1515
0.22	.0871	.4129	0.63	.2357	.2643	1.04	.3508	.1492
0.23	.0910	.4090	0.64	.2389	.2611	1.05	.3531	.1469
0.24	.0948	.4052	0.65	.2422	.2578	1.06	.3554	.1446
0.25	.0987	.4013	0.66	.2454	.2546	1.07	.3577	.1423
0.26	.1026	.3974	0.67	.2486	.2514	1.08	.3599	.1401
0.27	.1064	.3936	0.68	.2517	.2483	1.09	.3621	.1379
0.28	.1103	.3897	0.69	.2549	.2451	1.10	.3643	.1357
0.29	.1141	.3859	0.70	.2580	.2420	1.11	.3665	.1335
0.30	.1179	.3821	0.71	.2611	.2389	1.12	.3686	.1314
0.31	.1217	.3783	0.72	.2642	.2358	1.13	.3708	.1292
0.32	.1255	.3745	0.73	.2673	.2327	1.14	.3729	.1271
0.33	.1293	.3707	0.74	.2704	.2296	1.15	.3749	.1251
0.34	.1331	.3669	0.75	.2734	.2266	1.16	.3770	.1230
0.35	.1368	.3632	0.76	.2764	.2236	1.17	.3790	.1210
0.36	.1406	.3594	0.77	.2794	.2206	1.18	.3810	.1190
0.37	.1443	.3557	0.78	.2823	.2177	1.19	.3830	.1170
0.38	.1480	.3520	0.79	.2852	.2148	1.20	.3849	.1151
0.39	.1517	.3483	0.80	.2881	.2119	1.21	.3869	.1131
0.40	.1554	.3446	0.81	.2910	.2090	1.22	.3888	.1112

TABLE A: z Distribution Table (Normal Curve) (*continued*)

A	B	C	A	B	C	A	B	C
z	Area Between Mean and z	Area Beyond z	z	Area Between Mean and z	Area Beyond z	z	Area Between Mean and z	Area Beyond z
1.23	.3907	.1093	1.63	.4484	.0516	2.03	.4788	.0212
1.24	.3925	.1075	1.64	.4495	.0505	2.04	.4793	.0207
1.25	.3944	.1056	1.65	.4505	.0494	2.05	.4798	.0202
1.26	.3962	.1038	1.66	.4515	.0485	2.06	.4803	.0197
1.27	.3980	.1020	1.67	.4525	.0475	2.07	.4808	.0192
1.28	.3997	.1003	1.68	.4535	.0465	2.08	.4812	.0188
1.29	.4015	.0985	1.69	.4545	.0455	2.09	.4817	.0183
1.30	.4032	.0968	1.70	.4554	.0446	2.10	.4821	.0179
1.31	.4049	.0951	1.71	.4564	.0436	2.11	.4826	.0174
1.32	.4066	.0934	1.72	.4573	.0427	2.12	.4830	.0170
1.33	.4082	.0918	1.73	.4582	.0418	2.13	.4834	.0166
1.34	.4099	.0901	1.74	.4591	.0409	2.14	.4838	.0162
1.35	.4115	.0885	1.75	.4599	.0401	2.15	.4842	.0158
1.36	.4131	.0869	1.76	.4608	.0392	2.16	.4846	.0154
1.37	.4147	.0853	1.77	.4616	.0384	2.17	.4850	.0150
1.38	.4162	.0838	1.78	.4625	.0375	2.18	.4854	.0146
1.39	.4177	.0823	1.79	.4633	.0367	2.19	.4857	.0143
1.40	.4192	.0808	1.80	.4641	.0359	2.20	.4861	.0139
1.41	.4207	.0793	1.81	.4649	.0351	2.21	.4864	.0136
1.42	.4222	.0778	1.82	.4656	.0344	2.22	.4868	.0132
1.43	.4236	.0764	1.83	.4664	.0336	2.23	.4871	.0129
1.44	.4251	.0749	1.84	.4671	.0329	2.24	.4875	.0125
1.45	.4265	.0735	1.85	.4678	.0322	2.25	.4878	.0122
1.46	.4279	.0721	1.86	.4686	.0314	2.26	.4881	.0119
1.47	.4292	.0708	1.87	.4693	.0307	2.27	.4884	.0116
1.48	.4306	.0694	1.88	.4699	.0301	2.28	.4887	.0113
1.49	.4319	.0681	1.89	.4706	.0294	2.29	.4890	.0110
1.50	.4332	.0668	1.90	.4713	.0287	2.30	.4893	.0107
1.51	.4345	.0655	1.91	.4719	.0281	2.31	.4896	.0104
1.52	.4357	.0643	1.92	.4726	.0274	2.32	.4898	.0102
1.53	.4370	.0630	1.93	.4732	.0268	2.33	.4901	.0099
1.54	.4382	.0618	1.94	.4738	.0262	2.34	.4904	.0096
1.55	.4394	.0606	1.95	.4744	.0256	2.35	.4906	.0094
1.56	.4406	.0594	1.96	.4750	.0250	2.36	.4909	.0091
1.57	.4418	.0582	1.97	.4756	.0244	2.37	.4911	.0089
1.58	.4429	.0571	1.98	.4761	.0239	2.38	.4913	.0087
1.59	.4441	.0559	1.99	.4767	.0233	2.39	.4916	.0084
1.60	.4452	.0548	2.00	.4772	.0228	2.40	.4918	.0082
1.61	.4463	.0537	2.01	.4778	.0222	2.41	.4920	.0080
1.62	.4474	.0526	2.02	.4783	.0217	2.42	.4922	.0078

TABLE A: *z* Distribution Table (Normal Curve) (*continued*)

z	Area Between Mean and z	Area Beyond z	z	Area Between Mean and z	Area Beyond z	z	Area Between Mean and z	Area Beyond z
2.43	.4925	.0075	2.73	.4968	.0032	3.03	.4988	.0012
2.44	.4927	.0073	2.74	.4969	.0031	3.04	.4988	.0012
2.45	.4929	.0071	2.75	.4970	.0030	3.05	.4989	.0011
2.46	.4931	.0069	2.76	.4971	.0029	3.06	.4989	.0011
2.47	.4932	.0068	2.77	.4972	.0028	3.07	.4989	.0011
2.48	.4934	.0066	2.78	.4973	.0027	3.08	.4990	.0010
2.49	.4936	.0064	2.79	.4974	.0026	3.09	.4990	.0010
2.50	.4938	.0062	2.80	.4974	.0026	3.10	.4990	.0010
2.51	.4940	.0060	2.81	.4975	.0025	3.11	.4991	.0009
2.52	.4941	.0059	2.82	.4976	.0024	3.12	.4991	.0009
2.53	.4943	.0057	2.83	.4977	.0023	3.13	.4991	.0009
2.54	.4945	.0055	2.84	.4977	.0023	3.14	.4992	.0008
2.55	.4946	.0054	2.85	.4978	.0022	3.15	.4992	.0008
2.56	.4948	.0052	2.86	.4979	.0021	3.16	.4992	.0008
2.57	.4949	.0051	2.87	.4979	.0021	3.17	.4992	.0008
2.58	.4951	.0049	2.88	.4980	.0020	3.18	.4993	.0007
2.59	.4952	.0048	2.89	.4981	.0019	3.19	.4993	.0007
2.60	.4953	.0047	2.90	.4981	.0019	3.20	.4993	.0007
2.61	.4955	.0045	2.91	.4982	.0018	3.21	.4993	.0007
2.62	.4956	.0044	2.92	.4982	.0018	3.22	.4994	.0006
2.63	.4957	.0043	2.93	.4983	.0017	3.23	.4994	.0006
2.64	.4959	.0041	2.94	.4984	.0016	3.24	.4994	.0006
2.65	.4960	.0040	2.95	.4984	.0016	3.30	.4995	.0005
2.66	.4961	.0039	2.96	.4985	.0015	3.40	.4997	.0003
2.67	.4962	.0038	2.97	.4985	.0015	3.50	.4998	.0002
2.68	.4963	.0037	2.98	.4986	.0014	3.60	.4998	.0002
2.69	.4964	.0036	2.99	.4986	.0014	3.70	.4999	.0001
2.70	.4965	.0035	3.00	.4987	.0013	3.80	.49993	.00007
2.71	.4066	.0034	3.01	.4987	.0013	3.90	.49995	.00005
2.72	.4967	.0033	3.02	.4987	.0013	4.00	.49997	.00003
						∞	.5000	.00000

TABLE B: Critical Values of *t* $df = n_1 + n_2 - 2$ *t - test*

Significance Levels for Two-Tailed t Test				Significance Levels for One-Tailed t Test				
df	.10	.05	.01	.001	df	.10	.05	.01	.0005
1	6.31	12.71	63.66	636.62	1	3.08	6.31	31.82	636.62
2	2.92	4.30	9.93	31.60	2	1.886	2.92	6.97	31.60
3	2.35	3.18	5.84	12.92	3	1.64	2.35	4.54	12.92
4	2.13	2.78	4.60	8.61	4	1.53	2.13	3.75	8.61
5	2.02	2.57	4.03	6.87	5	1.48	2.02	3.37	6.87
6	1.94	2.45	3.71	5.96	6	1.44	1.94	3.14	5.96
7	1.90	2.37	3.50	5.41	7	1.42	1.90	3.00	5.41
8	1.86	2.31	3.36	5.04	8	1.40	1.86	2.90	5.04
9	1.83	2.26	3.25	4.78	9	1.38	1.83	2.82	4.78
10	1.81	2.23	3.17	4.59	10	1.37	1.81	2.76	4.59
11	1.80	2.20	3.11	4.44	11	1.36	1.80	2.72	4.44
12	1.78	2.18	3.06	4.32	12	1.36	1.78	2.68	4.32
13	1.77	2.16	3.01	4.22	13	1.35	1.77	2.65	4.22
14	1.76	2.15	2.98	4.14	14	1.35	1.76	2.62	4.14
15	1.75	2.13	2.95	4.07	15	1.34	1.75	2.60	4.07
16	1.75	2.12	2.92	4.02	16	1.34	1.75	2.58	4.02
17	1.74	2.11	2.90	3.97	17	1.33	1.74	2.57	3.97
18	1.73	2.10	2.88	3.92	18	1.33	1.73	2.55	3.92
19	1.73	2.09	2.86	3.88	19	1.33	1.73	2.54	3.88
20	1.73	2.09	2.85	3.85	20	1.33	1.73	2.53	3.85
21	1.72	2.08	2.83	3.82	21	1.32	1.72	2.52	3.82
22	1.72	2.07	2.82	3.79	22	1.32	1.72	2.51	3.79
23	1.71	2.07	2.81	3.77	23	1.32	1.71	2.50	3.77
24	1.71	2.06	2.80	3.75	24	1.32	1.71	2.49	3.75
25	1.71	2.06	2.79	3.73	25	1.32	1.71	2.49	3.73
26	1.71	2.06	2.78	3.71	26	1.32	1.71	2.48	3.71
27	1.70	2.05	2.77	3.69	27	1.31	1.70	2.47	3.69
28	1.70	2.05	2.76	3.67	28	1.31	1.70	2.47	3.67
29	1.70	2.05	2.76	3.66	29	1.31	1.70	2.46	3.66
30	1.70	2.04	2.75	3.65	30	1.31	1.70	2.46	3.65
40	1.68	2.02	2.70	3.55	40	1.30	1.68	2.42	3.55
60	1.67	2.00	2.66	3.46	60	1.30	1.67	2.39	3.46
120	1.66	1.98	2.62	3.37	120	1.29	1.66	2.36	3.37
∞	1.65	1.96	2.58	3.29	∞	1.28	1.65	2.33	3.29

Source: E. S. Pearson and H. O. Hartley. (1970). *Biometrika Tables for Statisticians, Vol. 1* (Oxford: Oxford University Press). Adapted with permission of the Biometrika trustees.

$df(r) = n - 2$

TABLE C: Critical Values of *r* at the .05 and .01 Significance Levels

directional

	Two-Tailed Test Significance Level (α)			One-Tailed Test Significance Level (α)	
df	.05	.01	df	.05	.01
1	1.00	1.00	1	.99	1.00
2	.95	.99	2	.90	.98
3	.88	.96	3	.81	.93
4	.81	.92	4	.73	.88
5	.75	.87	5	.67	.83
6	.71	.83	6	.63	.79
7	.67	.80	7	.58	.75
8	.63	.76	8	.55	.72
9	.60	.73	9	.52	.69
10	.58	.71	10	.50	.66
11	.55	.68	11	.48	.63
12	.53	.66	12	.46	.61
13	.51	.64	13	.44	.59
14	.50	.62	14	.43	.57
15	.48	.61	15	.41	.56
16	.47	.59	16	.40	.54
17	.46	.58	17	.39	.53
18	.44	.56	18	.38	.52
19	.43	.55	19	.37	.50
20	.42	.54	20	.36	.49
25	.38	.49	25	.32	.45
30	.35	.45	30	.30	.41
35	.32	.42	35	.27	.38
40	.30	.40	40	.26	.36
45	.29	.37	45	.24	.34
50	.27	.35	50	.23	.32
60	.25	.32	60	.21	.29
70	.23	.30	70	.20	.27
80	.22	.28	80	.18	.26
90	.21	.27	90	.17	.24
100	.19	.25	100	.16	.23

Source: Statistical Tables for Biological, Agricultural, and Medical Research. Copyright © 1963 R. A. Fisher and F. Yates. Reprinted by permission of Addison Wesley Longman Limited. Reprinted by permission of Pearson Education Limited.

Anova

TABLE D: Critical Values of F at the .05 Significance Level

df_{Within}	\multicolumn{9}{c}{$df_{Between}$}
	1	2	3	4	5	6	8	10	∞
1	161.45	199.50	215.71	224.58	230.16	233.99	238.88	241.88	254.31
2	18.51	19.00	19.16	19.25	19.30	19.33	19.37	19.40	19.50
3	10.13	9.55	9.28	9.12	9.01	8.94	8.85	8.79	8.53
4	7.71	6.94	6.59	6.39	6.26	6.16	6.04	5.96	5.63
5	6.61	5.79	5.41	5.19	5.05	4.95	4.82	4.74	4.37
6	5.99	5.14	4.76	4.53	4.39	4.28	4.15	4.06	3.67
7	5.59	4.74	4.35	4.12	3.97	3.87	3.73	3.64	3.23
8	5.32	4.46	4.07	3.84	3.69	3.58	3.44	3.35	2.93
9	5.12	4.26	3.86	3.63	3.48	3.37	3.23	3.14	2.71
10	4.96	4.10	3.71	3.48	3.33	3.22	3.07	2.98	2.54
11	4.84	3.98	3.59	3.36	3.20	3.09	2.95	2.85	2.40
12	4.75	3.89	3.49	3.26	3.11	3.00	2.85	2.75	2.30
13	4.67	3.81	3.41	3.18	3.03	2.92	2.77	2.67	2.21
14	4.60	3.74	3.34	3.11	2.96	2.85	2.70	2.60	2.13
15	4.54	3.68	3.29	3.06	2.90	2.79	2.64	2.54	2.07
16	4.49	3.63	3.24	3.01	2.85	2.74	2.59	2.49	2.01
17	4.45	3.59	3.20	2.96	2.81	2.70	2.55	2.45	1.96
18	4.41	3.55	3.16	2.93	2.77	2.66	2.51	2.41	1.92
19	4.38	3.52	3.13	2.90	2.74	2.63	2.48	2.38	1.88
20	4.35	3.49	3.10	2.87	2.71	2.60	2.45	2.35	1.84
21	4.32	3.47	3.07	2.84	2.68	2.57	2.42	2.32	1.81
22	4.30	3.44	3.05	2.82	2.66	2.55	2.40	2.30	1.78
23	4.28	3.42	3.03	2.80	2.64	2.53	2.37	2.27	1.76
24	4.26	3.40	3.01	2.78	2.62	2.51	2.36	2.25	1.73
25	4.24	3.39	2.99	2.76	2.60	2.49	2.34	2.24	1.71
26	4.23	3.37	2.98	2.74	2.59	2.47	2.32	2.22	1.69
27	4.21	3.35	2.96	2.73	2.57	2.46	2.31	2.20	1.67
28	4.20	3.34	2.95	2.71	2.56	2.45	2.29	2.19	1.65
29	4.18	3.33	2.93	2.70	2.55	2.43	2.28	2.18	1.64
30	4.17	3.32	2.92	2.69	2.53	2.42	2.27	2.16	1.62
40	4.08	3.23	2.84	2.61	2.45	2.34	2.18	2.08	1.51
60	4.00	3.15	2.76	2.53	2.37	2.25	2.10	1.99	1.39
120	3.92	3.07	2.68	2.45	2.29	2.18	2.02	1.91	1.25
∞	3.84	2.99	2.60	2.37	2.21	2.10	1.94	1.83	1.00

(Continued)

$$df_w = n - k$$
$$df_{b/w} = k - 1$$

TABLE D: Critical Values of *F* at the .01 Significance Level

df$_{Within}$	1	2	3	4	5	6	8	10	∞
1	4052.2	4999.5	5403.4	5624.6	5763.6	5859.0	5981.1	6055.8	6365.9
2	98.50	99.00	99.17	99.25	99.30	99.33	99.37	99.40	99.50
3	34.12	30.82	29.46	28.71	28.24	27.91	27.49	27.23	26.13
4	21.20	18.00	16.69	15.98	15.52	15.21	14.80	14.55	13.46
5	16.26	13.27	12.06	11.39	10.97	10.67	10.29	10.05	9.02
6	13.75	10.93	9.78	9.15	8.75	8.47	8.10	7.87	6.88
7	12.25	9.55	8.45	7.85	7.46	7.19	6.84	6.62	5.65
8	11.26	8.65	7.59	7.01	6.63	6.37	6.03	5.81	4.86
9	10.56	8.02	6.99	6.42	6.06	5.80	5.47	5.26	4.31
10	10.04	7.56	6.55	5.99	5.64	5.39	5.06	4.85	3.91
11	9.65	7.21	6.22	5.67	5.32	5.07	4.74	4.54	3.60
12	9.33	6.93	5.95	5.41	5.06	4.82	4.50	4.30	3.36
13	9.07	6.70	5.74	5.21	4.86	4.62	4.30	4.10	3.17
14	8.86	6.51	5.56	5.04	4.70	4.46	4.14	3.94	3.00
15	8.68	6.36	5.42	4.89	4.56	4.32	4.00	3.80	2.87
16	8.53	6.23	5.29	4.77	4.44	4.20	3.89	3.69	2.75
17	8.40	6.11	5.19	4.67	4.34	4.10	3.79	3.59	2.65
18	8.29	6.01	5.09	4.58	4.25	4.01	3.71	3.51	2.57
19	8.18	5.93	5.01	4.50	4.17	3.94	3.63	3.43	2.49
20	8.10	5.85	4.94	4.43	4.10	3.87	3.56	3.37	2.42
21	8.02	5.78	4.87	4.37	4.04	3.81	3.51	3.31	2.36
22	7.95	5.72	4.82	4.31	3.99	3.76	3.45	3.26	2.31
23	7.88	5.66	4.76	4.26	3.94	3.71	3.41	3.21	2.26
24	7.82	5.61	4.72	4.22	3.90	3.67	3.36	3.17	2.21
25	7.77	5.57	4.68	4.18	3.86	3.63	3.32	3.13	2.17
26	7.72	5.53	4.64	4.14	3.82	3.59	3.29	3.09	2.13
27	7.68	5.49	4.60	4.11	3.78	3.56	3.26	3.06	2.10
28	7.64	5.45	4.57	4.07	3.75	3.53	3.23	3.03	2.06
29	7.60	5.42	4.54	4.04	3.73	3.50	3.20	3.00	2.03
30	7.56	5.39	4.51	4.02	3.70	3.47	3.17	2.98	2.01
40	7.31	5.18	4.31	3.83	3.51	3.29	2.99	2.80	1.80
60	7.08	4.98	4.13	3.65	3.34	3.12	2.82	2.63	1.60
120	6.85	4.79	3.95	3.48	3.17	2.96	2.66	2.47	1.38
∞	6.63	4.61	3.78	3.32	3.02	2.80	2.51	2.32	1.00

df$_{Between}$

$$df = \frac{k}{A} k - 1 \ (\text{one-sample})$$
$$df = (R-1)(C-1) \rightarrow \text{two-sample}$$

Probability Distribution Tables 415

TABLE E: Critical Values of Chi-Square at the .10, .05, .01, and .001 Significance Levels

df	Significance Level (α)			
	.10	.05	.01	.001
1	2.71	3.84	6.64	10.83
2	4.61	5.99	9.21	13.82
3	6.25	7.82	11.35	16.27
4	7.78	9.49	13.28	18.48
5	9.24	11.07	15.09	20.52
6	10.65	12.59	16.81	22.46
7	12.02	14.07	18.48	24.32
8	13.36	15.51	20.09	26.13
9	14.68	16.92	21.67	27.88
10	15.99	18.31	23.21	29.59
11	17.28	19.68	24.73	31.26
12	18.55	21.03	26.23	32.91
13	19.81	22.36	27.69	34.53
14	21.06	23.69	29.14	36.12
15	22.31	24.99	30.58	37.70
16	23.54	26.30	32.00	39.25
17	24.77	27.59	33.41	40.79
18	25.99	28.87	34.81	42.31
19	27.20	30.14	36.19	43.82
20	28.41	31.41	37.57	45.32
21	29.62	32.67	38.93	46.80
22	30.81	33.92	40.29	48.27
23	32.01	35.17	41.64	49.73
24	33.20	36.42	42.98	51.18
25	34.38	37.65	44.31	52.62
26	35.56	38.89	45.64	54.05
27	36.74	40.11	46.96	55.48
28	37.92	41.34	48.28	56.89
29	39.01	42.56	49.59	58.30
30	40.26	43.77	50.89	59.70
40	51.81	55.76	63.69	73.40
50	63.17	67.51	76.15	86.66
60	74.40	79.08	88.38	99.61
70	85.53	90.53	100.43	112.32

Source: E. S. Pearson and H. O. Hartley. (1970). *Biometrika Tables for Statisticians, Vol. 1* (Oxford: Oxford University Press). Adapted with permission of the Biometrika trustees.

TABLE F: Critical Values of Studentized Range (*q*) at the .05 Significance Level

MS$_{within}$ df	Number of Means (k)									
	2	3	4	5	6	7	8	9	10	11
1	17.97	26.98	32.82	37.08	40.41	43.12	45.40	47.36	49.07	50.59
2	6.08	8.33	9.80	10.88	11.74	12.44	13.03	13.54	13.99	14.39
3	4.50	5.91	6.82	7.50	8.04	8.48	8.85	9.18	9.46	9.72
4	3.93	5.04	5.76	6.29	6.71	7.05	7.35	7.60	7.83	8.03
5	3.64	4.60	5.22	5.67	6.03	6.33	6.58	6.80	6.99	7.17
6	3.46	4.34	4.90	5.30	5.63	5.90	6.12	6.32	6.49	6.65
7	3.34	4.16	4.68	5.06	5.36	5.61	5.82	6.00	6.16	6.3
8	3.26	4.04	4.53	4.89	5.17	5.40	5.60	5.77	5.92	6.05
9	3.20	3.95	4.41	4.76	5.02	5.24	5.43	5.59	5.74	5.87
10	3.15	3.88	4.33	4.65	4.91	5.12	5.30	5.46	5.60	5.72
11	3.11	3.82	4.26	4.57	4.82	5.03	5.20	5.35	5.49	5.61
12	3.08	3.77	4.20	4.51	4.75	4.95	5.12	5.27	5.39	5.51
13	3.06	3.73	4.15	4.45	4.69	4.88	5.05	5.19	5.32	5.43
14	3.03	3.70	4.11	4.41	4.64	4.83	4.99	5.13	5.25	5.36
15	3.01	3.67	4.08	4.37	4.59	4.78	4.94	5.08	5.20	5.31
16	3.00	3.65	4.05	4.33	4.56	4.74	4.90	5.03	5.15	5.26
17	2.98	3.63	4.02	4.30	4.52	4.70	4.86	5.99	5.11	5.21
18	2.97	3.61	4.00	4.28	4.49	4.67	4.82	4.96	5.07	5.17
19	2.96	3.59	3.98	4.25	4.47	4.65	4.79	4.92	5.04	5.14
20	2.95	3.58	3.96	4.23	4.45	4.62	4.77	4.90	5.01	5.11
24	2.92	3.53	3.90	4.17	4.37	4.54	4.68	4.81	4.92	5.01
30	2.89	3.49	3.85	4.10	4.30	4.46	4.60	4.72	4.82	4.92
40	2.86	3.44	3.79	4.04	4.23	4.39	4.52	4.63	4.73	4.82
60	2.83	3.40	3.74	3.98	4.16	4.31	4.44	4.55	4.65	4.73
120	2.80	3.36	3.68	3.92	4.10	4.24	4.36	4.46	4.56	4.64
∞	2.77	3.31	3.63	3.86	4.03	4.17	4.29	4.39	4.47	4.55

TABLE F: Critical Values of Studentized Range (*q*) at the .01 Significance Level *(continued)*

MS_within df	Number of Means (k)									
	2	3	4	5	6	7	8	9	10	11
1	90.03	135	164.3	185.60	202.2	215.8	227.20	237.00	245.6	253.20
2	14.04	19.02	22.29	24.72	26.63	28.2	29.53	30.68	31.69	32.59
3	8.26	10.62	12.17	13.33	14.24	15.00	15.64	16.20	16.69	17.13
4	6.51	8.12	9.17	9.96	10.58	11.10	11.55	11.93	12.27	12.57
5	5.70	6.98	7.80	8.42	8.91	9.32	9.67	9.97	10.24	10.48
6	5.24	6.33	7.03	7.56	7.97	8.32	8.61	8.87	9.10	9.30
7	4.95	5.92	6.54	7.01	7.37	7.68	7.94	8.17	8.37	8.55
8	4.75	5.64	6.20	6.62	6.96	7.24	7.47	7.68	7.86	8.03
9	4.60	6.43	5.96	6.35	6.66	6.91	7.13	7.33	7.49	7.65
10	4.48	5.27	5.77	6.14	6.43	6.67	6.87	7.05	7.29	7.36
11	4.39	5.15	5.62	5.97	6.25	6.48	6.67	6.84	6.99	7.13
12	4.32	5.05	5.50	5.84	6.10	6.32	6.51	6.67	6.81	6.94
13	4.26	4.96	5.40	5.73	5.98	6.19	6.37	6.53	6.67	6.79
14	4.21	4.89	5.32	5.63	5.88	6.08	6.26	6.41	6.54	6.66
15	4.17	4.84	5.25	5.56	5.80	5.99	6.16	6.31	6.44	6.55
16	4.13	4.79	5.19	5.49	5.72	5.92	6.08	6.22	6.35	6.46
17	4.10	4.74	5.14	5.43	5.66	5.85	6.01	6.15	6.27	6.38
18	4.07	4.70	5.09	5.38	5.60	5.79	5.94	6.08	6.20	6.31
19	4.05	4.67	5.05	5.33	5.55	5.73	5.89	6.02	6.14	6.25
20	4.02	4.64	5.02	5.29	5.51	5.69	5.84	5.97	6.09	6.19
24	3.96	4.55	4.91	5.17	5.37	5.54	4.59	5.81	5.92	6.02
30	3.89	4.45	4.80	5.05	5.24	5.40	5.54	5.65	5.76	5.85
40	3.82	4.37	4.70	4.93	5.11	5.26	5.39	5.50	5.60	5.69
60	3.76	4.28	4.59	4.82	4.99	5.13	5.25	5.36	5.45	5.53
120	3.70	4.20	4.50	4.71	4.87	5.01	5.12	5.21	5.30	5.37
∞	3.64	4.12	4.40	4.60	4.76	4.88	4.99	5.08	5.16	5.23

TABLE G: Critical Values of Spearman's Rho (r_s)

Two-Tailed Test Significance Level (α)			One-Tailed Test Significance Level (α)		
n	.05	.01	n	.05	.01
5	1.00	—	5	.90	1.00
6	.89	1.00	6	.83	.94
7	.79	.93	7	.71	.89
8	.74	.88	8	.64	.83
9	.70	.83	9	.60	.78
10	.65	.79	10	.56	.75
11	.62	.76	11	.54	.71
12	.59	.74	12	.50	.70
13	.57	.70	13	.48	.67
14	.55	.68	14	.46	.65
15	.53	.66	15	.44	.62
16	.51	.64	16	.43	.60
17	.49	.62	17	.41	.58
18	.48	.60	18	.40	.56
19	.46	.59	19	.39	.55
20	.45	.57	20	.38	.53
21	.44	.56	21	.37	.52
22	.43	.54	22	.36	.51
23	.42	.53	23	.35	.50
24	.41	.52	24	.34	.49
25	.40	.51	25	.34	.48
26	.39	.50	26	.33	.47
27	.39	.49	27	.32	.46
28	.38	.48	28	.32	.45
29	.37	.48	29	.31	.44
30	.36	.47	30	.31	.43

Source: G. J. Glasser and R. F. Winter. (1961). Critical values of the coefficient of rank correlation for testing the hypothesis of independence. *Biometrika, 48:*444. Adapted with permission of the Biometrika trustees.

Chapter Solutions
for Odd Questions

Solutions to Chapter 2 Problems

1. a) descriptive, b) applied, c) explanatory, d) descriptive

3. Dependent variable = trial verdict, Independent variables = type of attorney, prior record, and making bail
   Hypothesis 1: Offenders with private attorneys are more likely to be acquitted than are offenders with public defenders.
   Hypothesis 2: Offenders who make bail are less likely to be found guilty than are offenders who do not make bail.
   Hypothesis 3: Prior record influences trial verdict.

5. a) nominal, b) ordinal, c) nominal, d) ordinal

7. Nominal—Have you ever received a misconduct report?
   1) Yes   2) No
   Ordinal—How frequently do you receive misconduct reports?
   1) Infrequently   2) Frequently   3) Very frequently
   Interval—On a 1–to–10 scale, how severe are the misconduct reports you have received?
   1 = Not at all severe   10 = Very severe
   Ratio—How many misconduct reports have you received?

9. Dependent variable = officer satisfaction—interval measure, Independent variable = merit awards—ordinal measure

Solutions to Chapter 3 Problems

1. | *Crime* | *Frequency* |
   |---|---|
   | Theft | 12 |
   | Burglary | 8 |
   | Robbery | 6 |
   | Assault | 4 |

3. | *Crime* | *Frequency* |
   |---|---|
   | Violent | 10 |
   | Property | 20 |

   Ratio of property offenders to violent offenders is 2 to 1.

5. Independent variable = Drug Counseling (X), Dependent Variable = Probation Outcome (Y)

7.

Sentence Length	Frequency	Percentage	cmfreq	cm%
1–12 months	9,086	23.65	38,419	100
13–35 months	11,054	28.77	29,333	76.35
36–60 months	7,547	19.64	18,279	47.58
Over 60 months	10,732	27.93	10,732	27.94

9.

Lost Days	Frequency
25–30	15
20–24	14
15–19	16
10–14	21
5–9	42
0–4	49

11. Line Chart of Prior DUI Arrests

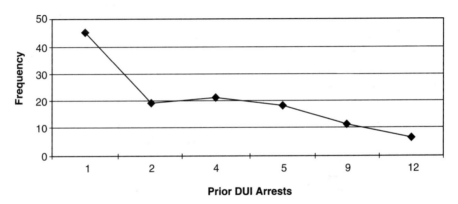

13.

	A	B	C	D	E	F	G
1	High School	Population	Expulsions	Disciplinary Hearings	Expulsion Rate	Disciplinary Hearing Rate	Ratio
2	Sammamish	1,400	5	20	0.36	1.43	0.25
3	Hudson	800	4	18	0.50	2.25	0.22
4	Penn	3,000	8	28	0.27	0.93	0.29
5	Westfield	1,300	4	35	0.31	2.69	0.11
6	Inglemoore	950	3	42	0.32	4.42	0.07

Solutions to Chapter 4 Problems

1. a) Mode = 0,   b) Median = 2,   c) Mean = 4.67

3.

	A	B	C	D	E
1	Exam Score (X)	Frequency (f)	Midpoint (m)	fm	cf
2	90–100	132	95	12540	370
3	80–89	109	84.5	9210.50	238
4	70–79	76	74.5	5662	129
5	60–69	34	64.5	2193	53
6	50–59	19	54.5	1035.50	19
7	**Sum**	**370**		**30641**	
8	**Mode (Mo)**	**95**			
9	**Median (Md)**	**83.84**			
10	**Mean $\bar{X}$**	**82.81**			

5.

	A	B	C
1	Prior Incarcerations (X)	Frequency (f)	fX
2	6	1	6
3	5	2	10
4	4	2	8
5	3	15	45
6	2	35	70
7	1	85	85
8	0	312	0
9	**Sum**	**452**	**224**
10	**Mode (Mo)**	**0**	
11	**Median (Md)**	**0**	
12	**Mean $\bar{X}$**	**0.50**	

7. Mode

9. Symmetrical

11. a) Mode, b) Mode, Median, or Mean, c) Mode or Median

Solutions to Chapter 5 Problems

1. a) Range = 11, b) Interquartile Range = 4, c) Variance = 12.57,
   d) Standard Deviation = 3.55

3.

	A	B	C	D	E	F	G
1	Days in Jail (X)	Frequency (f)	Midpoint (m)	fm	$(m - \bar{X})$	$(m - \bar{X})^2$	$f(m - \bar{X})^2$
2	61–100	5	80.5	402.5	55.35	3063.62	15318.11
3	46–60	23	53	1219	27.85	775.62	17839.32
4	31–45	32	38	1216	12.85	165.12	5283.92
5	15–30	70	22.5	1575	-2.65	7.02	491.57
6	8–15	45	11.5	517.5	-13.65	186.32	8384.51
7	1–7	25	4	100	-21.15	447.32	11183.06
8	Sum	200		5030			58500.50
9	Mean $\bar{X}$	25.15					
10	Variance (s^2)	293.97					
11	Standard deviation (s)	17.15					

5. a) Range = 6, b) Variance = .81, c) Standard Deviation = .90

7. Range

9. 95%

11. The standard deviation is equal to 0, because all of the values are the same. That is, there is no variability in the scores.

13.

	A	B
1	Monetary Loss (*X*)	
2	$ 500.00	$ 575.00
3	$ 1,200.00	$ 1,250.00
4	$ 850.00	$ 1,000.00
5	$ 45.00	$ 1,200.00
6	$ 30.00	$ 900.00
7	$ 580.00	$ 1,000.00
8	$ 450.00	$ 1,000.00
9	Range	$ 1,220.00
10	Variance (*s²*)	$ 161,691.76
11	Standard deviation (*s*)	$ 402.11

Solutions to Chapter 6 Problems

1. Mean and Standard Deviation

3. a) 17.4, b) .39, c) .009, d) 47.7%

5. a) 21.8%, b) 9.9%, c) .08, d) .59

7. Bell-shaped—the curve resembles a bell; Unimodal—the curve has only one mode; Symmetrical—each half of the curve is an exact representation of the other half; Asymptotic—the tails of the curve never touch the horizontal axis.

9. a) .6826, b) .9544, c) .9972

11. 11.9%

13. The student did better in the criminal justice class with a *z*-score of 1.4 and percentile rank of 92%, compared to performance in the psychology class, where the student had a *z*-score of .73 and percentile rank of 77%.

15.

	A	B	C	D
1	City	Crime Rate	z-score	Percentile Rank
2	Ellensburg	123.45	0.45	67.34%
3	Whitewater	145.65	1.01	84.39%
4	Kalamazoo	110.56	0.12	54.92%
5	Agawam	106.57	0.02	50.91%
6	Beaverton	98.43	-0.18	42.74%
7	Beatrice	101.45	-0.11	45.75%
8	Buckley	87.65	-0.46	32.44%
9	Juniper	99.01	-0.17	43.32%
10	Custer	105.31	-0.01	49.64%
11	Blaine	100.21	-0.14	44.51%
12	**Mean ($\bar{X}$)**	**105.67**		
13	**Standard deviation (s)**	**39.56**		

Solutions to Chapter 7 Problems

1. a) .004, b) .02, c) .07, d) .09, e) .14

3. a) 1.0, b) 1.15, c) 1.29, d) 1.65, e) 1.96, f) 2.17, g) 2.58

5. a) .11, b) .24, c) .52, d) .03, e) .21

7. We are 95% confident that the actual percentage of college students in the population who have violated university rules regarding alcohol use is between 55.1% and 59.7%.

9. Criminal Justice: 95% CI = 79.66 – 88.94; 99% CI = 77.83 – 90.77
Sociology: 95% CI = 77.16 – 87.65; 99% CI = 75.00 – 89.80
Psychology: 95% CI = 76.67 – 84.93; 99% CI = 75.11 – 86.49

11. The actual percentage of people in the population who own a gun is between 35.0% and 41.8%.

13.

	A	B	C	D	E	F	G
1		Mean ($\bar{X}$)	Standard Deviation (s)	Sample Size (n)	Standard Error ($s_{\bar{x}}$)	95% C.L.	
2	a.	2.56	2.11	12	0.64	0.61	4.51
3	b.	89.21	25.67	8	9.70	56.61	121.81
4	c.	10.98	5.45	15	1.46	6.68	15.28
5	d.	15.32	7.00	21	1.57	10.89	19.75

15.

	A	B	C	D	E
1		Frequency (f)	Proportion (p)	95% C.L.	
2	Accept Gratuities	54	0.45	36%	54%
3	Reject Gratuities	66	0.55		
4	Total	120			
5					
6	Standard error of proportion (Sp)	0.05			

Solutions to Chapter 8 Problems

1. a) directional, b) one-tailed test

3. Type II error

5. a) H_1: There is a difference in disciplinary infractions between inmates who participated in an anger management program and inmates who did not participate.
   H_0: There is no difference in disciplinary infractions between program participants and nonparticipants.
   b) $H_1: \bar{X} \neq \mu; H_0: \bar{X} = \mu$

7. a) calculated $z = -2.00$, b) critical $z = 1.96$, c) reject the null hypothesis

9. equal or exceed

11. a) H_1: The proportion of correctional officers who favor the death penalty is
    higher than the proportion of police officers who favor the death penalty.
    H_0: The proportion of correctional officers who favor the death penalty is equal
    to or less than the proportion of police officers who favor the death penalty.
    b) $H_1: p_1 > p_2; H_0: p_1 \leq p_2$

13. a) calculated $z = 1.38$, b) critical $z = 1.64$, c) accept the null hypothesis

15. a) reject the null, b) accept the null, c) reject the null, d) accept the null

17.

	A	B	C	D	E	F	G
1	$H_1: \bar{X} < \mu$ $H_0: \bar{X} \geq \mu$	Citations (X)	Frequency (f)	fX	$f(X-\bar{X})^2$		
2		5	7	35	90.72		
3		2	8	16	2.88		
4		1	5	5	0.80		
5		0	20	0	39.20		
6	Sum		40	56	133.6		
7	Population mean (μ)	2.20					
8	Sample mean ($\bar{X}$)	1.40					
9	Standard deviation (s)	3.43					
10	Standard error ($s_{\bar{x}}$)	0.55					
11	z statistic	-1.46					
12	z critical	-1.64					
13	**Interpretation:** Since the calculated z statistic is less than the critical z value, we are unable to reject the null hypothesis. Thus, we conclude that the difference between the sample mean and the population mean is the result of sampling error, and not the result of program effects.						

Solutions to Chapter 9 Problems

1. a) 6.64, b) 11.07, c) 11.35, d) 7.82, e) 23.21, f) 9.21

3. Cramer's V

5. Ordinal, Nominal

7. a) 1.00, b) .71, c) .74, d) .88, e) .38

9. Based on the above analysis, we would reject the null hypothesis (calculated $X^2 = 28.72 >$ critical $X^2 = 3.84$) and conclude that, among the entire population of students, graduate students are more likely to support the campus drinking policy than are the undergraduates.

11. a) 2, b) 15, c) 7, d) 25, e) 8

13. a) accept the null hypothesis, b) the difference in the rankings is attributed to sampling error and not actual differences between the population parameters

15.

	A	B	C	D	E	F	G	H
1	$H_1: f_1 \neq f_2$ $H_0: f_1 = f_2$							
2				Value of Automobile (X)				
3	Own Auto Alarm (Y)			$15,000 or less		over $15,000		row sum
4								
5		Yes		135		64		199
6		fe		142.83		56.17		
7		$(f_o\text{-}f_e)^2$		0.43		1.09		
8			column %	41.16%		49.61%		
9		No		193		65		258
10		fe		185.17		72.83		
11		$(f_o\text{-}f_e)^2$		0.33		0.84		
12			column %	58.84%		50.39%		
13	column sum			328		129		457
14								
15	X^2	2.69						
16	Phi	0.08						
17	**Interpretation:** The chi-square value of 2.69 is less than the critical value of 3.84. Therefore, we are unable to reject the null hypothesis. The differences in auto alarm ownership by car value is due to sampling error, and not the result of actual differences in the population.							

Solutions to Chapter 10 Problems

1. a) 2.98, b) 14, c) 2.15, d) reject the null hypothesis

3. Interval or ratio

5. a) independent samples *t* test, b) one-tailed test

7. a) a statistical technique used to assess the mean difference between two different groups drawn from the same sample

b) a statistical technique used to test the difference scores for a single sample of respondents

9. a) −2.52, b) 6, c) −1.94, d) reject the null hypothesis

11. a) 48, b) 2.02, c) accept the null hypothesis

13.

	A	B	C	D
1	$H_1: \mu_1 > \mu_2$ $H_0: \mu_1 \leq \mu_2$			
2	Area	No. Calls Before (X_1)	No. Calls After (X_2)	D^2
3	1	125	83	1764
4	2	150	175	625
5	3	93	94	1
6	4	100	90	100
7	5	110	81	841
8	6	75	65	100
9	7	80	90	100
10	8	120	100	400
11	sample	8		3931
12	Mean ($\bar{X}$)	106.62	97.25	
13	Standard deviation of Difference (s_D)	20.09		
14	Standard error of Difference ($s_{\bar{D}}$)	7.59		
15	*t* statistic	1.23		
16	*df*	7		
17	significance	0.13		
18	**Decision:** The calculated *t* statistic is not statistically significant; thus, we are unable to reject the null hypothesis. We conclude that directed patrols did not significantly reduce the number of calls.			

Solutions to Chapter 11 Problems

1. a) 3.06, b) 3.39, c) 5.39, d) 5.39, e) 2.75, f) 3.65

3. a) single-factor ANOVA, b) 2, c) 72, d) 4.98, e) 3.15

5. a) 4.05, b) 5.51, c) 4.89, d) 4.82, e) 6.14

7. a) fail to reject the null hypothesis b) reject the null hypothesis c) reject the null hypothesis d) fail to reject the null hypothesis

9. a) 3.55, b) fail to reject the null hypothesis

11. a) 9.85, b) 5.11, c) 12.03, d) 6.67

13. The scores are drawn randomly from normally distributed populations, the scores are independent of each other, the dependent variable is measured at the interval/ratio level, and the variances are homogeneous.

15.

	A	B	C	D	E	F	G
1	$H_1: \mu_1 \neq \mu_2 \neq \mu_3$ $H_0: \mu_1 = \mu_2 = \mu_3$	5'0"–5'10" (X_1)	5'11"–6'4" (X_2)	Over 6'4" (X_3)	5'0"–5'10" $(X_{iGroup}-\overline{X}_{Group1})^2$	5'11"–6'4" $(X_{iGroup}-\overline{X}_{Group2})^2$	Over 6'4" $(X_{iGroup}-\overline{X}_{Group3})^2$
2		0	0	2	1.21	0.49	0.25
3		3	0	3	3.61	0.49	2.25
4		1	1	1	0.01	0.09	0.25
5		1	2	0	0.01	1.69	2.25
6		0	0	0	1.21	0.49	2.25
7		2	0	3	0.81	0.49	2.25
8		2	1	3	0.81	0.09	2.25
9		0	1	1	1.21	0.09	0.25
10		2	2	1	0.81	1.69	0.25
11		0	0	1	1.21	0.49	0.25
12	Sample size (n)	10	10	10			
13	Sum (Σ)				10.90	6.10	12.50
14	Means ($\overline{X}_{group}$)	1.10	0.70	1.50			
15	Mean ($\overline{X}_{grand}$)	1.10					
16	$SS_{Between}$	3.20					
17	SS_{Within}	29.50					
18	SS_{Total}	32.70					
19	$df_{Between}$	2					

20	*df*_{Within}	27						
21	*MS*_{Between}	1.60						
22	*MS*_{Within}	1.09						
23	*F* Statistic	1.46						
24	Significance	0.25						
25	**Decision:** We are unable to reject the null hypothesis. Thus, we conclude that the differences between the three groups in terms of the average amount of times physical force was used is the result of sampling error and not of actual differences among the population parameters.							

Solutions to Chapter 12 Problems

1. a) The researcher is proposing a directional hypothesis by suggesting that as X increases, so does Y. A one-tailed test should be used, because her hypothesis suggests that the correlation between X and Y will be greater than zero (positively correlated).

   b) $r_{xy} = .73$. The correlation coefficient is in the hypothesized direction (positive), and is large enough to indicate a strong relationship between alcohol use and domestic violence.

   c) The correlation coefficient is significant at the .05 level (.73 calculated > .55 critical). We would conclude that increasing levels of alcohol use lead to increased incidences of domestic violence within the population.

3. a) one-tailed test indicating a negative relationship, b) two-tailed test, c) two-tailed test, d) one-tailed test indicating a negative relationship, e) one-tailed test indicating a positive relationship

5. $r_{xy \cdot z} = .37$. The partial correlation coefficient indicates that age accounts for some of the variance between TV viewing and fear of victimization, although only a small amount.

7. a) .57, b) .55, c) .54, d) .58, e) .32

9. strength, direction

11.

	A	B	C	D	E	F	G	H
1				Deviations		Product	Squared Deviations	
2	$H_1: p_{xy} < 0$ $H_0: p_{xy} \geq 0$	Income Level (X)	Delinquent Acts(Y)	d_x	d_y	$d_x d_y$	d_x^2	d_y^2
3		$ 45,000.00	3	$ 3,700.00	1.47	$ 5,426.67	$ 13,690,000.00	2.15
4		$ 56,000.00	2	$ 14,700.00	0.47	$ 6,860.00	$ 216,090,000.00	0.22
5		$ 28,000.00	4	$ (13,300.00)	247	$ (32,806.67)	$ 176,890,000.00	6.08
6		$ 25,000.00	2	$ (16,300.00)	0.47	$ (7,606.67)	$ 265,690,000.00	0.22
7		$ 55,000.00	1	$ 13,700.00	-0.53	$ (7,306.67)	$ 187,690,000.00	0.28
8		$ 45,000.00	1	$ 3,700.00	-0.53	$ (1,973.33)	$ 13,690,000.00	0.28
9		$ 40,000.00	0	$ (1,300.00)	-1.53	$ 1,993.33	$ 1,690,000.00	2.35
10		$ 37,500.00	3	$ (3,800.00)	1.47	$ (5,573.33)	$ 14,440,000.00	2.15
11		$ 39,000,00	1	$ (2,300.00)	-0.53	$ 1,226.67	$ 5,290,000.00	0.28
12		$ 67,000.00	0	$ 25,700.00	-1.53	$ (39,406.67)	$ 660,490,000.00	2.35
13		$ 50,000.00	1	$ 8,700.00	-0.53	$ (4,640.00)	$ 75,690,000.00	0.28
14		$ 28,000.00	1	$ (13,300.00)	-0.53	$ 7,093.33	$ 176,890,000.00	0.28
15		$ 35,000.00	0	$ (6,300.00)	-1.53	$ 9,660.00	$ 39,690,000.00	2.35
16		$ 30,000.00	3	$ (11,300.00)	1.47	$ (16,573.33)	$ 127,690,000.00	2.15
17		$ 39,000.00	1	$ (2,300.00)	-0.53	$ 1,226.67	$ 5,290,000.00	0.28
18								
19	Mean $(\bar{X})(\bar{Y})$	$ 41,300.00	1.53					
20	Sum					$ (82,400.00)	$1,980,900,000.00	21.73
21	r_{xy}	-0.40						
22	df	13						
23	Critical r	0.44						
24	**Decision:** We are unable to reject the null hypothesis. We must conclude that any association between Income Level and Delinquent Acts is the result of sampling error, and not an actual association among the population parameters.							

13.

	A	B	C	D	E
1	No. Arrests (Y_1)	No. Convictions (Y_2)	Education Level (X_1)	Income (X_2)	
2	3	2	9	$ 25,000.00	
3	2	0	8	$ 15,000.00	
4	2	1	11	$ 30,000.00	
5	1	0	12	$ 45,000.00	
6	1	0	14	$ 40,000.00	
7	3	3	10	$ 25,000.00	
8	3	2	12	$ 15,000.00	
9	1	0	12	$ 18,000.00	
10	1	1	12	$ 22,000.00	
11	5	3	9	$ 15,000.00	
12	4	2	10	$ 18,000.00	
13	5	3	9	$ 35,000.00	
14					
15		No. Arrests (Y_1)	No. Convictions (Y_2)	Education Level (X_1)	Income (X_2)
16	No. Arrests (Y_1)	-			
17	No. Convictions (Y_2)	.88**	-		
18	Education Level (X_1)	-.67*	-0.51	-	
19	Income (X_2)	-0.30	-0.26	0.41	-

*p ≤ .05 **p ≤ .01

Solutions to Chapter 13 Problems

1. a) 1.5, b) 2.6, c) 7, d) 12.5, e) 19.1

3. Bivariate regression

5. Slope, intercept, and error

7. a) 1.44, b) .64, c) .64, d) 4.84, e) 3.24, f) .16, g) 1.44

9. It is a highly predictive model, in that 92% of the variability in Y is accounted for or explained by X.

11. a) $H_1: \beta \neq 0$ $H_0: \beta = 0$
    b) $b = .28$ $a = 69.84$
    c) $r_{xy} = .39$ (critical r_{xy} [8 *df*, two-tailed test] $= .63$)
    d) We fail to reject the null hypothesis and conclude that the population slope is not significantly different than zero. In other words, there is no linear relationship between length of employment and stress among the population of correctional officers.
    e) $SS_{Total} = 604$, $SS_{Error} = 513.37$, $SS_{Regression} = 90.63$
    f) $MS_{Regression} = 90.63$, $MS_{Error} = 64.17$
    g) $F = 1.41$ $R^2 = .15$
    h) Only 15% of the variability in stress is explained or accounted for by length of employment.

13. Predicted

15.

	A	B	C	D	E	F
1	*a*	5.19				
2	*b*	-.37				
3	$\bar{Y}$	3.47				
4		Individual Scores		SS_{Total}	Regression Equation	SS_{Error}
5		X	Y	$(Y - \bar{Y})^2$	$\hat{Y} = a + b\,(X)$	$(Y - \hat{Y})^2$
6		1	7	12.48	4.82	4.75
7		2	8	20.55	4.45	12.59
8		1	8	20.55	4.82	10.10
9		2	5	2.35	4.45	0.30
10		4	5	2.35	3.71	1.66
11		6	2	2.15	2.97	0.94
12		3	2	2.15	4.08	4.33
13		10	2	2.15	1.49	0.26
14		8	1	6.08	2.23	1.52
15		8	1	6.08	2.23	1.52
16		3	1	6.08	4.08	9.49
17		9	3	0.22	1.86	1.30

18		9	4	0.28	1.86	4.57
19		3	1	6.08	4.08	9.49
20		1	2	2.15	4.82	7.96
21	**Sum**			**91.73**		**70.79**
22	**$SS_{Regression}$**	**20.94**				
23	**$df_{Regression}$**	**1**				
24	**df_{Error}**	**13**				
25	**$MS_{Regression}$**	**20.94**				
26	**MS_{Error}**	**5.45**				
27	**F statistic**	**3.85**				
28	**F critical**	**4.67**				
29	**R^2**	**0.23**				
30	**Note:** The regression model is not statistically significant, as the calculated *F* statistic (3.85) is less than the critical *F* value (4.67).					

17.

	A	B	C	D	E	F
1	Arrests (*Y*)	Education (X_1)	Unemployment (X_2)	Alcohol Use (X_3)		
2	2	12	3	8		
3	1	14	0	12		
4	1	12	5	5		
5	3	10	5	0		
6	5	12	5	0		
7	6	8	2	6		
8	6	9	8	6		
9	2	14	0	12		
10	1	12	2	4		
11	2	8	6	4		
12	4	12	6	0		
13	2	12	2	2		
14						
15	Summary Output					
16	Regression Statistics					
17	Multiple *R*	0.59				

18	R-square	0.35				
19	Adjusted R-square	0.10				
20	Standard error	1.78				
21	Observations	12				
22						
23	ANOVA					
24		df	SS	MS	F	Significance F
25	Regression	3	13.49	4.50	1.41	0.31
26	Residual	8	25.43	3.18		
27	Total	11	38.92			
28						
29		Coefficients	Standard Error	t Stat	P-value	
30	Intercept	6.90	4.47	1.55	0.16	
31	Education (X_1)	-0.40	0.32	-1.23	0.25	
32	Unemployment (X_2)	0.15	0.31	0.49	0.64	
33	Alcohol Use (X_3)	-0.01	0.16	-0.09	0.93	
34	**Interpretation:** The overall model is not statistically significant, as the significance level of .31 is greater than the required .05 level. In addition, none of the independent variables are statistically significant, as evidenced by the fact that the P-values are greater than .05. Thus, we are unable to reject any of the three null hypotheses. Finally, 35% of the variability in Y is accounted for by the set of X variables.					

Glossary

Addition rule: The probability of any number of outcomes occurring is equal to the sum of the separate probabilities of the number of outcomes (see Multiplication rule).

Alpha (see Significance level).

Analysis of variance (ANOVA): A class of techniques for testing if different groups or combinations of groups vary in terms of a continuous dependent measure.

Applied research: One of four general types of research. Applied research typically involves the evaluation of programs and/or policies (see Descriptive research, Explanatory research, Exploratory research).

Attributes: Qualities or quantities that describe a variable (see Variable).

Bar graph: A method of representing data in tabular form. A bar graph is a chart that describes a categorical variable in which the bars are separated by spacing and the height of the bars represents the percentages or frequencies of the attributes (see Frequency polygon, Histogram, Pie chart).

Bimodal distribution: A data distribution characterized by two scores that occur more often than any other score (see Multimodal distribution, Unimodal distribution).

Central limit theorem: The principle that the sampling distribution of a statistic will be normally distributed, regardless of the shape of the population distribution, provided that the sample is sufficiently large.

Chi-square: A statistical test used for assessing how well the distribution of observed frequencies of nominal-level variables fits the distribution of expected frequencies. A one-sample chi-square is used to examine how observations within a single sample will distribute across a set of categories. A two-sample chi-square is used to examine how observations with two samples distribute across a set of categories.

Coefficient of determination (r^2): The percentage of the variance in the Y variable that is explained by the X variable (see Coefficient of nondetermination).

Coefficient of multiple determination (R^2): The percentage of variance in the Y variable that is explained or accounted for by the set of independent variables.

Coefficient of nondetermination $(1 - r^2)$: The percentage of variance in the Y variable not explained by the X variable (see Coefficient of determination).

Confidence interval: The range of values in which the population parameter is estimated to lie.

Confidence level: The probability that a population parameter lies within a given confidence interval.

Correlational analysis: A statistical test to determine the extent to which two variables are related (see Pearson product-moment correlation coefficient, Spearman's rank correlation coefficient).

Correlational coefficient: A numerical summary of the direction and strength of the relationship between two variables.

Cramer's *V*: A statistic to examine the strength of the relationship between two nominal level variables. It is an appropriate measure of association for contingency tables larger than 2×2.

Critical value: The value in the probability distribution that marks the lower boundary of the critical region.

Crosstabulation: A table combining two separate frequency distributions to examine the impact of an independent variable on a dependent variable.

Cumulative frequency: The summed total of the frequency of any given numerical value or range of values plus the frequencies of all the other numerical values or range of values falling below it. This statistic is often used with grouped and ungrouped frequency distributions (see Cumulative percentage).

Cumulative percentage: The summed total of the percentage of any given numerical value or range of values plus the percentage of all the other numerical values or range of values falling below it. This statistic often is used with grouped and ungrouped frequency distributions (see Cumulative frequency).

Degrees of freedom (*df*): The number of values in a data set that are free to vary.

Dependent- or matched-samples *t* test: A statistical technique used to test the difference score for a single sample of respondents (see Independent samples *t* test).

Dependent variable: A variable that is influenced or affected by the independent variable (see Independent variable).

Descriptive statistics: A class of statistics used to describe and summarize observations, often involving the grouping of those observations and identifying a value or values best representing the observations (see Inferential statistics).

Descriptive research: One of four general types of research. Descriptive research primarily focuses on describing events and/or situations (see Applied research, Explanatory research, Exploratory research).

Directional hypothesis: A statement about the direction of the differences existing in the populations (see Nondirectional hypothesis).

Explanatory research: One of four general types of research. Explanatory research goes beyond description in an attempt to explain *why* (see Applied research, Descriptive research, Exploratory research).

Exploratory research: One of four general types of research. Exploratory research is usually reserved for the study of "new" behaviors and/or phenomena about which little is known (see Applied research, Descriptive research, Explanatory research).

Frequency distribution: A common type of distribution used to represent data. A frequency distribution typically is presented in a table listing the attributes of a variable along with their frequency of occurrence (see Grouped frequency distribution, Single data distribution).

Frequency polygon: A method of representing data in tabular form. A frequency polygon is a line graph that describes a numerical variable in which a dot over each attribute represents the frequency of that attribute. This type of graph is often referred to simply as a line graph (see Bar graph, Histogram, Pie chart).

Grouped frequency distribution: A type of frequency distribution in which single numerical values are grouped into class intervals or categories along with their frequency of occurrence (see Frequency distribution, Single data distribution).

Histogram: A method of representing data in tabular form. A histogram is a chart that describes a numerical variable in which the height of the bars represents the frequencies of the attributes (see Bar graph, Frequency polygon, Pie chart).

Hypothesis: A proposed relationship between two or more variables. A hypothesis often predicts how one variable will change depending on the influence of another variable (see Directional hypothesis, Nondirectional hypothesis, Null hypothesis, Research hypothesis, Research question).

Independence: A principle of the multiplication rule that stipulates that the occurrence of one outcome does not effect the likelihood of occurrence of any other outcome.

Independent samples *t* test: A statistical technique used to assess the mean difference between two different groups drawn from the same sample (see Dependent- or matched-samples *t* test).

Independent variable: A variable that produces a change in another variable; that is, it will influence, determine, or cause changes in the dependent variable (see Dependent variable).

Inferential statistics: A class of statistics used to make generalizations about what is happening in a given population based on a sample of observations (see Descriptive statistics).

Interaction effect: A kind of treatment effect in which the impact of one independent variable depends on the level of another independent variable (see Main effect).

Intercept: The point at which the regression line crosses the Y axis. It represents the predicted value of Y when the value of X is equal to 0 (see Regression analysis, Slope).

Interquartile range: An alternative range defined as the difference between the scores falling at the third quartile and the first quartile.

Interval-level: A level of measurement in which the variable has different attributes, an implied order among them, and equal intervals that can measure distances between the attributes (see Nominal-level, Ordinal-level, Ratio-level).

Law of large numbers: As the number of samples increases, the frequency distribution will more closely approximate the probability distribution.

Main effect: A kind of treatment effect in which the influence of one independent variable is examined apart from the influence of other independent variables in the design (see Interaction effect).

Margin of error: Is the difference between the sample mean and the population parameters based on the 95% confidence level (see Confidence interval, Confidence level).

Mean: A measure of central tendency defined as the average score among a group of scores (see Median, Mode).

Measures of central tendency: A group of indexes describing how scores in a distribution tend to cluster. These measures attempt to identify the score(s) that best represents the distribution. Mean, mode, and median are measures of central tendency (see Measures of dispersion).

Measures of dispersion: A group of indexes describing the typical range of values for a distribution of scores. Range, variance, and standard deviation are measures of dispersion (see Measures of central tendency).

Median: A measure of central tendency defined as the middle score in a data set (see Mean, Mode).

Mode: A measure of central tendency defined as the most frequently occurring score in a group of scores (see Mean, Median).

Multicollinearity: The correlation among a set of independent variables in a regression model that confounds the individual effects of the independent variables on the dependent variable.

Multimodal distribution: A data distribution characterized by three or more scores occurring more frequently than any other scores (see Bimodal distribution, Unimodal distribution).

Multiple correlation coefficient (Multiple R): A correlation coefficient, in a multiple regression analysis, that assesses the correlation between the set of independent variables and the dependent variable.

Multiple-factor analysis of variance (ANOVA): A statistical technique used for comparing sample means with research designs consisting of more than two independent variables (factors) with each variable consisting of two or more groups or levels (see Single-factor analysis of variance, Two-factor analysis of variance).

Multiple regression: A statistical technique to determine the predictive power of a set of independent variables on a single dependent variable.

Multiplication rule: The probability of obtaining two or more outcomes simultaneously is equal to the product of their separate probabilities (see Addition rule).

Multistage cluster sample: A type of sampling procedure that involves randomly selecting two or more clusters (e.g., groupings of individuals) followed by the final selection of elements typically using simple or systematic random sampling procedures (see Simple random sample, Stratified sample, Systematic sample).

Mutually exclusive: A principle of the addition rule stipulating that no more than one outcome can occur at a given time.

Negative correlation coefficient: Indicates that the two variables covary in the opposite direction. High values on one variable are associated with low values on another variable (see Positive correlation coefficient).

Negatively skewed distribution: A data distribution in which the majority of scores fall on the positive (right) end of the distribution, while the remaining scores are distributed on the negative (left) end of the distribution. Thus, the tail of the distribution lies on the negative end of the distribution (see Positively skewed distribution).

Nominal-level: A level of measurement in which the variable consists of a set of attributes that have different names or labels describing the categories (see Interval-level, Ordinal-level, Ratio-level).

Nondirectional hypothesis: A statement about the differences existing in the populations without specifying the direction of the differences (see Directional hypothesis).

Nonparametric statistics: Statistical tests that make no assumptions concerning the level of measurement or the distribution of the data in the population. Common nonparametric statistics include chi-square and Spearman rank-order correlation coefficient (see Parametric statistics).

Normal curve: A type of probability distribution mathematically defined as being unimodal, symmetrical, and asymptotic.

Null hypothesis: A statement of no difference or no association between an independent variable and a dependent variable (see Research hypothesis).

One-sample chi-square: A nonparametric statistical procedure that examines the way in which observations within a single sample will distribute across a set of categories (see Two-sample chi-square).

One-sample z test: A statistical technique that is used for testing a hypothesis about the relationship between a known population mean and a sample mean.

One-tailed test: A test of a directional hypothesis in which the critical region lies in one tail of the probability distribution (see Two-tailed test).

Ordinal-level: A level of measurement in which the variable has a set of different attributes with a rank-ordering among the categories (see Interval-level, Nominal-level, Ratio-level).

Outlier: An extreme or atypical case that distorts the data distribution.

Parameter: The value of a given variable in a population (see Statistic).

Parametric statistics: Statistical tests that involve some key assumptions concerning the level of measurement of the data as well as the distribution of the data in the population. These assumptions are that the data is measured at the interval or ratio level, and that the population distribution is normal. Some common parametric statistics include t test, ANOVA, and Pearson product-moment correlation coefficient (see Nonparametric statistics).

Partial correlation coefficient: A statistic used to analyze the correlation between two variables, while controlling for the influence of one or more other variables.

Partial slope: In a regression model, the partial slope represents the effect of an independent variable on a dependent variable controlling for the effects of the other independent variables in the model (see Slope).

Pearson's product-moment correlation coefficient: A statistical test to assess the relationship between two interval-ratio-level variables (also referred to simply as Pearson's r).

Percentage: The frequency of any single attribute divided by the total frequency of all the attributes, multiplied by 100. Percentage—a common type of descriptive statistic similar to proportion—is used to make meaningful comparisons among variables and their attributes (see Proportion, Rate, Ratio).

Percentile rank: A value that indicates the percentage of cases in a distribution falling below a particular score.

Phi: A statistic to examine the strength of the relationship between two nominal level variables each with two attributes. It is an appropriate measure of association for a 2 × 2 contingency table.

Pie chart: A circular graph divided into different sections representing the attributes of a variable (see Bar graph, Frequency polygon, Histogram).

Population: The entire collection of the people or objects of interest in the study (see Sample).

Positive correlation coefficient: Indicates that the variables covary in the same way. High values of one variable are associated with high values of another variable (see Negative correlation coefficient).

Positively skewed distribution: A data distribution in which the majority of the scores fall on the negative (left) end of the distribution, while the remaining scores are distributed on the positive (right) end of the distribution. Thus, the tail of the distribution lies on the positive end of the distribution (see Negatively skewed distribution).

Post hoc (posteriori) comparisons: Statistical procedures for isolating differences among sample means. These tests are conducted only after an overall significance test, such as ANOVA, detects a statistically significant finding (see Tukey's Honestly Significant Difference [HSD] test).

Probability: The number of times that a particular event or outcome can occur, divided by the number of times any event or outcome can occur.

Probability distribution: A distribution based on the theoretical assumption of which outcomes would be expected rather than which outcome is actually observed.

Probability sampling: A random method of selection, in which every member in the population has an equal and known probability of selection.

Proportion: The frequency of any single attribute divided by the total frequency of all the attributes. Proportion is a type of descriptive statistic used to make meaningful comparisons among variables and their attributes (see Percentage, Rate, Ratio).

Qualitative variable: A variable that consists of attributes that vary in quality or kind (see Quantitative variable).

Quantitative variable: A variable that consists of attributes that vary in degree or magnitude (see Qualitative variable).

Range: A measure of dispersion defined as the difference between the highest and lowest score in a distribution of scores (see Standard deviation, Variance).

Rate: A common method of comparison that controls for population differences. A rate is defined as the total frequency of cases that occurred, divided by the total possible frequency at risk of occurring, multiplied by any standard number (see Percentage, Proportion, Ratio).

Ratio: A type of descriptive statistic used to compare the frequency of one attribute with the frequency of another variable (see Percentage, Proportion, Rate).

Ratio-level: A level of measurement in which the variable has different attributes, an implied order among them, equal interval that can measure distances between the attributes, and an absolute zero point indicating the absence of the variable (see Interval-level, Nominal-level, Ordinal-level).

Regression analysis: A statistical technique used for predicting values of a dependent variable based on values of one or more independent variables.

Regression line (line of best fit): The best fitting line that accurately portrays the linear relationship between X and Y.

Repeated-measures analysis of variance (ANOVA): A statistical technique for comparing sample means of three or more dependent groups.

Research hypothesis: The hypothesized effect of an independent variable on a dependent variable that we believe to be true in the population (see Null hypothesis).

Research question: A formal question guiding our research inquiry often in terms of variable selection and hypothesis construction (see Hypothesis).

Residual error: The amount of variation in the dependent variable unexplained by the regression model. It is the difference between the predicted value of Y and the actual value of Y.

Sample: A subset of the people or objects of interest in the study, drawn from and representing the larger population (see Population).

Sampling distribution of means: A probability distribution of a statistic based on an infinite number of samples randomly selected from a given population.

Sampling error: The estimated difference between a sample statistic and a population parameter.

Sampling without replacement: A sampling technique that involves selecting sample elements from the population without replacing the selected element back into the population prior to selecting the next sample element (see Sampling with replacement).

Sampling with replacement: A sampling technique that involves replacing a selected sampling element back into the population prior to selecting the next element in the sample (see Sampling without replacement).

Sampling variation: The difference between the sample statistics as a result of differing sample characteristics.

Scatterplot: A graph that plots the values of the independent and dependent variable simultaneously for each observation.

Significance level (or alpha): The probability of making a Type I error.

Simple random sample: A type of random sample in which elements are selected randomly from a list of all elements of the population. Each element has an equal chance of selection (see Multistage cluster sample, Stratified sample, Systematic sample).

Single-data distribution: The simplest type of distribution for representing raw data, in which the number of listed attributes is equal to the number of subjects in the sample. Frequency or grouped frequency distributions are generally preferred to the single-data distribution (see Frequency distribution, Grouped frequency distribution).

Single-factor analysis of variance (one-way ANOVA): A statistical test for comparing three or more groups in terms of a continuous dependent measure.

Slope: In a regression model, the slope represents the amount of change in the value of the dependent variable per one unit change in the value of the independent variable (see Intercept, Partial slope, Regression analysis).

Spearman rank-order correlation coefficient (Spearman's rho): A nonparametric test to assess the correlation among ordinal (rank) variables.

Standard deviation: A measure of dispersion defined as the square root of the variance (see Range, Variance).

Standard error of the difference between means: An estimate of the variability or error in the sampling distribution of two samples.

Standard error of the mean: The standard deviation of the sampling distribution of means.

Standard error of the proportion: An estimate of the standard deviation of the sampling distribution of proportions.

Standardized score (see z-score).

Statistic: The value of a given variable in a sample (see Parameter).

Statistical inference: The process of using sample statistics to estimate population parameters.

Statistically significant: To say that a finding is statistically significant means that the differences observed between the sample statistics are the result of actual differences between the population parameters.

Statistics: A branch of science that involves collecting, describing, analyzing, and interpreting observations.

Stratified sample: A type of sampling procedure that categorizes a population in terms of a specific characteristic, and selects its elements—usually using simple random sample or systematic random sample procedures—from each of the different categories (see Multistage cluster sample, Simple random sample, Systematic sample).

Sums of squares between-group ($SS_{Between}$): A source of variability in analysis of variance (ANOVA), which refers to how much the means of each group deviate from the total mean.

Sums of squares total (SS_{Total}): The total amount of variability in analysis of variance (ANOVA), $SS_{Between} + SS_{Within} = SS_{Total}$ is the sum of the squared deviations of each individual score minus the grand mean.

Sums of squares within-group (SS_{Within}): A source of variability in analysis of variance (ANOVA), which refers to how much each score deviates from the mean of its own group.

Systematic sample: A type of random sample procedure in which every *k*th element from the population list is selected for entry into the study (see Multistage cluster sample, Simple random sample, Stratified sample).

Tukey's Honestly Significant Difference (HSD) test: A post hoc test for making comparisons after a significant *F* statistic is detected. This test involves comparing the difference between any two means to a critical difference score using a sampling distribution called the studentized range statistic (q).

Two-factor analysis of variance (ANOVA): A statistical procedure used for comparing sample means with research designs consisting of two independent variables (factors), each variable consisting of two or more groups or levels.

Two-sample chi-square: A nonparametric statistical procedure that examines the way in which observations within two samples distribute across a set of categories (see One-sample chi-square).

Two-tailed test: A test of a nondirectional hypothesis in which the critical region lies in both tails of the probability distribution (see One-tailed test).

Type I error: One of two types of incorrect decisions made in hypothesis testing. Type I error rejects the null hypothesis when the null hypothesis is true (see Type II error).

Type II error: One of two types of incorrect decisions made in hypothesis testing. Type II error accepts the null hypothesis when the null hypothesis is false (see Type I error).

Unbiased estimator: A statistic, the value of which gives an average over all possible random samples equal to the population value.

Unimodal distribution: A data distribution characterized by only one mode; that is, one score occurs more frequently than any other score in the distribution (see Bimodal distribution, Multimodal distribution).

Variable: Any characteristic that varies in quality and/or quantity among individuals (see Attributes, Quantitative variable, Qualitative variable).

Variance: A measure of dispersion defined as the average of the squared deviation scores (see Range, Standard deviation).

z test for proportions: A statistical technique used for comparing two population proportions.

z-score (standardized score): A score based on a standardized unit of measurement that indicates the direction and degree in which a raw score deviates from its mean in standard deviation units.

Bibliography

Agresti, A., and Finlay, B. (1997). *Statistical methods for the social sciences,* 3rd ed. Upper Saddle River, NJ: Prentice Hall.

Bureau of Justice Statistics. (1996). *Sourcebook of criminal justice statistics.* Washington, DC: U.S. Government Printing Office.

Bureau of Justice Statistics. (1998). *Sourcebook of criminal justice statistics.* Washington, DC: U.S. Government Printing Office.

Bureau of Justice Statistics. (2000, November 8). *Crime and victims statistics.* Online: www.ojp.usdoj.gov/bjs/cvict.htm

DeJong, C., and Jackson, K. C. (1998). Putting race into context: Race, juvenile justice processing, and urbanization. *Justice Quarterly, 15,* 487–504.

Ellsworth, T. (1990). The goal orientation of adult probation professionals: A study of probation systems. *Journal of Crime and Justice, 13,* 55–76.

Forde, D. R., and Kennedy, L. W. (1997). Risky lifestyles, routine activities, and the general theory of crime. *Justice Quarterly, 14,* 266–294.

Frey, L. R., Botan, C. H., and Kreps, G. L. (2000). *Investigating communication: An introduction to research methods.* Boston: Allyn and Bacon.

Gergen, D. (2000, June 26). Death by incompetence. *U.S. News and World Report,* p. 76.

Gottfredson, M. R., and Hirschi, T. (1990). *A general theory of crime.* Stanford, CA: Stanford University Press.

Hendricks, H. (1987). *Teaching to change lives.* Sisters, OR: Multnomah Press.

Hoover, K. (1988). *The elements of social scientific thinking,* 4th ed. New York: St. Martin's Press.

Johnson, B. R., Larson, D. B., and Pitts, T. C. (1997). Religious programs, institutional adjustment, and recidivism among former inmates in prison fellowship programs. *Justice Quarterly 14,* 145–166.

Johnson, M., Badzinski, D. M., and Proctor, J. L. (1999). *Media exposure and attention: Impact on knowledge of and support for Megan's Law.* Unpublished manuscript.

Judd, C. M., and McClelland, G. H. (1989). *Data analysis: A model comparison approach.* New York: Harcourt Brace Jovanovich.

Kingsnorth, R. F., Alvis, L., and Gavia, G. (1993). Specific deterrence and the DUI offender: The impact of a decade of reform. *Justice Quarterly, 10,* 265–288.

Kirk, R. E. (1982). *Experimental design,* 2nd ed. Belmont, CA: Brooks/Cole.

Leiber, M. J., Nalla, M. K., and Farnsworth, M. (1998). Explaining juveniles' attitudes towards police. *Justice Quarterly, 15,* 151–174.

MacNeil, J. S. (2000, June 26). Don't drink and smoke. *U.S. News and World Report,* p. 63.

Maxfield, M. G., and Babbie, E. (1998). *Research methods for criminal justice and criminology.* Belmont, CA: West / Wadsworth.

Melchionno, R., and Steinman, M. S. (1998). The 1996–2006 job outlook in brief. *Occupational Outlook Quarterly, 42*(1), 2–9.

Miller, L. S., and Whitehead, J. T. (1996). *Introduction to criminal justice research and statistics.* Cincinnati, OH: Anderson.

Proctor, J. L. (1999). The "new parole": An analysis of parole board decision making as a function of eligibility. *Journal of Crime and Justice, 22,* 193–217.

Rosellini, L. (2000, September 11). The sordid side of college sports. *U.S. News and World Report,* p. 102.

Scouting reports. (2000, August 14). *Sports Illustrated,* p. 52.

Shaw, C. R., and McKay, H. D. (1942). *Juvenile delinquency and urban areas.* Chicago: University of Chicago Press.

Sherman, L. (1992). *Policing domestic violence: Experiments and dilemmas.* New York: Free Press.

Sherman, L., and Berk, R. (1984). The specific deterrence effects of arrest for domestic assault. *American Sociological Review, 49,* 261–272.

Stepp, C. S. (1998, April). The fallout from too much crime coverage. *American Journalism Review, 20* (3), 55.

They're on death row. But should they be? (2000, June 12). *Newsweek,* p. 26.

Uniform Crime Reports (1998). *Crime in the United States.* Washington, DC: U.S. Government Printing Office.

Vold, G. B., and Bernard, T. J. (1986). *Theoretical criminology.* New York: Oxford University Press.

Williams, F. (1979). *Reasoning with statistics.* New York: Holt, Rinehart, and Winston.

Zhao, J., Thurman, Q., and He, N. (1999). Sources of job satisfaction among police officers: A test of demographic and work environment models. *Justice Quarterly, 16,* 153–173.

Index